ADVANCES IN WORLD ARCHAEOLOGY

VOLUME 1, 1982

Advisory Board

ADVANCES IN
World Archaeology

VOLUME 1, 1982

Edited by

Fred Wendorf
Angela E. Close
Department of Anthropology
Southern Methodist University
Dallas, Texas, U.S.A.

ACADEMIC PRESS
A Subsidiary of Harcourt Brace Jovanovich, Publishers
New York   London
Paris   San Diego   San Francisco   São Paulo   Sydney   Tokyo   Toronto

ACADEMIC PRESS, INC.
111 Fifth Avenue, New York, New York 10003

United Kingdom Edition published by
ACADEMIC PRESS, INC. (LONDON) LTD.
24/28 Oval Road, London NW1 7DX

86-10039

ISSN: 0733-5121

ISBN: 0-12-039901-6

PRINTED IN THE UNITED STATES OF AMERICA

82 83 84 85   9 8 7 6 5 4 3 2 1

Contents

Contributors

D. P. Agrawal, Archaeology Group, Physical Research Laboratory, Ahmedabad 380 009, India

Takeru Akazawa, Department of Anthropology and Prehistory, The University Museum, University of Tokyo, Hongo 7-3-1, Bunkyo-Ku, Tokyo, Japan

Sandra Bowdler,* Department of Prehistory, University of New England, Armidale, New South Wales 2351, Australia

J. M. Coles, Department of Archaeology, Cambridge University, Cambridge CB2 3DZ, England

Paul M. Dolukhanov, Institute of Archaeology, U.S.S.R. Academy of Sciences, 191041 Leningrad, U.S.S.R.

Patrick V. Kirch, Department of Anthropology, Bernice P. Bishop Museum, Honolulu, Hawaii 96819, U.S.A.

Sarah M. Nelson, Department of Anthropology, University of Denver, Denver, Colorado 80238, U.S.A.

*Present address: Department of Anthropology, University of Sydney, Sydney, New South Wales 2006, Australia.

Preface

We have seen a dramatic increase in archaeological activity in most areas of the world in recent years. There are many more practicing archaeologists, more excavations are carried out, more analyses of greater complexity are performed, and the amount of pure information generated each year would defeat the digestive powers of the most dedicated synthesizer among us. Indeed, syntheses of any kind seem very rare these days, except for those of book length; and when an entire book is devoted to the archaeology of a limited period within a very small area, the term "synthesis" hardly seems appropriate. Certainly, it is very difficult for specialists in other areas and other periods to find the time and financial resources to keep up with all such syntheses. And journals are frequently of little more help. Many new journals have been created to provide outlets for these new and multifarious archaeological activities, but their editorial policies and budgetary restrictions often combine to limit severely the length of papers that can be published. In addition, many journals favor reports of primary research over more synthetical approaches, and the smaller and more locally oriented journals are frequently not widely available or are published in languages not widely used in the international scholarly community.

In short, archaeologists seem to have reached a stage where most are able to keep up with developments within their own field of specialization, but where it has become very difficult to keep track of even the major findings of research into other areas and other periods, and quite impossible to keep abreast of all archaeological developments. Available syntheses tend to be too long and detailed for the nonspecialist in us or too short and superficial for the scholar, and few archaeologists are capable of creating their own syntheses of material with which they have no first-hand acquaintance.

Advances in World Archaeology has been created to meet a perceived need for a single and reliable source of syntheses of current archaeological knowledge from all over the world. These syntheses are longer and more detailed than those available in almost any journal, but more concise and more recent than the monographic versions. We believe that as *Advances* grows, archaeologists everywhere, whether scholars or teachers, will be able to turn here with confidence to find up-to-date accounts of the archaeology of almost any major area or period in the world.

With this goal before us, we present our first volume. The volume comprises seven chapters arranged in a more or less geographical order. Our areal and temporal coverages are not complete, but this is by chance rather than design. Taken together, the papers solicited and promised for *Advances* provide a full and balanced account of the major work going on within our discipline throughout the world. We have, however, adhered strictly to a policy of "first come first served" in selecting the papers to be included in this volume. This leaves our coverage in the one volume a little patchy but does expedite publication. We assure our readers that Africa and North America will be represented in future volumes.

We have also tried to pursue a policy of using syntheses only by those who are active in research in the relevant area or topic. All of our authors are working within the areas of which they write, and most of them are resident there. This, we feel, is proper. However, because of the various histories of, and approaches to, archaeology in different areas of the world, there is no single, common, theoretical stance within the volume, and this also we find proper. It would be presumptuous and unconstructive to suppose that all archaeology throughout the world should be practiced within one universal framework. Instead, we present the archaeology as it is done by those who are actually doing it. We hope our colleagues will find this instructive.

We thank those who have made this publication possible. Academic Press has shown the vision and originality we tend to associate with them, in dreaming that a series such as this might ever come to fruition. Without our authors it never would have. Them, we have tried not to abuse, but we confess to having bullied some and ridden roughshod over the sensibilities of others. We hope they agree it was for a good cause. Our Advisory Board has been (and continues to be) invaluable in providing us with contributors, reviews, and other points of view concerning what is significant in world archaeology. Most of our reviewers have been drawn from the general worldwide community of archaeologists. They have rendered us signal service, and their cover of anonymity was only reinforced by the expressed desire of some of our authors to know just who these people were.

French Abstracts

Chapter 1 Prehistoric Archaeology in Tasmania
SANDRA BOWDLER

Cet article fait l'état présent des connaissances relatives à la préhistoire des aborigènes tasmaniens. Après la description de l'environnement naturel de la Tasmanie, vient ensuite une brève relation sur les aborigènes tasmaniens dans la période historique. On passe en revue les recherches récentes dans plusieurs disciplines. D'abord, les recherches linguistiques s'avèrent ne pas révéler d'affinités démontrables entre les langues tasmaniennes et d'autres langues. Par contre, les études ostéologiques démontrent des ressemblances morphologiques entre les aborigènes tasmaniens et les aborigènes australiens. Des documents écrits provenant du 19ᵉ siècle ont servi de sources de renseignements pour des études ethnographiques traitant divers aspects de la culture tasmanienne. La plupart de cet article traite d'enquêtes archéologiques menées en Tasmanie au cours des 20 dernières années. Les premières excavations archéologiques modernes s'exécutèrent dans le nord-ouest de la Tasmanie au début des années 60, et démontrèrent que la Tasmanie était occupée depuis au moins 8.000 ans. Ce travail fut suivi par des excavations dans l'est de la Tasmanie, lesquelles montrèrent que certaines particularités de la séquence nord-ouest s'appliquaient aussi bien à l'autre côté de l'île. Des travaux executés sur l'île Hunter dans le nord-ouest firent reculer l'occupation humaine jusqu'en 23.000 B.P., et cette occupation pleistocène s'étendit au centre sud de la Tasmanie moyennant des excavations dans une caverne de la vallée Florentine. D'autres travaux archéologiques dans d'autres parties de la Tasmanie sont décrits. Pour terminer, l'article passe en revue différentes interprétations des données préhistoriques révélées jusqu'à présent. On en conclut que tous les chercheurs sont d'accord sur ce point: les aborigènes tasmaniens et les aborigènes australiens partagent un commun héritage génétique et culturel, et les différences perçues dans le présent ethnographique sont le résultat de 12.000 ans d'isolement tasmanien depuis la formation du détroit Bass.

Chapter 2   Advances in Polynesian Prehistory: Three Decades in Review
PATRICK V. KIRCH

Des excavations archéologiques en Polynésie, à partir de 1950, ont vite dissipé
la doctrine antérieure selon laquelle l'investigation de la sous-surface ne donnerait
pas de résultats. Depuis trente ans on a vu un nombre croissant d'études archéologiques, dans tous les principaux groupements d'îles. Ce travail a contribué, d'abord
à une meilleure compréhension des origines polynésiennes. La thèse de la migration,
qui voyait les sociétés polynésiennes comme des amalgames de traits diffusés, a été
remplacée par des données empiriques concernant la dispersion et la colonisation de
nouveaux archipels, ainsi que l'adaptation de peuples océaniques à leurs écosystèmes
insulaires. La culture polynésienne se développa dans le Pacifique du sud-ouest,
d'ancêtres Lapita et Asiatiques, comme réponse à des pressions socio-environne-
mentales particulières de sélection. La dispersion de Polynésiens dans toute la
grande région triangulaire bornée par le Hawaï, la Nouvelle-Zélande et l'île de Pa-
ques, commençca vers 1500 av. J.-C. et fut complétée dès 800 après J.-C. La préhistoire polynésienne s'occupe de problèmes anthropologiques plus généraux, y
compris la documentation et l'explication de modèles d'adaptation et de différen-
ciation culturelles. Des changements dans la technologie, les systèmes de production
et l'organisation de l'habitation ont été assez longuement traités. Le plus récemment, les archéologues ont commencé à considérer la nature de l'évolution socio-
politique, et les rapports de celle-ci avec la croissance de la population, la dégra-
dation de l'environnement, l'intensification agricole, et la guerre. Au cours de la
décennie à venir, on verra sans doute, dans la préhistoire polynésienne, des essais
intéressants de vérification archéologique directe de tels modèles de changement
socio-politique.

Chapter 3   Recent Progress in Korean Archaeology
SARAH M. NELSON

Il y a eu de nombreuses découvertes importantes dans l'archéologie coréenne
depuis dix ans, dont les principales sont décrites ici. Comme il n'existe pas d'état
présent récent, en aucune langue occidentale, de l'archéologie coréenne jusqu'à la
fin de l'époque des Trois Royaumes, les nouvelles découvertes sont placées dans le
contexte de ce qu'on savait auparavant. Vu que la plupart des découvertes principales ont une importance chronologique, un format chronologique a été adopté,
avec des esquisses des périodes paléolithique, néolithique, âge du bronze, âge du fer,
et Trois Royaumes. Sont décrits, dans chaque section, diverses espèces d'objets
façonnés, localités, sépultures, et d'autres classes de gisements. De récentes découvertes sont discutées par rapport aux travaux antérieurs, et des dates radiocarbone

calibrées sont présentées. Des rapports avec d'autres régions de l'Asie orientale sont inclus, là où l'on possède des connaissances comparables. Les découvertes les plus importantes comprennent un gisement de hache à main du Paléolithique, des dates dans le sixième millénaire avant J.-C. pour la période Chulmun (néolithique), et du riz provenant d'un gisement Mumun (âge du bronze) du treizième siècle avant J.-C. En outre, de nombreuses tombes d'ères proto-historiques et historiques ont été récemment excavées, ce qui fournit de nouvelles dimensions à l'étude de ces périodes.

Chapter 4 Cultural Change in Prehistoric Japan: Receptivity to Rice Agriculture in the Japanese Archipelago
TAKERU AKAZAWA

Il s'agit dans cet article de la dichotomisation culturelle survenue dans l'archipel japonais pendant la période Jomon et prolongée jusqu'aux époques ultérieures, peut-être jusqu'au présent, et, en plus, de l'explication de ces phénomènes d'après les processus d'adaptation de différents groupes Jomon. Ceci nous conduit à mieux comprendre le rapport de l'homme avec son environnement et aussi le rôle, dans l'histoire humaine, de la transformation culturelle en société agricole. L'étude se compose de quatre sections. D'abord, on examine les données générales de l'environnement de l'archipel japonais pour montrer des différences régionales dans les conditions biophysiques exploitées par les sociétés de cueillette et chasse de la préhistoire. Deuxièmement, on examine les commencements et la diffusion de la culture du riz dans l'archipel japonais. On souligne le fait que les groupes Jomon du littoral du Japon oriental ont apparemment résisté à cette culture du riz. En troisième lieu, on traite des différences dans l'adaptation à la pêche de la part des Jomons. On insiste sur la concentration des sites Jomon dûe à l'économie de pêche. La conclusion examine comment et pourquoi différents groupes de Jomons ont suivi des chemins divergents, et d'une allure variable, dans la transition vers une vie agricole sédentaire. Ici s'examine la dichotomisation culturelle du Japon occidental et oriental, survenue au cours de la période Jomon: dans celui-ci fleurirent des sociétés spécialisées; en pêche; dans celui-là fleurirent des sociétés de cueillette intensive et/ou des sociétés agricoles naissantes, avec moins d'activités de pêche. Ces faits nous conduisent à envisager l'histoire du Japon comme caractérisée par deux chemins différents : l'innovation agricole fut résistée et/ou acceptée lentement par les Jomons orientaux, mais elle fut acceptée et développée de façon régulière par les Jomons occidentaux. Cette sorte de transition, de cueillette et chasse à la production agricole, s'accorde avec le modèle opératoire de la révolution non-spécialisée dans les origines de la domestication des cultures dans l'histoire humaine.

Chapter 5   The Indian Bronze Age Cultures and Their Metal Technology
D. P. AGRAWAL

Entre l'âge néolithique et l'âge du fer, les sociétés se servant de cuivre en Inde peuvent se grouper de façon approximative en trois catégories: les pré Harappans et Harappans; les Chalcolithiques; et les sociétés « Copper Hoards » (Dépôts de Cuivre). A l'exception des Harappans, toutes étaient des sociétés non-urbaines, villageoises. La culture Harappan (civilisation de l'Indus) s'étendit sur une vaste superficie de plus d'un million de kilomètres carrés, mais garda une uniformité remarquable dans les objets à usage général, les poids et les mesures. Leurs villes étaient caractérisées par des rues en gril et un système d'égouts. A partir du milieu du troisième millénaire avant J.-C., la culture Harappan dura 500–600 ans, et la culture actuelle de l'Inde lui doit beaucoup.

Le sociétés chalcolithiques utilisaient des lames de pierre et un peu de cuivre mais ne semblent pas urbanisées. Du Rajasthan de l'est, la culture Banas (environ 3950–3350 B.P.) s'étendit dans Madhya Pradesh; la culture Kayatha (environ 3950–3750 B.P.) se bornait pour la plupart à Madhya Pradesh et pourrait avoir des rapports avec les Pré-Harappans; la culture Malwa (environ 3650–3350 B.P.) se produisit à la fois dans Madhya Pradesh et dans Maharashtra; la culture Jorwe (environ 3350–3050 B.P.) se bornait plutôt à Maharashtra. Ces sociétés sont marquées par une poterie très distinctive et par un riche répertoire de motifs.

La vallée Gangetic (le Doab) fut colonisée par les peuples à poterie ocre (PPO). Il semble actuellement que le PPO n'est pas une seule tradition unifiée mais qu'elle a au moins deux variétés distinctes. Dans plusieurs gisements du Doab, on a trouvé, en dépôts, de nombreux objets de cuivre, d'où la désignation de culture « Copper Hoards ». Il y a des preuves indirectes que le type PPO de l'est s'associe aux « Copper Hoards ». Des dates établies au moyen de la thermoluminescence suggèrent environ 1100 avant J.-C. pour le PPO de l'est. L'alliage fait à l'arsénique, qui caractérise exclusivement les « Copper hoards », suggère une tradition autochtone.

Chapter 6   The Bronze Age in Northwestern Europe: Problems and Advances
J. M. COLES

Les études au sujet de l'âge du bronze de l'Europe du nord-ouest ont subi dernièrement des changements dramatiques. Auparavant, on envisagea le développement de l'âge du bronze comme une série de phases évolutionnaires dans la production d'objets en métal, et on considéra que la seule autre source de renseignements était les milliers de monuments funéraires excavés depuis trois siècles. Ces dernières années, une forte réaction contre ces sources restreintes a eu comme résultat de nombreuses études au sujet d'environnements, d'économies, d'habitations et de structures sociales des communautés de l'âge du bronze dans l'Europe du nord-ouest. La collaboration avec d'autres disciplines, l'utilisation généralisée de la photographie aérienne et d'intensifs travaux sur place ont rapporté d'abondantes preuves de l'existence dans l'âge du bronze de la gestion et l'exploitation de terrains. A cela se sont ajoutées des études imaginatives au sujet de cimetières, d'industries métallurgiques et d'habitations, et aujourd'hui l'âge du bronze peut se considérer comme une phase significative de la préhistoire européenne, ainsi qu'une époque où se sont produits des changements à la fois dans le paysage et dans l'organisation sociale qui continuent à se faire voir dans la société européene même aujourd'hui. L'article esquisse les sources traditionnelles de renseignements sur l'âge du bronze et fournit un commentaire sur les développements récents avec des suggestions pour des recherches à l'avenir.

Chapter 7   Upper Pleistocene and Holocene Cultures of the Russian Plain and Caucasus: Ecology, Economy, and Settlement Pattern
PAUL M. DOLUKHANOV

A partir de données paléogéographiques, géochronologiques, et écologiques, la tentative est faite pour tracer les changements dans l'environnement, l'économie et le modèle d'habitation de cultures préhistoriques dans le Caucase et sur la Plaine Russe durant le Pleistocène supérieur et le Holocène ancien et moyen (environ 70.000–4.000 B.P.). Les étapes suivantes peuvent se distinguer : (1) 70.000–35.000 B.P. : prédominance d'un climat frais avec des oscillations plus chaudes et plus froides; développement de cultures moustériennes; haute densité de population dans le Caucase; population peu élevée sur la Plaine Russe; (2) 35.000–10.000 B.P. : point culminant du refroidissement; développement de cultures de type Paléolithique supérieur; haute densité de population sur la plaine Russe; population peu élevée dans le Caucase; (3) 10.000–8.000 B.P. : commencement de l'optimum climatologique post-glaciaire; développement de cultures mésolithiques; population peu élevée dans les deux régions; (4) 8.000–4.000 B.P. : l'optimum climatologique post-glaciaire; l'émergence d'économies agricoles dans plusieurs régions du Caucase et dans la partie sud-ouest de la Plaine Russe; des migrations à grande échelle dans les deux régions. Restriction de zones agricoles dûe à l'aridité croissante vers 4.500–4.000 B.P.

German Abstracts

Chapter 1 Prehistoric Archaeology in Tasmania
SANDRA BOWDLER

Diese Arbeit will den zur Zeit gültigen Stand der Wissenschaft auf dem Gebiete der Vorgeschichte tasmanischer Ureinwohner aufzeigen. Nach einer Beschreibung der natürlichen tasmanischen Umwelt folgt eine kurze Darstellung der Ureinwohner Tasmaniens im geschichtlichen Zeitraum. Die jüngste Forschung auf verschiedenen Gebieten wird überprüft. Zunächst hat die linguistische Forschung, wie gezeigt wird, keine erweislichen Ähnlichkeiten zwischen den tasmanischen und irgendwelchen anderen Sprachen feststellen können. Auf der anderen Seite zeigen knochenkundliche Untersuchungen morphologische Ähnlichkeiten zwischen tasmanischen und australischen Ureinwohnern auf. Schriftliche Urkunden des 19. Jahrhunderts wurden als Informationsquelle verwendet, von der ethnographische Untersuchungen verschiedener Aspekte tasmanischer Kultur kollationiert werden konnten. Der Hauptteil dieses Artikels befaßt sich mit der Beschreibung der während der vergangenen 20 Jahre in Tasmanien durchgeführten archeologischen Untersuchen. Die ersten modernen archeologischen Ausgrabungen wurden im Nordwesten Tasmaniens in den ersten sechziger Jahren des 20. Jahrhunderts vorgenommen und führten zu dem Beweis, daß Tasmanien mindestens 8000 Jahre bewohnt gewesen sein muß. Danach folgten Ausgrabungen im östlichen Tasmanien, welche sichtbar machten, daß einige nordwestliche Merkmale sich über die ganze Insel erstreckten. Die Arbeit auf Hunter Island im Nordwesten Tasmaniens rückte menschliche Besetzung des Landes bis ins Jahr 23.000 B.P. zurück, und diese Pleistozän Besetzung erstreckte sich bis ins südlich zentrale Tasmanien, wie durch Ausgrabungen am Höhlenplatz im Florentiner Tal sichtbar wurde.—Weitere archeologische Arbeit in verschieden Teilen Tasmaniens wird beschrieben. Der Artikel schließt mit einem

Überblick verschiedener Deutungen der bisher offenbar gewordenen vorgeschichtlichen Aufzeichnungen. Es wird festgestellt, daß alle Forscher in einem Punkt
übereinstimmen: tasmanische und australische Ureinwohner haben genetische und
kulturelle Vorfahren gemeinsam, und die in der ethnographischen Gegenwart wahr-
genommenen Unterschiede rührten davon her, daß Tasmanien nach der Bildung der
Bass Meerenge 12.000 Jahre lang isoliert war.

Chapter 2   Advances in Polynesian Prehistory: Three Decades in Review
PATRICK V. KIRCH

    Archeologische Ausgrabungen in Polynesien ließen mit dem Jahre 1950 schnell
die Ansicht verblassen, es ließen sich durch Untergrunduntersuchungen keine neuen
Erkenntnisse gewinnen. In den vergangenen drei Jahrzehnten sind auf allen
größeren Inselgruppen in wachsender Anzahl archeologische Studien betrieben
worden, was zunächst zu einem klareren Verständnis der polynesischen Ursprünge
geführt hat. Die „Völkerwanderungsmentalität,'' die polynesische Kulturen als
Mischungen zerstreut auftretender Merkmale ansah, ist durch empirische Daten
bezüglich der Zerstreuung und Kolonisation neuer Archipele ersetzt worden, sowie
durch die Anpassung ozeanischer Menschen an ihre Ökosysteme. Die polynesische
Kultur entwickelte sich im südwestlichen Pazifik, von ihren Lapita und letzten
Endes südost-asiatischen Vorfahren, und zwar als Resultat eines örtlich sozio-
umweltlichen Auslesedruckes. Die Zerstreuung der Polynesier über das ganze große
Dreiecksgebiet, das durch Hawaii, Neuseeland und Easter Island begrenzt wird, fing
ca. 1500 v.Chr. an und war um 800 n.Chr. abgeschlossen. Polynesische Vorgeschichte umfaßt aber auch allgemeinere anthropologische Probleme, wie z.B. die
Dokumentation und Erklärung von Mustern kultureller Anpassung und Differen-
zierung. Die Veränderungen in der Technologie, in den Produktionssystemen und in
Siedlungsmustern haben beträchtliche Beachtung gefunden. In jüngster Zeit haben
Archeologen begonnen, das Wesen sozio-politischer Evolution und seine Beziehung
zum Bevölkerungswachstum, zur Umweltsabnutzung, zur wirtschaftlichen Ver-
stärkung und zur Kreigsführung anzusprechen. Das nächste Jahrzehnt polynesischer
Vorgeschichtsstudien wird wohl in wachsendem Maße Versuche hervorbringen,
solche Modelle sozio-politischer Änderungen archeologisch direkt zu testen.

Chapter 3   Recent Progress in Korean Archaeology
SARAH M. NELSON

    Das letzte Jahrzehnt in der koreanischen Archeologie erlebte eine Unmenge
wichtiger Entdeckungen. Die Hauptfunde werden hier beschrieben. Da es in irgend-

einer westlichen Sprache keine jüngere allgemeine Zusammenfassung koreanischer Archeologie gibt, die in die Drei-Königreich Zeit reicht, werden die neuen Entdeckungen in den Zusammenhang des bereits Bekannten gestellt. Eine chronologische Methode mit Abrissen des Paläolithikums, des Neolithikums, der Bronzezeit, der Eisenzeit und der Drei-Königreich Zeit ist besonders deshalb angewendet worden, weil die meisten der wichtigen Funde chronologische Bedeutung haben. In jedem Abschnitt werden Gegenstände verschiedener Kategorien, Siedlungen, Grabstätten und andere Arten von Stätten beschrieben. Jüngere Entdeckungen werden unter Bezugnahme auf vorangegangene Arbeiten diskutiert, und kalibrierte ^{14}C Daten bereichern die Diskussion darüber hinaus. Wo vergleichbares Material bekannt und vorhanden ist, werden Beziehungen zu anderen ost-asiatischen Gegenden miteingeschlossen. Die wichtigsten Funde schließen eine Handaxt Stätte im Paläolithikum ein, datierend vom sechsten Jahrtausend v.Chr. in der Chŭlmun Zeit (Neolithikum), außerdem Reis von einer Mumun (Bronzezeit) Stätte, die ins 13. Jahrhundert v.Chr. datiert. Außerdem sind vor kurzem eine große Anzahl von Grabstätten aus protogeschichtlichen und geschichtlichen Zeiträumen ausgegraben worden, was dem Studium dieser Zeiten neue Dimensionen verleiht.

Chapter 4 Cultural Change in Prehistoric Japan: Receptivity to Rice Agriculture in the Japanese Archipelago

TAKERU AKAZAWA

Diese Arbeit bespricht die während des Jomon Zeitraumes vorgefallene kulturelle Aufgabelung im japanischen Archipel, die sich bis in spätere Zeiten—wahrscheinlich sogar bis in die Gegenwart—gehalten hat und führt dieses Phänomen auf den Anpassungsprozeß verschiedener Jomon Gruppen zurück. Eine solche Erscheinung ermöglicht es uns, die Beziehung des Menschen zu seiner Umwelt, sowie den kulturellen Übergang zur Landwirtschaft in der Menschheitsgeschichte besser zu verstehen. Die Studie setzt sich aus vier Teilen zusammen. Im ersten Teil wird der allgemeine Umweltswerdegang des japanischen Archipels analysiert, um regionale Unterschiede der von vorgeschichtlichen Jäger-Sammlern genutzten biophysischen Gegebenheiten anzuzeigen. Zweitens wird der Anfang und die Ausdehnung des Reisanbaus im japanischen Archipel untersucht. Dieser Teil konzentriert sich auf den Umstand, daß sich die Jomon Gruppen in den Küstengegenden des östlichen Japan scheinbar dagegen wehrten, die Reiskultur anzunehmen. Der dritte Teil der Untersuchung beschäftigt sich mit den Unterschieden in der Anpassung der Jomon Menschen an die Fischerei. Dieser Teil konzentriert sich auf die Häufung der Jomon Wohnstätten aufgrund der Fischerei Wirtschaft. Der Schlußteil untersucht die Frage, wie und warum verschiedene Jomon Gruppen auf dem Übergang zu einem seßhaften Leben in der Landwirtschaft abweichende Wege mit schwanken der Geschwindigkeit beschritten. In diesem Zusammenhang wird die während des Jomon Zeitraumes vorgefallene kulturelle Aufgabelung zwischen dem

östlichen und dem westlichen Japan untersucht: in jenem gediehen Fischereigemein-
schaften, in diesem Pflanzensammel- und/oder im Entstehen begriffene Pflanzen-
baugemeinschaften mit weniger ausgeprägten Fischereitätigkeiten. Diese Tatsachen
erlauben es uns, japanische Geschichte als von zwei verschiedenen Wegen gekennzeichnet zu verstehen: Jomon Menschen im Osten wehrten sich gegen landwirt-
schaftliche Erneuerungen oder nahmen sie nur langsam an, während sie von Jomon
Menschen im Westen akzeptiert und reibungslos weiterentwickelt wurden. Diese Art
des Überganges vom Jagd-Sammeln zur Nahrungsmittelerzeugung stimmt mit dem
,,broad spectrum'' Arbeitsmodell überein, wonach eine solche Revolution in den
Ursprüngen früher Eingewöhnung in der menschlichen Geschichte zu suchen ist.

Chapter 5   The Indian Bronze Age Cultures and Their Metal Technology
D. P. AGRAWAL

Die kupferverarbeitenden Kulturen Indiens können zwischen dem Neolithikum
und der Eisenzeit im allgemeinen in drei Kategorien aufgeteilt werden: Vorharappa
und Harappa, Chalkolithikum und die Kupfervorratslager Kulturen. Außer der
Harappa Kultur waren alle anderen nicht städtische Dorfkulturen. Die Harappa
Kultur (Indus Zivilisation) erstreckte sich über ein weites Gebiet von mehr als einer
Million Quadratkilometern, behielt jedoch eine bemerkenswerte Gleichförmigkeit in
Dingen des Massengebrauchs, sowie der Gewichte und Maße. Ihre Städte zeichneten
sich durch wie Balkenroste angelegte Straßen und durch Untergrund Entwässerungs-
anlagen aus. Die Harappa Kultur fing ungefähr um die Mitte des 3. Jahrtausends
vor Chr. an und behauptete sich etwa 500-600 Jahre, und die indische Kultur
unserer Zeit kann von ihr zum großen Teil abgeleitet werden.

Die Kulturen des Chalkolithikums gebrauchten Steinklingen und etwas Kupfer,
scheinen aber nicht städtisch gewesen zu sein. Die Banas Kultur (ca. 3950–3350 vor
der Gegenwart) dehnte sich auf Madhya Pradesh aus; die Kayatha Kultur (ca.
3950–3750 vor der Gegenwart) beschränkte sich meist auf Madhya Pradesh und ist
vielleicht mit der Vor-Harappa Kultur verwandt; die Malwa Kultur (ca. 3650–3350
vor der Gegenwart) trat sowohl in Madhya Pradesh wie auch in Maharashtra auf;
die Jorwe Kultur (ca. 3350–3050 vor der Gegenwart) war fast nur auf Maharashtra
beschränkt. Diese Kulturen sind durch äußerst ausgeprägte Tongefäße und ein
reichhaltiges Motivinventar gekennzeichnet.

Das Gangestal (Doab) wurde von Menschen kolonialisiert, die ockerfarbene
Tongefäße (Ocher-Colored Pottery [OCP]) gebrauchten. Es scheint jetzt, daß OCP
keine vereinheitlichte Tradition darstellt, sondern sich aus zwei verschiedenen Arten
zusammensetzt. Eine große Anzahl von Kupfergegenständen sind in den Vorratslagern verschiedener Stätten gefunden worden, und deshalb der Name Vor-
ratslager Kultur. Es bestehen Indizienbeweise, daß die östliche Art des OCP mit

Vorratslagern in Verbindung gebracht wird. Thermolumineszenz Daten setzen ca. 1100 vor Chr. für die OCP an. Die ausschließliche Arsenlegierung der Kupfervorräte läßt eine ureingesessene Tradition vermuten.

Chapter 6   The Bronze Age in Northwestern Europe: Problems and Advances
J. M. COLES

Untersuchungen der Bronzezeit im nordwestlichen Europa sind seit kurzem drastischen Wandlungen unterworfen gewesen. Die Entwicklung der Bronzezeit wurde ursprünglich als eine Folge evolutionärer Phasen in der Herstellung metallener Gegenstände angesehen, und man hielt die vielen tausenden, in den vergangenen dreihundert Jahren ausgegrabenen Grabstätten für die einzig weitere Informationsqeuelle. In den letzten Jahren hat die starke Reaktion gegen diese begrenzten Informationsquellen zu ausgedehnten Untersuchungen der Umweltbedingungen, Wirtschaftsformen, Siedlungen und Gesellschaftsstrukturen der Bronzezeit-Gemeinschaften im nordwestlichen Europa geführt. Zusammenarbeit mit anderen Fachgebieten, konzentrierte Anwendung von Luftphotographie, sowie intensive Arbeit im Gelände selbst haben reichhaltiges Zeugnis abgegeben für die Verwaltung und Benutzung von Grund und Boden in der Bronzezeit. Darüber hinaus hat man gedankenreiche Untersuchungen von Grabstätten, Metallverarbeitungsstätten und Siedlungen durchgeführt, damit die Bronzezeit heute als bedeutsame Phase der europäischen Vorgeschichte angesehen werden kann—und all dies zu einer Zeit, als diejenigen Änderungen im Landschafts- und Gesellschaftsgefüge auftraten, die man noch heute in der europäischen Gesellschaft dargestellt findet. Die vorliegende Arbeit umreißt die traditionellen Informationsquellen über die Bronzezeit, bietet einen Kommentar über die jüngsten Erkenntnisse und schlägt noch zu bewältigende Arbeitsgebiete vor.

Chapter 7   Upper Pleistocene and Holocene Cultures of the Russian Plain and Caucasus: Ecology, Economy, and Settlement Pattern
PAUL M. DOLUKHANOV

Mit Hilfe paleogeographischer, geochronologischer und ökologischer Daten wird versucht, die Umweltsveränderungen sowie Wirtschafts- und Siedlungsmuster vorgeschichtlicher Kulturen im Kaukasus und in der russischen Tiefebene nachzuzeichnen, die während der oberen Pleistozän und früheren und mittleren Holozän Zeit (ca. 70.000–4.000 vor der Gegenwart) vor sich gingen. Es wird zwischen den folgenden Stadien unterschieden: (1) 70.000–35.000 vor der Gegenwart: vorwiegend kühles Klima mit wärmeren und kälteren Schwankungen; Entwicklung von Mousterien Kulturen; starke Bevölkerungsdichte im Kaukasus; geringe Bevölkerung in der russischen Tiefebene; (2) 35.000–10.000 vor der Gegenwart: maximale Abkühlung; Entwicklung von Jung Paläolithikum Kulturen; große Bevölkerungsdichte in der russischen Tiefebene; niedrige Bevölkerung im Kaukasus; (3) 10.000–8.000 vor der Gegenwart: Anfang des nacheiszeitlichen klimatischen Optimums; Entwicklung mittelsteinzeitlicher Kulturen; geringe Bevölkerungsdichte in beiden Gebieten; (4) 8.000–4.000 vor der Gegenwahrt; klimatisches Optimum der Nacheiszeit; Aufkommen von Nahrungsmittel schaffenden Wirtschaften in mehreren Gegenden des Kaukausus und im südwestlichen Teil der russischen Tiefebene; Massenvölkerwanderungen in beiden Gebieten. Einschränkung der Ackerbaugebiete wegen wachsender Trockenheit ca. 4.500–4.00 vor der Gegenwart.

Russian Abstracts

Chapter 1 Prehistoric Archaeology in Tasmania
SANDRA BOWDLER

В этой работе дается совокупность сведений о доисторической эпохе аборигенов Тасмании. После изложения естественных условий Тасмании, следует краткий обзор аборигенов Тасмании за исторический период. Для некоторых дисциплин дается положение последних изысканий. Во-первых, это лингвистические исследования, которые не дают явных сходств между тасманскими языками и другими, а с другой стороны, остеологическия исследования указывают на морфологические сходства между аборигенами Тасмании и Австралии. Для сопоставления, с разных точек зрения этнографических изысканий тасманской культуры, исследовались письменные данные девятнадцатого века. Главная часть этой работы состоит из описания археологических раскопок в Тасмании за последние 20 лет. Первые современные раскопки в северазаподной Тасмании производились в первой половине 60-тых годов, которые паказали, что Тасмания была заселена по крайней мере 8 000 лет. За этой работой следовали раскопки в восточной Тасмании, которые показали, что некоторые хронологические условия северозапада существовали и на востоке. Раскопки в северозападной Тасмании на острове Хантер показали, что человек жил там 23 000 лет до н.э. Эта обитаемость в плейстоценовом периоде была также установлена раскопками в южноцентральной Тасмании в районе пещер флорентийской долины. Тут также описываются дальнейшие археологические работы в различных частях Тасмании. В заключение дается обзор разных интерпретаций уже известных данных доисторической эпохи. Тут подтверждается, что все научные работники сходятся на одной точке зрения, а именно, что аборигены Тасмании и Австралии имеют общее генетическое и культурное прошлое и, что разница ощущаемая в этнографическом настоящем произошла из-за того, что в течении 12 000 лет Тасмания изолирована Бассовым проливом.

Chapter 2   Advances in Polynesian Prehistory: Three Decades in Review
PATRICK V. KIRCH

Начиная с 1950 года археологические раскопки в Полинезии опровергли существующую до тех пор догму, что подпочвенные раскопки ничего не дают. За последнее тридцатилетие, на всех трех главных группах этих островов, сильно увеличилось число археологических исследований. Главным образом эти работы дали лучшее понимание происхождения полинезийцев. «Психоз миграции,» который объяснял полинезийские культуры, как амальгамирование характерных черт человека, был заменен эмпирическими данными распростронения жителей Океании и колонизации новых островов и их адоптация к островской экономической системе. В результате влияния выбора местной социальной среды, полинезийская культура произошла в юго-западной части Тихого океана от лапитов и в конечном итоге от юго-восточных азиатских предков. В треугольном районе ограниченным Гавайскими островами, Новой Зеландией и островом Пасхи, распространение полинезийцев началось около 1 500 лет до н.э. и закончилось в начале 8-го века н.э. Доисторический период Полинезии также включает в себя вопросы более общего антропологического характера, включая документацию и объяснение форм культурной адоптации и дифференциации. Большое внимание уделяется изменениям в технологии, в системах производства и в видах заселения. В настоящее время археологи стали больше интересоваться сущностью социально-политического развития и зависимостью его от роста населения, загрязнения окружающей среды, интенсификации сельского хозяйства и войн. В следующем десятилетии должны быть предприняты меры прямого архиологического исследования таких моделей, как моделей социально-политических изменений в доисторическом периоде Полинезии.

Chapter 3   Recent Progress in Korean Archaeology
SARAH M. NELSON

За последнее десятилетие в археологии Кореи произошло много важных открытий. Главные из них описываются в этой работе. Так как ни на одном западном языке не имеется современной общей сводки археологии Кореи за период «Три королевства», новые открытия относятся в контекст об уже известных открытиях. Хронологический порядок соблюдался описывая периоды: полеолитический, неолитический, бронзовый, железный и Трех королевств. В каждом отделе описываются остатки разных категорий материальной культуры древнего человека, поселения, места погребения и другие типы местонахождений. Современные открытия описываются в плане предыдущих работ и дальше к описанию добавляются стандартизованные данные С-14. Связь с другими районами восточной Азии включена там, где сравниваемый материал известен. Самыми главными открытиями являются местонахождения ручного топора в палеолитическом периоде; даты относящиеся к 6 000 лет до н.э. для чульмунского периода /неолит/, и рис из мумунской стоянки /бронзовый век/, датированного 1 300 лет до н.э. Кроме того очень много могил исторической эры были раскопаны в недавнем прошлом, таким образом пополнив исследования вышеуказанных периодов.

Chapter 4   Cultural Change in Prehistoric Japan: Receptivity to Rice Agriculture in the Japanese Archipelago
TAKERU AKAZAWA

В этой работе разбирается разделение культуры на две части, происшедшее на японских островах во время жомонского периода и, сохранившееся до более позднего времени, возможно что и до настояшего. Также тут даются пояснения этих явлений с точки зрения адоптации разных жомонских групп. Эти проявления приводят к лучшему пониманию связи между человеком и его окружающей средой, а также культурного перехода к сельскому хозяйству в плане истории человека. Это исследование состоит из четырех отделов. В первом отделе, дается анализ разбирающий общий фон окружающей среды японского архипелага, для того чтобы дать региональные различия биофизических условий, использованных доисторическими охотниками. Второй отдел, анализирует начало и распространение культивации риса на японских островах. Эта часть останавливается на факте, что жомонские группы в прибрежных районах восточной Японии явно противились культивации риса. В третьем отделе говорится о различии в адаптации рыболовства среди жомонских народов. Эта часть сосредотачивается на том, что из-за рыболовной экономики жомонские стоянки заселялись группами. В последнем отделе разбирается вопрос, как и почему разные группы жомонских народов следовали по разновидным путям и, с разным темпом в переходе на оседлую жизнь сельского хозяйства. Тут рассматривается культурная дихотомизация между восточной и западной Японией, которая произошла во время жомонского периода. Рыболовное общество процветало в восточной Японии, а в западной Японии процветал интенсивный сбор растений и зарождающееся культивирование растений, а рыболовство было менее цивилизованным. Эти факты дают нам возможность понять историю Японии, характерную двум разным путям развития: усовершенствование сельского хозяйства в начале вызвало сопротивление, а потом медленно начало входить в жизнь восточных жомонских народов. Западные жомонские племена восприняли и развили его без всяких затруднений. Переход такого рода от охоты-сбора к производству пищи согласуется с рабочей моделью « широкого диапозона » революции в раннем зачатке оседлого образца жизни и одомашнивания в истории человека.

Chapter 5   The Indian Bronze Age Cultures and Their Metal Technology
D. P. AGRAWAL

Культуры, которые в Индии использовали медь между неолитическим веком и железным, можно разделить на три категории: дохараппскую и хараппскую; халколитическую, и культуры хранилищ меди. Все они, за исключением хараппской, были сельскими культурами. Хараппская /индусская цивилизация/ культура очень широко распространялась в районе более одного миллиона km², но замечательно сохранила единообразие изделий массового употребления, единицы веса и мер. Их города характеризовались сеткообразно расположенными улицами и подземными стоками. Начиная с середины 3 000 лет до н.э. хараппская культура существовала 500–600 лет. Современная индусская культура многое заимствовала от нее.

Халколические культуры пользовались каменными клинками и немного медью, но не меняли сельскую жизнь на городскую. Банская культура /около 3 950–3 350 лет до н.э./ распространилась от восточного Раджастана в Мадхья Прадеш. Каятская культура /около 3 950–3 750 лет до н.э./ главным образом ограничилась в Мадхья Прадеш и может быть родственной дохараппской; мальваская культура /около 3 650–3 350 лет до н.э./ появилась в обоих местах Мадхья Прадеш и Махараштра. Джорвская культура /около 3 350–3 050 до н.э./ главным образом относится к Махараштра. Эти культуры отличаются друг от друга очень характерными гончарными изделиями с очень богатыми узорами.

Долина реки Гонга /Доаб/ была заселена народами, которые употребляли гончарные изделия охровой окраски. Теперь оказывается, что эти изделия не были только одной традицией, но имели по крайней мере два резких варианта. Во многих стоянках с хранилищами меди, в районе Доаб, было найдено большое количество медных изделий, откуда и идет название культуры хранилищ меди. Имеются косвенные доказательства, что восточная разновидность изделий охровой окраски, связана с хранилищами меди. Термолюминесценционное датирование относит восточные охроокрашенные изделия к прибл. 1 100 лет до н.э. Особый мышьяковый сплав медных запасов указывает на местную традицию.

Chapter 6   The Bronze Age in Northwestern Europe: Problems and Advances
J. M. COLES

В последнее время исследования бронзового века в северо-западной Европе подверглись драматическим изменениям. Развитие бронзового века первоначально рассматривалось, как ряд эволюционных этапов в производстве металлических изделий материальной культуры древнего человека. За последние три столетия, считались единственным источником информации многотысячные раскопки кладбищ. Против этих ограниченных источников в настоящее время появилась сильная реакция. Она проявляется в изучении окружающей среды, экономики, стоянок древнего человека и социальной структуры поселений северо-западной Европы в бронзовом веке. В сотрудничестве с учеными других наук, применяя аэросъемку и интенсивные полевые работы, получено большое количество материала, указывающего на управление землей и использование ее во время бронзового века. Этот материал пополнен комплексными исследованиями мест погребения, металлической промышленности и стоянок древнего человека. Таким образом, бронзовый век можно рассматривать как важный период доисторической Европы, во время которого произошли изменения как ландшафта, так и социального порядка, которые и до сих пор наблюдаются в Европейском обществе. В этой работе приводятся главные источники информации об этом веке. Тут также комментируется положение в настоящее время и даются предложения для последующих работ.

Chapter 7   Upper Pleistocene and Holocene Cultures of the Russian Plain and Caucasus: Ecology, Economy, and Settlement Pattern
PAUL M. DOLUKHANOV

Была сделана попытка проследить изменения в окружающей среде, экономике и образе заселения Кавказа и Русской равнины во время верхнего плейстоцена, а также раннего и среднего голоцена /прибл. 70 000–4 000 лет до н.э./ основываясь на палеографических, геохронологических и экологических данных. Тут различаются следующие периоды: 1/ 70 000–35 000 лет до н.э.; климат, главным образом, прохладный с теплыми и холодными колебаниями; развитие мустьерских культур; плотность населения на Кавказе высокая, а низкая на Русской равнине. 2/ 35 000–10 000 лет до н.э.; тут происходит максимальное охлаждение климата; развитие верхне-палеолитических культур; высокая заселенность Русской равнины и низкая заселенность Кавказа. 3/ 10 000–8 000 лет до н.э.; начало после-ледникового климатического оптимума; развитие мезолитовых культур; редкая заселенность обоих районов; 4/ 8 000–4 000 лет до н.э.; после-ледниковые наиболее благоприятные климатические условия ; появление пищепроизводственной экономики в разных районах Кавказа, а также в юго-западной части Русской равнины ; значительное переселение народов в обоих районах. В связи с возрастающей сухостью приблизительно в 4 500–4 000 лет до н.э. происходит ограничение сельскохозяйственных площадей.

ADVANCES IN WORLD ARCHAEOLOGY

VOLUME 1, 1982

1

Prehistoric Archaeology in Tasmania

SANDRA BOWDLER

INTRODUCTION

Tasmania is Australia's largest offshore island. It is named after Abel Janszoon Tasman, a Dutch navigator who discovered it on behalf of Western civilization in 1642. He named it Van Diemen's Land, in honor of Anthony Van Diemen, who was the governor-general of Batavia at the time; this name was used officially until 1856.

Tasmania is separated from the mainland of Australia by Bass Strait (Figure 1.1), named after George Bass. In 1798, Bass, in company with Matthew Flinders, sailed around Tasmania in the sloop *Norfolk* and proved it to be an island, a fact previously in some dispute among the European newcomers.

The first European settlement of Australia was by the British at Port Jackson, at what was to become the modern city of Sydney, in 1788. The first European settlement of Tasmania emanated from Port Jackson. In 1803, a small party of soldiers and convicts established a camp at Risdon Cove, near the later city of Hobart in southeast Tasmania; further settlement followed. The fact that Tasmania, and indeed Australia, were already occupied was swept aside as a minor nuisance.

The modern state of Tasmania incorporates the islands of Bass Strait, which is about 240 km wide, and numerous islands to the south and east of the main island. All the islands of Tasmania are continental islands. At times of lowered sea level during the Pleistocene, all the modern Tasmanian islands were incorporated into the extended continent of Greater Australia, as were New Guinea in the north, Kangaroo Island near the modern city of Adelaide, and most of the other offshore islands of Australia. Biogeographically, therefore, we would expect Tasmania to be essentially Australian and, generally, this is so.

1

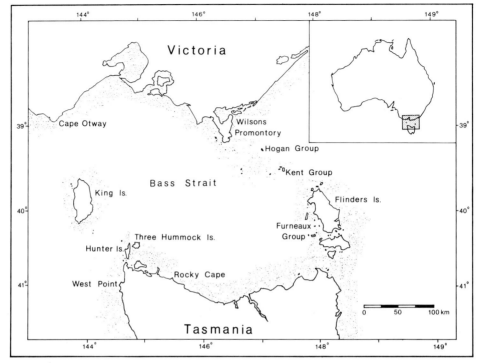

Figure 1.1   Bass Strait.

Tasmania* lies between southern latitudes 40° and 44°, and between longitudes 144° and 149°. No part of mainland Australia occupies such high latitudes, and thus differences between them might be expected as well as continuities. Tasmania has an area of about 67,900 km², and is considerably more rugged in topography than most of Australia. The coastal plains are narrow, especially in the west, and much of the interior is occupied by plateaus and mountains rising to heights over 1500 m above sea level (Figure 1.2).

Not surprisingly, Tasmania's climate is temperate and marine (Langford 1965); the marine aspect leads to mild winters and cool summers. There is a marked rainfall gradient from west to east, both because the prevailing winds are westerly, and because of the higher altitudes in the west (Figure 1.3). A marked rain shadow effect is thus seen in the east and there is a subsequent ecological dichotomy between east and west. In the west, where the average yearly rainfall exceeds 1375 mm, *Nothofagus* (southern beech) rain forest tends to be the dominant vegetation, but in the drier east, open sclerophyll forest or woodland is more prevalent (Figure 1.4). At higher altitudes moorland is found, and coastal heath occurs in narrow bands on the coast, especially in the north-

*I shall use *Tasmania* to mean the main island unless otherwise specified.

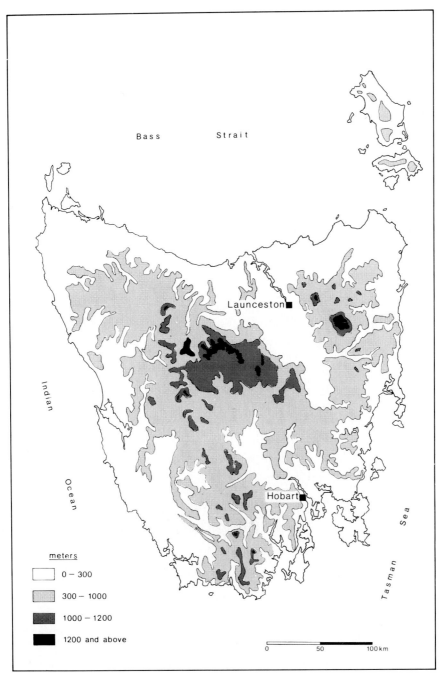

Figure 1.2 Tasmanian topography.

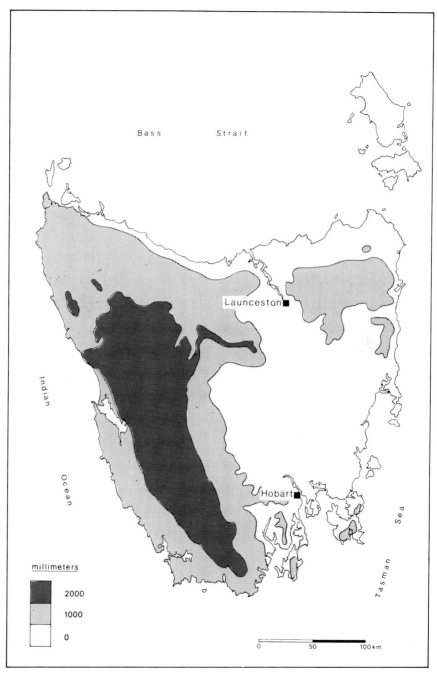

Figure 1.3 Tasmanian rainfall.

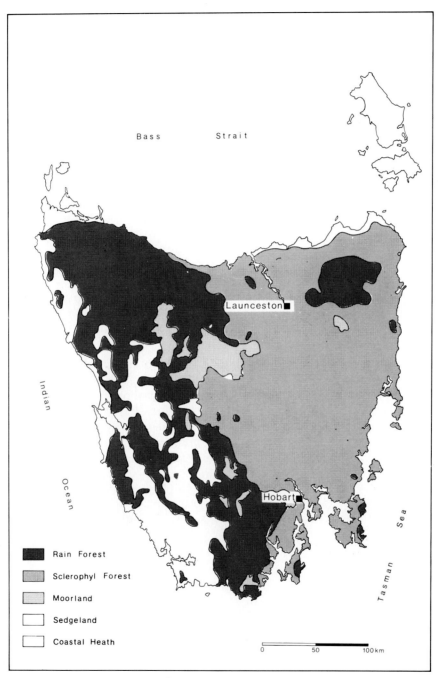

Figure 1.4 Tasmanian vegetation.

west and northeast. This is a greatly simplified picture, and ignores for the
moment the effects of human activities on vegetation in prehistory and history.
The flora itself is a mixture of Australian (e.g., *Eucalyptus* species forming sclerophyll woodlands) and Southern Oceanic (e.g., *Nothofagus*) components (Jackson 1965).

The Tasmanian fauna is essentially a depauperate Australian fauna, and unlike the flora, includes few endemics (Guiler 1965). There are numerous species
of birds, and seabirds are abundant on the coasts. Mention must be made of the
Tasmanian muttonbird (short-tailed shearwater, *Puffinus tenuirostris*), perhaps
Australia's most abundant species of bird. Muttonbirds breed in the southern
summer on offshore islands, in burrows in the sand within dense rookeries, and
spend the southern winter in the northern hemisphere.

Terrestrial mammals that have not been introduced in historical times consist
predominantly of marsupials. These include several macropods (the kangaroo
family); two species of bandicoot; brushtail, ringtail, and pygmy possums; a
wombat; and a number of carnivorous and predatory forms. Of this last category, the Tasmanian devil (*Sarcophilus harrisii*) and the Tasmanian wolf or tiger
(*Thylacinus cynocephalus*) were not found alive on the Australian mainland in the
historical period. It seems likely that the Tasmanian wolf is now extinct in
Tasmania, and thus the world. The dingo (the Australian semidomestic dog,
Canis familiaris) was not found in Tasmania during the historical period, nor is
there evidence for its presence in pre-European times (Jones 1970). The mono-
tremes, platypus and echidna, are found in Tasmania. Several species of native
rodent are also found in Tasmania. In general, Tasmanian mammals are most
abundant in sclerophyll forest and woodland, coastal heath, and moorland environments. Few occur in the rain forest, which Guiler (1965:37) characterizes as
"distinguished by its stillness and lack of conspicuous life."

Tasmanian freshwater fauna are not abundant, comprising only occasional
eels, small fish in the many perennial rivers and streams, and crustaceans in the
high mountain tarns and streams. The littoral on the other hand is generously
supplied. The Tasmanian intertidal marine fauna forms part of a province that
includes southern Victoria, and which has close ecological affinities with the
fauna of New Zealand, Namibia, and Chile. Animals of relevance include shellfish, especially two large species of abalone, crayfish (*Jasus lalandii*, also known
as spiny lobster, but lacking the large claws of northern lobsters), and several
species of scale fish, including wrasses (family Labridae), known locally as par-
rotfish. In pre-European times, many marine mammals abounded in Tasmanian
waters, including three species of seal, the southern elephant seal (*Mirounga
leonina*), the Australian fur seal (*Arctocephalus doriferus*), and the New Zealand fur
seal (*A. fosteri*) (O'Connor 1980).

Prior to the advent of Europeans in the Antipodes, Tasmania was occupied by
human beings, usually referred to as the Tasmanian Aborigines. For convenience, I shall refer to these indigenous inhabitants as Tasmanians or Tasmanian
Aborigines. The transient French navigators of the late-eighteenth and early-

nineteenth centuries, who had personal contact with the eastern Tasmanians, regarded them with some delight (e.g., Peron 1807:220–231). The British settlers, who were in direct competition for the land, regarded them first with contempt, and later, as the Tasmanians fought back, with fear and hatred. The Tasmanian population between 1803 and 1830 was more than decimated by the gun, disease, and "ecological dislocation" (Jones 1971a,b:10–11).

In 1828, George Arthur, the governor of Tasmania, declared martial law. He initiated military measures aimed at securing all those Aborigines still at large. Unsuccessful at this attempt, Arthur heeded the advice of George Augustus Robinson, an erstwhile bricklayer and fervent Christian who was then managing a government Aboriginal station on Bruny Island (off the east coast of Tasmania). Robinson proposed to Arthur that he, Robinson, would go off into the unsettled bush, and persuade the Aborigines to come in. He was granted official support in this after his first successful foray. Robinson spent most of 1829 to 1834 in the bush, persuading what Aborigines remained at large to return with him to the benefits of civilization. Three hundred Tasmanians were rounded up (out of an estimated population of 3000) and were virtually incarcerated, first on Flinders Island, later at Oyster Cove, near Hobart. During this time their numbers steadily declined. In 1876, Truganini (or Truggernanner) of Bruny Island, who had accompanied Robinson on all his expeditions, died in Hobart. She is often regarded as the last Tasmanian. It is more correct to say that she was probably the last person of unmixed Tasmanian descent to die in Tasmania.

At the time of Truganini's death, there were some 100 Tasmanians alive on the Bass Strait Islands, in Victoria, and indeed on the Tasmanian mainland (Ryan 1972). These Tasmanians were the descendants of Tasmanian women who had lived with European sealers in Bass Strait. The sealers themselves lived a tenuous existence on the fringe of society; they had obtained women from northwest and northeast Tasmania by kidnapping them or by means of exchange with the tribes. The women were acquired not only for sexual purposes, but for economic reasons; they assisted the sealers in their precarious livelihood, and also got food for them from the sea and the bush. Robinson deplored the lot of these women, on the grounds both of the immorality of their situation, and the brutality they were subjected to. It is also true that their removal from their own society did nothing to help the dwindling birth rate among the tribes. But by removing themselves from the ambit of white officialdom, which thanks to Robinson meant the whole of Tasmania, the Tasmanian women who consorted with sealers were able to survive themselves, and to produce surviving offspring. Their descendants today number in excess of 4000 people, and many identify themselves as Tasmanian Aborigines.

The Tasmanians who were removed to the Flinders Island establishment were subjected to a program which tried to divest them of their traditional culture, and turn them into civilized Christians. The success of the program is hard to judge; they all died. The Tasmanians who survived in the Bass Strait islands did so at the expense of much of their cultural heritage. Their descendants speak

English, albeit an English with its own distinctive character, and while some traditional skills have been retained, many have been lost in the fight for survival in a white Australia. Salvage ethnography may still be feasible, although whether the modern Tasmanians would wish to divulge their surviving traditional lore to white outsiders is another matter (cf. Kelly 1980).

As the Tasmanian population declined in the nineteenth century, and as the traditional culture disappeared, scientific interest in the people and the culture grew. This is ironic, but perhaps to be expected, in that only when the Tasmanians ceased to be a threat did the white community have the "objectivity" for scientific pursuits (cf. Ryan 1975:9). Jones (1971b:17) proposes two reasons for the extreme interest shown in the Tasmanians by scientists in many parts of the world. On the one hand, he suggests that other tribesmen "survived too long to be glamorous"; on the other hand, he sees the Tasmanians as being like the Tierra del Fuegans, in that both "represented an extreme position in the human condition, a datum point from which to speculate about the nature of man."

The questions that most piqued nineteenth-century curiosity were, who were the Tasmanians and where had they come from? The debate has been usefully summarized by Jones (1971b:17–27), and polarized around two theories. One was that the Tasmanians had originated in island Melanesia, most likely New Caledonia, and had come to Tasmania directly by sea. This idea was propounded by Huxley (1869), and was prompted by observable physical characteristics of the Tasmanians, namely woolly hair and short stocky stature. The Tasmanians were thus classified as a branch of the negroid race, and viewed as quite different from the Australians.

The alternative school of thought, led by Mathew (1889), proposed that the Tasmanians came from nearby Australia. This theory looked more closely at cultural traits, such as languages and artifacts, and circumvented the problem of physical and other differences by seeing the Tasmanians as representing the earliest inhabitants of Australia, isolated and preserved in Tasmania, but swamped by more recent arrivals on the mainland. While there were obvious advantages in proposing an Australian origin, the mode of arrival was unclear. Most writers thought Tasmanian watercraft to have been unsuitable for crossing Bass Strait, much less the voyage from New Caledonia, and canvassed the idea of a land linkage between Tasmania and Australia. The kinds of evidence available that could be brought to bear on the controversy were limited. Only in the past 20 years has new evidence, and new ways of looking at the evidence generally, allowed headway to be made, not only with the classic "problem of the Tasmanians," but with new problems more suited to the new phase of research.

In the field of Tasmanian Aboriginal studies, anthropological, historical, and archaeological research have tended to go hand-in-hand, for reasons that should become apparent. Some specializations have been preserved, however, and it will be useful to look first at some distinct areas of research other than archaeological.

LINGUISTICS

Not surprisingly, research into traditional Tasmanian languages has been hampered by lack of detailed texts. In 1971, Tryon observed that all attempts to demonstrate affinities between Tasmanian languages and any Australian or other languages had failed (Tryon 1971:349, 351). Research into the available material to establish its internal relationships has been summarized by Jones, who concludes:

> There is a consensus that within Tasmania there were at least five related languages or dialects. One school favors five languages separated into an eastern and a western group; and the other favors two languages, one of which contained four dialects (Jones 1974:323).

The publication of Plomley's word list (1976), which incorporates the newly available material from the Robinson papers (see the following), may clarify these internal relationships. Dixon (1980:229) in his work on Australian languages, stands outside the earlier consensus, suggesting that "a slightly informed guess" indicates somewhere between eight and twelve Tasmanian languages. He further comments that "the phonological system we have inferred for Tasmania accords exactly with the Australian type" (Dixon 1980:232) and finishes "all that we can conclude is this—there is NO evidence that the Tasmanian languages were NOT of the regular Australian types" (Dixon 1980:233).

OSTEOLOGY

Problems of authenticity, provenance, and documentation have long bedevilled all Tasmanian osteological studies. Ethical problems in the study of human skeletal material have a long history in Tasmania, and are likely to continue. Despite this, however, the literature on this topic is vast. A particularly valuable guide to the data and their interpretation was published by Macintosh and Barker (1965). This monograph reviewed the data and the literature, and attempted to present a summary of all previous work, with an indication of Macintosh and Barker's thoughts on the matter.

Macintosh and Barker (1965:49) suggested that despite apparent conflict within the literature, there is "a substantial proportion of agreement." The areas of agreement were seen to lie in the numerical analysis of the data, and there were thought to be good agreements in certain differences observed between Tasmanian and Australian skulls, and also in observed similarities. Dispute, they observed, lay not in the facts, but in interpretation of the facts: "Is the weighing up of difference compared with similarity sufficient or not sufficient to separate Tasmanians from Australians?" (Macintosh and Barker 1965:49). No consensus was apparent, although Birdsell's then-predominating tri-hybrid theory of Australian Aboriginal origins, which is still in very wide currency, supported the case of Tasmanian distinctness.

Birdsell (1949, 1967) held that three separate groups of people, all originally from Asia, had colonized Australia. These were the Negritoes, the Murrayans, and the Carpentarians, in that chronological order. Negritoes survived in the Cairns rain forests of northeast Queensland and in Tasmania. In Tasmania, however, later migration brought Murrayans, and the Tasmanian Aborigines of the ethnographic present are seen as a hybrid form: predominantly Murrayan with Negrite elements. I shall not review Birdsell's tri-hybrid theory in toto, but it should be noted that he really only allows two factors to account for regional variation among Australian Aboriginal populations: hybridization and "arrested evolution" (Birdsell 1967:153). It should be further noted that Birdsell relies heavily on characteristics recorded from recent populations; the formulation of his theory was little influenced by dated, prehistoric fossil material.

Recent discoveries of well-dated, well-provenanced, indubitably prehistoric human skeletal material from modern, controlled archaeological excavations have shed new light on the problem. A number of specimens were recovered from the West Point midden (see the following). These represented about eight individuals, but because they had been cremated, the remains were badly calcined and heavily fragmented. They derived from contexts dated between about 1000 and 2000 B.P. They have been analyzed by Thorne, who comments that while no complete skull could be reconstructed, comparisons could be made on the basis of isolated characters, mostly nonmetrical (1971:318). Thorne was unable to discern in this material the special characteristics that had often in the past been assumed to be particularly Tasmanian. He concluded as follows:

> On the evidence, assuming for the moment one was not aware of the source of the material or its radiocarbon age, there would be no reasons to identify it as Tasmanian. Indeed, there would be strong grounds for saying the morphology was very consistent with individuals from coastal New South Wales in the recent past.... My present attitude is to regard the Tasmanian Aborigines as local variants of a south Australian population, based on a morphology existing about the time of Tasmania's connection and subsequent separation from the mainland. The degree of individuality developed by the islanders has been heightened by environmental stimulus and accelerated genetic effects due to population size (Thorne 1971:318–319).

A more recent, single specimen was discovered eroding from a sand dune on the west coast of Tasmania (Wallace and Doran 1976). This skull is far more complete than the West Point specimens, and although there is some blackening, it is not excessively charred. A radiocarbon date was obtained on a pooled specimen of charcoal flecks, discrete lumps, and remnants of possible sticks, all found in the immediate vicinity of the skull, but not associated in a strict archaeological sense. The date obtained was 4260 ± 360 years B.P. (ANU–1136). From their detailed osteological analysis of this specimen, the authors echoed the conclusions of Thorne in stating that:

> The skull ... displays many of those features which most authors would consider typically but not exclusively Tasmanian. No single feature, however, appears to fall outside the Australian Aboriginal range and this new material lends support to the concept of the essential kinship of the Tasmanian and Australian Aboriginals (Wallace and Doran 1976:182).

ETHNOGRAPHIC EVIDENCE

While ethnographic evidence cannot, of itself, shed light on the origins of the Tasmanians, such evidence must be considered in any initial attempt to define cultural affinities. It is also of importance in considering questions of a more general anthropological nature. This evidence is of two kinds. On the one hand, there are items of material culture that survive in museums or private collections. These are items, often of a perishable nature, collected from the traditional functioning society, as distinct from surface collections of articles essentially archaeological. Ethnographic items from Tasmania that survive are not abundant (Plomley 1962) and certainly do not represent the entire range of Tasmanian material culture items in use in the ethnographic present. In conjunction with this source of information, we might also consider pictorial representations of material culture items, drawn or otherwise rendered by European observers in the early historical period. Examples are Lesueur's illustration of five Tasmanian items—spear, waddy, kelp container, basket, and shell necklace (reproduced in Jones 1977: Fig. 5) and Labillardière's rendition of a canoe/catamaran (1800: Vol. II: plate XLVI).

By far the most important source of ethnographic information about the traditional Tasmanian culture is the corpus of observations of European navigators, explorers, and settlers contained in the early historical records. This ethnohistorical corpus is of varying quality, as might be expected. Hiatt (1967) reviews this literature and suggests a useful division into periods. Lourandos (1970:97) follows a similar scheme, with minor differences. The first group of observers are those navigators and explorers who preceded European settlement in Tasmania; their observations are regarded as pertaining to an undisturbed society. This group includes the observations of Tasman in 1642 (although he saw no *people*), Marion du Fresne in 1771, Labillardière who sailed with d'Entrecasteaux in 1792, Cook in 1773, Bass and Flinders in 1798, and Peron and Baudin in 1802. Lourandos would include in this group the 1803–1838 diaries of Robert Knopwood, the chaplain attached to the first settlement in Hobart (Nicholls 1977). While some of his observations were made at a very early date, it should be noted that they pertain to a society already under stress.

The second group of observations was made after settlement had begun, by persons now settled in Tasmania, or for some reason exploring within it. Examples are Captain James Kelly, who circumnavigated Tasmania in a whaleboat in 1816 (Bowden 1964) and the explorers in the employ of the Van Diemen's Land Company, who often ventured into territory not occupied by Europeans, especially in the northwest (Meston 1958). Such people made useful observations of Aborigines in regions not yet settled, but some disruption of traditional society can be assumed to have been taking place.

In a class by itself is the published record of the Tasmanian journals of George Augustus Robinson (Plomley 1966). Robinson, it will be recalled, the self-appointed "conciliator," was granted government support and recognition in his attempt, largely successful, to round up peacefully the Tasmanians remaining at large in the period 1829–1834. This task was accomplished by Robinson, unarmed, on foot, and accompanied only by Tasmanians already "converted." During these years, Robinson made many journeys across nearly all of Tasmania, and kept detailed journals on all his travels. He gleaned information about Tasmanian society and culture by recording information from his Aboriginal companions, the Aborigines he encountered, and his own observations. The society he observed was hardly functioning in its original state, especially as he managed to round up only some 300 people of a presumed original population in excess of 3000 (see the following). What he learned by way of informant testimony however was extensive, and covered many aspects of the original culture. Robinson's journals and papers were in private hands until 1949, when they passed to the Mitchell Library in Sydney. Thanks to the dedication and patience of N. J. B. Plomley, Robinson's journals became available in published form (Plomley 1966).

Several writers made observations of Tasmanian culture about the same time as Robinson. Their accounts are based, like his, mainly on informant testimony, but without his close knowledge of the people, nor his long-term contact with them. Such accounts include that of the visiting Quaker, James Backhouse (1843). In the late-nineteenth century, general accounts of Tasmanian life and culture began to appear. Most of these either are based entirely on second-hand information, or contain some information gleaned from the institutionalized Aborigines on Flinders Island. That accepted as the most authoritative is the compendium of Roth (1899), which included all information known at the time of publication. Roth, however, did not have the benefit of the Robinson journals and, moreover, approached the sources available to him most uncritically. Unfortunately, similar works still appear, utilizing nineteenth-century accounts and ignoring modern research (e.g., Davies 1973).

Since the publication of the Robinson journals, several attempts have been made to reconstruct particular aspects of Tasmanian culture, in the light of modern anthropological and archaeological research interests.

Material Culture

Items of material culture may be identified by their physical survival, figurative depiction, or a written description. They are in some ways the most accessible and easily interpreted aspects of any culture, but their role in a functioning society is sometimes obscure, particularly in the Tasmanian situation. Much has been written about Tasmanian stone tools, but these are essentially archaeological; paradoxically, as Jones (1971b:471) points out, "we do not have surviving, a single implement which was unquestionably used for a known purpose."

In a review of surviving objects and information, Davidson (1937) made the important point that every known aspect of the Tasmanian material culture had an analogue in mainland Aboriginal culture. Conversely however many Australian items were not found in Tasmania, such as spearthrowers, boomerangs, ground-edge axes, and compound tools involving a method of hafting.

Some recent studies have looked at particular items and attempted to define their role in the functioning society. Hiatt (1967) for instance looked at equipment used in the procurement and preparation of food, in the course of a general investigation into the food quest (see the following). Lourandos (1970:104–116) has collated information about hut types and sizes and the relationship of these variables to group size. Jones (1976) has brought together information about Tasmanian maritime technology. He found that in many parts of Tasmania, canoe–rafts or catamarans were made from bundles of bark or reeds, and were surprisingly effective in crossing rivers and conveying people to nearby offshore islands. In northeast Tasmania, however, no form of watercraft was made or used (Jones 1976:239–249).

Economy

Hiatt (1967) tackled the question of Tasmanian economy and diet, as revealed by ethnohistorical accounts, being careful to distinguish "direct" observations from "gossip" accounts. Hiatt also discussed the distribution of the population, the size and movements of local groups, material culture, and religious observances. With regard to diet, she concluded that the Tasmanians in the ethnographic present ate most of the animal and vegetable resources which were available to them, with one notable exception. The Tasmanians did not eat scale fish. Apart from this, their diet was seen to be similar to that of mainland Aborigines, although some groups of the latter ate more vegetable foods. The division of labor between the sexes was also described as similar to that of the mainland; reliable items were supplied by women, and Tasmanian men were responsible for less reliable elements. Hiatt also highlighted the fact that the Tasmanians modified their environment considerably by the use of fire:

> In Tasmania, some Aborigines modified their environment so much that the normal vegetation and food supply were changed. For example, the inhabitants of the west coast extended their narrow coastal environment by burning rain forest areas which in some places came down to the sea. The resultant sedgeland provided much more food than the rain forest. Similar burning occurred in other parts of Tasmania and in most cases it changed existing vegetation into one which provided more or different food sources (Hiatt 1967:219; see also Jones 1969).

Hiatt found no marked economic dichotomy between the east and west coasts.

Lourandos (1968, 1970) argued that there *was* a marked dichotomy between the east and west coasts, in terms of overall economy and concomitant cultural aspects. He suggests that Hiatt's division of Tasmania into "east" and "west" ignored the distribution of ecological zones and cut across them, and that she did not distinguish with sufficient clarity between observations of Aborigines in pre-European contact situations and observations of Aborigines operating in a Europeanized situation (Lourandos 1970:95–06). Lourandos accordingly re-analyzed the ethnohistorical literature, distinguishing the dry sclerophyll regions of the east and southeast from the heath and wet sclerophyll zone of the northeast. He concluded that settlement and economic activities in western

Tasmania were concentrated on the coast, due mainly to the dense rain forest hinterland. On the east coast, however, settlement and economic activities were more dispersed into the interior, due to the open nature of the dry sclerophyll hinterland (1970:118 and passim; see also Lourandos 1968, 1977).

Social Organization and Land Use

One important aspect of Tasmanian culture that is perhaps only susceptible to ethnographic analysis is social organization. Again drawing primarily on the Robinson journals, Jones (1974) has attempted a reconstruction of the Tasmanian social organization at the tribe–local group level. This painstaking piece of research is probably as far as we will ever be able to go in this direction. Jones describes what is known of the Tasmanian family, pointing out that it differed from mainland Aboriginal marriage practices in that the Tasmanians were "almost invariably monogamous," and that both men and women married when they reached maturity, and were usually of comparable ages when wed (Jones 1974:324). Jones described the unit that camped together and cooked around a single fire as a "hearth group":

> Its core was a single family consisting of man, wife, children, aged relatives, and sometimes friends or other relatives; it ranged in size from two to about seven or eight people, and we have many descriptions of such hearth groups. They were the domestic and possibly foraging unit, and they often corresponded to the group occupying a single hut, particularly in the west coast camps (Jones 1974:324).

At a higher level of organization was the "band": "a group of people who called themselves by a particular name and were known by that or other names to other people" (Jones 1974:324). This band corresponds to the mainland Aboriginal local group designated the "horde" by Radcliffe-Brown (1930; see also Stanner 1965), but whether its core was agnatic in Tasmania is unknown, and in any case this concept has been challenged for mainland groups (Hiatt 1962). Jones (1974:324–325) says that the band "owned a territory," but

> Such ownership was formal, for although a band based its residence in the vicinity of its country and could often be found there, it also foraged widely on the territories of both bands (Jones 1974:325).

In the latter case, however, the other bands usually belonged to the same tribe. Bands were usually exogamous (Jones 1974:327). Jones (1974:325) thinks there were originally 70–85 bands in Tasmania, and that the average band consisted of about 40–50 people. Using these figures, he suggests the original population of Tasmania was between 3000 and 4000 people. Ryan (1975:19–20), following Plomley (1966:969; 1971), feels the bands were larger in size but fewer in number, with the overall population being about the same as Jones's estimate.

Jones thinks there were nine Tasmanian tribes, larger units of social organization which subsumed the bands. A tribe is defined as

> that agglomeration of bands that lived in contiguous regions, spoke the same language or dialect, shared the same cultural traits, usually intermarried, had a similar pattern of seasonal

movement, habitually met together for economic and other reasons, the pattern of whose peaceful relations were within the agglomeration, and of whose enmities and military adventures were directed outside it. Such a tribe had a territory, consisting of the sum of the land owned by its constituent bands (Jones 1974:328).

Jones's tribes and their territories are depicted in Figure 1.5. He has detailed the composition, pattern of seasonal movements, and distinctive cultural traits of each tribe (Jones 1974). It is noteworthy that there are more tribes than identifiable language groups (see preceding); while the evidence suggests that each tribe was linguistically homogeneous, some tribes must have shared a language. Jones feels that it is likely that each tribe was distinguished from its neighbors by "some differences in speech" (Jones 1974:328).

Jones concluded that the average number of bands in a tribe was 9, with a range from 5 or 6 up to 15. Using his figures of 40–50 people per band produces an average of 360–450 people per tribe, with a range between 250 and 700 people. For the whole of Tasmania, using these figures, he estimates an overall population of between 3000 and 4000 people in Tasmania just before European contact (Jones 1974:328–329). This is the same as the figure calculated from bands only. This is hardly a sophisticated exercise in demography, but it is probably the best that can be done with our present information.

Jones makes some important overall comments about the tribal economic patterns. All tribal territories were oriented in such a way that a large range of economic zones was able to be exploited. Each tribe had a complex pattern of seasonal movements involving seasonally available foods, and specialized resources such as ochre. In a general sense, the fact that Tasmania is an island was exploited: "Within Tasmania, there was no tribe nor group of bands that lived totally inland and did not at some time of the year forage on the seashore" (Jones 1974:329).

Hunter Island is only 24 km long by 6 km wide, lying just off the northwest tip of Tasmania. It and others of the Hunter Group (see Figure 1.12) fell within the territory of Jones's North West Tribe, and during the historical period was visited by Kelly and surveyors for the Van Diemen's Land Company. Robinson made two visits there, a brief one in 1830 and a longer one in 1832. The ethnohistorical accounts have been compiled by Bowdler (1980a) to form a picture of pre-European Aboriginal land use. She concluded that there was a band based on nearby Robbins Island, easily accessible from the Tasmanian mainland by foot at low tide. The other islands of the group, and the Tasmanian mainland, were visited by members of the Robbins Island band; the Hunter Islands were reciprocally visited by members of most of the west coast bands. It seems that groups of up to 50 people may have visited the larger islands of the group (Hunter, Three Hummock) in groups composed of men, women, and children.

A fairly dangerous water crossing had to be made to reach the Hunter Islands, apart from Robbins Island. While there are accounts of Aborigines swimming between islands, the tides and currents ensure that the initial trip from the mainland was by catamaran. There seems no question of permanent occupation of any of the Hunter Islands, except perhaps Robbins Island. Visits to the other

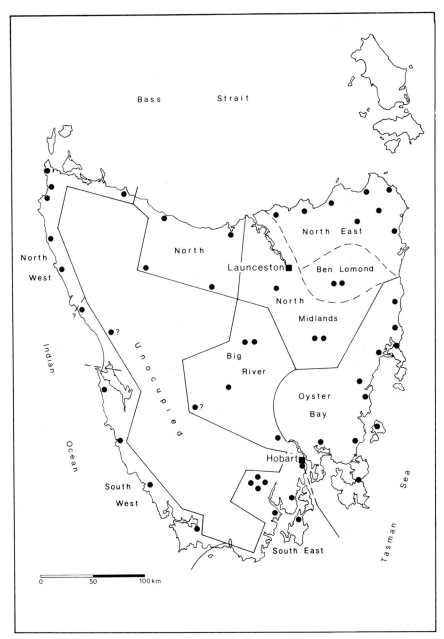

Figure 1.5 Tasmanian tribes. Local residence of a band (●), tribal boundary (—). (From Jones 1974.)

islands seem to have been of short duration, and to have taken place in summer, when muttonbirds, their eggs, and chicks were available. Some comments made to Robinson suggest that few if any visits were made in winter (Bowdler 1980a:12–13). The exploitation of Hunter Island is interpreted as one aspect of the general seasonal pattern of the North West Tribe.

Mortuary Rites and Religious Practices

Hiatt has compiled the available ethnohistorical information on Tasmanian mortuary practices (Hiatt 1969). She focused particularly on cremation, as not only was this the rite most commonly described for Tasmania, but it was also common in southeastern Australia. She concluded that it was most likely that cremation in southeastern Australia and Tasmania "is a survival from a time when both areas shared the same culture" (Hiatt 1969:113).

Horton has collected the available written information about myth, ritual, and ceremony, and concludes that "some evidence for communal religious activity is . . . present in Robinson's journals" (1979:32). He cites examples of extended ceremonial events, variety in the Tasmanian ritual life, rituals involving large numbers of people, and examples of "ceremonial sculpture" (Horton 1979:33). Hiatt (1967:217) has also commented that "evidence for dancing, singing and myth among the Tasmanian groups resembles the pattern of a culture that has a totemic religion."

PALEOENVIRONMENTAL RESEARCH

If prehistoric research in Tasmania has gone hand-in-hand with historical and ethnographic research, it has been no less closely intertwined with paleoenvironmental research, including palynology, paleontology, and geomorphology. Of crucial importance to the prehistory of the Tasmanians is the effect of Pleistocene eustatic sea level changes. The submarine topography of Bass Strait has been elucidated by Jennings (1959, 1971), and, in conjunction with the recent work on sea level change in the Australasian region (e.g., Chappell 1976) enables us to estimate with some confidence those times when Tasmania was part of Greater Australasia, and the times when it has been completely severed (the last 12,000 years).

Tasmania has been more directly subject to glacial effects than other parts of Australia, due to its high altitudes and high latitudes. It has therefore received considerable attention from geomorphologists interested in glacial landforms and associated phenomena. Research until 1968 was usefully summarized by Jones (1968), in the context of a general discussion of late Pleistocene environments in Tasmania and Australia. Jones concluded that much of Tasmania would have been uninhabitable during the last glacial maximum, about 18,000–20,000 B.P., as it would have been in the grip of full glacial or periglacial conditions, leaving only a "narrow forested fringe around the coast" (Jones 1968:192). More recent research does not dispute that much of Tasmania was glaciated, but rather than a narrow forested coastal corridor, it now seems that non-glaciated regions in southeast Australia generally were covered with an open, grassy savannah-like environment, as a result of a cold, dry climatic regime (Colhoun 1975, 1978; Hope 1978). Macphail's work on several pollen sequences has allowed the reconstruction of Tasmanian Holocene vegetational histories in some detail (Macphail 1979).

ARCHAEOLOGY

Prehistoric Archaeology in Australia

The prehistory of human beings in Tasmania is clearly inextricably linked with the prehistory of human beings in Australia, and prehistoric research in Tasmania is historically linked with the progress of such research in Australia, so a brief résumé of the latter may be helpful. An early and exemplary controlled excavation of a prehistoric archaeological site in the lower Murray Valley, South Australia was conducted in the 1920s by Hale and Tindale (1930). Like Hero of Alexander's steam engine, however, it was clearly too much ahead of its time and had no sequel. Not until the early 1960s did such research begin to be conducted in a concerted way. Mulvaney's (1964) announcement of a firmly dated Pleistocene antiquity for people in Australia attracted new interest to the subject, and the 15 or so years since then have seen a virtual explosion in the subject in Australian universities and other institutions. Research in that period has demonstrated a 40,000-year antiquity for Aboriginal occupation of Australia; and while there are regional differences, some pan-continental phenomena have been identified. The earliest human arrivals into Australia must have come by sea, from southeastern Asia, and were probably therefore coastally oriented (Bowdler 1977). Their material culture included artifacts of both bone and stone, the latter comprising a large-sized component of core tools and pebble tools, and a small-sized component including steep-edged scrapers (Mulvaney 1975:174). Their mortuary rites included both cremation (cf. Hiatt 1969) and interment (Mulvaney 1975:152; Bowler and Thorne 1976). In the tropical regions, they had ground-edge axes (White 1967).

Between 3000 and 5000 B.P., a new suite of stone tools appeared everywhere in mainland Australia. Dubbed the "Australian Small Tool Tradition" by Gould (1969:233), it manifests itself differently in various regions. In a general sense, one can say that in southern temperate Australia, this new suite of stone tools is characterized by small backed implements, including geometric microliths like those of the European and Middle Eastern Mesolithic industries. In northern Australia, it is typified by unifacial and bifacial projectile points. In arid Australia, it is characterized by an implement resembling an abruptly retouched scraper that is hafted onto a handle (often a spearthrower) and used as a wood-working chisel called a *tula* adze. These tool types do not have exclusive distributions (see Mulvaney 1975:224–225), and do not replace earlier types; in most places, they appear to have been supplemental to the pre-existing industries. Mulvaney initially suggested (Mulvaney and Joyce 1965) that the earlier industries represented a non-hafted phase, and the introduction of the new types indicated the invention or introduction of hafting. This view was criticized in the light of the discovery of grooved ground-edge axes in Pleistocene contexts in Arnhem Land (White 1971), which were grooved presumably to allow a handle to be attached. Gould (1969:233), however, has pointed out that Mulvaney's proposition is valid insofar as the new tools represent the earliest evidence for hafting with an adhesive.

Archaeology in Tasmania before 1963

It may be something of a non sequitur to say at this point that modern archaeology did not begin in Tasmania until 1963. There were however a number of activities taking place in Tasmania which should be called archaeological, even though they did not involve controlled archaeological excavation. Jones (1971b:35–54) has traced the history of these interests, especially as they focused on the Rocky Cape caves, and also as they reflected the intellectual currents of Australia and the rest of the scientific world.

From 1908, a number of people, trained and employed in other subjects, collected Tasmanian stone artifacts, and also wrote about them (Crowther 1950; Legge 1929, 1930; Meston 1937; Noetling 1908, 1910; Pulleine 1929). They also commented on the kinds of sites, middens, quarries, and caves that they located in the field. In the 1930s, examples of Tasmanian Aboriginal art were discovered on the west coast and in the northwest. These consisted of circles and other abstract motifs pecked in rock (Meston 1932, 1933, 1934; Sims 1977). The point of most of this research was seen as being to amplify the ethnographic accounts of Tasmanian culture. The discovery of bone tools (Crowther 1925) and fish bones (Meston 1956) at archeological sites indicated that the ethnohistorical records were deficient, as they described neither the manufacturing of bone tools nor the eating of scale fish.

Controlled excavations were seen to be not worthwhile, because researchers interested in Tasmanian culture believed, as did their mainland counterparts, that the Aborigines in Tasmania, as in Australia, were an "unchanging people in an unchanging environment" (Pulleine 1929:310). Holes however were dug, especially at the Rocky Cape cave; the aim of these early diggings seems simply to have been the acquisition of specimens. As provenance was of no account, excavation techniques were, quite simply, appalling. Jones has traced the history of holes at Rocky Cape back to the turn of the century (Jones 1971b:35). No inkling of what we would regard as an archaeological interpretation began to emerge until a visit was paid to Rocky Cape by Norman Tindale in the 1930s. In the south cave, one of the earlier burrowers' trenches was open, and Tindale thought he detected a division in the stratigraphy and in the implements from them. While Tindale's suggested sequence (1937) has not stood the test of time, it was the first time it had been suggested that evidence for cultural change might exist in the Tasmanian archaeological record.

Perhaps the real turning point in Tasmanian archaeological studies, as on the mainland, came with the invention and widespread availability of radiocarbon dating. In the early 1960s, radio astronomer Grote Reber, an American pioneer in his own field who had taken up residence in Tasmania, began to collect charcoal samples from midden sites. His excavation technique was hardly so-phisticated; he simply cut slits into a number of middens and extracted charcoal from the very bottom of each. Reber himself described it as "a rather expensive brute force approach" (Reber 1965:264). The middens sampled were located on the west coast, in the northwest, the east coast, and the Derwent estuary; they ranged from 1000 to over 8000 B.P. From a midden at Carlton on the east coast, a date of 8700 ± 200 years B.P. (I–323) was obtained, and from the Rocky Cape South cave, in the northwest, a date of 8120 ± 200 years B.P. (GXO–266; Reber 1965, 1967). Reber saw clearly what the next development should be:

> Now full-scale excavations are required to learn about the cultural content and its change within this time period. Clearly, action by professional archaeologists is indicated, and will be richly rewarding to the diligent and competent (Reber 1965:268).

Archaeology in Tasmania since 1963

Modern archaeology began in Tasmania with the advent of Rhys Jones, who in 1963 accepted a position at Sydney University, and in the summer undertook an archaeological reconnaissance trip to Tasmania. Since that time, a consider-able amount of field work has occurred in Tasmania, and still continues. Much of the work has not as yet been fully reported, and most of what has, is only available in thesis form. Some of what follows will undoubtedly require future revision, and a more mature synthesis will be possible at a later time.

Jones's strategy on his initial Tasmanian trip (1963–1964) was to locate as many promising sites as possible, in the east, west, and midlands, and sample them, with an eye to returning to carry out more detailed investigations in the follow-ing summer (Jones 1965). In the course of this first trip, quite a large excavation was carried out at a cave at Sisters' Creek in northwest Tasmania. The Rocky Cape caves were inspected, and a section of the unfilled pit left by previous diggers in the South cave was cleaned back. Jones concluded that there was undisturbed, stratified deposit remaining in situ here, and that it was similar to that at Sisters' Creek (Jones 1971b:60). A large, stabilized open midden site at West Point on the west coast of Tasmania was located and sampled. On his return in the summer of 1964–1965, Jones carried out extensive excavations at West Point and at two caves at Rocky Cape, the North cave and the South Cave (Figure 1.6).

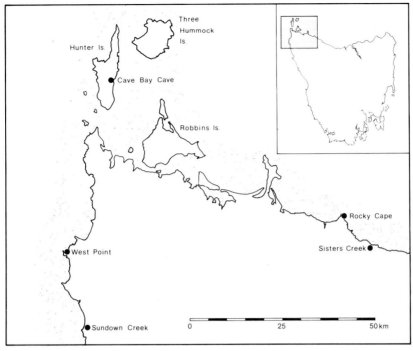

Figure 1.6   Northwest Tasmania, showing sites mentioned in text.

Jones thus conducted quite large excavations at four sites: West Point, Sisters' Creek, Rocky Cape South, and Rocky Cape North. Only the excavations at the Rocky Cape caves have been reported in detail, but preliminary accounts and radiocarbon dates are available for the other two sites.

Rocky Cape

Rocky Cape itself is a promontory of pre-Cambrian quartzite extending into Bass Strait from the north coast of Tasmania. Several caves are located along this stretch of coast where quartzite forms the country rock. Rocky Cape South is the cave that has been best known and most vandalized since the turn of the century. The detailed report on these excavations forms the subject of Jones's Ph.D. dissertation (Jones 1971b), but brief accounts are also available (Jones 1966, 1978).

Rocky Cape South is on the east side of the peninsula, about 110 m from the foreshore, and 21 m above it. Like the others in the region, it is a stranded sea cave. It consists of two chambers, one of which was sealed by accumulated deposit until recently. Jones's excavations revealed more than 3 m of undisturbed archaeological deposit. This deposit was entirely anthropogenic and consisted of shell midden which was not homogeneous. It exhibited a complex microstratigraphy of interleaving shell lenses, ashy lenses, hearths, and white phosphatic lenses. Three major stratigraphic units could be identified however (Stratigraphic Units P, Q, and R) which Jones then specified as Analytical Units 5, 6, and 7. A series of radiocarbon dates was obtained from Jones's excavations, and those of Reber and earlier diggers were incorporated into Jones's sequence. Two dates were obtained for the bottom of Analytical Unit 7 (Stratigraphic Unit R): 7465 ± 150 B.P. (V–86) and 8120 ± 165 B.P. (GXO–226). Two dates were obtained from the middle of Analytical Unit 7: 6445 ± 80 B.P. (V–51) and 6745 ± 145 B.P. (V–97). One date was obtained for the top of Analytical Unit 7: 6145 ± 200 B.P. (V–85). The mean depth of this unit is 1.5 m. The bottom of Analytical Unit 6 (Stratigraphic Unit Q) is dated 5075 ± 250 B.P. (V–84); this unit is about 75 cm thick. The top of Analytical Unit 5 (Stratigraphic Unit P) is dated 3795 ± 100 B.P. (V–83); it is about 1.5 m thick. Thus, there is a continuous sequence indicating reasonably even deposition (Jones 1971b:195–198).

The deposit contained stone artifacts including finished implements, animal bones, shellfish remains, and charcoal throughout. Bone tools were found throughout these deposits, as also were fish bones. The deposit overlay archaeologically sterile basal grit.

In his analysis of the material from the Rocky Cape caves, Jones concentrated on the stone tools in considering the basic culture-historical problem. This was because he felt that the most pressing question with regard to the Tasmanians was still: "Who were they? Where had they come from?" His excavations and the radiocarbon dates acquired by Reber and others, showed that people had been using Tasmanian coastal sites since at least 8000 B.P. Clearly the most economical explanation for these dates was that during the late Pleistocene, people had been living on the Pleistocene shoreline practicing a coastal economy. When sea level rose after the glacial retreat, people moved with the coastline until it reached its present position, when they occupied the Rocky Cape South cave for the first time, as well as the Carlton midden in east Tasmania. The evidence from the lowest level of the Rocky Cape South Cave indicates a well-developed littoral economy, featuring shellfish, fish, and seals. Older sites would thus be on the Pleistocene shoreline, under the present level of the sea (Jones 1968:200). By implication, therefore, people had been in Tasmania since the time it was joined to Australia prior to 12,000 B.P., and shared with the mainland Aborigines a common ancestry. This should be evident from an analysis of cultural items, in this case, stone tools. Jones felt it was time that

> Tasmania's history rested on a detailed documentation of its culture sequences, and it was rapidly apparent that the relationship between mainland and island stone assemblages could no longer rest on unsupported assertions (Jones 1971b:65).

Jones concentrated on erecting a typology of the stone implements from Rocky Cape. Implements were defined as "any piece of stone, be it a flake or a block, that has on it one or more worked edges" (Jones 1971b:325). The types were derived using an analysis which Jones saw as a "compromise between a traditional approach and one based on newer statistical techniques" (Jones 1971b:319–320). Five types were identified (Figures 1.7–1.9):

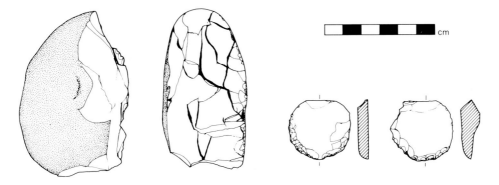

Pebble choppers   Type 1   Round–edge scraper

Figure 1.7   Rocky Cape stone tool types: pebble chopper and round-edge scraper. (From Jones 1971b.)

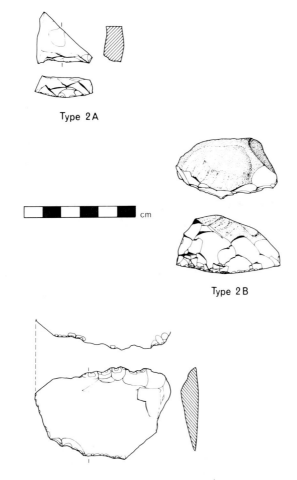

Type 2A

Type 2B

Type 3

Figure 1.8   Rocky Cape stone tool types: small steep-edge scraper (type 2A), large steep-edge scraper (type 2B), flat straight-edge scraper (type 3). (From Jones 1971b.)

Type	Scraper characteristics
1	Round-edge
2	Steep-edge
	2A small (or low)
	2B large (or high)
3	Flat, straight–edge
4	Notched
5	Concave and nosed

Pebble choppers were also identified, from the older deposits; they were omitted from the major part of Jones's analysis because there were too few of them (Jones 1971b:296).

Overall, Jones comments that the Rocky Cape stone tool sequence "documents the internal evolution of a single, historically related technological tradition, over a period of 8000 years" (Jones 1971b:607). In examining its relationship with industries of mainland Australia, he looks to the earlier, pre-Australian Small Tool Tradition industries, referred to here as the "Australian core tool and scraper tradition":

> Tasmania formed one of the regional provinces of this core tool and scraper tradition. Tasmanian industries, while sharing the basic technology of steep edge scrapers, were characterised by a higher proportion of notched and concave and nosed scrapers, and by the absence or rarity of specialised horsehoof core scrapers, though analogous forms do exist. There was no greater difference between Tasmanian and mainland assemblages than there was internally between some mainland provinces (Jones 1971b:627).

While there was an overall single tradition, there were also internal changes within the implement sequence. Not all the identified types were present in equal proportions throughout. Round-edge scrapers (type 1) increased from the older levels to the more recent levels. Small steep-edge scrapers (type 2A) remained constant, but large steep-edge scrapers (type 2B) declined, as did

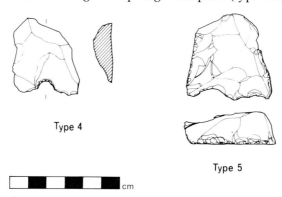

Type 4

Type 5

cm

Figure 1.9   Rocky Cape stone tool types: notched scraper (type 4), concave and nosed scraper (type 5). (From Jones 1971b.)

notched scrapers (type 4). Concave and nosed scrapers (type 5) increased, concomitant with the decline in type 4. Jones interprets this latter inverse relationship as indicating that types 4 and 5 filled "an analogous functional role within the technological armoury" (Jones 1971b:445–446).

There is also a change through time in the raw materials from which the tools were made. In the lower levels, local quartzites are the most commonly used stone; in later levels, cherts and a fine-grained siliceous stone called "spongolite," which must have come from the west coast of Tasmania, were favored. There is also a general decrease in the size of the tools. Overall, Jones sees the observed changes within types, and within the suite of types, and the changes in raw materials used, as reflecting a steady increase of efficiency in the use of raw material, "coincident with, and probably related to the steady replacement of the use of locally obtained blocks of poor raw materials by the importation of superior ones from quarries, several days' walk away from the site" (Jones 1971b:448).

The most marked change in the prehistoric sequence for the Rocky Cape caves is the absence of fish bones and bone tools from the later part of the sequence. From Analytical Units 5, 6, and 7 in the South Cave came many thousands of fish bones, representing almost exclusively parrot fish (wrasses, family Labridae). Also from these units came many bone artifacts (Figure 1.10). Small numbers of both were found in the lower levels (Analytical Units 3 and 4) of the North Cave, but neither occurred in contexts younger than 3500 B.P. The disappearance of these objects from the archaeological record, supported by the evidence from other sites, as we shall see, has excited much controversy. This will be discussed further.

Sisters' Creek

This is another cave in the Precambrian quartzite of northwest Tasmania, located about 11 km east of Rocky Cape, also on the coast, with the cave entrance about 30 m above sea level. The deposits resembled those of both Rocky Cape sites, consisting of interleaving bands and lenses of shell and ash and phosphate concentrations, all laid down over archaeologically sterile basal grit. A radiocarbon date for the bottom of the midden deposits was obtained: 6050 ± 88 B.P. (NSW–17). The site still awaits detailed analysis and description, but preliminary comments are available (Jones 1966:5–6, 1968:198, 1978:37).

The Sisters' Creek finds resemble those of Analytical Units 5 and 6 of Rocky Cape South, with which they are at least in part contemporaneous. Stone artifacts including finished implements, animal bones, shellfish remains, and charcoal were found throughout. Stone raw materials were mostly local. Bone tools were found, and numerous parrot fish bones also.

West Point

The excavation of this site is also largely undescribed; preliminary accounts may be found in Jones (1966:6–7, 1967, 1978:37), and a detailed analysis of

Figure 1.10 Rocky Cape bone artifacts. (Photo by Dragi Markovic, from Jones 1971b.)

shellfish samples was conducted by Coleman (1966). The site is a large established open shell midden on West Point on the west coast of Tasmania. It caps a dune on the northern margin of a small rocky inlet, and covers almost half a km². On its surface, 7 circular depressions were evident, measuring 3–5 m in diameter. These depressions occur on other large middens in west Tasmania, and correlate well with the huts described by Robinson for the area (Jones 1947, Lourandos 1968, Jones 1971a, Ranson 1978).

Jones's excavations here in 1965 revealed some 2.5 m of midden deposit, stratigraphically divisible into an upper, dense midden layer, and a lower, somewhat sandier midden layer, the two being separated by an intermittent sandy band (Jones 1966:6).

Jones obtained a date for the bottom of his excavated deposits of 1850 ± 80 B.P. (V–69) and one for the top of 1330 ± 80 B.P. (V–66), (Jones 1971b:609). Reber (1965) had also obtained a date for the bottom of this site, prior to Jones's excavations, of 2350 ± 266 B.P. (I–322). The deposits were extremely rich in stone artifacts, with many finished tools mostly made from fine-grained spongolite, which here constitutes a local stone. Typologically, the tools are considered to resemble those from the upper layers of Rocky Cape North. Also found were many animal bones (especially those of southern elephant seal, *Mirounga leonina*), shellfish remains, and charcoal. No bone tools were found, and, out of a total of some 20,000 separate bones, only 4 or 5 were fish bones.

Little Swanport

An oyster midden at Little Swanport was excavated as part of the second program of modern archaeological research to be conducted in Tasmania, begun by Lourandos in 1967 (Lourandos 1968, 1970, 1977). Lourandos carried out a program of survey and excavation in eastern Tasmania to investigate the similarities and differences there might be between the east and the northwest. Two sites were excavated, the midden at Little Swanport and an island site at Crown Lagoon (Figure 1.11).

Little Swanport is a sheltered estuary on the east coast of Tasmania, both sides of which are lined by a series of shell middens. One was chosen for excavation, a stabilized, conical-shaped midden, about 2800 m² in area. Excavation revealed the midden to be composed of a series of interleaving shell lenses up to 2 m deep. Small ashy hearths were present. A thin but continuous lens of mussel shell occurred over most of the site at a depth of about 1.3 m, dividing the deposit into an upper layer (the upper two-thirds) and a lower layer (the bottom third). A basal radiocarbon date was obtained: 4490 ± 120 B.P. (ANU–356). The mussel layer was dated 3660 ± 95 B.P. (ANU–357), and a date was obtained for just below the top of the midden of 1660 ± 85 B.P. (ANU–355) (Lourandos 1970:52–53, and personal communication 1980).

The deposits consisted primarily of estuarine shellfish; other components were meager in occurrence. They included flaked stone, mostly used pieces and

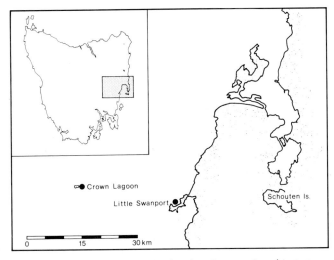

Figure 1.11 East Tasmania, showing sites mentioned in text.

finished implements, animal bone, and charcoal. The animal bone included fish bone, but only in the lower layer. Bone tools also occurred and were likewise limited to the lower layer. This site thus confirmed one aspect of the Rocky Cape sequence: Fish were not eaten, and bone tools were not made, after about 3500 B.P., although both these activities had taken place before that time. The evidence from Little Swanport implied that the cessation of fish eating and bone toolmaking was a pan-Tasmanian phenomenon (Lourandos 1970:54–55).

Crown Lagoon

This was the first lunette (fossil sand dune: cf. Lake Mungo) site to be excavated in Australia. Crown Lagoon itself is now drained, but once formed part of the upper drainage system of the Little Swanport River. It is about 25 km inland, directly west from Little Swanport, and is in dry sclerophyll country about 600–700 m above sea level.

The cultural deposit consists of stone tools and charcoal stratified mainly within a dark red sandy layer in the dune. Its top is dated to 4170 ± 80 B.P. (ANU–279) and its bottom to 4860 ± 95 B.P. (ANU–278). Charcoal was concentrated in small hearths, and the stone artifacts formed recognizable flaking floors. Animal bone was found throughout, but in a poor state of preservation; where it could be identified it was of the large kangaroo (*Macropus giganteus*) (Lourandos 1970:60–67, 1977).

Lourandos has interpreted the observed differences between Little Swanport and Crown Lagoon as follows:

> the Crown Lagoon assemblage, together with the supporting faunal and structural evidence, suggest that the site consisted of a series of temporary camps oriented chiefly around the maintenance and utilisation of flaked stone tools used to manufacture and maintain wooden implements which were themselves associated with the hunting of forest animals. In contrast the Little Swanport assemblage in form and frequency indicates both the less frequent and less complex nature of such activities at a site whose main orientation was towards the waters of the estuary (Lourandos 1977:222).

In other words, at Little Swanport the main activity represented is the gathering of shellfish, but at Crown Lagoon, the main activities represented are the making of spears and hunting of land animals. Lourandos sees this dichotomy as reflecting an overall east Tasmanian adaptation involving activities being dispersed from the coast back across a wide hinterland. Lourandos contrasts this with the west coast, where activities were much more tightly coastal, and localized at large base camps such as West Point, where a whole gamut of activities is represented (Lourandos 1968, 1977).

In viewing the overall sequence in northwest Tasmania, Jones (1977) argued that the initial occupation of Rocky Cape involved the occupation of hitherto unknown territory, and that over the subsequent 8000 years, the archaeological sequence documents increasing knowledge of, and adaptation to, the new environment: "Tasmanian society managed to assert, or perhaps re-assert, a regionally co-ordinated economic system in the north-west" (Jones 1977:195; see also Jones 1974). Lourandos, comparing the eastern sequence revealed by his research with that of Jones in the northwest, concluded that for Tasmania in general, after the sea reached its present level, there was a process of independent cultural adaptation to separate environments (Lourandos 1977:223).

Hunter Island

In 1973, Bowdler began a research project on Hunter Island, which lies just off the tip of northwest Tasmania. This project was seen as a natural extension of the work of Jones in northwest Tasmania (Bowdler 1974a, 1979). A site survey of the island was carried out, and five sites were excavated. Some of the other islands in the group (called the Hunter Islands) were briefly examined. Hunter Island itself lies about 5 km off the Tasmanian mainland (Figure 1.12). As mentioned previously, historical records (including Robinson's journals) tell us that the Hunter Islands were visited by Tasmanian Aborigines in the ethnographic present (Bowdler 1980a).

The oldest site excavated was Cave Bay Cave, on the east coast of Hunter Island. Like the Rocky Cape caves, it is a stranded sea cave, and occurs in a siltstone which is geologically related to the Precambrian quartzites of northwest Tasmania. The modern floor of the cave is about 25 m directly above the foreshore; the entrance looks southeast. Excavations were carried out here in the summers of 1974 and 1975. Its major immediate significance is that it produced the first firmly dated evidence of the presence of people in Tasmania during the Pleistocene (Bowdler 1974b).

Unlike the Rocky Cape and Sisters' Creek sites, the deposit here did not consist entirely of anthropogenic, dense shell midden. Instead we find a complex sequence of archaeological and nonarchaeological deposits, and some of the archaeological deposits are very sparse. Mainly because of large siltstone boulders embedded throughout the deposit, bedrock was not reached; it is therefore possible (if not highly likely) that occupational deposit older than that found may be present. The lowest levels reached, at a depth of about 2.4 m, consisted of an archaeologically sterile, light brownish gray silty sand. Overlying this was a series of black hearthy layers containing stone artifacts, mainly waste, animal bones, and charcoal. The few stone tools have a generalized resemblance to those from some Australian mainland sites of similar antiquity. The lowest of these layers was dated 22,750 ± 420 B.P. (ANU–1498); the uppermost was dated 20,850 ± 290 B.P. (ANU–1612). Over these hearthy layers were deposits characterized by large blocks of roof–fall and containing sparse archaeological material. Dates for these deposits from different trenches within the cave are: 19,520 ± 300 B.P. (ANU–1774) and 18,550 ± 600 B.P. (ANU–1361). Included in the sparse archaeological material associated with these dates were bone tools comparable to those from mainland Australian sites of similar age (Figure 1.13), and stone artifacts. These deposits are thus contemporary with the period of full glaciation in the Tasmanian highlands, and the large amount of roof–fall at this time might be due to frost-wedging caused by low temperatures. Silty deposits overlie this

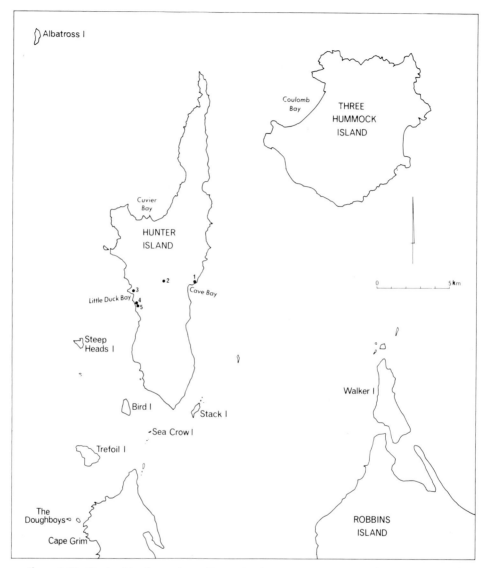

Figure 1.12 Hunter Islands, northwest Tasmania, showing sites mentioned in text. Cave Bay Cave (1), Stockyard Site (2), Little Duck Bay (3), Rookery Rockshelter (4), Muttonbird Midden (5).

layer, containing no archaeological deposits except one small, isolated hearth dated 15,400 ± 330 B.P. (ANU–1613). After this, deposition slowed considerably, until the time when the sea reached its present level, when a thin but dense layer of shell midden was deposited. The bottom of this has three dates: 7180 ± 90 B.P. (ANU–1552), 6600 ± 90 B.P. (ANU–1773), and 6640 ± 100 B.P. (ANU–1797). The last two are preferred for stratigraphic reasons and their close agreement; they make a very good fit for other estimates of when the sea reached its present level in Australia (Thom and Chappel 1975). A small, isolated hearth immediately above this midden layer has been dated to 3960 ± 110 B.P. (ANU–1614), and another archaeologically sterile layer follows. The top part of the deposit consists of a shallow series of hearths and shell lenses, the bottom of which is dated 2580 ± 70 B.P. (ANU–1362) and the top part is dated 990 ± 90 B.P. (ANU–1616). Both the midden layers contain stone artifacts with some finished tools, animal bones, shellfish remains, and charcoal. The lower midden layer (6600–4000 years old) contains bone tools and some fish bones; the upper midden layer (2500–1000 years old) does not contain these elements (Bowdler 1979:80–82, 94–97).

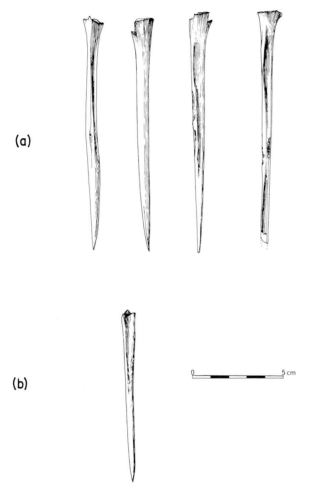

(a)

(b)

Figure 1.13 Cave Bay Cave, bone artifacts: (a) from lower midden layer dated between 6600 and 4000 B.P.; (b) from Pleistocene layer dated 18,550 B.P.

Animal bones were preserved throughout the deposits, including those which were archaeologically sterile. While they present a problem in interpretation of which were left by people and which by scavenging or predatory animals, they provide useful environmental information. In the layers beneath the 6600-year-old midden layer, they consist mainly of land mammal bones including many species not now found on Hunter Island, indicating a period when in fact Hunter Island was Hunter Hill, situated on the land bridge between Tasmania and Australia. It should be noted, however, that all mammals identified were extant in Tasmania in the historical period. In the deposits more recent than 6000 B.P., the suite of land mammals is much reduced, and bones of sea birds occur in great quantities, indicating island conditions. Also preserved throughout the sequence are pollen grains, which have been studied by Hope (1978), and which also give useful palaeoenvironmental information. One useful piece of information yielded by the pollen analysis is a striking correlation between archaeologically sterile layers of Pleistocene age and very high levels of some fern spores, presumed to be from epiphytes inside the cave which were probably sensitive to fires and trampling. Their complete absence from the Holocene layers is attributable to salt spray (Bowdler 1979:466, Hope 1978).

This rather complex sequence is interpreted as follows. Between 23,000 and 21,000 years ago the cave was occasionally used as an inland hunting bivouac by people with a basically coastal economy, foraging inland away from their base camps. The open vegetation indicated by the pollen analysis demonstrates that humans need not have been restricted to the coast, as on the west coast in the Holocene. As the last glaciation spread in central Tasmania, the sea levels fell, the coast retreated, and use of the cave became less frequent. After the glaciation reached its maximum extent and the coast also retreated to its maximum distance away, the site was effectively abandoned for some 12,000 years, with the exception of very rare and fleeting visits, as shown by the one small hearth dated 15,400 B.P. (Bowdler 1977, 1979).

When the sea reached its present level 6000 years ago, people came with it, practicing a well-developed coastal economy. About 4000 years ago or earlier, the site was again abandoned. Two explanations are possible. Hunter Island may not have come completely into being when the sea reached its present level, but was still connected to Tasmania by a sand pit. When the fierce tide severed this spit, the island was abandoned until rediscovered by sea 2500 years ago. Alternatively, people may have been stranded on the new island 6600 years ago, and then either escaped or died out. This is the scenario envisaged for the other larger Bass Strait islands (see following discussion). What is perhaps most significant here is the fact that 2500 years ago, Hunter Island was incorporated into the northwest Tasmanian economic system by maritime Tasmanians.

The latter part of the Cave Bay Cave sequence receives support from the evidence of the other sites excavated on Hunter Island. A small rockshelter on the west coast of Hunter Island was excavated, and named the Rookery Rockshelter due to its situation in a muttonbird rookery. Muttonbirds nest in burrows and, in consequence, the deposits of this shelter have been somewhat disturbed. A coherent sequence can be identified however. The oldest definite stone artifacts in this site occurred about 55–60 cm below the surface; associated charcoal has been dated 4620 ± 360 B.P. (ANU–1617). Above this, little deposition occurred. The next occupational level was a layer of shell midden 25–35 cm below the surface dated 1370 ± 70 B.P. (ANU–1699). The uppermost midden layer was dated 870 ± 70 B.P. (ANU–1698) (Bowdler 1979:324).

Three other sites have been excavated on Hunter Island, all open midden sites, and all apparently occupied for the first time within the past 1600 years. The Muttonbird Midden is located on the west coast of the island, in a gully overlooked by the Rookery Rockshelter. It is not a rich site, except in shellfish and charcoal. Interest lies in the fact that the midden appears to have accumulated on a muttonbird rookery, and has a muttonbird rookery on top of it now. It contained, however, few muttonbird bones. It might be suggested that muttonbird eggs, which leave no archaeological trace, were being exploited. The bottom of this site is dated 1610 ± 160 B.P. (ANU–1363), the top 420 ± 70 B.P. (ANU–1621) (Bowdler 1979:315). Also on the west coast of the island is Little Duck Bay, a midden site similar to a small version of West Point. On its surface are two circular depressions of the kind thought to be hut sites. This site is rich in bone including seal bones, shellfish remains, and stone artifacts, mainly waste. The bottom of the midden deposit was dated 1000 ± 60 B.P. (ANU–1778), the top 900 ± 90 B.P. (ANU–1618); the 50 cm or so of deposit had thus accumulated quite rapidly. A deciduous human tooth was found in this site (Bowdler 1979:309–312).

The Stockyard Site is located in the center of Hunter Island. A small excavation was originally carried out here in 1973–1974, but in the summer of 1980, a large-scale excavation was conducted at this site (Bowdler 1981, O'Connor 1980, Geering 1980). This site is rich in animal bones including both land mammals, especially small wallabies, and seals, shellfish remains, stone artifacts including many finished implements, and charcoal. There is about 60 cm of deposit; a date from about 20 cm below the surface was obtained: 760 ± 70 B.P. (ANU–1620).

All three open midden sites on Hunter Island thus date to within the last 1600 years, and demonstrate systematic exploitation of coastal and other resources on the island. Archaeological research supports the implications of the ethnohistorical record that the island was visited in summer by groups composed of men (wallaby hunting), women (shellfish gathering), and children (the deciduous tooth from Little Duck Bay). The recovery of a few small, obviously wellworked over, scraps of chert and spongolite are direct indications of contact with the Tasmanian mainland. Overall, it is unlikely that Hunter Island was permanently occupied.

Beginners Luck Cave

The Florentine Valley is located in that area of south-central Tasmania which was covered with dense rain forest during the Holocene, and which was not

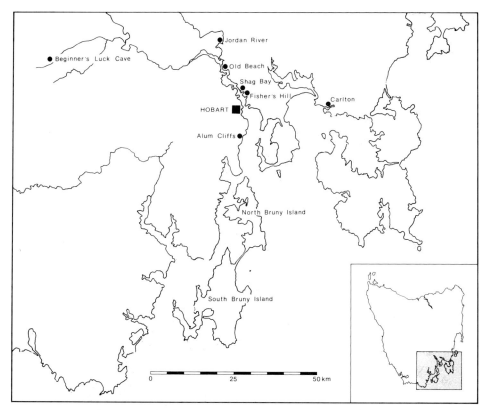

Figure 1.14   Southeast Tasmania, showing sites mentioned in text.

occupied by Tasmanian Aborigines in the ethnographic present (Figure 1.14). Recent research (Murray *et al.*, 1980) however indicates that such was not the case during the different climatic regime of the Pleistocene. Beginners Luck Cave is a limestone cave located in the valley of the Florentine River, which drains into the upper Derwent River. Evidence of human occupation has been found in a limestone breccia, an entrance facies deposit transported to its present position within the cave from a previous entrance. Some caution is therefore indicated as to the association of materials within this deposit.

Archaeological evidence consists of less than 20 stone artifacts in apparent association with flecks of charcoal and abundant fossil land mammal bone. The stone artifacts include some raw materials exotic to the region, and consist predominantly of typologically crude, thick, amorphous flake implements. The faunal remains consist of the bones of modern Tasmanian species, with one exception. A particularly large cuboid is suggested to belong to the extinct macropodid, *Macropus titan*. Some·of the bone is quite heavily burnt.

A radiocarbon date was obtained from bone, and assayed to be 20,650 ± 1790 B.P. (GaK–7081). An aspartic acid racemization date was also obtained from bone material, and divulged a remarkably similar result, of 21,000 (Sample AG20). The site was thus occupied contemporaneously with the lower levels of Cave Bay Cave, just prior to the onset of the last glacial maximum. Faunal remains from other, purely paleontological sites in the Florentine Valley indicate the presence of a varied marsupial fauna in an open environment during the late Pleistocene. With the generally colder and drier conditions envisaged for Tasmania in this period, the limestone soils here would have supported grassland and herbfield vegetation interspersed with alpine shrubbery. The overall evidence indicates a not particularly intensive human occupation of this region during the time when changed vegetation cover made it both accessible and productive for hunters. Access to this part of the interior would easily have been gained via the corridor of the Derwent Valley (Murray *et al.*, 1980).

Derwent Valley

The Derwent River is the major river in southeast Tasmania. The modern city of Hobart and the first site of European settlement in Tasmania are located near the mouth of the Derwent River, with two major effects. First, disruption of traditional Aboriginal culture and economy happened very early here. Second, modern urban and industrial development has been both disclosing and disturbing archaeological sites in the region. More work needs to be done here, but a remarkably consistent pattern of Holocene occupation has emerged (Figure 1.14).

A claim has been put forward for the Pleistocene occupation of the Old Beach site, some 35 km up the Derwent estuary. All that can be confidently said about this is that a half-dozen stone artifacts were found in a wind-deposited sand horizon in excess of 6000 years old; certainly there are none of the well-defined hearths and activity areas described by Lourandos for Crown Lagoon (previously discussed), and the dating of the relevant stratigraphic unit at Old Beach remains problematical (Sigleo and Colhoun 1975, cf. Lourandos 1970:64–66). The *terminus ante quem* for the supposed Pleistocene unit here is provided by two small, recent, indubitably Aboriginal hearths containing mussel shell. The radiocarbon dates are 5800 ± 130 B.P. (SUA–306) and 5600 ± 100 B.P. (SUA–307). Many other sites in the Lower Derwent valley are similarly dated.

One of Reber's (1965) charcoal samples was obtained from a small midden near the Old Beach site, and is dated 5220 ± 110 B.P. (I–324). An open midden site at Fishers Hill about 25 km up the estuary, of which little information is available except that it contained some stone artifacts, provided a shell date, presumably due to lack of charcoal. The shell carbonate was dated 5520 ± 85 B.P. (ANU–1090A), the acid insoluble organic fraction was dated 5890 ± 90 B.P. (ANU–1090B). Just inside the estuary at Alum Cliffs, an open midden was excavated that contained marine shell, unlike the other Derwent sites, which all contain estuarine species of mussel and oyster. This site is dated 3875 ± 160 B.P. (SUA–599) (Stockton and Wallace 1979:83).

Two other sites in the lower Derwent Valley have been reported in somewhat more detail. One is an open midden on the Jordan River, a small tributary which drains into the Derwent just north of Old Beach. The Jordan River midden is undated. Two square meters of it were excavated, and produced many shellfish remains and charcoal, but only seven stone artifacts and no animal bones whatsoever were found (Gaffney and Stockton 1980). Further downstream near Fisher's Hill, a small rockshelter at Shag Bay was excavated by Vanderwal (1977). Much of the deposit within the rockshelter consisted of archaeologically sterile rooffall, but stratified within this was a 25-cm-thick band of cultural debris, mostly estuarine shellfish remains. Three square meters were excavated, but only two stone artifacts were found, and, again, no animal bones whatsoever in the cultural deposit. The top of this was dated 4720 ± 110 B.P. (GaK–5424), and the bottom 5300 ± 120 B.P. (GaK–5425).

It should be noted that all these sites, except the Alum Cliffs site, have basal dates falling between 5200 and 5800 years ago—quite a good fit for the time when the sea reached its present level. It should be further noted that all these sites seem to be highly specialized, containing estuarine shellfish remains and very little else. They are thus seen to conform well to Lourandos's model for eastern Tasmania, and are interpreted as representing but one aspect of a nomadic, geographically dispersed economy (Vanderwal 1977:168, Gaffney and Stockton 1980:76). Perhaps it is time to seek the sites that represent the other aspects of this economy, to ascertain whether they are located inland, on the open coast, or both.

Louisa Bay

Research has been carried out on the southernmost coast of Tasmania by Vanderwal (1978), whose final report is awaited (Figure 1.15). A series of sites were excavated around the coastal perimeter of Louisa Bay, which lies directly beneath the western slopes of the formidable Ironbound Mountains; the hinterland is thus limited. A series of sites or at least cultural events has been identified within a long eroding sand dune at the east end of the bay. The oldest cultural components in the series were identified as shallow lenses indicating ephemeral use; later components are said to be more substantial. No charcoal was found in the older deposits, so a "basal organically enriched soil sample" was submitted for dating, and a date of 2970 ± 200 B.P. (ANU–1771) was obtained. In a context interpreted on stratigraphic and other grounds as being more recent, a bone tool was found similar to those from Rocky Cape South, Cave Bay Cave, and elsewhere. There are three possibilites: (a) the dating is wrong or the stratigraphic interpretation is wrong; (b) bone tools at Louisa Bay continued to be made well after they ceased to be made and used elsewhere in Tasmania; and (c) this artifact was a relic, saved or scavenged from an earlier context. A more recent part of the cultural sequence within the dune was dated 630 ± 90 B.P. (GaK–6599) (Vanderwal 1978:40).

A small rockshelter site containing 30 cm of deposit was dated 870 ± 90 B.P. (GaK–5990). Another sand dune site at the other end of the bay has been dated 1250 ± 100 B.P. (GaK–5989) (Vanderwal 1978:118). All sites showed exploitation

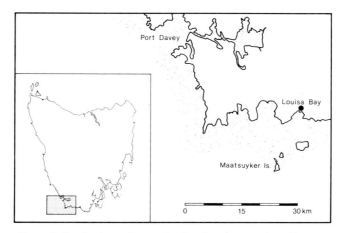

Figure 1.15   Southwest Tasmania, showing sites mentioned in text.

of shellfish, seabirds, and land mammals. Apart from the enigmatic presence of the bone tool, the evidence does not suggest that Louisa Bay was occupied before about 3000 years ago, or at least not with any intensity. The evidence suggests to Vanderwal that occupation increased in intensity within the last 1000 years (Vanderwal 1978:120).

Maatsuyker Island

Maatsuyker Island, 13 km from the south coast near Louisa Bay (Figure 1.15), has also been investigated by Vanderwal. One open site contained mostly seal and muttonbird bones, suggesting what drew people to embark on a dangerous sea crossing. Two dates were obtained: 400 ± 90 B.P. (GaK–5988) and 570 ± 100 B.P. (GaK–5987). Maatsuyker Island thus appears to have been visited only in recent times, well within the chronology of occupation at Louisa Bay (Vanderwal 1978:119).

Sundown Creek

Ranson (1978, and personal communication 1979) has been carrying out a project of archaeological survey and excavation in the region of the mouth of Sundown Creek on the west coast of Tasmania, some 20 km south of West Point. Ranson's research has concentrated on the complete excavation of a "dough-nut" midden consisting of a single raised ring of deposit around a lower inner area, with the circular depression also containing deposit. This work has verified that such circular depressions do indeed represent hut sites. The midden at Sundown Creek is modern in age, overlapping the historical period.

King and Flinders Islands

Unlike the Hunter Islands, the large islands of Bass Strait were unoccupied and unvisited by Aborigines from Tasmania or Victoria in the ethnographic present. Surface finds have long been known from Flinders and Cape Barren

Islands in eastern Bass Strait, but their status has always been problematical (e.g., Jones 1976:257–259). Sparse shell midden sites in eroding sand dunes on the north end of Flinders Island at Palana have been excavated. These contained rather amorphous stone artifacts, marine shell, and charcoal. A date of 9890 ± 175 B.P. (SUA–640) appears to be from a horizon pre-dating occupation. Two dates obtained from within occupation deposits are 7150 ± 135 B.P. (SUA–641) and 6520 ± 130 B.P. (SUA–642). Once again we have evidence for coastal occupation and exploitation coinciding with the time the sea reached its present level (Orchiston and Glenie 1978).

King Island, in western Bass Strait, had never produced even surface finds of artifacts until recently. Jones, on a one-day stopover, discovered stone tools in the extreme southwest of the island. They were eroding from a dune formation from which Jones was able to collect a charcoal sample that has yielded a preliminary date of 7670 ± 150 B.P. (ANU–2189). Jones compares the stone artifact assemblage to that from the lower levels of Cave Bay Cave. No associated faunal remains were found (Jones 1979).

INTERPRETATIONS

All current researchers agree that the Tasmanian Aborigines share a common ancestry with mainland Australian Aborigines. The date of 23,000 B.P. for the occupation of what is now Hunter Island by people with stone and bone tools resembling those of mainland Pleistocene Australian assemblages confirms this view. Recent osteological studies also support it.

Both cultural and physical differences between Tasmania and Australia can be explained in terms of Tasmania's 12,000 years of isolation from the rest of Australia. This is the date when the land link was severed, and all the evidence indicates that no further contact took place between the inhabitants on either side of Bass Strait.

The new stone tool types that make up the Australian Small Tool Tradition spread to all parts of Australia, but none of these types has ever been found in Tasmania; the same can be said regarding the distribution of dogs. Furthermore, the survival of the Tasmanian devil (*Sarcophilus harrissi*) and the Tasmanian wolf or tiger (*Thylacinus cynocephalus*) into the historical period in Tasmania is seen as further evidence that the dog was never present here, as these marsupial carnivores seem to have died out on the mainland after the arrival of their ecological competitor (Milham and Thompson 1976).

Other areas of interpretation have been subject to controversy. One concerns the relative lack of Pleistocene sites in Tasmania. Jones suggested (1968:200) that during the Pleistocene, people were confined to the coast by dense rain forest, thus, most Pleistocene sites are beneath the sea. Subsequent work on paleoenvironments has established that this was unlikely, insofar as most vegetation communities in Tasmania during the Pleistocene were open grasslands or savannahs and the climate cold and dry, rather than cold and wet. Bowdler (1977) agreed with Jones that most Pleistocene sites are beneath the present sea level, but suggests that people were coastally adapted, not in any way confined to the Pleistocene coast line. She argued (1977, 1979:431–436) that, like all Tasmanian tribes in the ethnographic present, Pleistocene Tasmanians (and Australians) had an economic pattern which involved a coastal (or aquatic) component, but which allowed exploitation of a wide hinterland, as shown by the lower levels of Cave Bay Cave. Only under conditions of environmental change after the last glacial maximum did some Australian groups begin to exploit territories not including coasts or major river systems.

Murray *et al.* (1980) disagree that people in Tasmania during the Pleistocene were confined to the coasts. They argue, on the basis of their evidence from the Florentine valley, that at least some specialized hunting economies existed in interior Tasmania, and that these people turned to coastal alternatives as a consequence of the forestation of the river valleys. They suggest that incipient marine littoral adaptations may have taken place about 12,000–10,000 years ago. Unfortunately we have no archaeological evidence from Tasmania dating to between about 18,000 and 8000 years ago; and we are still only talking about two, or perhaps three, Pleistocene sites altogether. While it is possible that this is an artifact of limited survey and research, there is still a ratio of something in excess of 500 to 1 known Holocene, indeed post-8000 B.P., sites to Pleistocene sites in Tasmania.

The apparent recent occupation of the west coast and some islands has also been a subject for discussion. No archaeological sites older than 3000 B.P. have been reported from the west coast of Tasmania. No middens yet found there appear to contain fish bones or bone tools. This is also true of Louisa Bay on the south coast, if we ignore the single contra-indication of one bone tool, apparently in a post-3000 B.P. context. No one would wish to argue that no single Tasmanian person had set foot on the west coast during the Holocene before 3000 years ago, but it would appear that no systematic occupation or exploitation of these regions took place, such as would lead to identifiable archaeological remains. It is of course possible that environmental conditions here, more severe than on the east coast, have led to the obliteration of older evidence.

On Hunter Island, all evidence for intensive occupation and systematic exploitation dates within the past 2500 years, or less. Similarly, Maatsuyker Island only appears to have been visited within the last 600 years. Vanderwal (1978) considers the island evidence in conjunction with the fact that watercraft were not used in northeast Tasmania, and suggests that the Tasmanian catamaran was a recent invention. These were made of bark or reeds, and required no special tool (as far as is known), so their recovery from archaeological contexts, directly or indirectly, is not likely. Vanderwal suggests that their absence in northeast Tasmania is attributable to the fact that they were not part of the original Tasmanian technology, and that their invention led to the recent occupation of Louisa Bay and regular seasonal visitations to Hunter and Maatsuyker islands.

Evidence from Bruny Island off the east coast of Tasmania can be interpreted

both in support of, and against, this suggestion. It consists of sites, not excavated by professional archaeologists, but dated by Reber (1965, 1967) in the early 1960s. One is a midden dated 6050 ± 350 B.P. (I–316). The other is a midden whose base has two dates: one is 5235 ± 280 B.P. (GXO–419), the other is 5270 ± 90 B.P. (R–1520/3). The site is described as consisting of 2 m of shell. Another sample from 30 cm below the surface of the midden was dated 5220 ± 200 B.P. (R–1520/2). Another sample, however, from the edge of the site was dated 1987 ± 90 B.P. (R–1520/1). These dates can be interpreted to mean either that Bruny Island was occupied briefly after the sea reached its present level, then abandoned until about 2000 years ago, like Hunter Island; or it can be interpreted to mean that occupation was continuous and probably involved crossing from the mainland over that whole period, as it did in the ethnographic present. In the first instance, the idea of a recent invention of watercraft is sustained; in the second instance, it is not. Clearly more work needs to be done on Bruny Island to establish a good archaeological sequence.

An alternative suggestion has been proposed by Bowdler (1979:424–427). The particular adaptation seen on the west coast in the ethnographic present (Lourandos 1968, 1977; Jones 1974) is characterized as semi-sedentary, with large localized base camps, such as the West Point midden. People were restricted to a narrow coastal corridor because of the rain forest, but an important factor in their economy is the fact that they could manipulate this rain forest. They did this by fire, keeping a wider hinterland open than would naturally be the case: a fire disclimax of sedgeland which supports a larger mammal biomass than rain forest. There is also considerable evidence for the Tasmanians maintaining tracks through the rain forest, again by the use of fire (Jones 1969, 1975:26).

Analysis of pollen from the Cave Bay Cave deposits, where rain forest pollen only featured as long distance elements, led Hope (1978) to comment, first, that it was probably established to its present extent by 7000 B.P. in northwest Tasmania, but was virtually nonexistent between 25,000 and 12,000 years ago. Second, Hope comments (1978:507) that the rain forest elements appear to be "marginally more important before 3300 B.P." It is possible that the initial expansion of the rain forest was something with which people were unable to cope. Tasmanian rain forest is dense and damp, and its manipulation by fire is no mean feat, and would hardly have been learned overnight. The decrease in pollen elements after 3300 B.P. may reflect successful rain forest manipulation, which allowed people to make an intensive adaptation to the south and west coasts. Along the north coast, rain forest came right down to the coast in places (Figure 1.4; Jones, 1975). To visit Hunter Island regularly, it is possible that paths to suitable embarkation points had to be kept open by firing. Thus, it is perhaps only after the rain forest is able to be manipulated that we see the emergence of Jones's coordinated northwest regional system; it is only after 3000 years ago that west coast spongolite begins to appear at Rocky Cape.

Perhaps the most controversial point of view about Tasmanian prehistory has emerged from what is at one level a trivial fact: 3500 years ago, the Tasmanians stopped eating fish. Employing this and related facts, Jones (especially 1977,

1978) has built a complex edifice of interpretation, which sees the Tasmanians as suffering from "the world's longest isolation, the world's simplest technology" (1977:200), and a technology which became simpler through time, leading perhaps to their doom, with or without European intervention. Such an idea has of course problematical political implications. Not surprisingly, Jones has been attacked on this ground, also on the basis of his archaeological–ethnographic analysis, interpretation, and theory. A brief review of his argument, and the counterarguments, will be offered.

Fish stopped being eaten by Tasmanians 3500 years ago, and at about the same time, bone tools stopped being made. Making comparisons with mainland Aboriginal culture in the ethnographic present, Jones points to the absence in Tasmania of various items. Some of these items are unlikely ever to have been present in Tasmania, such as the small tools hafted with adhesive to spears and spearthrowers. Others are said to have originally been part of Tasmanian technology, but to have been lost: These include ground-edge axes, boomerangs, and barbed spears (Jones 1977:196). The basis for this claim is that ground-edge axes have been found in northern Australia in Pleistocene contexts (White 1967), and barbed spears and boomerangs have been found in a swamp in South Australia, dated between 10,200 ± 150 B.P. (ANU–1292) and 8990 ± 120 B.P. (ANU–1293) (Luebbers 1975).

Jones (1978:46) likens the isolated Tasmanian culture of the last 12,000 years to a "closed system": one which was running down. It is particularly the loss of fish from the diet which Jones emphasizes:

> With this abnegation, part of the economic heritage of early Tasmanians slipped away. An intellectual event caused a contraction in their ecological space (Jones 1977:190).

Not just an event, but "an intellectual decision which had the result of constricting their ecological universe" (Jones 1978:44). And the net result:

> Like a blow above the heart, it took a long time to take effect, but slowly but surely there was a simplification in the tool kit, a diminution in the range of foods eaten, perhaps a squeezing of intellectuality.... Were 4000 people enough to propel forever the cultural inheritance of Late Pleistocene Australia? Even if Abel Tasman had not sailed the winds of the Roaring Forties in 1642, were they in fact doomed—doomed to a slow strangulation of the mind? (Jones 1977:200).

Jones also indicates, however, that the role of fish in the Tasmanian diet in the early Holocene was not greatly significant (1978:35–36).

Jones has also developed what Horton (1979:28) calls his "secondary thesis" to account for an apparent contradiction: Jones has estimated that Tasmanian population densities were equal to those of mainland Aboriginal groups in similar environments, despite the evident technological superiority of the latter. He argues that the new tools which entered mainland Aboriginal society, and presumably the old ones "lost" by the Tasmanians, allowed the development of large-scale religious events that were not part of Tasmanian culture (Jones 1977:200).

This edifice has been attacked at several levels (Vanderwal 1978; Allen 1979;

Horton 1979; Bowdler, 1980b). At the factual level, the foundations of the edifice lie in the "simplification of the tool kit." Some of the evidence here is far from solid. Ground-edge axes are not found anywhere in Australia south of the tropics before the advent of the Small Tool Tradition approximately 4000–3000 years ago (Mulvaney 1975:194); there is no reason why they should have been part of the original Tasmanian inheritance. The discovery of boomerangs and barbed spear heads in South Australia dated to some 2000 years after Tasmania was severed from the mainland also does not indicate their presence in Tasmania prior to that event. This leaves fish and bone tools. Jones (1971b:510) argues that the two are not functionally connected, because of the following points.

1. Bone tools and fish do not have an identical distribution through the sequence.
2. The use wear on the bone tools is not consistent with their function as spear points.
3. Although most bone tools have been found in coastal shell middens, there are sites where fishing would not have been carried out which contained these objects.

Bowdler (1979:297–300) has argued against these points, as follows.

1. While there is not an *identical* distribution, there is in fact a general agreement.
2. An alternative functional interpretation is that the bone tools could have been netting needles; the size and species selectivity of fish caught at Rocky Cape indicates their capture by nets.
3. This argument does not distinguish between manufacture and use: Tools may be made at sites where they are not used.

Jones, however, prefers the interpretation that bone tools were used primarily for making fur cloaks (1971b:513–524).

Vanderwal (1978) has argued that if watercraft were a recent invention, the Tasmanian technology was not diminishing but rather increasing. The evidence for this is, as we have seen, tenuous. Jones, in fact, prefers the hypothesis that watercraft were dropped from the technological repertoire of northeast Tasmanians, thus supporting his diminution hypothesis (Jones 1976:250). Vanderwal also argues that the Tasmanians in the past 3000 years were enlarging their universe by moving in on Louisa Bay and voyaging out to islands previously unvisited. Bowdler agrees with this view, in light of the maritime rediscovery of Hunter Island, and also the possibility that rain forest manipulation by fire allowed a stable adaptation to the west coast in the same period (1979:426–427, in press). Vanderwal also argues (1978:123) that if bone tools were used for making fur cloaks, the loss of such cloaks might be seen as adaptive, in that ochre and grease might have been more effective in recent Tasmanian climatic conditions.

In a similar vein, Allen (1979) has argued that the dropping of not particularly fatty fish from the diet is an adaptive move for Tasmanians. He draws comparisons with hunting societies in similar latitudes, where fatty foods are important for metabolic as well as economic reasons. Allen suggests that a minor climatic fluctuation led to a greater emphasis on oil-rich foods such as seals and muttonbirds.

Horton (1979) similarly suggests that Jones has overemphasized the importance of fish in the Tasmanian diet. Only at Rocky Cape South and Sisters' Creek are fish bones present in any abundance; at other coastal sites with deposits older than 3500 B.P. (Cave Bay Cave, Little Swanport, and Rocky Cape North) only a small number of fish remains occurs. Horton emphasizes the evidence for the importance of seals in the Tasmanian diet, the abundance of seals in prehistoric Tasmanian waters, and the advantages conferred by eating seal in the Tasmanian climate as against fish (Horton 1979:30). With regard to the simplicity of the Tasmanian tool kit, he sees this as adaptive: "in a rich environment a simple technology is sufficient" (Horton 1979:31). Overall, he concludes that the differences perceived between Tasmania and the rest of Australia are no more significant than differences perceived between culture areas within Australia (Horton 1979:34).

Jones's secondary thesis has been attacked on two fronts. Lourandos (1980) has produced evidence which in fact renders it unnecessary. He has shown, by an analysis of ethnohistorical records (which include Robinson's Victorian journals), that the population densities in coastal Victoria in the ethnographic present were considerably higher than those estimated for Tasmania. Coastal Victoria probably shares more similarities with Tasmania environmentally than any other part of Australia. Furthermore, Horton (1979:32–33), on examining Robinson's journals, concludes that evidence does exist to suggest that the Tasmanians did have large-scale religious ceremonies.

Bowdler (1980b) examines the theoretical underpinning of Jones's position, and concludes that it is based on an evolutionary model only one step removed from nineteenth century social Darwinism, one that puts all societies in the ethnographic present on a scale of technological complexity, with the Tasmanians at the bottom. She also argues that Jones's concept of "culture" as random is counterproductive for archaeologists, and that it is more illuminating to see culture as a form of adaptation. This is in implicit agreement with Horton and Allen who seek an adaptive interpretation of why the Tasmanians ceased to eat fish. Jones sees this event as "maladaptive" (Jones 1978:46); Bowdler (1980b) argues that if culture is a form of adaptation, then maladaptations will be like bad genes in physical evolution: "Either the genes go, or the species goes." The Tasmanians stopped eating fish, and survived for another 3000 years.

While these debates may have, like earlier debates on the Tasmanians, engendered much heat and little light (Mulvaney 1975:162), they may perhaps be said to differ from the earlier debates in that they result from less than 20 years of active field work, and entail the setting up of hypotheses which are yet to be archaeologically tested. In some ways it may be fair to say that the last 20 years have advanced our understanding of the Tasmanian culture more than the previous 80 or so years of study. The Tasmanians should no longer be seen as a unique, almost romantic, "lost" culture of obscure origins, but as collateral relatives of the Australian Aborigines, isolated on an island and successfully adapted to a high latitude, marine environment until the advent of Europeans with gunpowder and an unstoppable imperialist mentality.

ACKNOWLEDGMENTS

I would like to thank Peter White for giving me the opportunity to write this paper. I am grateful to Sharon Sullivan and Harry Lourandos for their comments on an early draft. The text was typed by Wendy Chappell. Figures 1.1, 1.5, 1.7–1.9, 1.12, and 1.13 were drawn by Winifred Mumford. Figures 1.2–1.4, 1.6, 1.11, 1.14, and 1.15 were drawn by Doug Hobbs. I thank Rhys Jones for copies of Figures 1.7–1.10. Although they were not directly involved with the production of this paper, I am grateful to Rhys Jones, the Maguires of Hunter Island, and all the people living in Tasmania itself or working in the field of Tasmanian studies who have been so helpful.

REFERENCES

Allen, Harry
    1979   Left out in the cold: why the Tasmanians stopped eating fish. *The Artefact* **4**:1–10.
Backhouse, James
    1843   *A narrative of a visit to the Australian colonies.* London: Hamilton, Adams.
Birdsell, J. B.
    1949   The racial origin of the extinct Tasmanians. *Records of the Queen Victoria Museum*, Launceston, Tasmania. Vol. 2, No. 3. Pp. 105–122.
    1967   Preliminary data on the trihybrid origin of the Australian Aborigines. *Archaeology and Physical Anthropology in Oceania* **2**:100–155.
Bowden, K. M.
    1964   *Captain James Kelly of Hobart Town.* Melbourne: Melbourne University Press.
Bowdler, Sandra
    1974a   An account of an archaeological reconnaissance of Hunter's Isles, north-west Tasmania 1973/4. *Records of the Queen Victoria Museum*, Launceston, Tasmania, new series, No. 54.
    1974b   Pleistocene date for man in Tasmania. *Nature* **252**:697–698.
    1977   The coastal colonisation of Australia. In *Sunda and Sahul*, edited by J. Allen, J. Golson, and R. Jones. London: Academic Press. Pp. 205–246.
    1979   Hunter Hill, Hunter Island. Unpublished Ph.D. dissertation, Department of Prehistory Research, School of Pacific Studies, Australian National University.
    1980a   Hunters and farmers in the Hunter Islands: Aboriginal and European land-use of north-west Tasmanian Islands in the historical period. *Records of the Queen Victoria Museum*, Launceston, Tasmania, new series, No. 70.
    1980b   Fish and culture: A Tasmanian polemic. *Mankind* **12**:334–340.
    1981   Stone tools, style and function: Some evidence from the Stockyard Site, Hunter Island. *Archaeology in Oceania* **16**:64–69.
Bowler, J. M., and A. G. Thorne
    1976   Human remains from Lake Mungo: discovery and excavation of Lake Mungo III. In *The Origin of the Australians*, edited by R. C. Kirk and A. G. Thorne. Canberra: Australian Institute of Aboriginal Studies. Pp. 127–138.

Chappell, J. M. A.
    1976   Aspects of late Quaternary palaeogeography of the Australian–East Indonesian region. In *The Origin of the Australians,* edited by R. L. Kirk and A. G. Thorne. Canberra: Australian Institute of Aboriginal Studies. Pp. 11–22.

Coleman, Emily
    1966   An analysis of small samples from the West Point shell midden. Unpublished B.A. (Honours) thesis, Department of Anthropology, University of Sydney.

Colhoun, Eric A.
    1975   A Quaternary climatic curve for Tasmania. Paper presented at the Australasian Conference on Climate and Climatic change. Royal Meteorological Society, Monash University, Melbourne.
    1978   The late Quaternary environment of Tasmania as a backdrop to man's occupance. *Records of the Queen Victoria Museum,* Launceston, Tasmania, new series, No. 61.

Crowther, W. L.
    1925   Notes on the habits of the extinct Tasmanian race. I. The uses and manufacture of bone implements. *Papers and Proceedings of the Royal Society of Tasmania for 1924.* Pp. 136–139.
    1950   On the formation and dispersal of a collection. *Papers and Proceedings of the Royal Society of Tasmania for 1949.* Pp. 83–92.

Davidson, D. F.
    1937   The relationship of Tasmanian and Australian cultures. *Twenty-fifth Anniversary Studies, Philadelphia Anthropological Society,* Vol. 1. Pp. 47–62.

Davies, David
    1973   *The last of the Tasmanians.* Sydney: Shakespeare Head Press.

Dixon, R. M. W.
    1980   *The languages of Australia.* Cambridge: Cambridge University Press.

Gaffney, Lisa, and Jim Stockton
    1980   Results of the Jordan River midden excavation. *Australian Archaeology* (Newsletter of the Australian Archaeological Association) No. 10:68–78.

Geering, Katrina
    1980   *An attempt to establish the seasonality of occupation of the Stockyard Site, Hunter Island.* Unpublished B.A. (Honours) thesis, Department of Prehistory and Anthropology, University of New England (Armidale, New South Wales, Australia).

Gould, R. A.
    1969   Puntutjarpa rockshelter: a reply to Messrs. Glover and Lampert. *Archaeology and Physical Anthropology in Oceania* 4:229–237.

Guiler, E. R.
    1965   Animals. In *Atlas of Tasmania,* edited by J. L. Davies. Hobart: Lands and Surveys Department. Pp. 36–37.

Hale, H. M., and N. B. Tindale
    1930   Notes on some human remains in the Lower Murray Valley, South Australia. *Records of the South Australian Museum* (Vol. 4). Pp. 145–218.

Hiatt, Betty
    1967   The food quest and the economy of the Tasmanian Aborigines. *Oceania* 38:99–133, 190–219.
    1969   Cremation in Aboriginal Australia. *Mankind* 7:104–119.

Hiatt, L. R.
    1962   Local organisation among the Australian Aborigines. *Oceania* 32:267–286.

Hope, G. S.
    1978   A late Pleistocene and Holocene vegetational history from a rock shelter deposit, Hunter Island, north-western Tasmania. *Australian Journal of Botany* 26:493–514.

Horton, D. R.
    1979   Tasmanian adaptation. *Mankind* 12:28–34.

Huxley, T. H.
      1869   On the distribution of the races of mankind and its bearing on the antiquity of man. *International Congress for Prehistoric Archaeology* (1868), **3**:92–105.
Jackson, W. D.
      1965   Vegetation. In *Atlas of Tasmania,* edited by J. L. Davies. Hobart: Lands and Surveys Department. Pp. 30–37.
Jennings, J. N.
      1959   The submarine topography of Bass Strait. *Proceedings of the Royal Society of Victoria* **71**:49–72.
      1971   Sea level changes and land links. In *Aboriginal man and environment in Australia,* edited by J. Golson and D. J. Mulvaney. Canberra: Australian National University Press. Pp. 1–13.
Jones, J. F.
      1947   Huts of Tasmanian Aborigines. *Papers and Proceedings of the Royal Society of Tasmania for 1946,* 133.
Jones, Rhys
      1965   Archaeological reconnaissance in Tasmania, summer 1963–1964. *Oceania* **35**:191–201.
      1966   A speculative archaeological sequence for north-west Tasmania. *Records of the Queen Victoria Museum,* Launceston, Tasmania, new series, No. 25.
      1967   Middens and man in Tasmania. *Australian Natural History* **18**:359–364.
      1968   The geographical background to the arrival of man in Australia and Tasmania. *Archaeology and Physical Anthropology in Oceania* **3**:186–215.
      1969   Fire-stick farming. *Australian Natural History* **16**:224–228.
      1970   Tasmanian Aborigines and dogs. *Mankind* **7**:256–271.
      1971a   A demography of hunters and farmers in Tasmania. In *Aboriginal man and environment in Australia,* edited by J. Golson and D. J. Mulvaney. Canberra: Australian National University Press. Pp. 271–287.
      1971b   *Rocky Cape and the problem of the Tasmanians.* Unpublished Ph.D. dissertation, Department of Anthropology, University of Sydney, Australia.
      1974   Tasmanian tribes. Appendix to *Aboriginal tribes of Australia* by N. B. Tindale. Canberra: Australian National University Press. Pp. 319–354.
      1975   The Neolithic, Palaeolithic and the hunting gardners: man and land in the Antipodes. In *Quaternary studies,* edited by R. P. Suggate and M. M. Cresswell. Wellington, New Zealand: The Royal Society of New Zealand. Pp. 21–34.
      1976   Tasmania: aquatic machines and off-shore islands. In *Problems in economic and social archaeology,* edited by G. de G. Sieveking, I. H. Longworth, and K. E. Wilson. London: Duckworth. Pp. 235–263.
      1977   The Tasmanian paradox. In *Stone tools as cultural markers,* edited by R. V. S. Wright. Canberra: Australian Institute of Aboriginal Studies. Pp. 189–204.
      1978   Why did the Tasmanians stop eating fish? In *Explorations in ethno-archaeology,* edited by R. A. Gould. Albuquerque: University of New Mexico Press and Santa Fe: School of American Research. Pp. 11–47.
      1979   A note on the discovery of stone tools and a stratified prehistoric site on King Island, Bass Strait. *Australian Archaeology* (Newsletter of the Australian Archaeological Association) No. 9:87–94.
Kelly, Ray
      1980   A revival of Aboriginal culture. *Parks and Wildlife* **2**(5):79–80.
Labillardière, M.
      1800   *Voyage in search of La Perouse . . .* (2 vols), translated from the French. London: John Stockdale.
Langford, J.
      1965   Weather and climate. In *Atlas of Tasmania,* edited by J. L. Davies. Hobart: Lands and Surveys Department. Pp. 2–11.

Legge, R. W.
  1929   On some diminutive types of Tasmanian stone implements. *Papers and Proceedings of the Royal Society of Tasmania for 1928*, pp. 87–92.
  1930   Tasmanian stone culture. Some notes on distinctive types, spokeshaves, borers and chipping tools, and their probable usages. *Papers and Proceedings of the Royal Society of Tasmania for 1929*, pp. 39–43.

Lourandos, Harry
  1968   Dispersal of activities—the east Tasmanian Aboriginal sites. *Papers and Proceedings of the Royal Society of Tasmania*, **102**:41–46.
  1970   Coast and Hinterland: the archaeological sites of Eastern Tasmania. Unpublished M.A. thesis, Department of Prehistory, Research School of Pacific Studies, Australian National University, Canberra.
  1977   Stone tools, settlement, adaptation: a Tasmanian example. In *Stone tools as cultural markers*, edited by R. V. S. Wright. Canberra: Australian Institute of Aboriginal Studies. Pp. 219–224.
  1980   Change or stability? Hydraulics, hunter–gathers and population in temperate Australia. *World Archaeology* **11**:245–264.

Luebbers, R. A.
  1975   Ancient boomerangs discovered in South Australia. *Nature* **253**:39.

Macintosh, N. W. G., and B. C. W. Barker
  1965   The osteology of Aboriginal man in Tasmania. *Oceania Monographs*, 12. Sydney: University of Sydney.

Macphail, Michael K.
  1979   Vegetation and climate in southern Tasmania since the last glaciation. *Quaternary Research* **11**:306–341.

Mathew, J.
  1889   The Australian Aborigines. *Journal of the Royal Society of New South Wales* **23**:335–349.

Meston, A. L.
  1932   Aboriginal rock-carvings on the north-west coast of Tasmania. *Papers and Proceedings of the Royal Society of Tasmania for 1931*, pp. 12–19.
  1933   Aboriginal rock carvings in Tasmania—Part II. *Papers and Proceedings of the Royal Society of Tasmania for 1932*, pp. 1–16.
  1934   Aboriginal rock-carvings in Tasmania. *Antiquity* **8**:179–184.
  1937   Tasmanian stone implements. *Mankind* **2**:80–82.
  1956   Miscellaneous notes on the culture of the Tasmanian Aboriginal. *Memoirs of the National Museum of Victoria* (Vol. 20). Pp. 191–199.
  1958   The Van Diemen's Land Company, 1825–1842. *Records of the Queen Victoria Museum*, Launceston, Tasmania, new series, No. 9.

Milham, Paul, and Peter Thompson
  1976   Relative antiquity of human occupation and extinct fauna at Madura Cave, south-eastern Western Australia. *Mankind* **10**:175–180.

Mulvaney, D. J.
  1964   The Pleistocene colonisation of Australia. *Antiquity* **38**:263–267.
  1975   *The Prehistory of Australia* (2nd edition). Harmondsworth: Penguin.

Mulvaney, D. J., and E. B. Joyce
  1965   Archaeological and geomorphological investigations on Mt. Moffatt Station, Queensland. *Proceedings of the Prehistoric Society*, **31**:147–212.

Murray, P., A. Goede, and J. Bada
  1980   Pleistocene human occupation at Beginners Luck Cave, Florentine Valley, Tasmania. *Archaeology and Physical Anthropology in Oceania* **15**:142–152.

Nicholls, Mary (editor)
  1977   *The diary of the Reverend Robert Knopwood, 1803–1838*. Hobart: Tasmanian Historical Research Association.

Noetling, F.
    1908   Notes on the Tasmanian amorpholiths. *Papers and Proceedings of the Royal Society of Tasmania for 1906–1907,* pp. 1–37.
    1910   A peculiar group of tronattas. *Papers and Proceedings of the Royal Society of Tasmania for 1908,* pp. 1–8.

O'Connor, Sue
    1980   Bringing it all back home: analysis of the vertebrate faunal remains from the Stockyard Site, Hunter Island, Northwest Tasmania. Unpublished B.A. (Honours) thesis, Department of Prehistory and Archaeology, University of New England (Armidale, New South Wales, Australia).

Orchiston, D. Wayne, and R. C. Glenie
    1978   Residual Holocene populations in Bassiania: Aboriginal man at Palana, northern Flinders Island. *Australian Archaeology* (Newsletter of the Australian Archaeological Association) No. 8:127–137.

Peron, F.
    1807   *Voyage de découvertes aux Terres Australes* (vol. 1). Paris: Imprimerie Royale.

Plomley, N. J. B.
    1962   A list of Tasmanian Aboriginal material in collections in Europe. *Records of the Queen Victoria Museum,* Launceston, Tasmania, new series, No. 15.

Plomley, N. J. B. (editor)
    1966   *Friendly mission: The Tasmanian journals and papers of George Augustus Robinson 1829–1834.* Hobart: Tasmanian Historical Research Association.
    1971   *Friendly mission. The Tasmanian journals and papers of George August Robinson 1829–1834: a supplement.* Hobart: Tasmanian Historical Research Association.
    1976   *A word-list of the Tasmanian Aboriginal languages.* Hobart: the author with the assistance of the Government of Tasmania.

Pulleine, R. H.
    1929   The Tasmanians and their stone culture. *Report of the Australian Association for the Advancement of Science* **19**:294–314.

Radcliffe-Brown, A.
    1930   The social organisation of Australian Tribes. *Oceania* **1**:34–63ff.

Ranson, Don
    1978   A preliminary examination of prehistoric coastal settlement at Nelson Bay, west coast of Tasmania. *Australian Archaeology* (Newsletter of the Australian Archaeological Association) No. 8:149–158.

Reber, Grote
    1965   Aboriginal carbon dates from Tasmania. *Mankind* **6**:264–268.
    1967   New Aboriginal carbon dates from Tasmania. *Mankind* **6**:435–437.

Roth, H. Ling
    1899   *The Aborigines of Tasmania.* Halifax: King and Sons.

Ryan, Lyndall
    1972   Outcasts in White Tasmania. *Mankind* **8**:249–254.
    1975   The Aborigines in Tasmania 1800–1974 and their problems with the Europeans. Ph.D. dissertation, School of Historical, Philosophical, and Political Science, Macquarie University, Sydney.

Sigleo, W. R., and E. A. Colhoun
    1975   Glacial age man in south-eastern Tasmania: evidence from the old Beach site. *Search* **6**:300–302.

Sims, Peter
    1977   Variations in Tasmanian petroglyphs. In *Form in Indigenous Art,* edited by P. J. Ucko. Canberra: Australian Institute of Aboriginal Studies. Pp. 429–438.

Stanner, W. E. H.
    1965   Aboriginal territorial organisation: estate, range, domain and regime. *Oceania* **36**:1–26.

Stockton, Jim, and Alan Wallace
  1979   Towards a human prehistory in the lower Derwent River area, south-eastern Tasmania, Australia. *Papers and Proceedings of the Royal Society of Tasmania* **113**:81–84.
Thom, B. G., and J. Chappell
  1975   Holocene sea levels relative to Australia. *Search* **6**:90–93.
Thorne, A. G.
  1971   The racial affinities and origins of the Australian Aborigines. In *Aboriginal man and environment in Australia,* edited by Jack Golson and D. J. Mulvaney. Canberra: Australian National University Press. Pp. 316–325.
Tindale, N. B.
  1937   Relationship of extinct Kangaroo Island culture with cultures of Australia, Tasmania and Malaya. *Records of the South Australian Museum* (Vol. 6), pp. 39–60.
Tryon, D. T.
  1971   Linguistic evidence and Aboriginal origins. In *Aboriginal man and environment in Australia,* edited by Jack Golson and D. J. Mulvaney. Canberra: Australian National University Press. Pp. 344–355.
Vanderwal, R. L.
  1977   The Shag Bay rockshelter, Tasmania. *The Artefact* **2**:161–170.
  1978   Adaptive technology in southwest Tasmania. *Australian Archaeology* (Newsletter of the Australian Archaeological Association) No. 8:107–127.
Wallace, A. G., and G. A. Doran
  1976   Early man in Tasmania: new skeletal evidence. In *The origin of the Australians,* edited by R. L. Kirk and A. G. Thorne. Canberra: Australian Institute of Aboriginal Studies. Pp. 173–182.
White, Carmel
  1967   Early stone axes in Arnhem Land. *Antiquity* **41**:149–152.
  1971   Man and environment in Northwest Arnhem Land. In *Aboriginal man and environment in Australia,* edited by Jack Golson and D. J. Mulvaney. Canberra: Australian National University Press. Pp. 141–157.

2

Advances in Polynesian Prehistory: Three Decades in Review

PATRICK V. KIRCH

> Pardon me, noble chiefs and lineages,
> For the searching place is now far and difficult;
> The old plantations once scattered on the roads
> Have now quite disappeared and gone with them their generation;
> But although they now lie in very thick bush,
> Search will be made at any rate
> For Touiafutuna, the first rock
> Where our origins began
>
> Verse composed by the Tongan chief Tafolo (Gifford 1924:6).

In the spring of 1950, a class in archaeological field techniques under the tutelage of K. P. Emory began excavations in a bluff shelter at Kuli'ou'ou, Oahu, which yielded an unanticipated abundance and variety of prehistoric artifacts. Taking advantage of W. Libby's offer to date charcoal using the then still-experimental ^{14}C method, Emory obtained a result even more damaging to established dogmas: the occupation of Kuli'ou'ou shelter by at least A.D. 1004 (946 ± 180 B.P., C-540; Emory, *et al.*, 1959:x) pushed back the settlement of Hawaii beyond expectations.

Coming on the heels of W. C. Gifford's pioneering archaeological work in Fiji in 1947, and Spoehr's demonstration of at least 3500 years of West Micronesian prehistory (Gifford 1951; Spoehr 1957), Emory's Hawaiian results left no doubt that it was time to abandon the older paradigm of Oceanic prehistory. This paradigm, which had held sway for some three decades, maintained that there was little or nothing to be gained through subsurface excavation in the Pacific Islands. Such a dogma—amazing today—resulted from several assumptions: (*a*) man was too recent an arrival in Oceania to have left substantial archaeological

51

ADVANCES IN WORLD ARCHAEOLOGY
Volume 1

deposits; (*b*) hurricanes and tidal waves would have scoured any potential sites along island coasts; (*c*) acidic soils would not preserve any but stone artifacts, of which the world's museums already had abundant collections; and (*d*) with pottery absent, it would be impossible to establish relative chronological sequences. The prevailing attitude was summed up by Piddington, who while grudgingly admitting that archaeological methods were "valid" in Polynesia, questioned whether "the systematic exhumation of pre-European Polynesian artifacts is a profitable and urgent task for science today" (Williamson and Piddington 1939:335).

Thirty years of increasingly intensive archaeological work since Emory's pioneering sondage have sent each of these assumptions to their proper graveyard. The pace of archaeological investigations quickened during the later 1960s and throughout the 1970s, with younger researchers from the United States, New Zealand, Australia, and Japan adding their names to the field rejuvenated by Emory, Duff, Sinoto, Suggs, Golson, and Green. Not only has Polynesia emerged from the realm of archaeological terra incognita, but it has begun to offer contributions to archaeological method and theory that transcend sequences bound to time and place. And, as the new Pacific nations emerge from colonial restraints, the pace of "development" begins to create a real urgency for the conservation and preservation of the region's prehistory.

THE POLYNESIAN WORLD

Polynesia is simultaneously a study in structural homogeneity and in cultural variability. The essential homogeneity of Polynesia stands in contrast to the remarkable ethnic and linguistic heterogeneity of Melanesia and Micronesia (cf. Mead 1967). James Cook, the English explorer who charted Polynesia so thoroughly, rightly concluded on the basis of linguistic similarities (in many instances, mutual intelligibility) that the island inhabitants had a common genesis. At Easter Island in 1774, he remarked, "It is extraordinary that the same Nation should have spread themselves over all the isles in this vast Ocean from New Zealand to this island which is almost a fourth part of the circumference of the Globe" (Beaglehole 1961:354). Exhaustive ethnographic, linguistic, biologic, and archaeological studies leave no doubt that this underlying structural homogeneity in Polynesia resulted from a common ancestry. At the same time, there is tremendous cultural and behavioral variability from island to island and archipelago to archipelago. This variation reflects, in part, environmental diversity within the region: atoll to near-continent, tropical to temperate. Not all cultural variation, of course, can be ascribed to the segregative effects of environment, and we must take into account random changes associated with isolation over long distances—the "founder effect" applied to culture (Vayda and Rappaport 1963:133–135).

In essence, it is this pattern of cultural variability overlying a fundamental structural homogeneity that has so often attracted anthropologists to Polynesia, and has led some to impute a "laboratory-like" status for the region (e.g., Clark and Terrell 1978; Kirch 1980b). The common ancestry shared by all Polynesian cultures provides an element of *control* frequently lacking in other "culture areas." Sahlins (1958:ix) drew an evolutionary analogy when he wrote that Polynesian cultures "are members of a single cultural genus that has filled in and adapted to a variety of local habitats." If we, as prehistorians, are ever to succeed in isolating processes of cultural adaptation and evolution, Polynesia is certainly one of our best evolutionary and ecological theaters.

The common structural bases of all Polynesian cultures are readily discernible through ethnographic comparison (cf. Williamson and Piddington 1939; Sahlins 1958; Goldman 1970). Technologically, Polynesian cultures were (at the time of European contact) Neolithic, in both the "classic" sense of ground stone tools, and in the economic connotation of a sedentary, agrarian subsistence base. The Polynesians made ingenious use not only of stone and wood, but raw materials including marine shell; sea urchin spines; animal bone and teeth; plant leaves, fibers, and bark; feathers; and more. Polynesian material culture was highly developed in terms of the variety of tools, garments, houses, fishing gear, and so forth (see, e.g., Buck 1930). Polynesian art forms reached a high level of sophistication in carving, weaving, dyeing, and tattooing (Kaeppler 1978). Pottery, the one strikingly absent item, was not manufactured anywhere in Polynesia at the time of European contact.

Although Polynesian societies exhibited a wide latitude in sociopolitical organization, all were chiefdoms and all were structured around the principles of genealogical seniority and dominantly agnatic inheritance of ranked titles. Terms for chief (**qariki*) and for a local, land-holding descent group (**kainanga*), or ramage (Sahlins 1958), may be reconstructed to Proto-Polynesian language. As Earle (1978:10) has suggested, the prototypical Polynesian social organization likely consisted of localized ramages, each derived by a branching process of segmentation from a common ancestor, and embedded in a conical clan structure. Each ramage would occupy its own geographical area; on oceanic islands, this frequently led to the pattern of sector-shaped land divisions running from the mountain core across lowlands, lagoon, and reef (e.g., the Hawaiian *ahupua'a* system). In many Polynesian societies, the fundamental class distinction between chiefs and commoners had been greatly elaborated by the time of European intrusion. The chieftainship itself was closely integrated with religion, and with the concepts of *mana* (supernatural power that was vested in the chief) and of *tapu* (sanctity or taboo), and Polynesian polities were to some extent theocracies.

Predictably in an island world, Polynesian production systems were dualistic, with agriculture and marine exploitation playing equal roles (Kirch 1979b). Polynesian crop plants, all adventive and purposefully introduced to the islands, were dominantly tropical and Southeast Asian in origin. Chief among these were taro, yam, bananas, and breadfruit. Domestic animals comprised the pig, dog, and fowl (*Gallus gallus*). The sea provided the greatest amount of protein, and Polynesian technology for marine exploitation was highly developed, including nets, spears, hooks, traps, poisons, weirs, and so on (Kirch and Dye 1979).

During the settlement of the inner Pacific region, the diversity of ecological constraints (Thomas 1963) required local adaptation of the fundamental Polynesian pattern of Neolithic chiefdoms organized upon a dual economic base. The islands range in type and size from atolls (e.g., Pukapuka), to upraised coral-limestone islands (e.g., Makatea), to "high" volcanic islands with stream valleys and fertile soil (e.g., Tahiti), to the largest of all, New Zealand, which is "continental" in its geological and biotic complexity. Differences in island size alone are staggering, as in the case of Anuta with a scant 40 ha of land area, and New Zealand's 501,776 km² encompassing more land than the rest of Polynesia combined. Crosscutting this physical spectrum is a climatic continuum from tropical (the majority of Polynesian islands) through subtropical (e.g., Hawaii), to fully temperate in the case of southern New Zealand and the Chatham Islands. Marine environments are similarly varied, with the extensive lagoons of tropical Polynesia, rich in variety and abundance of fish and shellfish, contrasting with the rocky cliffs of Easter Island or the Marquesas, or of the "roaring forties" seas that lash the Chathams. The ancestral Polynesians who first colonized the tropical western archipelagoes around 1500 B.C. could never have imagined the extremes of environmental variation that their descendants would encounter and to which they would adapt successfully.

On the basis of linguistic differences, there were at least 35 separate Polynesian cultures. Table 2.1 lists the principal islands and archipelagoes according to three area divisions. Polynesia proper, often referred to as Triangle Polynesia, lies within the triangular region whose apexes are Hawaii, New Zealand, and Easter Island (Figure 2.1). This is further divided into Western Polynesia, dominated by Samoa and Tonga, and Eastern Polynesia. The east–west distinction is more than geographic; certain cultural traits differentiate these subgroups (Burrows 1939b). These differences have been shown by linguistic and archaeological studies (Green 1968) to have an historical basis, which I review shortly. The third major subgroup is the Polynesian Outliers (Bayard 1976), a group of small islands situated on the fringe of Melanesia, from West Uvea in the Loyalty Islands to Nukuoro in the southern Caroline Islands of Micronesia. How these Polynesian isolates came to be dispersed across a dominantly Melanesian sea is a problem just beginning to succumb to archaeological probing.

ORIGINS

Speculations as to Polynesian origins began almost immediately after European discovery of the islands. Early theorists, frequently biased by Biblical predilections, were tempted to correlate the Polynesians with the Babylonians, or

TABLE 2.1

Principal Islands and Archipelagoes of Polynesia

Island or group	Type and number of islands	Area (km²)	Estimated population[a]	Major archaeological studies[b]
West Polynesia				
Tonga	Raised coral, atoll, high (160)	647	25,000	McKern 1929; Poulsen 1968; Kirch 1978b
Samoa	High (10)	3,134	50,000	Green and Davidson 1969, 1974; Jennings et al. 1976
Futuna	High (2)	65	2,500	Kirch 1976
Uvea	High (1)	59	4,000	Kirch 1976
Niue	Raised coral (1)	259	4,500	
Outliers (Total 18)				
Anuta	High (1)	0.4	150	Kirch and Rosendahl 1973
Tikopia	High (1)	5	1,250	Kirch and Yen 1980
Bellona	Raised coral (1)	20	450	Poulsen 1972
Nukuoro	Atoll (1)	1.7	150	Davidson 1971
East Polynesia				
Society Islands	High, atolls (11)	1,536	45,000	Emory 1933, 1979; Green et al. 1967; Sinoto and McCoy 1975
Marquesas	High (10)	1,057	20,000	Suggs 1961; Sinoto 1966
Hawaii	High (8)	16,692	250,000	Tuggle 1979; Kirch and Kelly 1975; Green 1980
New Zealand	"Continental" (2)	501,776	100,000	Davidson 1979; Duff 1956; Leach and Leach 1979
Tuamotus	Atolls (76)	790	7,000	Emory 1934b; Chazine 1977
Easter Island	High (1)	142	5,000	Heyerdahl and Ferdon 1961; McCoy 1976; Ayres 1973
Australs	High (5)	132	5,000	Verin 1969; Ferdon 1965
Cook Islands	High, atolls (15)	240	15,000	Bellwood 1978
Mangareva	High (8)	15	4,000	Emory 1939

[a] Estimate of population at time of European contact.

[b] Selected references to major archaeological surveys or excavations; not meant to be exhaustive.

with the lost tribes of Israel (Howard 1967). Some scholars, however, like the philologist Horatio Hale, derived theories not too divergent from present views. By 1938, when Sir Peter Buck published *Vikings of the Sunrise,* the weight of anthropological, linguistic, physical anthropological, and ethnobotanical evidence had firmly convinced most scientists that Polynesian origins lay in Southeast Asia and/or South China, although considerable debate still centered on whether the route to Polynesia had been via Melanesia or Micronesia. Underlying Buck's and other theories, however, was an assumption that the ancestral Polynesians had crossed the Pacific in migratory "waves," but more or less as a single ethnic unit that was separate from other Oceanic peoples. Thor Heyerdahl, whose rather one-sidedly argued theory received great popular attention

Figure 2.1   Oceania, showing the principal archipelagoes of Polynesia, and other major islands discussed in the text. The shaded area delineates the distribution of the Polynesian-speaking peoples.

after the Kon-Tiki expedition, was likewise in the grip of the migration mentality, differing from the others only in that he chose to ignore the bulk of accumulated evidence and advocated the Americas as the homeland.

Excavations in Fiji, New Caledonia, and the Marianas in the late 1940s and early 1950s (Gifford 1951; Spoehr 1957) first began to demonstrate that the traditional cultural divisions between Polynesia, Micronesia, and Melanesia lose their heuristic value as we penetrate deeper into the Oceanic past. Rather than viewing the settlement of the Pacific as a series of rapid and populous migrations that quickly led to an ethnic status quo, archaeology has been able to contribute the perspective that the region's settlement history is both lengthy and complex.

The progression of man into Oceania may be viewed as a gradual process of generally west-to-east movement (but with significant counter movements and "eddies"), beginning probably not long after the end of the Pleistocene, and completed only within the last millennium. Furthermore, this progression was more than the colonization of new islands; it encompassed a continual process of adaptation to an increasingly oceanic world. As one moves from the island arcs of Melanesia into the remote tracts of the Pacific, the islands become not only more isolated, but geologically simpler, and frequently biotically depauperate. These constraints led to the adaptive development of new cognitive and behavioral patterns. Thus the contribution of a prehistoric perspective has been to show that those cultural patterns characteristic of Polynesia were not carried intact along migration routes, but developed in situ. The Polynesians *became* Polynesians in Oceania, over the course of several thousands of years of adaptive change.

The Lapita Cultural Complex

Archaeologically, Polynesian origins have been clearly traced to the Lapita Cultural Complex (Green 1978, 1979), apparently representing the first major intrusion of man into the deeper reaches of Oceania (i.e., the island arcs lying beyond New Guinea and its immediate neighbors). Archaeological assemblages belonging to this complex are distributed from the Bismark archipelago in Western Melanesia, through the Santa Cruz Islands, New Hebrides, and New Caledonia, to Fiji, Tonga, and Samoa. Temporally, the Lapita complex spans the period from approximately 1600 to 500 B.C. (Green 1979:Table 2.1).

Given the relatively embryonic state of Southeast Asian archaeology, the further origins of the Lapita complex itself, doubtless in the general area of West New Guinea, Celebes, Philippines, and East Indonesia, remain hazy. Recent excavations in this presumed homeland region, however, have yielded evidence of ceramic-using cultures with a range of stone and shell artifacts quite similar to their Lapita equivalents, dating from the second and third millennia B.C. (Bellwood 1979:203–231). What seems evident, if as yet only minimally attested archaeologically, is the presence throughout island Southeast Asia by the third millennium B.C. of one or more groups of "Neolithic," pottery-making horticulturalists, who had already achieved certain adaptations to island existence (cf. Shutler and Marck 1975). The development of suitable watercraft, specifically the outrigger sailing canoe, was the critical adaptation that permitted these Oceanic ancestors to penetrate beyond the sheltered coasts of New Guinea.

The Lapita Cultural Complex is minimally defined on the basis of its characteristic dentate-stamped pottery. Because there is both spatial and temporal variability in Lapita ceramics, it has proved useful to employ a concept of a Lapitoid Ceramic Series (Golson 1971; Kirch 1978b), emphasizing that Lapita assemblages partake of aspects of both *horizon* and *tradition*, as used in American archaeological terminology. Lapitoid ceramics are generally well-fired, frequently calcareous-sand tempered, paddle-and-anvil finished, earthenware vessels (including shouldered pots, jars, bowls, flat-bottomed dishes, and plates). Although there are usually substantial quantities of plain ware, the decorative component is highly distinctive, and has been exhaustively analyzed by S. Mead and others (Mead *et al.* 1973; Donovan 1973). Mead has shown that this largely geometric decorative system can be reduced to a small set of basic design elements, which are consistently combined into approximately 120 motifs according to a set of transformation rules. That a substantial number of these motifs are shared over the entire region of Lapita distribution is convincing evidence for the cultural continuity of the Lapita Cultural Complex (Green 1978). It is also possible, however, to determine regional subgroups based on uniquely shared design motifs. Thus Green (1978, 1979) has demonstrated that two major subgroups, Western Lapita and Eastern Lapita, have considerable significance for the origins of ethnic diversity in the southwestern Pacific. The Eastern Lapita group, occupying the archipelagoes of Fiji, Tonga, and Samoa, seems to have become effectively isolated from its.Western counterpart due to the large ocean gap (850 km) between Fiji and the New Hebrides, which reduced the feasibility for maintaining two-way voyaging contact. The adaptations undergone by this Eastern Lapita population, in the Fijian-Samoan-Tongan region, over approximately 1500 years, resulted in what we term *Polynesian* culture.

Oceania has proven to be an especially fruitful area for the interplay of archaeology and historical linguistics, and the evidence of the Lapita Cultural Complex is rather closely approximated by recent studies in the subgrouping of Austronesian languages (Shutler and Marck 1975; Pawley and Green 1973). The Austronesian language family (formerly termed Malayo-Polynesian) is spread from Madagascar to Easter Island and comprises about 500 modern languages, including all those of Oceania and island Southeast Asia (except the Papuan languages spoken in parts of New Guinea and the Solomons). Pawley and Green (1973), among others, have convincingly argued that the intrusion of Lapita settlements into the southwestern Pacific may be correlated with the dispersal of Austronesian speakers, particularly those belonging to the Oceanic subgroup (Figure 2.2). The breakup of Proto-Eastern Oceanic language was probably associated with the isolation of the Western and Eastern Lapita groups. Further linguistic change within the Eastern Lapita group led to the differentiation of Proto-Fijian and Proto-Polynesian from Proto-Central Pacific. It can be clearly seen from this model that the Lapita Cultural Complex is of importance not only for Polynesian origins, but for the diverse cultures of eastern Melanesia and Micronesia as well. For the immediate purpose of reviewing Polynesian prehistory, however, a discussion of Eastern Lapita and the Fiji–Tonga–Samoa region is valuable.

Eastern Lapita and Polynesian Origins

Lapita pottery was discovered in 1920 in Tonga (McKern 1929), but its significance for Polynesian origins was not realized at the time. Not until Golson's discovery of plain ceramics in Samoa in 1956, and Gifford's excavations of deco-

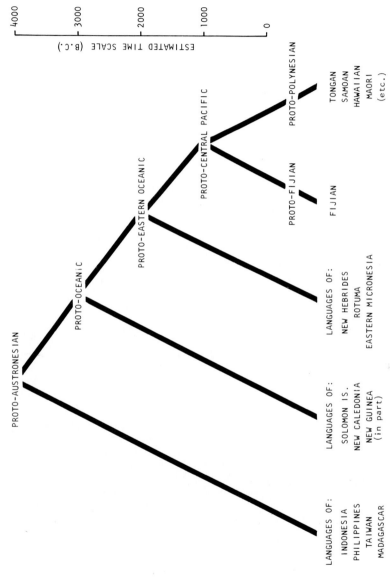

Figure 2.2 Simplified "family tree" of the Austronesian languages, showing the position of the Polynesian language group.

rated Lapita in Fiji (Gifford 1951), did a consistent framework begin to emerge (Golson 1971). Subsequently, a number of intensive investigations of Lapitoid-ceramic bearing sites in Fiji, the Lau Islands, Tongatapu, Niuatoputapu, Samoa, Futuna, and Uvea have provided a great deal of new evidence for the 1500-year transition from initial Eastern Lapita to what we may term *Archaic Polynesian* culture (Kirch 1980b). Table 2.2 lists the major excavated sites and associated ages.

TABLE 2.2

Sites With Lapitoid Pottery in West Polynesia and Fiji

Island and site	Type	^{14}C age[a]	Ceramic phase represented	Reference
Viti Levu (Fiji)				
Natunuku (VL1/1)	Midden	3240 ± 100 (GaK–1218)	Early Eastern Lapita	
Yanuca (VL16/81)	Rockshelter	2980 ± 90 (GaK–1226)	Early to Late Eastern Lapita	Hunt 1980
Sigatoka (VL16/1)	Sand dune	2460 ± 90 (GaK–946)	Late Eastern Lapita	Birks 1973
Tongatapu				
TO-2	Midden	3090 ± 95 (ANU–541)	Early Eastern Lapita	Poulsen 1968
Mangaia Mound	Midden	2630 ± 50 (NZ–727A)	Early Eastern Lapita	McKern 1929; Groube 1971
Vuki's Mound	Midden	2440 ± 110 (ANU–441)	Late Eastern Lapita	Groube 1971
TO-6	Midden	2380 ± 51 (NZ–636A)	Late Eastern Lapita	Poulsen 1968
Niuatoputapu				
Lolokoka (NT-90)	Midden	3210 ± 85 (I–10633)	Early Eastern Lapita	Kirch 1978b
Lotoā (NT-100)	Midden	—	Late Eastern Lapita	Kirch 1978b
Pome'e (NT-93)	Midden	—	Polynesian Plain Ware	Kirch 1978b
Upolu (Samoa)				
Ferry Berth	Submerged midden	2890 ± 80	Early Eastern Lapita	Green & Davidson 1974
Sasoa'a (SU-Sa-3)	Inland site	1840 ± 100	Polynesian Plain Ware	Green & Davidson 1974
Vailele (SU-Va-1)	Mound site	1880 ± 60 (NZ–361)	Polynesian Plain Ware	Green & Davidson 1969
Futuna				
Tavai (FU-11)	Midden (buried)	2120 ± 80 (I–8355)	Late Eastern Lapita	Kirch 1976

[a] Age B.P. (1950), T1/2 = 5568 years. The age given is frequently only one of a series, and has been chosen to best represent *initial* occupation. The laboratory number is given in parentheses.

The earliest known Eastern Lapita sites are those of Natunuku and Yanuca on Viti Levu in Fiji, and site TO-2 on Tongatapu, indicating settlement in the Fiji-Tonga area by the end of the second millennium B.C. These sites, and several others slightly later in time (e.g., Ferry Berth, Lolokoka), contain characteristic dentate-stamped pottery that may be designated Early Eastern Lapita. A second set of sites, dating the middle of the first millennium B.C. (e.g., Sigatoka, TO-6, Lotoaa, Tavai), generally lacks the dentate-stamped decoration, but retains certain vessel forms and notched-rim decoration, and may be termed Late Eastern Lapita. Finally, a third set of sites has ceramic assemblages restricted entirely to undecorated, simple bowls, and dates from the end of the first millennium B.C. to as late as A.D. 300 (e.g., Pome'e, Vailele). This last ceramic group has been termed Polynesian Plain Ware (Green and Davidson 1969) and represents the final stage in the local devolution of the Eastern Lapita Ceramic Series. Ceramics ceased to be produced anywhere in Polynesia after about A.D. 300. The division of what was actually a continuous process in the devolution of ceramic technology into three phases is, of course, somewhat arbitrary, but nonetheless useful. This devolutionary sequence is graphed in Figure 2.3. Explanations for the unique loss of the potter's art in Polynesia remain at the level of speculation. Absence of materials can be ruled out, because both clay and temper are abundant on all high islands in the region. It is likely that this devolution was a complex process, involving more than a single causal mechanism.

Nonceramic portable artifacts from Lapita sites show a continuity of development over time. With the settlement of Samoa and Tonga, Austronesian man for the first time crossed a major geological boundary—the Andesite Line, which separates older, island-arc petrographic suites in the west from younger, oceanic basalts in the east. The immediate implication is a great reduction in the variety of rock types available for stone tool production. The initial Lapita settlers of Samoa and Tonga were forced, therefore, to adapt their lithic technology to basalt and volcanic glass alone, and this may account for several significant changes in the adz kit (Green 1971).

The range of portable artifacts in Lapita sites is quite wide, and includes a variety of shell ornaments (*Trochus* and *Conus* shell rings, beads, bi-perforate beads or bracelet segments, *Trochus* shell armbands), one-piece fishhooks of *Turbo* shell, files of branch coral and sea urchin spines, scrapers for food preparation, bone awls, tattooing needles, adzes of both stone and *Tridacna* shell, and cores and flakes of obsidian and chert. A selection of typical artifacts is illustrated in Figure 2.4.

One characteristic aspect of the Lapita Cultural Complex throughout its distribution is the presence in most sites of imported materials, interpreted by Green (1979:38) as representing, at the minimum, "a network of reciprocal exchanges between isolated communities that maintained frequent contact." The Early Eastern Lapita sites in Niuatoputapu and Tongatapu fit this pattern, with the presence of such imported items as chert, obsidian, stone adzes, and perhaps pottery. Such exotic items, however, cease to be present in sites of Late

62   Patrick V. Kirch

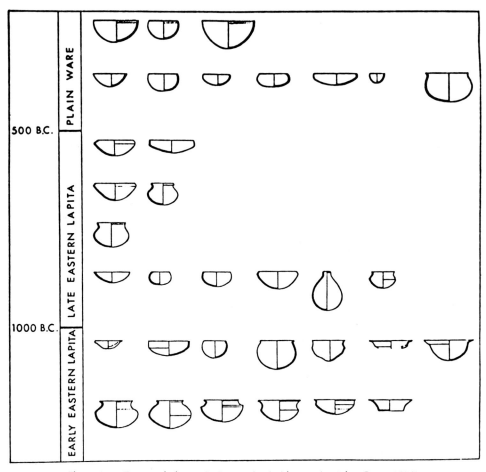

Figure 2.3 Temporal change in Eastern Lapitoid ceramics (after Green 1979).

Eastern Lapita age, suggesting that local communities had become self-sufficient and no longer required the importation of resources. It is conceivable that the abandonment of reciprocal exchange networks, and consequent reduction in the frequency of two-way voyaging, helped to accelerate the processes of linguistic and cultural differentiation between isolated settlements in the Fiji–Tonga–Samoa region. Linguistic evidence, for example, indicates that Proto-Polynesian language had separated into distinct Tongic and Nuclear Polynesian subgroups by approximately 500 B.C.

Lapita sites generally are either coastal or associated with geomorphological features indicative of former shorelines. Relative sea level has undergone significant changes over the past 4000 years in the Tonga–Samoa area, due more to local tectonic emergence or submergence than to eustatic change (the Andesite Line corresponds with a major tectonic plate boundary). The Ferry Berth site on

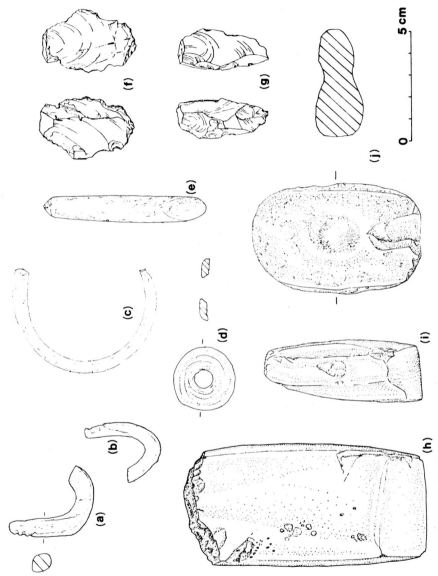

Figure 2.4 Artifacts from Eastern Lapita sites on Niuatoputapu Island: (a,b) one-piece fishhooks of *Turbo* shell, (c) *Trochus*-shell armband, (d) *Conus*-shell ornament, (e) abrader of sea urchin spine, (f,g) flakes of volcanic glass, (h,i) *Tridacna*-shell adzes, (j) hammerstone with pecked finger-grips.

Upolu thus is below modern sea level, while the Niuatoputapu sites are situated behind an elevated shoreline now as much as 2 km inland. The first evidence for truly inland settlement dates to the terminal Polynesian Plain Ware phase of the Lapitoid Series, specifically the Sasoa'a site situated some 3 km up the Falefa Valley of Upolu (Green and Davidson 1974).

The sites themselves are usually open middens (with abundant shellfish remains), although some rockshelters were occupied (e.g., Yanuca). The open sites frequently range from 1000 to 10,000 m² in area (Green 1979:30–31). Features excavated in these sites include basin-shaped earth ovens with cooking stones, scoop fire pits, postholes (no house plans have been determined as yet), small pits, and in one instance, a well (at Lolokoka).

Questions concerning the nature of Lapita subsistence ecology and economic orientation inspired a fair amount of controversy over the past decade, centered particularly on the issue of whether or not the initial Lapita colonizers were agriculturalists (cf. Green 1979; Groube 1971; Kirch 1978b, 1979b). Data from recent excavations, although partly indirect, seem to have largely resolved the issue in favor of Lapita economy as a broad-based, generalist set of strategies including agriculture, animal husbandry, and marine exploitation. Domestic pig, dog, and fowl were all part of the cultural "baggage" transported by the initial settlers. An agricultural subsistence base is suggested not only by the pig, but by the sendentary nature of Lapita villages, the presence of food scrapers and peelers, and of probable starchy food fermentation pits. It is evident, nonetheless, that the first settlers on any island intensively exploited the marine biota which would have been abundant prior to initial incursion of humans. Thus, the Lolokoka site on Niuatoputapu, for example, contains five times as much turtle bone, and four times as much shellfish (per excavated unit) as the later Pome'e site (Kirch and Dye 1979).

The archaeological picture of ancestral Polynesian culture from 1500 B.C. to A.D. 300, outlined previously, may be further amplified by drawing from the method of historical linguistics. Biggs and others (Walsh and Biggs 1966; Clark 1979; Pawley and Green 1971) have reconstructed a substantial Proto-Polynesian vocabulary, part of the ancestral language spoken at the western gateway to Polynesia prior to the differentiation of Tongic and Nuclear Polynesian linguistic subgroups. A few of these reconstructed items relating to significant aspects of society, economy, material culture, and settlement pattern are given in Table 2.3. The interpretation of Lapita as agriculturally based is well supported by these data. Furthermore, it is clear that certain features of Polynesian social organization (stratification, descent groups) were already in existence.

In summary, archaeological and linguistic data agree closely in associating the immediate origins of Polynesian culture with the Lapita Cultural Complex, itself representing the initial incursion of Austronesian-speaking man into the southwestern Pacific. An Eastern Lapita subgroup, situated in the Fiji–Tonga–Samoa region, underwent a sequence of adaptive change from approximately 1500 B.C. to the first few centuries of the Christian era, a sequence resulting in an Archaic

TABLE 2.3

Some Proto-Polynesian Reconstructions Relating to Ancestral Polynesian Culture

Gloss	Proto-Polynesian term	Tongan reflex[a]	Hawaiian reflex[b]
Society			
Chief	*qariki	'eiki	ali'i
Ramage group	*kainanga	kainga	maka'ainana
Seaman, navigator	*tautai	toutai	'aukai
Spirit, diety	*qa(n)tua	'otua	akua
Assembly of people	*fono	fono	['aha][c]
Economy			
Taro	*talo	talo	kalo
Yam	*qufi	'ufi	uhi
Breadfruit	*kulu	[mei]	'ulu
Banana	*futi	fusi	[mai'a]
Garden	*ma'ala	ma'ala	māla
Pig	*puaka	puaka	pua'a
Dog	*kulī	kulī	['īlio]
Material culture			
Adz	*toki	toki	ko'i
Canoe	*waka	vaka	wa'a
Wooden bowl	*kumete	kumete	'umeke
Barkcloth	*tapa	[ngatu]	kapa
Basket	*kete	kete	'eke
Fishhook	*mata'u	māta'u	makau
Fishnet	*kupenga	kupenga	'upena
Fishtrap	*finaki	finaki	hīna'i
Settlement pattern			
House	*fale	fale	hale
Ceremonial area	*mala'e	mala'e	—
Fortress	*kolo	kolo	—
Canoe Shed	*folau	—	hālau

[a] Chosen to represent the Tongic subgroup.
[b] Chosen to represent the Nuclear Polynesian subgroup.
[c] Terms in brackets are innovations, not reflexes of the Proto-Polynesian term.

Polynesian culture. The stage had been set for what may have been the great seafaring saga of all time—the dispersal of Polynesian-speaking colonizers to every habitable island over more than 20 million km² of Pacific Ocean.

DISPERSAL AND COLONIZATION

The first settlement of Eastern Polynesia was accomplished no later than A.D. 300, and several ^{14}C ages from the Marquesan site of Ha'atuatua (Table 2.4) (Suggs 1961) suggest that this event possibly occurred as early as 150 B.C. The sites of Ha'atuatua and Hane (Sinoto 1966) in the Northern Marquesas Islands

66   Patrick V. Kirch

TABLE 2.4

Early East Polynesian Sites

Island and site	Type	^{14}C age[a]	Reference
Marquesas			
Ha'atuatua (NHaal)	Dune site	2080 ± 150 (I–394B)	Suggs 1961
Hane (MUH 1)	Dune site	1750 ± 140 (WSU–524)	Sinoto 1966
Societies			
Maupiti	Burial site	1090 ± 85 (GXO–207)	Emory and Sinoto 1964
Vaito'otia (ScH1-1)	Waterlogged site	1100 ± 70 (GaK–4629)	Sinoto and McCoy 1975
Hawaiian Islands			
Bellows (O18)	Dune site	1600 ± 90 (GaK–1818)	Pearson et al. 1971
Halawa (Mo-A1-3)	Dune site	1380 ± 90 (GaK–2743)	Kirch and Kelly 1975
Waiahukini (H8)	Shelter cave	1195 ± 210 (WSU–487)	Emory, Bonk, and Sinoto 1959
New Zealand			
Wairau Bar	Midden with burials	940 ± 110 (n.a.)	Duff 1956
Washpool	Midden	760 ± 41 (NZ–1505)	Leach and Leach 1979
Cook Islands			
Ureia (AIT.10)	Beach midden	969 ± 83 (NZ–1252)	Bellwood 1978

[a] Age B.P. (1950), T1/2 = 5568. The age given is frequently only one of a series, and has been chosen to best represent *initial* occupation. Laboratory number given in parentheses.

are, to date, the earliest excavated East Polynesian settlements, and are the only sites known to contain Polynesian Plain Ware ceramics. In both cases, only a handful of shards were excavated, and Dickinson and Shutler (1974) have presented evidence to suggest that at least some of these pots may have been imports from Western Polynesia or Fiji. In any event, the use of ceramics in the Marquesas ceased almost immediately after colonization, paralleling the loss of ceramics in the west.

On archaeological grounds, any of the West Polynesian islands could have served as the springboard for the long eastward voyage (approximately 3500 km) to the Marquesas. Linguistic evidence, however, would rule out the southern Tongan islands, since all East Polynesian languages are associable with the Nuclear Polynesian rather than the Tongic branch. The Samoas, Niuatoputapu, Niuafo'ou, Futuna, or Uvea are all potential candidates for this immediate Eastern Polynesian homeland. (The legendary "Havaiki" of Polynesian myth [Buck 1938] has been correlated by some with the Samoan island of Savai'i [the terms are lexical equivalents] but such tentative evidence must be viewed with extreme caution.)

The Society Islands, which are 1200 km southwest of the Marquesas, were settled by A.D. 600 (Emory 1979), and it is possible that yet earlier sites will be discovered there in the future. Although ceramics are absent, the artifact assemblages of the early Maupiti and Vaito'otia sites (Emory and Sinoto 1964; Sinoto and McCoy 1975) virtually replicate those of Hane and Ha'atuatua in the Marquesas, and prompted Sinoto (1979) to define an *Archaic East Polynesian* culture. The technological repertoire of this Archaic East Polynesian culture (Figure 2.5) displays certain differences and innovations with respect to its Archaic Polynesian ancestor in Samoa and Tonga, presumably reflecting adaptation to new conditions as well as random changes resulting from isolation.

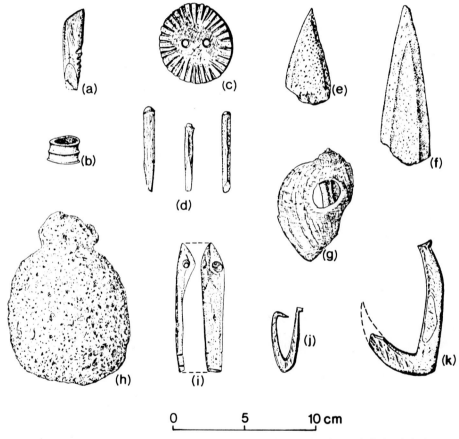

Figure 2.5 Archaic East Polynesian artifacts from the Marquesas Islands: (a) shell chisel; (b) bone reel ornament; (c) pearl-shell ornament; (d) three abraders of sea-urchin spines; (e,f) abraders of *Porites* coral; (g) vegetable peeler of *Tonna* shell; (h) stone plummet sinker; (i) pearl-shell trolling lure; (j,k) one-piece fishhooks of pearl-shell. (After Suggs 1961.)

Dispersal of Archaic East Polynesian populations to the most remote corners of the Polynesian Triangle occurred during a relatively short time span from approximately A.D. 300 to 800, a virtual "burst" of exploration and discovery. Archaeological as well as linguistic evidence suggests that both the Marquesas and Societies acted as dispersal centers, and it is frequently difficult to pinpoint either as a discrete origin point. Easter Island was perhaps one of the first remote outposts to be colonized, by A.D. 400 (McCoy 1979). The island's language retains several archaic components (e.g., the velar nasal) apparently lost prior to the settlement of the remainder of East Polynesia. The Hawaiian chain was certainly occupied by A.D. 600, and quite likely one or two centuries earlier (Kirch 1974), while New Zealand had been discovered by A.D. 800 (Davison 1979). We as yet lack early settlement sites for the Tuamotus, Mangareva, and Australs, but there is no reason to believe that these archipelagoes, more proximal to the Marquesan and Society dispersal centers, were colonized any later than the remoter outposts.

The other major regional subgroup of Polynesia, the outliers, had a lengthy and complex settlement sequence, as yet imperfectly known. Excavations have been undertaken on Nukuoro (Davidson 1971), Bellona (Poulsen 1972), Anuta (Kirch and Rosendahl 1973), and Tikopia (Kirch and Yen, n.d.), a small sample given the total of 18 outliers. To date, only Anuta and Tikopia have yielded relatively complete cultural sequences, in both cases beginning with later Lapitoid ceramics, approximately 900 B.C. Whereas the Anutan sequence appears to have a major hiatus (during which time the island is presumed to have been unoccupied), that of Tikopia is continuous.In Tikopia, Lapitoid ceramics are replaced early in the Christian era with an incised, imported "trade" ware of Mangaasi type (Garanger 1972) from the New Hebrides. The Tikopian sequence is aceramic after about A.D. 1200, and is characterized in its final stages by certain diagnostically West Polynesian artifacts (e.g., untanged adzes of oceanic basalt, West Polynesian type trolling lures). The complexities of Outlier settlement histories may reflect, in part, the continued impact of drift voyages from West Polynesia, attested ethnographically. It will require a good deal more excavation on other Outliers before a comprehensive picture can be synthesized.

While archaeological investigations have provided a reasonably clear outline of the colonization of Eastern Polynesia, and have begun to elucidate the position of the Outliers, Polynesian prehistorians have hardly begun to address the broader questions of: (a) what were the inducements that led the Polynesians to settle such an immense area of the globe in the course of a few centuries; and (b) what colonization strategies permitted the successful establishment of new communities on remote and previously unpopulated islands? Answers to such important questions can be addressed archaeologically, but also require such diverse inputs as computer simulation of drift voyaging and of population growth, or the experimental replication of purposeful voyaging.

Various causes have been posited for the departure of colonizing expeditions from Polynesian islands, among them population pressure and expulsion following defeat in war. While both of these were seemingly important in some cases, I doubt that they alone would have led to the extraordinary dispersal that Polynesia represents. While it might appear unscientific or romantic to refer to "wanderlust" as an underlying motive for migration, some sort of culturally ingrained ethic of exploration and discovery may well have played a vital role in Polynesian dispersal. As Levison *et al.* (1973:4) remarked, "In the first and second millennia B.C. the ocean to the east, north, and south of eastern Melanesia was a space frontier as the solar system is today." Yet, it is certain that the colonization of the "undiscovered lands beyond the horizon" was a matter of purposeful voyaging, and not mere chance landfalls of drifting canoes and castaways. The exhaustive computer simulations of Levison *et al.* (1973) have demonstrated that the probabilities of drifting to such remote islands as Easter or Hawaii are virtually zero. Moving through the island arcs of the southwestern Pacific over the course of several thousand years, Polynesian ancestors may have conceived of the Pacific as a sea of islands. Thus the Polynesian explorer might well have "set sail . . . in search of new land, confident in the belief that, as usual, islands would rise over the horizon to meet him" (Levison *et al.* 1973:64).

The ocean-going capabilities of Polynesian double canoes have been the focus of recent experimentation, the most spectacular being the several successful voyages of the "Hokule'a" (Finney 1977). At the uniquely waterlogged site of Vaito'otia on Huahine, Sinoto (1978) excavated a wooden steering paddle (3.8 m long), foreboom, and two adz-hewn platform planks from a double-canoe at least 24 m in length, dating about A.D. 850–1200. Such craft were certainly capable of transporting organized expeditions of colonization, complete with stocks of domestic animals and crop plants. A successful landfall, however, was only the first phase of the colonization strategy. Since Polynesian islands were virtually barren of useful food plants, the establishment of imported stocks of cultigens would have received the greatest priority upon arrival. Not surprisingly, early settlement sites indicate a heavy reliance on wild bird, shellfish, turtle, and fish resources during the initial phase of occuation (e.g., Kirch 1973).

The size and age–sex composition of the human propagule itself was critical in determining whether the new colony would survive and grow, or head irreversibly toward extinction. Demographic simulations (McArthur *et al.* 1976) demonstrate that there are substantial differences in survival probabilities of propagules of 6, 10, and 14 persons (3, 5, and 7 couples). With a propagule of 6, in which the only marriage rule was a ban on incest, probability of extinction was as high as 77%, whereas increasing the initial propagule to 14 persons lowered the extinction probability to 19%. It would clearly have been advantageous for the colonizing group to remain at a high population growth rate until the survival of the group was assured (cf. Kirch 1980b on r/K selection models in Polynesia).

While Polynesian colonization strategies appear, on the whole, to have been highly successful, there are several intriguing instances, attested archaeologically, of founding populations that went to extinction. These cases are the so-called "mystery islands" of Polynesia, with archaeological traces of settlement, yet devoid of humans at the time of European contact. Included here are the islands of Pitcairn, Henderson, the Line Islands (Fanning, Christmas, and others [Emory 1934a]), Nihoa, and Necker (Emory 1928). All of these islands share one characteristic—small size—although they vary considerably in the degree to which they can be considered ecologically limiting or marginal. Pitcairn, though small (less than 6 km²) is reasonably fertile and well-watered, while Necker (.17 km²) is a mere rocky pinnacle with but a single, heavily guano-tainted seep for a water source. It seems likely that the extinction or extirpation of the former human populations of these islands was due to their limited carrying capacities, possibly compounded by human-induced degradations of already marginal environments.

MODELS OF PREHISTORIC CHANGE IN POLYNESIA

The varied Polynesian cultures as witnessed at their indigenous developmental endpoints by European explorers were each the product of dispersal, subsequent isolation, and divergence from an Archaic Polynesian ancestor. Following initial colonization, each island or archipelago was characterized by its own particular sequence of cultural change. While each sequence is, in certain respects, unique, there were at the same time a number of parallel patterns common to all or a sizable number of these sequences:

1. The period following initial colonization seems frequently to have been one of "reassortment" of technological and economic systems, reflecting the extent to which a new environment differed from the ancestral homeland.
2. Although initial propagules were small, rapid population growth brought populations up to levels of relatively high density by the time of, or even prior to, European contact. In some instances there is evidence of stabilization, oscillation, or decline in population levels.
3. Polynesian populations were responsible for significant impacts upon their island environments, impacts which sometimes bordered on extreme degradation. Human-induced environmental change thus induced new selection pressures requiring cultural adaptation or adjustment.
4. In most Polynesian production and exploitation systems there is evidence for a trend toward increasing intensification, in both terrestrial and marine aspects.
5. There are frequently trends toward elaboration of sociopolitical organization, increase in degree of class stratification, and in the frequency and intensity of between-group competition and warfare. These trends are furthermore accompanied by what Mead (1967) has called "hypertrophy" or efflorescence of highly stylized behavior, whether expressed in material culture or social behavior.

In the investigation of island sequences, two fundamental aims are evident: to document the course of prehistoric change for any particular island or archipelago, and to seek explanations for the alternative pathways of change represented by these sequences. It is in pursuit of the second objective, the search for underlying processes of cultural change, that Polynesian archaeologists are most likely to contribute to questions of broad anthropological concern. The successful prosecution of both objectives, however, depends considerably upon one's theoretical conception of how prehistoric change should be modeled.

One approach to sequence–modeling in Polynesia centers upon artifactual change, and is strongly typological in outlook. This approach is perhaps best exemplified by the work of Emory and Sinoto, including the well-known Hawaiian fishook chronology (Emory *et al.* 1959) and Sinoto's Northern Marquesas cultural sequence (Sinoto 1966, 1979). This approach aims to establish periods or phases characterized by clusters or associations of distinctive artifact types. Although Sinoto has concentrated upon portable artifacts, his Marquesan sequence also incorporates architectural styles, burial types, and to some extent economic orientation. No attempt, however, is made to correlate artifactual change with social, demographic, or ecological processes; this approach is thus oriented primarily toward documentation of change rather than explanation. One problem with the artifactual approach lies in its typological emphasis, which tends to obscure variability in technology (cf. Kirch 1980c). Nevertheless, the school has successfully documented artifactual change, if largely ignoring why change occurred.

In contrast, several Polynesian workers have attempted to establish "developmental" sequences for various island groups. One of the first to apply a developmental scheme was Suggs (1961), who criticized earlier Polynesianists for a "tendency towards denial of cultural processes of independent invention, convergence, stimulus diffusion, and obsolescence" (1961:11). Influenced by the then-prevailing American culture-historical school (e.g., Willey and Phillips 1958), Suggs established a four-period sequence for the Marquesas Islands, based on "socio-political, demographical, economic, and technological factors" (1961:21). His terminology (Settlement, Development, Expansion, and Classic Periods) was meant to convey significant aspects of cultural development within the Marquesan environmental setting. A similar developmental sequence was proposed by Ayres (1973) for Easter Island, while Newman (1969) and Cordy (1974) each proposed sequences for the Hawaiian Islands (neither of the latter has enjoyed much acceptance from other prehistorians active in the Hawaiian field).

Nowhere in Polynesia has there been more debate concerning culture sequence models than in New Zealand. There recognition of prehistoric change came early (von Haast 1871), due to the excitement sparked by discoveries of human artifacts in association with the bones of extinct, flightless *moa* birds. Duff (1956) convincingly demonstrated that these early, moa-associated remains were of East Polynesian affinity (and not representatives of some Paleolithic era), and proposed the Moa–Hunter Period of Maori Culture. Golson (1959), using a largely typological-artifactual approach, established a sequence with the transition from Archaic (= Moa–Hunter) to Classic Maori due to possible alternatives of in situ change, or of the impact of an intruding (East Polynesian) culture. Green (1963) elaborated Golson's sequence for the Iwitini region with an explicitly developmental approach rather like that of Suggs, incorporating settlement pattern and economic orientation. Particular attention was paid by Green to the role of sweet potato agriculture, following Yen's (1961) speculations on the adaptation of *kumara* cultivation to the temperate New Zealand environment. Groube (1967) reviewed these "stadial" and "stagel" models, and offered a "strophic" alternative, focusing on peaks or "strophes" of cultural activity. Green (1974) reconsidered the New Zealand sequence, explicitly in terms of adaptation to ecological conditions, examining change as "the response in isolation of a Polynesian culture to a non-tropical environment" (1974:38).

In striking contrast to the developmental models, is the approach of Green and Davidson (1974) to prehistoric change in Samoa. Summarizing an extensive project involving some 17 archaeologists, Green and Davidson wrote:

> we have not discovered in these data, nor found reason to impose on them, a particular scheme of temporal divisions. In large part this is because neither cultural peaks, abrupt changes in cultural content, nor significant clustering of distinctive materials are as yet in evidence (1974:213). Change there was, and it would be wrong to deny it. . . . Still, it can be documented without recourse to a period or stage model. Without such a model, the principal feature of the Samoan sequence is its continuity (1974:224).

In their review of Oceanic archaeology, Clark and Terrell (1978) appear to launch an attack on the whole notion of sequence-building, or what they term "culture-historical scenarios." Their objections, however, center not so much upon the validity of any particular sequence model, but upon the frequent failure to present alternatives suited to hypothesis testing.

> It is usually not made clear that more than one scenario is possible for the very same evidence. Indeed it is not uncommon for a new scenario to be presented as if it eliminated all previous models simply because its author believes it does greater justice to the facts as he understands them (1978:301).

Clark and Terrell therefore propose that Oceanic archaeologists concentrate on defining alternative working models that are subject to modification, elimination, or verification through hypothesis testing. In essence, they simply propose to extend Chamberlin's (1965) classic method of alternative working hypotheses to the level of model construction.

One approach to the construction and testing of alternative models of change centers upon the concept of cultural adaptation (Kirch 1980b, 1980c). The adaptational approach seeks to link specific aspects of behavioral change with socioenvironmental selection pressures that were responsible for the retention of these particular aspects out of a wider range of behavioral variability. This perspective has, for example, suggested an explanation for the great variability in Marquesan Settlement Period fishing gear, a model which yields testable hypotheses capable of confirmation or rejection. An adaptational approach, however, cannot account for all kinds of prehistoric change, since a good deal of change is apparently random and "adaptively-neutral" (Kirch, 1980c; see also

Groube 1967:9). Dunnell (1978) has similarly referred to the fundamental dichotomy between "style" and "function" and rightly stresses that prehistorians must develop models appropriate to each kind of phenomenon. It is likely that no single theoretical school can, alone, provide models of prehistoric change which are wholly satisfying. Each has offered its own special insights, and will continue to do so.

Although each Polynesian sequence is unique, parallel patterns of change recurred many times. The following section examines patterns of cultural adaptation and differentiation in three broad areas: technology, production systems, and settlement patterns. The approach is comparative, and aims to elucidate some of the general processes which propelled Polynesian societies along their alternate, yet frequently parallel, pathways of change.

PATTERNS OF ADAPTATION AND DIFFERENTIATION

Technology

Archaic Polynesian technology, itself the product of adaptive and stylistic change from a Lapita ancestor, underwent further modifications as it was carried by colonizing Polynesians to the environmentally diverse corners of the triangle. While some changes seem clearly to represent adaptive response to new environmental selection pressures, others appear to reflect stylistic ("random") differentiation following isolation. The problem is compounded when, as is frequently the case, both functional and stylistic change occurs within a single artifact class. Two of the most important oceanic artifact classes, fishhooks and adzes, exemplify the processes of technological change in Polynesia. These two items are particularly worthy of attention since they have been used more than any others as the basis for establishing cultural sequences and for positing interisland contacts and relationships.

Reinman (1970:50–56) suggested that adaptive change in fishing gear resulted from the interplay of three variables: (a) structural properties of the raw materials (shell, bone, wood, etc.); (b) functional behavior of the hook, including its action in relation to fish-jaw morphology; and (c) ecological properties of the local marine environment (depth of water, reef development, etc.). These variables of structure, function, and ecology are all important in assessing fishhook change throughout the Polynesian region.

The earliest known fishhooks of Western Polynesia are made of *Turbo* shell (Kirch and Dye 1979; Green and Davidson 1969; Poulsen 1968), the cross-laminated calcite layers of which are resistant to stresses between point and shank. Early colonizers to the Marquesas and Society groups found large species of *Turbo* shell absent, but discovered an excellent substitute in giant pearlshell (*Pinctada* sp.). Subsequent dispersal to the margins of Eastern Polynesia posed further problems with raw materials, as most peripheral islands lacked both large *Turbo* and *Pinctada*. In Hawaii and New Zealand, considerable emphasis was placed upon bone, and also on abalone (*Haliotis* sp.) in the latter area. On Easter Island, which also lacks large shellfish, fishhook technology was adapted to stone as well as to bone. Neither bone nor stone, however, has the resistance of laminated shell to shear stress. Large hooks of these materials are likely to break at the hook bend. This problem was solved, evidently independently in all three areas, by separating shank and point as discrete components joined at the bend by flexible lashing capable of withstanding stress.

Other changes in fishhook morphology may be correlated with ecological differences between island groups. Elsewhere (Kirch 1980b) I have argued that the great morphological variability in early Marquesan fishing gear reflects a phase of experimentation with angling technology in a situation of adaptive stress. Colonizers from the Tonga–Samoa region arriving in the Marquesas Islands were confronted with a new set of environmental constraints (rocky coasts, absence of developed reefs and lagoons) not suited to the fishing strategies (netting, spearing, poisoning) that had been applicable in the western, tropical islands. A phase of experimentation followed, represented archaeologically by extreme variability in form. Later in the sequence, Marquesan hooks become remarkably uniform, suggesting that the standardized jabbing hook had proved most effective in exploiting fish along the archipelago's rocky coasts and headlands.

The stone adz may justifiably be called the Polynesian's most important tool, serving both maintenance and extractive functions. Green (1971; Green and Davidson 1974) has masterfully surveyed the evidence for the development of the early Polynesian adz kit, from Lapita prototypes. The initial settlement of Eastern Polynesia was accompanied by three major innovations in adz morphology, which led to differences in the later adzes of Eastern and Western Polynesia: (*a*) development of reversed triangular-section forms; (*b*) development of thicker-bodied quadrangular forms; and (*c*) application of a variety of grip modifications, or "tangs" to assist in lashing (Green 1971:36). The latter innovation is clearly of functional significance, while the first two cannot yet be explained on adaptive principles, and could be stylistic.

In a seminal study which may presage further experimental research on adz function, Best (1977) has advanced a plausible explanation for morphological change in the New Zealand adz kit. Based on "function tests" (angle of attack and gouge depth), stress tests, and lithic material studies (hardness, static strength, edge damage), Best concluded that change in adz form paralleled a shift from a dominantly maritime economy (with emphasis on canoe construction) to a more terrestrially oriented economy. "The maritime facet of the early economy is held to be the most likely reason for the existence of adzes which were mainly for shaping and trimming, while the clearing of large tracts of forest and the erection of wooden defences is likewise the most reasonable explanation for the later adze" (1977:334). Best's experimental orientation is currently being duplicated in ongoing research on Hawaiian adz production (P. Cleghorn, personal communication 1980). These studies may provide some basis for assessing the extent to which changes in adz morphology reflect different socio-environmental selection pressures.

Production Systems

A major thrust of Polynesian prehistory has centered upon the region's varied production systems and their archaeological manifestations. Beginning with the faunal and floral remains of Polynesian middens (e.g., Green *et al.* 1967; Green and Davidson 1969; Kirch 1973, 1979a; Leach and Leach 1979; Shawcross 1967, 1972; Terrell 1967), investigations have expanded to include other manifestations both of agricultural production (H. Leach in Leach and Leach 1979; Riley 1975; Rosendahl 1972; Yen *et al.* 1972), and of marine exploitation (Coutts 1975; Kikuchi 1976; Kirch 1979a; Kirch and Dye 1979; Reinman 1970). In certain less acculturated Polynesian groups, indigenous subsistence systems are yet extant, and ethnobotanical and ethnoarchaeological research have helped to inform the more narrowly defined archaeological studies (Barrau 1965; Kirch 1976, 1978a; Yen 1973).

The inseparable dualism of Polynesian economies integrated exploitation of the sea with production from the land. While the former required the adaptation of technology to new environmental constraints, the establishment of agricultural systems on newly colonized islands depended not only on technological adjustment, but on transfer of the entire crop inventory as well. Throughout the tropical "core" of Polynesia, most high volcanic islands closely replicated the ecological templates of the dominant crop plants (for a list of Polynesian crops see Kirch 1979b:Table 12.1). The low, coral atolls, and the marginal, subtropical or temperate islands, however, posed immediate problems of agronomic adaptation. As Yen (1973:76) succinctly phrased the problem:

> The portable features of agriculture [plant materials, tools, ethnobiological concepts] . . . together with the elements of natural exploitation, have to undergo a reassortment or re-segregation as a first step in the colonization of a new island as an Introductory-Developmental sequence whose progress is dictated by the ultimate constraints offered by the new environment and the genetic flexibility of the introduced species.

Archaeological evidence from Hawaii, the Marquesas, New Zealand, and Tonga all suggest a dominant reliance on marine exploitation during this initial phase of establishment of the agricultural sector, a ratio which gradually changed in favor of terrestrial production.

The segregative effects of island environments are especially evident with respect to water control and the cultivation of taro. Taro (*Colocasia esculenta*) is a hydrophile of tropical Southeast Asian origin; though it will tolerate a certain degree of dryness, taro thrives under irrigation. Throughout tropical and subtropical Polynesia, on high islands with developed stream drainage, are found archaeological remains of irrigated pondfield systems, the most elaborate of which are in Hawaii (Earle 1978; Riley 1975; Yen *et al.* 1972) and Futuna (Kirch 1976). An absence of permanent streamflow, however, was a constraint rather ingeniously overcome, either by drainage of coastal swamps as in Uvea and Mangaia, or by the excavation, on atolls, of pits which exposed the freshwater Ghyben-Herzberg lens (Chazine 1977:Fig. 5).

Temperate New Zealand presented the greatest environmental challenge to Polynesian colonists from the tropical eastern islands. At the time of European contact, only North Island supported an agricultural economy, based on the annually producing sweet potato (*Ipomoea batatas*). The harsher conditions of South Island, and of the outlying Chatham group, dictated a hunting–gathering–fishing subsistence base unique in Polynesia. Even in the milder climate of North Island, the reassortment of agricultural systems must have been dramatic, and would have had a major impact within the first year's seasonal cycle. The majority of tropical plants, such as coconut, breadfruit, kava, and the like, obviously did not survive this initial reassortment.

The sweet potato, however, possessed sufficient adaptability to become the dominant staple of the only annually-based (seasonal) Polynesian agricultural system. In particular, the ability to store sweet potato tubers in subterranean pits, and the propagation of the new year's crop from these stored root stocks (Yen 1974:300) permitted this conversion of perennial–tropical to annual–temperate systems. Yen's model of the adaptation of kumara agriculture (1961, 1974), with *introductory, experimental,* and *systematic* phases, was based largely on ethnobotanical data, with only indirect confirmation from archaeology. However, the work of Helen Leach at Palliser Bay (Leach and Leach 1979) has documented in considerable detail the archaeological manifestations of early kumara cultivation, including the use of stone-walled gardens and fields, and of stone mounds, agronomic practices with parallels elsewhere in Polynesia.

Polynesian archaeologists have become increasingly aware of the tremendous impact wrought by the islanders on their often fragile ecosystems. These impacts, including extinction of local biota, introduction of weeds and pests, deforestation, and erosion, are perhaps of greater magnitude on small, circumscribed islands, and set up new constraints and selection pressures requiring further technological, demographic, and sociopolitical adaptation.

In New Zealand, the extinction of the flightless moa (Figure 2.6) and deforestation of large tracts apparently went hand in hand. Cumberland outlined a scenario of *Brandwirtschaft* with "catastrophic consequences" including "widespread extension of grassland," erosion, and sedimentation (1962:162–3). Direct evidence for deforestation resulting from burning has subsequently come from pollen cores, as at Hawkes Bay (McGlone 1978).

On smaller islands, forest removal was even more devastating: both Easter Island and Mangareva were stripped bare of trees and their vegetations reduced to grasslands. Futuna and Uvea, as well as the Marquesas, had large tracts of pyrophytic fernland, called *toafa,* which are evidently anthropogenic. Borings in closed basins on Lakeba Island in the Lau archipelago (Hughes *et al.* 1979)

Figure 2.6 Conjectural reconstructions of several species of extinct moa birds, shown with a "moahunter." From left to right, the species are *Dinornis maximus, Aptornis* sp., *Euryapteryx gravis,* and *Cnemiornis* sp. (From Cumberland 1962.)

demonstrate the creation of such pyrophytic associations through burning and erosion. Such extensive modifications of the Polynesians' island ecosystems had significant consequences for the productive ability of subsistence systems, and must be considered in any attempt to model prehistoric change.

Beyond the initial segregation and adaptation of production systems at the time of transfer to a new island environment, there is the matter of their further development, especially in relation to demographic and social pressures. This problem of *intensification* and its relations with other aspects of cultural systems is a dominant theme of current archaeological research in Polynesia and elsewhere in Oceania. The Hawaiian Islands offer an especially interesting, and well documented, case of alternative pathways to intensification.

Hawaiian agricultural systems can be categorized into two major "types," corresponding with gross environmental contrasts. In valleys with permanent streamflow, emphasis was placed on pondfield irrigation of taro, although a non-irrigated, "swidden" component was also present on higher slopes above the irrigation systems. On leeward, undissected slopes lacking permanent watercourses, the swidden component was developed into a permanent field system characterized by stone-walled divisions. Intensive archaeological studies, at Halawa (Kirch and Kelly 1975), Makaha (Green 1980; Yen *et al.* 1972), Lapakahi (Rosendahl 1972; Tuggle and Griffin 1973) and elsewhere, have provided temporal control for the development of these intensified agricultural systems—on the one hand irrigation, on the other permanent field rotation. Predictably, the well-watered valleys evidence earliest occupation, although large-scale irrigation networks do not appear until relatively late in the prehistoric sequence. Leeward regions, however, were generally not settled until 8 to 10 centuries later (approximately A.D. 1200 to 1400), and their dryland field systems can be shown to have developed within a rather rapid span of 200–300 years. In both cases, a correspondence between agricultural intensification and population growth is evident. We should be cautious, though, of attempting simplistic correlations between demography and production. Although there is clearly a relation, it may be a more complex equation than that of a "prime mover." Sociopolitical structures, technological innovation, environmental degradation, climatic fluctuation, and other inputs may all have affected the intensification process.

Although intensification is most clearly manifested in agricultural systems, there is evidence for a parallel process in the maritime sector of the economy. Hawaiian fishponds, stone walled enclosures up to 211 ha in area built onto the reef flats, represent an Oceanic apogee in the use of weirs and traps (Kikuchi 1976). In Hawaii, the simple weir was converted to an artificial ecosystem, suited to the raising of mullet (*Mugil cephalus*) and other brackish-water fish. Many of these ponds required considerable labor expenditures for their construction, and the correlations with demography and sociopolitical structures are again evident.

Settlement Patterns and Social Groups

Concomitantly with their interest in production systems, Polynesian archaeologists have stressed intensive site surveys and analysis of settlement patterns. An impressive settlement pattern literature encompasses most major island groups, including Samoa (Green and Davidson 1969, 1974; Jennings *et al.* 1976), Cook Islands (Bellwood 1971, 1978), Societies (Gerard 1974; Green *et al.* 1967), Marquesas (Bellwood 1972; Kellum-Ottino 1971), Easter Island (McCoy 1976), Rapa (Ferdon 1965), Hawaii (Green 1980; Kirch and Kelly 1975; Rosendahl 1972), and New Zealand (Cassels 1972; Groube 1965; Leach and Leach 1979), as well as several general syntheses (Green 1970; Gathercole 1972; Bellwood 1979). As with settlement pattern studies elsewhere, these investigations have focused on the distribution of sites both in relation to topography and resources, and as a reflection of social groups and networks responsible for site patterning. As Bellwood (1979:319) observes, however, it is frequently difficult and "perhaps pointless" to attempt to isolate social and ecological factors separately, since "social factors . . . operate within the ecological framework to determine individual settlement location in terms of clustering and dispersal."

This interplay of social and ecological determinants is especially evident in island-wide site distribution patterns, indicative of the division of arable land and other resources among a series of social groups, themselves often hierarchically nested. The classic high-island pattern divided an island into radial units, each occupied by a corporate social group, usually under the control of a hereditary chief. A number of such units were often linked politically to form a higher-level district or island group, under the charge of a paramount chief. This radial pattern is well documented for such archipelagoes as Hawaii (the ahupua'a pattern), Society Islands, Marquesas, and Cooks.

Radial units obviously utilize resources most efficiently, for they transect all major microenvironmental zones: reef, lagoon, alluvial lowlands, valley interiors, and forested crests. The linkage between inland and coast is summed up in the Samoan proverb, *a ua sala uta, ia tonu tai*, "a mistake made inland, will be rectified by the seaside" (Green and Davidson 1974:242). Although ideally every radial unit contained all necessary resources, the vagaries of local topography, vegetation, etc., resulted in considerable resource variation, which in some cases may have been alleviated by intergroup trade or exchange, and by redistribution at the level of the paramount chief (Sahlins 1958).

Polynesian settlement patterns were more often dispersed than nucleated, although there are several important cases of nucleation. In some islands, a shift over time from small, nucleated hamlets (generally coastal) to dispersed settlement is evidenced. In Halawa Valley, Molokai (Kirch and Kelly 1975), initial settlement (around A.D. 600) consisted of a coastal hamlet, with a change to dispersed inland residence after approximately A.D. 1250. A similar pattern has been documented for the Hane Valley on Ua Huka, Marquesas (Kellum-Ottino 1971). The fortified *pa* settlements of New Zealand (Fox 1976), and possibly the Rapan hill–forts (Ferdon 1965), are other exceptions to the general dispersed settlement pattern type.

McCoy (1976) analyzed a dispersed pattern on Easter Island, based on an intensive survey of 1738 sites in an area of 19.7 km². The fundamental settlement unit consisted of a household, manifested archaeologically by a dwelling site (stone-curb outlined) plus a constellation of associated features including earth ovens, chicken houses, and garden enclosures. A number of these dispersed household clusters (evidently related sociologically) were then associated with a religious site (*ahu*) and a communal center consisting of chief's and priest's houses. This settlement pattern is diagrammed in Figure 2.7.

Considerable variability existed throughout Polynesia in the form of individual settlement pattern components ("sites"), both at household and community levels. A few examples of domestic architecture may exemplify this variability. In Samoa, round-ended dwelling houses were frequently built upon gravel-paved mounds averaging about 100 m² in area. Marquesan dwellings, rectangular in plan, topped stone platforms (*paepae*), usually with two levels: a paved terrace (often with stone-lined pit incorporated) and an elevated sleeping platform. Stones used in such platforms range up to several hundred pounds in weight, and the riser slabs separating the two levels were usually cut-and-dressed, sometimes decorated with relief images. Hawaiian residential sites are of several types, including stone-faced, earthen-filled terraces on valley slopes, and stone-walled "C-shaped" structures typical of leeward areas. In New Zealand, the temperate climate stimulated development of sturdy rectangular houses built partly of hewn planks, with interior stone-lined hearths.

Community architecture, particularly religious structures such as the great

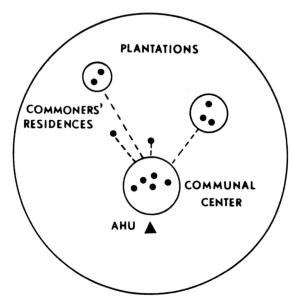

Figure 2.7   Diagrammatic representation of the late prehistoric settlement pattern of Easter Island. (From McCoy 1976.)

statuary temples of Easter Island, have interested archaeologists for decades (not to mention laymen with bizarre theories to peddle). The concept of a communal ceremonial area is quite ancient in Polynesia, indicated by the Proto-Polynesian term *mala'e,* an open meeting ground. In Western Polynesia the *mala'e* remained simple, an open ground with perhaps a row of upright stone slabs (representing deified ancestors) along one edge, upon which the ceremonial *kava* ritual and food distributions were held. In Eastern Polynesia, the *malae* concept was elaborated into a more formal religious structure, the basic elements of which are an enclosed or otherwise delineated courtyard, elevated altar area (*ahu*), and upright stone slabs or carved images representing deities. The Society Islands *marae* (Figure 2.8), Easter Island *ahu,* Marquesan *me'ae,* and Hawaiian *heiau* all derive from this basic temple concept. There is a tremendous range in size and degree of elaboration of these structures, which can generally be correlated with the social status or rank of the associated chief. Green *et al.* (1967) thus demonstrated that Society Island *marae* may be analyzed in terms of their component attributes (structural features) to derive a reconstruction of sociopolitical organization. This approach holds considerable promise for other Eastern Polynesian groups as well.

The propensity of Polynesians for intergroup warfare is well documented in the ethnohistoric literature, and it is not surprising therefore that fortifications are an important component of most Polynesian archaeological landscapes. In many areas, fortifications were inhabited only temporarily, in times of conflict, as with the fairly simple Hawaiian ridge-crest forts. In the Marquesas, ridge-

Figure 2.8 The *marae* of Ahu o Mahina in the Opunohu Valley, Mo'orea, Society Islands, after restoration. (Photo by Y. Sinoto, Bishop Museum.)

crest forts were somewhat more elaborate, with house terraces and large food-storage pits, enabling the defenders to withstand a lengthy siege. On certain islands, however, fortifications were permanently occupied, the most notable case being the Maori *pa* villages of New Zealand (Fox 1976), and the hill–forts of Rapa (see Figure 2.9) (Ferdon 1965). Caves modified as places of refuge are also known, from Hawaii, Samoa (Green and Davidson 1969:267), and Easter Island (McCoy 1976:36–7). These refuge caves have walled entrances, usually permitting only single-file access, and evidence of temporary habitation within.

SOCIOPOLITICAL EVOLUTION

Due in part to the "laboratory-like" aspects of control cited previously, Polynesia has several times served as a test case for anthropological theories of sociopolitical development or evolution. The classic syntheses of Williamson and Piddington (1939) first attempted to account for Polynesian social, economic, and religious systems as functional developments, rather than as an

Figure 2.9   The fortified ridge-top settlement of Moronga-uta, Rapa Island. (Bishop Museum photo by J. F. G. Stokes 1920.)

amalgam of "traits" diffused from various localities by a series of migrations. Burrows (1939a), drawing from fieldwork experience in Western Polynesia, advanced a processual theory for the encroachment of territorially based social groups ("border") over kinship-based groupings ("breed"), with rivalry over land as a major variable. The now classic (though refuted) attempt by Sahlins (1958) to correlate degree of social stratification with dispersion of resources influenced archaeological theory several times (e.g., Flannery and Coe 1968; Peebles and Kus 1977). Goldman's synthesis (1970), although less well received (Howard 1972), has also had its impact on social stratification theory. The Polynesian chiefdoms, at least those of the larger archipelagoes (e.g., Hawaii, Societies, Tonga, and Samoa), are especially intriguing to sociopolitical theorists, because they appear to be at the critical interface between chiefdoms and states (Service 1975).

Polynesian societies, although all chiefdoms, exhibited a considerable range of variability in degree of social stratification and of political integration. For example, there were societies like that of Pukapuka, in which chiefs were related as kinsmen to commoners, and production was undertaken and regulated almost entirely on the household level. At the other extreme is the Hawaiian case, where the chiefly class claimed descent separate from commoners, was internally ranked into seven or eight levels (and practiced hypergamy to maintain the highest possible rank), and where the political order not only regulated production and mobilized corvée labor, but had managed to alienate land entirely from ownership by commoners. Linguistic reconstruction (see Table 2.3) and ethnographic comparison indicate that Archaic Polynesian society was already organized at a chiefdom level, with the fundamental social group being some form of corporate, land-holding descent group (Proto-Polynesian *kainanga*). From this ancestral structure was derived the range of variations exhibited at the time of European contact.

Facing Polynesian prehistorians is the dual task of documenting changes in sociopolitical structure within each island group over the span of its cultural sequence, and of attempting to isolate the underlying processes or mechanisms which led in several instances to increased stratification and elaboration of the chiefly hierarchy. Although Polynesian archaeologists have been slow in applying the data of prehistory to the problem of sociopolitical evolution, a number of recent studies (particularly in the Hawaiian Islands) suggest that the topic will emerge as a dominant research concern within the next decade. Howard (1972:822) presaged the potential role of archaeology when he wrote that the ethnographic theorists had provided the archaeologists "with a richer set of competing possibilities concerning social change around which to orient their efforts, and if they do their job well we may yet accumulate sufficient data to produce compelling reconstructions."

The Demographic Factor

I have already alluded to the important role of population in the intensification of production systems, and most Polynesian prehistorians would agree that demographic variables were fundamental to processes of sociopolitical change. To begin, it is empirically obvious that degree of social stratification was positively correlated with the population size of the chiefdom. This correlation can be seen in Figure 2.10, where population size is plotted against Sahlins' four classes of stratification for 11 Polynesian societies. The mere documentation of a correlation, however, is hardly sufficient grounds for postulating a causal relationship. Lacking direct historical evidence, one could argue either the primacy of population growth as a spur to increased stratification, or, conceivably, the converse, that increased stratification allowed chiefs to bring neighboring groups under their sway thus swelling the size of the chiefdom. (Furthermore, these two scenarios are not necessarily mutually exclusive.) Clearly, what we need are accurate diachronic data for prehistoric populations: their size, growth rates, and densities, data which can then be compared with parallel temporal evidence for social stratification (from mortuary remains, settlement pattern studies, and the like).

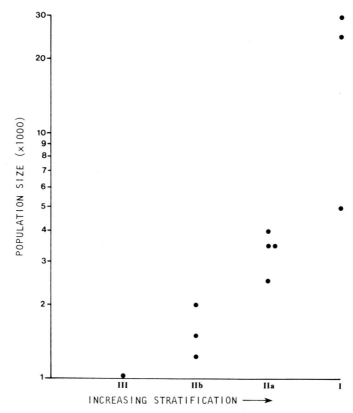

Figure 2.10 Relationship between population size and social stratification in 11 Polynesian societies, based on Sahlins' (1958) categories of stratification (III, least stratified; I, most highly stratified).

Such paleodemographic data have only recently begun to be forthcoming for Polynesia. Attempts at estimating total population sizes, based on some variation of the carrying-capacity approach (e.g., Bellwood 1972) are of little utility since they inherently fail to produce meaningful diachronic data. Several recent studies from the Hawaiian Islands, however, have attempted to measure population size and growth rates based on an ·"archaeological census taking" approach (Hommon 1976; Cordy 1978; Kirch 1980a). These studies are based on the quantification of habitation sites per interval of time, and thus assume a proportional relationship between number of sites and population. Given that prehistoric Hawaiian habitation sites are discrete, and appear in most cases to have been occupied by minimal household groups, such an assumption is reasonable. (In some cases, additional corrections have been made for floor area of residences, cf. Cordy 1978.) Additional paleodemographic data of relevance to population growth have been generated by analysis of skeletal populations, through the use of reconstructed life-tables (Kirch 1980a).

The temporal picture of prehistoric Hawaiian population growth revealed by these recent analyses portrays a modified logistic growth process (Figure 2.11). Population increased more or less exponentially for the first 1000 years following settlement; however, because the founding propagule was small, an archipelago-wide population of about 50,000 was not reached until about A.D. 1200–1300. Over the next three centuries, population increased an estimated six-to-seven-fold, although the actual rate of growth r declined over this period, and a peak population was achieved around A.D. 1600–1700. During the final century prior to European contact, the archaeological evidence suggests population decline or oscillation.

Clearly, the centuries from about A.D. 1300 to 1600 were a time of population growth and expansion, and it is to this period that we should perhaps look for archaeological evidence of increased sociopolitical complexity. There are now ample data to indicate that agricultural production systems were greatly intensified during this time, with expansion into more marginal, leeward environments, and development of the large-scale field systems mentioned earlier. Although limited, data on religious structures (*heiau*) indicate an increase in size and complexity during this phase. Hommon (1976) has also shown, through a detailed analysis of oral traditions, that the seventeenth and eighteenth cen-

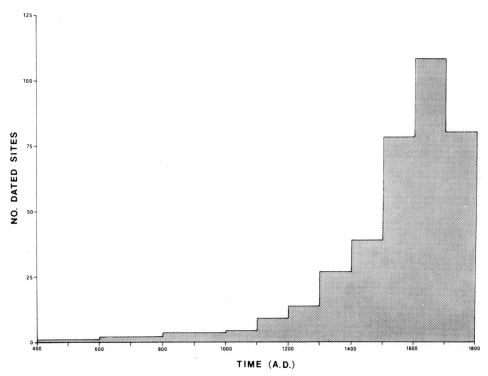

Figure 2.11   "Site population" growth curve based upon a sample of 170 dated habitation sites in the Hawaiian Islands.

turies were marked by increasing competition between rival political units, with frequent warfare, conquest, and amalgamation of smaller units into large chiefdoms.

Although we have only begun to accumulate the supportive evidence, it is possible to sketch the outlines of a model relating rapid population growth within the circumscribed confines of insular ecosystems to increases in sociopolitical complexity. The extremely rapid increases in population size indicated for Hawaii would have resulted in several stresses, especially for land and increased production, that would have favored the rise of more powerful chiefs, acting both as economic managers and as war leaders. The cybernetic model of Peebles and Kus (1977) may be applicable as well, because the chiefly political apparatus would have needed to develop its capacity to process "information" regarding the status and well-being of its supporting (and growing) population. Polynesian religious systems, which were intimately linked with the chiefly office, served as regulatory mechanisms for the islands' production systems (cf. Rappaport 1971). The elaboration of Hawaiian religion, especially the Lono rituals and the Makahiki (Peebles and Kus 1977) can perhaps best be understood from such a cybernetic perspective.

One criticism leveled at population-based models of sociopolitical evolution is that they frequently fail to explain why population should have grown in the first place (Flannery 1972:406). In Polynesia, not only is it empirically demonstrable that populations did grow (and rapidly), but reasons for growth are obvious. With the colonization of any new island or archipelago, the human propagule not only encountered an environment lacking constraints on growth (i.e., no competing populations, and extremely low initial density), but a high growth rate would have been essential to a successful colonization strategy. The probability of extinction for a propagule is diminished as the size of the group increases (McArthur *et al.* 1976). Thus the earlier part of any Polynesian cultural sequence was predictably characterized by population growth (cf. Kirch 1980b:41–43).

While rapid population growth was likely a stimulus to sociopolitical evolution, once situations of high density had been achieved on any island, growth itself would largely cease. Instead, population "pressure," including the need to intensify production and intergroup competition over limited land and resources, would replace growth as significant variables influencing the political armature. Indeed, as the Polynesian ethnographic record testifies, population regulation became in some cases a matter of politico-religious control, which may itself have enhanced the power of the chieftainship.

Such a model of population growth as a major stimulus to sociopolitical change has received support from the ethnographer Douglas Oliver, who concluded regarding the evolution of Tahitian society that "the principal influence upon social change . . . was population increase, and not so much by immigration as by steady internal pressure" (1974:1123). Polynesian archaeologists in the future can be expected to rise to the challenge of testing this proposition on the basis of empirical paleodemographic data from a variety of island groups.

Refining the Models

Population growth is surely a fundamental variable in the evolution of Polynesian sociopolitical systems, but it alone cannot constitute a sufficient explanatory model. It is doubtful that any single "prime mover" can account for the complexities of Polynesian social change. Thus, while recognizing the important role of demography, it will be necessary to consider a number of other, potentially significant variables, including ecological constraints, agricultural innovation, warfare, and the structural proclivities of Polynesian societies themselves (e.g., emphasis on segmentation, importance of redistribution, etc.). Furthermore, it is unlikely that any one model will apply to all Polynesian situations. As Flannery (1972:409) pointed out, while certain processes and mechanisms in the evolution of complex systems may be universal, the particular socioenvironmental stresses selecting for a particular combination of processes and mechanisms are unique to the region and society under consideration. Thus, while population growth occurred in all Polynesian islands, particular growth rates, maximum sizes, and densities would depend on such local environmental factors as island area and resource variability. While it took the prehistoric Hawaiian population some 1200 years to occupy extensively all of the lowland areas of that archipelago, a similar density could have been achieved at the same growth rates on some of the smaller islands and, especially, atolls within one or two centuries.

The importance of local ecological conditions and of the constraints and stresses they pose is evident when we examine the various alternate pathways to agricultural intensification in Polynesia, and the potential impact of intensification upon social stratification. Broadly speaking, Polynesian agricultural systems are of two kinds: those based on water control (either irrigation or drainage, especially for taro cultivation) and those known commonly as shifting cultivation. Of course, either of these may be combined in any locale, depending on environmental conditions. Both systems may be intensified, either by the construction of larger and more elaborate water control networks, or by the conversion of long-fallow shifting cultivation into a labor-intensive rotational field-system. Examples of both kinds of intensification are, as we have seen, archaeologically attested in Polynesia.

Earle (1978) has recently analyzed in detail a case of irrigation intensification in the Halelea district of Kauai. He rejects the Wittfogelian view that "scale and complexity of irrigation determine the degree of political centralization," because "there was virtually no evidence that Hawaiian irrigation would have required centralized management" (1978:193). Chiefly intervention, however, could have been necessary to determine water allocation at times of lower than normal streamflow (cf. Riley 1975). Earle also rejects resource diversity and redistribution as a stimulus to irrigation intensification, since Hawaiian territorial units (*ahupua'a*) were largely self-sufficient. He furthermore suggests that population pressure and warfare were not important causes of "regional centralization" because population was "apparently well below any potential carrying capacity" (Earle 1978:194). Earle's conclusion here is open to question, since recent surveys in the Halelea valleys revealed evidence of extensive dryland cultivation on even extremely steep slopes above the irrigated fields (P. Cleghorn and T. Dye, personal communication, 1980), evidence apparently missed by Earle. Nevertheless, Earle's primary thesis, that the significance of irrigation was not in its organizational requirements, but in its "central role in the maximizing political economy characteristic of chiefdoms" (1978:195) merits consideration. "Irrigation, through intensification, and warfare, through expansion, increased the flow of staples collected by the centralized redistributive hierarchy" (1978:195). A positive feedback loop was thus established, in which excess production from irrigation encouraged the elaboration of structural principles already inherent in Polynesian social organization.

Where local environmental constraints did not permit the establishment or intensification of irrigation or other forms of water control, the intensification of dryland cultivation systems may have provided even greater stimuli to social stratification. Interestingly, the most elaborate and highly stratified Polynesian chiefdoms arose in areas dependent upon shifting cultivation, rather than irrigation. In the Hawaiian Islands, for example, the most powerful chiefly lines developed on East Maui and West Hawaii islands, both characterized by the presence of intensive dryland field systems. Likewise, the Tongan chiefdom, rivaling that of Hawaii in degree of complexity, was supported entirely by an intensified type of shifting cultivation. Elsewhere (Kirch 1980b:46–47, Fig. 6) I have sketched a model of the systemic relations between shifting cultivation, population increase, and social stratification. An increasing population of shifting cultivators will find it necessary either to expand their area under cultivation, or to intensify in the direction of field rotation. Intensification, however, is not an endless alternative (and the possibility of serious soil degradation and erosion always looms large). Thus, given several local social groups occupying adjacent territories, each with growing populations, competition and conflict over arable land is inevitable. The role of chiefs as war leaders thus is enhanced, as is their role as economic managers and redistributors of surplus production deriving from intensification.

In sum, the two major alternatives to agricultural intensification in Polynesia, each depending on local environmental selection pressures, can both be hypothesized as leading to increased sociopolitical complexity. Furthermore, rather than simple prime mover causality, it is evident that we are dealing with multivariate, complex systems, with both negative and positive feedback loops. Figure 2.12 outlines my partial model for the evolution of complex Polynesian sociopolitical systems, a model which incorporates several variables equally: population growth, agricultural intensification, circumscription of land, warfare, and cybernetic regulation of production. This model, of course, suffers from the same defect that befalls all models, namely that a complex real-world system is greatly simplified. As a general model, it doubtless requires modifications, in some cases probably substantial, when applied to any specific island situation. It is also evident, however, that the construction and testing of such models is a

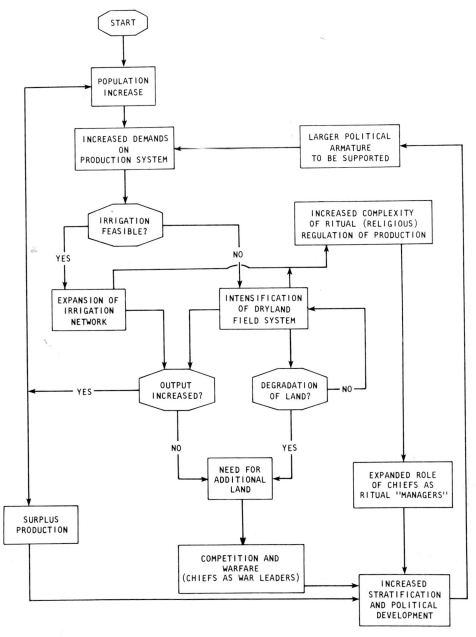

Figure 2.12 A multivariate model of Polynesian sociopolitical evolution, incorporating ecological constraints, agricultural intensification, warfare, and ritual regulation.

necessary first step in attempting to meet our eventual goal of explaining variability in Polynesian social and political organization.

THE FUTURE OF POLYNESIA'S PAST

Polynesian archaeology has in the course of three decades undergone a considerable evolution. Emory's pioneering Kuli'ou'ou excavation revealed glimpses of a prehistory both older and more complex than previous dogmas had allowed. An early·concern with tracing Polynesian origins and dispersals, and with establishing culture-historical sequences for the major island groups, has been joined by more anthropologically oriented research goals. Elucidation of the structures of prehistoric Polynesian populations, their social groupings and distribution over the landscape, their agricultural and maritime subsistence strategies, their adaptation of technology over a great range of environmental constraints, their voyaging and colonization capabilities, and the evolution of their political systems are the dominant concerns of contemporary archaeology in Polynesia. At the same time that our research efforts are intensifying and becoming more sophisticated, however, the finite data base of archaeological sites is decreasing, in some areas at a frightening pace. The alteration of ancient landscapes increases each year, spurred by urbanization, tourism, agricultural development, and other factors of our global economy. It is deplorable that such destruction of the Polynesian heritage is occurring now, just as the peoples of the emerging, new Pacific nations are finding in the vestiges of their past some cultural foundations on which to build their future.

Yet, the interest and concern of island people for their own past is increasing. As Michael Somare, first Chief Minister of Papua New Guinea, wrote of Oceanic peoples generally, "there is a burning desire among our people that our ancient values, wisdom, and unique forms of artistic expression should be preserved. . . . Oceania is a big region. It is only right that our civilizations and our achievements should become recognized in the world community" (in S. Mead 1979:xv). For occidental anthropologists, Polynesia has long been a fertile garden of intellectual insights. With the long overdue, emerging interest of the islanders themselves, the future of Polynesia's past may yet be secure.

REFERENCES

Ayres, W.
   1973   *The Cultural context of Easter Island religious structures*. Ph.D. dissertation, Department of Anthropology, Tulane University of Louisiana, New Orleans.
Barrau, J.
   1965   Histoire et préhistoire horticoles de l'Océanie tropicale. *Journal de la Société des Océanistes,* **21**:55–78.
Bayard, D.
   1976   The cultural relationships of the Polynesian Outliers. *University of Otago Studies in Prehistoric Anthropology* 9.

Beaglehole, J. C. (editor)
  1961   *The journals of Captain James Cook. The voyage of the resolution and adventure, 1772–1775.* Cambridge, England: Hakluyt Society.
Bellwood, P.
  1971   Varieties of ecological adaptation in the southern Cook Islands. *Archaeology and Physical Anthropology in Oceania* **6:**145–169.
  1972   Settlement pattern survey of Hanatekua Valley, Marquesas. *Pacific Anthropological Records* 17. Honolulu: Bishop Museum.
  1978   Archaeological research in the Cook Islands. *Pacific Anthropological Records* 27. Honolulu: Bishop Museum.
  1979   Settlement patterns. In *The prehistory of Polynesia,* edited by J. Jennings. Cambridge, Massachusetts: Harvard University Press.
Best, S.
  1977   The Maori adz: an explanation for change. *Journal of .the Polynesian Society* **86:**307–337.
Birks, L.
  1973   Archaeological excavations at Sigatoka Dune Site, Fiji. *Fiji Museum Bulletin 1.* Suva: Fiji Museum.
Buck, P.
  1930   Samoan material culture. *B. P. Bishop Museum Bulletin* 75. Honolulu.
  1938   *Vikings of the sunrise.* New York: A. Stokes.
Burrows, E.
  1939a Breed and border in Polynesia. *American Anthropologist* **41:**1–21.
  1939b Western Polynesia: A study in cultural differentiation. *Ethnological Studies* 7. Gothenburg.
Cassels, R.
  1972   Locational analysis of prehistoric settlement in New Zealand. *Mankind* **8:**212–222.
Chamberlin, T. C.
  1965   The method of multiple working hypotheses. *Science* **148:**754–759. (Originally published 1890.)
Chazine, J-M.
  1977   Prospections archéologiques à Takapoto. *Journal de la Société des Océanistes* **56–57:**191–214.
Clark, R.
  1979   Language. In *The prehistory of Polynesia,* edited by J. Jennings. Cambridge, Massachusetts: Harvard University Press. Pp. 249–270.
Clark, J. T., and J. Terrell
  1978   Archaeology in Oceania. *Annual Review of Anthropology* **7:**293–319.
Cordy, R.
  1974   Cultural adaptation and evolution in Hawaii: a suggested new sequence. *Journal of the Polynesian Society* **83:**180–191.
  1978   A study of prehistoric social change: the development of complex societies in the Hawaiian Islands. Ph.D. dissertation, Department of Anthropology, University of Hawaii, Honolulu.
Coutts, P. J.
  1975   Marine fishing in archaeological perspective: techniques for determining fishing strategies. In *Maritime adaptations of the Pacific,* edited by R. Casteel and G. Quimby. The Hague: Mouton. Pp. 265–306.
Cumberland, K. B.
  1962   Moas and men: New Zealand about A.D. 1250. *The Geographical Review* **52:**151–173.
Davidson, J. M.
  1971   Archaeology on Nukuoro Atoll. *Auckland Institute and Museum Bulletin* 9. Auckland, New Zealand.
  1979   New Zealand. In *The prehistory of Polynesia,* edited by J. Jennings. Cambridge, Massachusetts: Harvard University Press. Pp. 222–248.

Dickinson, W. R., and R. Shutler, Jr.
  1974   Probable Fijian origin of quartzose temper sands in prehistoric pottery from Tonga and the Marquesas. *Science* **185**:454–457.
Donovan, L. J.
  1973   A study of the decorative system of the Lapita potters in reefs and Santa Cruz Islands. Master's thesis, Department of Anthropology, University of Auckland, New Zealand.
Duff, R.
  1956   *The Moa Hunter Period of Maori culture.* Wellington: Government Printer.
Dunnell, R. C.
  1978   Style and function: a fundamental dichotomy. *American Antiquity* **43**:192–202.
Earle, T.
  1978   Economic and social organization of a complex chiefdom: the Halelea District, Kauai, Hawaii. *Anthropological Papers of the Museum of Anthropology, University of Michigan* No. 63.
Emory, K. P.
  1928   Archaeology of Nihoa and Necker Islands. *B. P. Bishop Museum Bulletin* 53.
  1933   Stone remains in the Society Islands. *B. P. Bishop Museum Bulletin* 116.
  1934a   Archaeology of the Pacific Equatorial Islands. *B. P. Bishop Museum Bulletin* 123.
  1934b   Tuamotuan stone structures. *B. P. Bishop Museum Bulletin* 118.
  1939   Archaeology of Mangareva and neighboring atolls. *B. P. Bishop Museum Bulletin* 163.
  1979   The Societies. In *The prehistory of Polynesia,* edited by J. Jennings. Cambridge, Massachusetts: Harvard University Press. Pp. 200–221.
Emory, K. P., W. J. Bonk, and Y. Sinoto
  1959   Hawaiian archaeology: fishhooks. *B. P. Bishop Museum Special Publication* 47.
Emory, K. P., and Y. Sinoto
  1964   Eastern Polynesian burials at Maupiti. *Journal of the Polynesian Society* **73**:143–160.
Ferdon, E. N., Jr.
  1965   A summary of Rapa Iti fortified villages. In Reports of the Norwegian archaeological expedition to Easter Island and the East Pacific (Vol. 2), edited by T. Heyerdahl and N. Ferdon, Jr. *Monographs of the School of American Research and the Kon-Tiki Museum* (Vol. 24), Part 2. Pp. 69–76.
Finney, B. R.
  1977   Voyaging canoes and the settlement of Polynesia. *Science* **196**:1277–1285.
Flannery, K. V.
  1972   The cultural evolution of civilizations. *Annual Review of Anthropology* **3**:399–426.
Flannery, K. V., and M. Coe
  1968   Social and economic systems in Formative Mesoamerica. In *New perspectives in archaeology,* edited by S. and L. Binford. Chicago: Aldine. Pp. 267–284.
Fox, A.
  1976   *Prehistoric Maori fortifications.* Auckland: Longman Paul.
Garanger, J.
  1972   Archéologie des Nouvelles-Hebrides. *Publications de la Société des Océanistes* No. 30. Paris.
Gathercole, P.
  1972   The study of settlement patterns in Polynesia. In *Man, settlement, and urbanism,* edited by P. Ucko, R. Tringham, and G. Dimbleby. Cambridge, England: Schenkman. Pp. 55–60.
Gerard, B.
  1974   Origine traditionelle et rôle social des marae aux îles de la Société. *Cahiers de l'Office de la Recherche Scientifique et Technique d'Outre Mer: Sciences Humaines* (Vol. II). Pp. 211–226
Gifford, E. W.
  1924   Tongan myths and tales. *B. P. Bishop Museum Bulletin* 8.

1951   Archaeological excavations in Fiji. *University of California Anthropological Records* (Vol. 13), pp. 189–288.

Goldman, I.
1970   *Ancient Polynesian society.* Chicago: University of Chicago Press.

Golson, J.
1959   Culture change in prehistoric New Zealand. In *Anthropology in the South Seas,* edited by J. Freeman and W. Geddes. New Plymouth: Avery. Pp. 29–74.
1971   Lapita ware and its transformations. In Studies in Oceanic culture history, Vol. 2, edited by R. Green and M. Kelly. *Pacific Anthropological Records* 12. Honolulu: Bishop Museum.

Green, R. C.
1963   A Review of the prehistoric sequence of the Auckland Province. *New Zealand Archaeological Association Monograph* No. 2.
1968   West Polynesian prehistory. In *Prehistoric culture in Oceania,* edited by I. Yawata and Y. Sinoto. Honolulu: Bishop Museum Press. Pp. 99–109.
1970   Settlement pattern archaeology in Polynesia. In Studies in Oceanic culture history (Vol. 1), edited by R. Green and M. Kelley. *Pacific Anthropological Records* 11. Honolulu: Bishop Museum.
1971   Evidence for the development of the early Polynesian adz kit. *New Zealand Archaeological Association Newsletter* **14:**12–44.
1974   Adaptation and change in Maori culture. In *Ecology and biogeography in New Zealand,* edited by G. Kuschel. The Hague: W. Junk.
1978   New Sites with Lapita Pottery and their implications for an understanding of the settlement of the Western Pacific. *Auckland University Working Papers in Anthropology* No. 51.
1979   Lapita. In *The prehistory of Polynesia,* edited by J. Jennings. Cambridge, Massachusetts: Harvard University Press. Pp. 27–60.
1980   Makaha before 1880 A.D. *Pacific Anthropological Records* 31. Honolulu: Bishop Museum.

Green, R. C., and J. M. Davidson (editors)
1969   Archaeology in Western Samoa (Vol. 1). *Auckland Institute and Museum Bulletin* 6.
1974   Archaeology in Western Samoa (Vol. 2). *Auckland Institute and Museum Bulletin.*

Green, R. C., R. Rappaport, A. Rappaport, and J. Davidson
1967   Archaeology on the Island of Mo'orea, French Polynesia. *Anthropological Papers of the American Museum of Natural History,* Vol. 51, Part 2.

Groube, L.
1965   Settlement Patterns in New Zealand. *Occasional Papers in Archaeology* No. 1, University of Otago.
1967   Models in prehistory. *Archaeology and Physical Anthropology in Oceania* 2:1–27.
1971   Tonga, Lapita pottery, and Polynesian origins. *Journal of the Polynesian Society* **80:**278–316.

Heyerdahl, T., and E. Ferdon, Jr. (editors)
1961   Archaeology of Easter Island. Reports of the Norwegian Archaeological Expedition to Easter Island and the East Pacific, Vol. 1. *Monographs of the School of American Research* No. 24, Part 1.

Hommon, R. J.
1976   The formation of primitive states in pre-contact Hawaii. Ph.D. dissertation, Department of Anthropology, University of Arizona, Tucson.

Howard, A.
1967   Polynesian origins and migrations: a review of two centuries of speculation and theory. In *Polynesian culture history,* edited by G. A. Highland, R. Force, A. Howard, M. Kelly, and Y. Sinoto. Honolulu: Bishop Museum Special Publication 56. Pp. 45–102.
1972   Polynesian social stratification revisited: reflections on castles built of sand (and a few bits of coral). *American Anthropologist* **74:**811–823.

Hughes, P., G. Hope, M. Latham, and M. Brookfield
    1979   Prehistoric man-induced degradation of the Lakeba landscape: evidence from two
            inland swamps. In *Lakeba: environmental change, population dynamics, and resource use*,
            edited by H. Brookfield. Paris: UNESCO. Pp. 93–110.
Hunt, T.
    1980   *Toward Fiji's past: archaeological research on southwestern Viti Levu.* Master's thesis, Depart-
            ment of Anthropology, University of Auckland, New Zealand.
Jennings, J. (editor)
    1979   *The prehistory of Polynesia.* Cambridge, Massachusetts: Harvard University Press.
Jennings, J., R. Holmer, J. Janetski, and H. Smith
    1976   Excavations on Upolu, Western Samoa. *Pacific Anthropological Records* 25. Honolulu:
            Bishop Museum.
Kaeppler, A. L.
    1978   Artificial curiosities: an expositional of native manufactures. *B. P. Bishop Museum Special
            Publication* 65.
Kellum-Ottino, M.
    1971   Archéologie d'une Vallée des îles Marquises. *Publications de la Société des Océanistes* No.
            26.
Kikuchi, W. K.
    1976   Prehistoric Hawaiian fishponds. *Science* **193:**295–299.
Kirch, P. V.
    1973   Prehistoric subsistence patterns in the northern Marquesas Islands, French Polynesia.
            Archaeology and Physical Anthropology in Oceania **8:**24–40.
    1974   The chronology of early Hawaiian settlement. *Archaeology and Physical Anthropology in
            Oceania* **9:**110–119.
    1976   Ethno-archaeological investigations in Futuna and Uvea (Western Polynesia): a prelimi-
            nary report. *Journal of the Polynesian Society* **85:**27–69.
    1978a   Ethnoarchaeology and the study of agricultural adaptation in the humid tropics. In
            Explorations in ethnoarchaeology, edited by R. Gould. Albuquerque: University of New
            Mexico Press. Pp. 103–125.
    1978b   The Lapitoid period in West Polynesia: excavations and survey in Niuatoputapu,
            Tonga. *Journal of Field Archaeology* **5:**1–13.
    1979a   Marine exploitation in prehistoric Hawaii. *Pacific Anthropological Records* 29. Honolulu:
            Bishop Museum.
    1979b   Subsistence and ecology. In *The prehistory of Polynesia,* edited by J. Jennings.
            Cambridge, Massachusetts: Harvard University Press. Pp. 286–307.
    1980a   Demographic archaeology in an isolated ecosystem: the dynamics of population
            growth in prehistoric Hawaii. Ms. on file, Department of Anthropology, B. P. Bishop
            Museum.
    1980b   Polynesian prehistory: cultural adaptation in island ecosystems. *American Scientist*
            68:39–48.
    1980c   The archaeological study of adaptation: theoretical and methodological issues. In *Ad-
            vances in archaeological method and theory* (Vol. 3), edited by M. B. Schiffer. New York:
            Academic Press.
Kirch, P. V., and T. S. Dye
    1979   Ethnoarchaeology and the development of Polynesian fishing strategies. *Journal of the
            Polynesian Society* **88:**53–76.
Kirch, P. V., and M. Kelly (editors)
    1975   Prehistory and ecology in a windward Hawaiian valley: Halawa Valley, Molokai. *Pacific
            Anthropological Records* 24. Honolulu: Bishop Museum.
Kirch, P. V., and P. Rosendahl
    1973   Archaeological investigation of Anuta. In Anuta: a Polynesian outlier in the Solomon

Islands, edited by D. Yen and J. Gordon. *Pacific Anthropological Records* 21. Honolulu: Bishop Museum. Pp. 25–108.

Kirch, P. V., and D. E. Yen
n.d.   Tikopia: prehistory and ecology of a Polynesian outlier. Honolulu: B. P. Bishop Museum Bulletin. (Forthcoming.)

Leach, B. F., and H. Leach (editors)
1979   Prehistoric man in Palliser Bay. *National Museum of New Zealand Bulletin* 21.

Levison, M., R. G. Ward, and J. W. Webb
1973   *The settlement of Polynesia: a computer simulation.* Minneapolis: University of Minnesota Press.

McArthur, N., I. Saunders, and R. Tweedie
1976   Small population isolates: a micro-simulation study. *Journal of the Polynesian Society* **85**:307–326.

McCoy, P. C.
1976   Easter Island settlement patterns in the Late Prehistoric and Protohistoric Periods. *International Fund for Monuments, Easter Island Committee, Bulletin 5.*
1979   Easter Island. In *The prehistory of Polynesia,* edited by J. Jennings. Cambridge, Massachusetts: Harvard University Press. Pp. 135–166.

McGlone, M. S.
1978   Forest destruction by early Polynesians, Lake Poukawa, Hawkes Bay, New Zealand. *Journal of the Royal Society of New Zealand* **8**:275–281.

McKern, W. C.
1929   The archaeology of Tonga. *B. P. Bishop Museum Bulletin* 60.

Mead, M.
1967   Homogeneity and hypertrophy. In *Polynesian culture history,* edited by G. A. Highland, R. Force, A. Howard, M. Kelly, and Y. Sinoto. Honolulu: Bishop Museum Special Publication 56. Pp. 121–140.

Mead, S. (editor)
1979   *Exploring the visual art of Oceania.* Honolulu: University of Hawaii Press.

Mead, S. M., L. Birks, H. Birks, and E. Shaw
1973   The Lapita style of Fiji and its associations. *Polynesian Society Memoir* 38.

Newman, T. S.
1969   Cultural adaptations to the island of Hawaii ecosystem. *Asian and Pacific Archaeology Series* (Vol. 3). Honolulu: Social Science Research Institute. Pp. 3–14.

Oliver, D.
1974   *Ancient Tahitian society.* Honolulu: University of Hawaii Press.

Pawley, A., and K. Green
1971   Lexical evidence for the Proto-Polynesian homeland. *Te Reo* **14**:1–36.

Pawley, A., and R. Green
1973   Dating the dispersal of the Oceanic languages. *Working papers in linguistics* (Vol. 5). Honolulu: University of Hawaii. Pp. 1–48.

Pearson, R., P. V. Kirch, and M. Pietrusewsky
1971   An early prehistoric site at Bellows Beach, Waimanalo, Oahu, Hawaiian Islands. *Archaeology and Physical Anthropology in Oceania* **6**:204–234.

Peebles, C., and S. Kus
1977   Some archaeological correlates of ranked societies. *American Antiquity* **42**:421–448.

Poulsen, J.
1968   Archaeological excavations on Tongatapu. In *Prehistoric culture in Oceania,* edited by I. Yawata and Y. Sinoto. Honolulu: Bishop Museum Press. Pp. 85–92.
1972   Outlier archaeology: Bellona. *Archaeology and Physical Anthropology in Oceania* **7**:184–205.

Rappaport, R. A.
1971   The sacred in human evolution. *Annual Review of Ecology and Systematics* **2**:23–44.

Reinman, F. M.
    1970   Fishhook variability: implications for the history and distribution of fishing gear in
            Oceania. In Studies in Oceanic Culture History, Vol. 1, edited by R. Green and M.
            Kelly. *Pacific Anthropological Records* 11. Honolulu: Bishop Museum. Pp. 47–60.
Riley, T. J.
    1975   Survey and excavations of the aboriginal agricultural system. In Prehistory and Ecology
            in a Windward Hawaiian Valley: Halawa Valley, Molokai, edited by P. Kirch and M.
            Kelly. *Pacific Anthropological Records* 24. Honolulu: Bishop Museum.
Rosendahl, P. H.
    1972   Aboriginal agriculture and residence patterns in upland Lapakahi, Island of Hawaii.
            Ph.D. dissertation, Department of Anthropology, University of Hawaii, Honolulu.
Sahlins, M. D.
    1958   *Social stratification in Polynesia.* Seattle: American Ethnological Society.
Service, E. R.
    1975   *Origins of the state and civilization.* New York: Norton.
Shawcross, W.
    1967   An investigation of prehistoric diet and economy on a coastal site at Galatea Bay, New
            Zealand. *Proceedings of the Prehistoric Society* **33**:107–131.
    1972   Energy and ecology: thermodynamic models in archaeology. In *Models in archaeology,*
            edited by D. L. Clark. London: Methuen. Pp. 577–622.
Shutler, R., Jr., and J. Marck
    1975   On the dispersal of the Austronesian horticulturalists. *Archaeology and Physical An-
            thropology in Oceania* **10**:81–113.
Sinoto, Y. H.
    1966   A tentative prehistoric cultural sequence in the Northern Marquesas Islands, French
            Polynesia. *Journal of the Polynesian Society* **75**:287–303.
    1978   Preliminary report on the salvage excavations at Fa'ahia, Fare, Huahine Island, Society
            Islands. Ms. on file, Department of Anthropology, B. P. Bishop Museum.
    1979   The Marquesas. In *The prehistory of Polynesia,* edited by J. Jennings. Cambridge, Mas-
            sachusetts: Harvard University Press. Pp. 110–134.
Sinoto, Y. H., and P. McCoy
    1975   Report on the preliminary excavation of an early habitation site on Huahine, Society
            Islands. *Journal de la Société des Océanistes,* **47**:143–186.
Spoehr, A.
    1957   Marianas prehistory. *Fieldiana: Anthropology* **48**.
Suggs, R. C.
    1961   Archaeology of Nuku Hiva, Marquesas Islands, French Polynesia. *Anthropological Pa-
            pers of the American Museum of Natural History* (Vol. 49), Part 1.
Terrell, J.
    1967   Galatea Bay: the excavation of a beach-stream midden site on Ponui Island in the
            Hauraki Gulf, New Zealand. *Transactions of the Royal Society of New Zealand, General
            Series* (Vol. 2). Pp. 31–70.
Thomas, W. L.
    1963   The variety of physical environments among Pacific Islands. In *Man's place in the island
            ecosystem,* edited by F. Fosberg. Honolulu: Bishop Museum Press. Pp. 7–38.
Tuggle, H. D.
    1979   Hawaii. In *The prehistory of Polynesia,* edited by J. Jennings. Cambridge, Massachusetts:
            Harvard University Press. Pp. 167–199.
Tuggle, H. D., and P. B. Griffin (editors)
    1973   Lapakahi, Hawaii: archaeological studies. *Asian and Pacific Archaeology Series* 5. Honolu-
            lu: Social Science Research Institute.

Vayda, A., and R. Rappaport
    1963   Island cultures. In *Man's place in the island ecosystem,* edited by R. Fosberg. Honolulu: Bishop Museum Press. Pp. 133–142.

Verin, P.
    1969   L'Ancienne Civilisation de Rurutu. *Mémoires de l'Office de la Recherche Scientifique et Technique d'Outre Mer* No. 33.

von Haast, J.
    1871   Moas and moa hunters. *Transactions of the New Zealand Institute* **4**:66–107.

Walsh, D. S., and B. Biggs
    1966   *Proto-Polynesian World List I.* Auckland: Linguistic Society of New Zealand.

Willey, G., and P. Phillips
    1958   *Method and theory in American archaeology.* Chicago: University of Chicago Press.

Williamson, R. W., and R. Piddington
    1939   *Essays in Polynesian ethnology.* Cambridge, England: The University Press.

Yen, D. E.
    1961   The adaptation of kumara by the New Zealand Maori. *Journal of the Polynesian Society* **70**:338–348.
    1973   The origins of Oceanic agriculture. *Archaeology and Physical Anthropology in Oceania* **8**:68–85.
    1974   The sweet potato and Oceania. *B. P. Bishop Museum Bulletin* 236.

Yen, D. E., P. V. Kirch, P. Rosendahl, and T. Riley
    1972   Prehistoric agriculture in the upper valley of Makaha, Oahu. In Makaha Valley Historical Project, Interim Report No. 3, edited by E. Ladd and D. Yen. *Pacific Anthropological Records* 18. Honolulu: Bishop Museum. Pp. 59–94.

3

Recent Progress in Korean Archaeology

SARAH M. NELSON

Within the last decade new discoveries in almost every time period in Korean archæology have necessitated rethinking the internal patterns as well as the relationships of Korean prehistory to that of its neighbors on all sides. This remarkable progress has come about despite many difficulties, not the least of which is the division of the peninsula into two separate political entities. Recent publications in the south have been considerably more numerous than those from the north, and thus new discoveries from the Republic of Korea (South Korea) are more prominently reported here than those from the Democratic People's Republic of Korea (North Korea). The peninsula must be perceived as a whole, however, and as much as possible, North Korean archaeological progress is included as well.

Some of the most important new finds include (*a*) a site with Acheulian-style tools; (*b*) the earliest ^{14}C date so far for the Chulmun period, which demonstrates contemporaneity with the Yangshao period in China; (*c*) rice and other grains from a Bronze Age site dated to the thirteenth century B.C.; and (*d*) "Liaoning" bronze daggers found in situ for the first time in southern Korean burials. Archaeological work for the Three Kingdoms period has included (*a*) excavation of the first intact Paekche tomb from the last Paekche capital, (*b*) several early Paekche tombs in the Seoul area, which demonstrate the accuracy of the legendary connection between the royal house of Paekche and Koguryo, (*c*) a number of Kaya pit burials, and (*d*) the first known paintings from Silla tombs. Tomb 98 in Kyongju, a double mound where king and queen had separate burials, brought to light new examples of the lavish grave goods of Silla royalty. In this case the queen's accoutrements outshone the king's, although both had exotic items identified as having been manufactured as far away as Alexandria, Egypt.

99

ADVANCES IN WORLD ARCHAEOLOGY
Volume 1

Much of this archaeological activity has been of a "salvage" nature, with increasing industrialization, road building, and the accelerating urban sprawl of the cities, especially Seoul. This work has been carried out with care and caution insofar as circumstances permitted. Many of the larger projects were joint expeditions of several universities and museums, which has allowed new techniques to spread rapidly. Problem-oriented archaeology has also been carried out, although the problems have been more chronological than processual. It is difficult, if not impossible, to study process before the spatial and temporal framework is firmly in place. Within the past decade most of the larger picture has become clear, and it is now possible to reconstruct some of the finer details.

Because the new discoveries are almost all of chronological significance, in addition to other important aspects, this chapter is arranged chronologically. The Paleolithic section includes recently excavated aceramic sites, and is discussed from presumed earliest to latest. There are no sites designated as Mesolithic in Korea. The Neolithic section includes the earliest ceramic sites, from the sixth to perhaps the second millennium B.C. Although sometimes translated into English as Combware or Geometric, I prefer to use the term Chulmun for this time period, by analogy with Jomon in Japan. The Bronze Age features megalithic monuments, bronze weaponry, a variety of burial styles, polished stone implements, and new types of pottery. The Iron Age section might well have been labeled Protohistoric, but while the latter term fits the Samhan or Chinguk period in southern Korea for which little written documentation exists, it is a less appropriate term for northern Korea. The Chinese commanderies and Koguryo followed Ancient Choson, for which some events are recorded in detail in Chinese historic writings. The Iron Age, as designated here, therefore covers the time period in Korea contemporaneous with the Warring States period in China, when Yen coins are widely found in the north, through the end of the Han dynasty and the collapse of Lolang, the last Chinese commandery remaining in Korea, in A.D. 313. Historians are not agreed on the founding dates of the Three Kingdoms, but the traditional dates of 37 B.C. for Koguryo, 18 B.C. for Paekche, and 57 B.C. for Silla (National Museum of Korea 1970:16) are usually agreed to be too early, especially for the two southern kingdoms. However, beginning the Three Kingdoms period with the fall of Lolang should be seen as an archaeological convenience because, of these few sites that have been dated with any precision, most are the later sites containing inscriptions. Archaeology of post-Three Kingdoms dynasties certainly exists, but the temptation to include Koryo celadon kilns and United Silla palaces here has been resisted. What follows includes only the archaeology from those time periods for which more is known from excavations than from written documents.

Korean names are spelled according to the McCune-Reischauer system, except where another spelling is more commonly used (e.g., Seoul). This has been preferred over the official Republic of Korea usage because it allows English speakers to approximate closely the Korean sounds, and can be easily transposed back into *Han'gul*. Since Korean place names are likely to be unfamiliar to

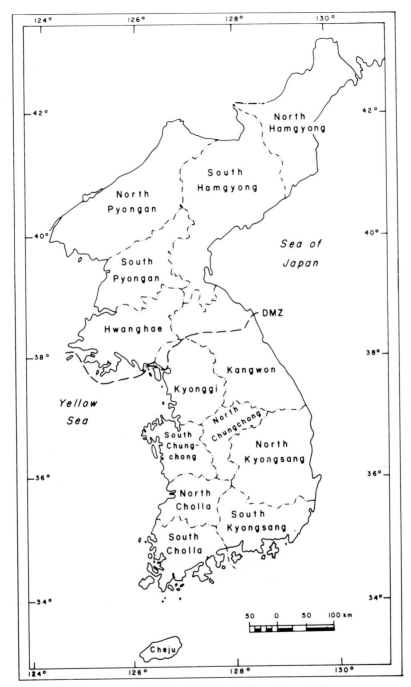

Figure 3.1 Map showing the historical provinces in Korea.

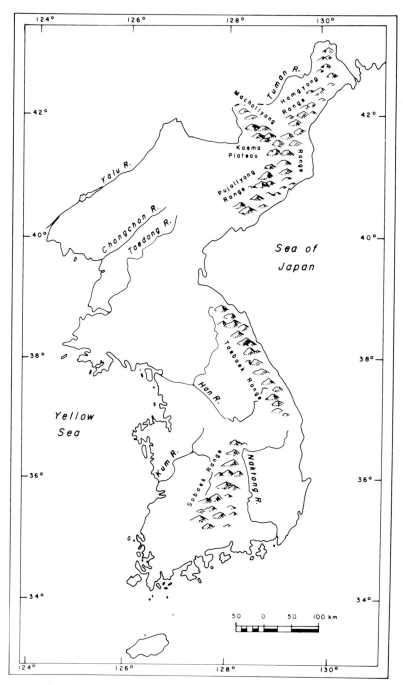

Figure 3.2 Map showing the principal rivers and mountains of Korea.

most readers, a map has been provided with the historical provinces (Figure 3.1), and another shows the principal rivers and mountains (Figure 3.2).

PALEOLITHIC

Several dozen Paleolithic sites have been discovered in Korea within the last decade, and there can no longer be any doubt that Korea was inhabited by *Homo* during the Pleistocene. Little more than that, however, can be said with much certainty. The sites are both too diverse and too sketchily reported even to begin attempting a discussion of patterns of artifact distributions, subsistence, or habitat. Even the terminology used is difficult to correlate, for terms and concepts have been borrowed from European, Chinese, and Russian archaeologists by scholars working in Korea. Nevertheless, the new data tentatively can be fitted into the worldwide scheme, raising interesting questions for East Asian archaeology, in terms of time depth, areal distribution, and relationships of tool types to subsistence activities. Paleolithic sites mentioned below can be located on the map in Figure 3.3.

Lower Paleolithic

Claims of Lower Paleolithic age have been made for four sites in the Korean peninsula. The most recent of these sites to be excavated and reported is Chon'gong-ni, in central Korea northeast of Seoul. The site was first recognized by Bowen (1979), who collected hand axes and other bifacial tools from the surface (Figure 3.4). Several Korean institutions have cooperated in excavating the site. A total of 46 tools are reported by Kim and Chung (1979) with measurements and photographs of 8 presumably representative tools. Chung describes these as Acheulian tools, including hand axes, choppers, chopping tools, cleavers, polyhedrals, and scrapers. On the basis of photographs sent to him, Bordes has confirmed that these are typologically Acheulian, and continues that stratigraphic confirmations of the age would make it a very important find (Kim WY and Chung YH 1979:7, footnote 3).

The stratigraphy has proved to be suggestive of Lower Paleolithic age, but is far from conclusive. The site is about a kilometer in extent, consisting of several different localities (Kim WY and Chung YH 1979). It is on a terrace about 30 m above the Handan River (Serizawa 1980). At Locality 2, a test pit revealed five strata: (1) a humus layer .15–.20 m in thickness, (2) a brownish yellow-red layer of .44–.50 m, (3) a yellow-brown layer .15–.77 m in thickness, (4) a thin layer (.09–.20 m) of brown sand, and (5) a basal layer of brown sand mixed with gravel, .15–.28 m thick. The total depth to bedrock is 1.5 m. Layers 2, 3, and 5 contained artifacts, but most of the artifacts in Chung and Kim's report came from the top of Layer 2, which was exposed by a bulldozer. The strata rest on basaltic bedrock, and pre-Cambrian granite underlies the basalt. Chung believes

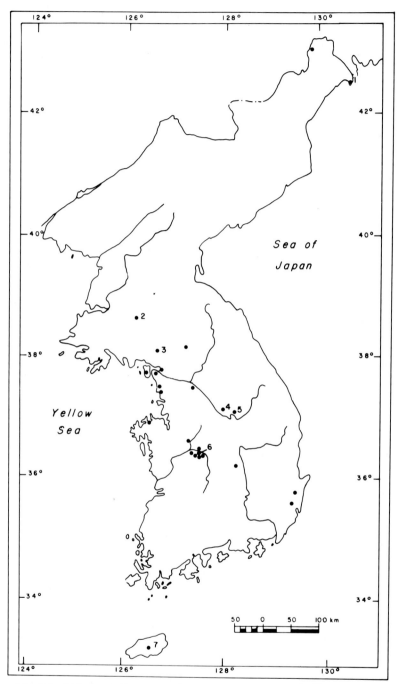

Figure 3.3 Paleolithic sites in Korea: (1) Kulp'o-ri; (2) Sangwon Cave; (3) Chon'gong-ni; (4) Chommal Cave; (5) Durubong Cave; (6) Sokchang-ni; and (7) Billemot Cave.

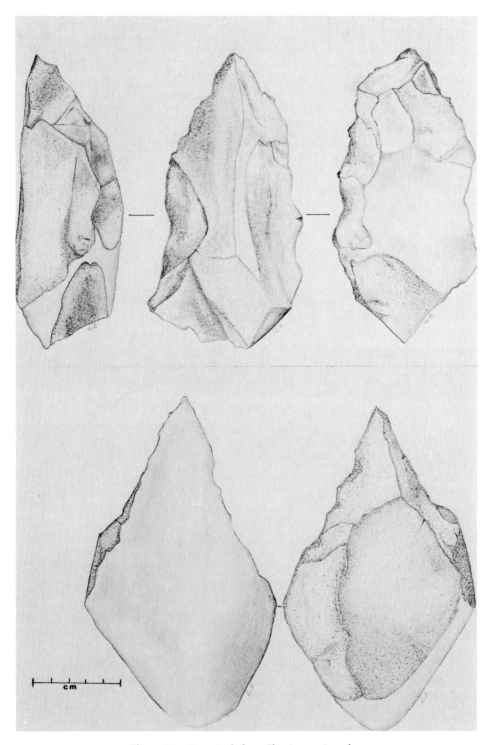

Figure 3.4 Stone tools from Chon'gong-ni, surface.

the site dates to "Mindel/Riss" interglacial or "Riss" glacial age, between 350,000 and 150,000 years ago, but the geology of Korea is as yet insufficiently studied to make age determinations on the basis of these strata. (Alpine glacial terms have been used in this chapter because they are in common usage in Korea, and the Korean Quaternary remains unstudied. The terms are to be understood as general time-frames only.)

Bowen (1979:48) describes the site location as the "third and uppermost flood plain," potentially a very significant observation. Multiple river terraces are not common in Korea. The geological processes that formed the Korean topography "like a sea in a heavy gale" (McCune 1956) are complex, and include tilting of the block up on the eastern edge where the higher peaks are found, and down toward the Yellow Sea (Bartz 1972). Glaciers did not play a significant part in the shaping of Korea, nor did the deposition of loess. The processes of land formation need to be studied in order to interpret river terraces in Korea. Sea level fluctuations may have been the major Pleistocene change and may help to account for the terraces.

Although Chon'gong-ni is the first Korean site with large numbers of hand axes to be excavated, there are also excavated sites of the chopper–chopping tool tradition for which early Paleolithic age has been claimed. One of these is Sokchang-ni, a stratified site on the Kum River in western Korea (Sohn 1972, 1978a). Layers 15a to 27, 6–11 m below ground surface, are thought to be Lower Paleolithic. The tools are large and crude, mostly bifacial, and made from cobbles of quartz. These lower strata are quite reduced in areal extent due to narrowing of the excavation unit, so few tools were found.

Chommal Cave on the western slope of the Taebaek range in North Chungchong province was also excavated by Sohn. Reports from the excavations include faunal and pollen identifications, as well as soil types, by level (Sohn 1975, 1978b). Many bone tools were found, but only a few stone tools except in the lower levels (Kim WY 1977a). Particle size analysis was used to create a temperature curve, which was more successful than the pollen analysis, because too few pollen grains were present for the results to be statistically reliable. All the arboreal species are consistent with a deciduous forest environment throughout the Pleistocene, varying only in percentages. A ^{14}C date of 13,700 ± 700 B.P. (Kim WY 1977b:10) corresponds to a cold period in Sohn's chart (Sohn 1975:Fig. 4). Table 3.1 correlates the environmental information from Chommal Cave.

Sangwon Cave, 40 km southeast of P'yongyang in North Korea, has five identified layers. The stratum just above bedrock is believed to be more than 400,000 years old on the basis of *Mimomys* sp., a field mouse which became extinct at that time (Foreign Languages Publishing House 1977:3; Sohn 1974).

These four sites do not yield good comparative data, because they are not reported in comparable ways. None of these sites can be said without question to be Lower Paleolithic, but the possibility of documenting these or other sites as Lower Paleolithic seems likely. It would extend the known range of *Homo erectus*

TABLE 3.1

Chommal Cave Fauna and Pollen

Cultural levels	Depth (cm)	Time period	Pollen	1	2	3	4	5	6	7	8	9	10	11	12
															Fauna[a]
1	0–60	Holocene	*Pinus*		X					X	X	X	X	X	X
2	74–100	Würm[b]	*Abies, Salix, Pinus*					X	X	X	X		X	X	X
3	103–120	Würm	*Pinus*			X		X	X	X	X			X	
4	129–134	Würm	*Pinus*			X			X	X	X				
5	142–155	Würm	*Pinus, Abies*						X	X	X				
6	164–175	Third Interglacial		X						X	X				
7	184–187	Third Interglacial									X				
8	194–200	Third Interglacial					X				X				
9	206–212	Third Interglacial									X				
10	218–230	Third Interglacial													
11	239–248	Third Interglacial	*Pinus*								X				
12															
13															

[a] Key to Fauna: 1 = macaque, *Macaca sp.*; 2 = black bear, *Ursus thibetarinus* (?); 3 = cave bear, *Ursus spelaeus* (?); 4 = badger, *Meles meles melancgenys*; 5 = mountain lemming, *Lepus sinensis coreanus*; 6 = red deer, *Cervus manchuricus*; 7 = spotted deer, *Cervus nippon*; 8 = deer, *Cervus nippon*; 9 = musk deer, *Moschus moschiferus*; 10 = roe deer, *Capreolus capreolus*; 11 = hedgehog, *Ericaceus coreensis*; 12 = hyena, *Hyaena* (?). (Sohn 1974:10.)

[b] ^{14}C date: 13,700 ± 700 B.P. (Kim WY 1977:10).

beyond northeastern China, and lend more credibility to sites in Japan and Manchuria that are also believed by some (Derevianko 1978; Serizawa 1978) to be possibly as early as the penultimate interglacial.

Studies of the function of hand axes and their associated artifacts and ecofacts would shed light on whether those in Korea are related directly or indirectly to those on the western side of the Eurasian land mass, or whether they represent an independent invention. Present evidence points to a persistent deciduous forest environment in Korea that might have required different tools and living arrangements from those of the tundra, taiga, or steppe. It seems unlikely that there would be any direct connection with European traditions; perhaps functional identity would explain the morphological similarities.

Upper Paleolithic

A few sites have been designated "Mousterian" or Middle Paleolithic on the basis of the occurrence of predominantly flake tools. The usefulness of such designations for East Asia has been rightly questioned by Ikawa-Smith (1978), and nothing is added to our understanding of processes in Korea by such designations. However, insofar as superposition is indicative of temporal relationships, the sequence of core to flake to blade tools does seem to hold in a very general way at Sokchang-ni, which is the only site to contain all three manufacturing techniques. Middle layers of the Sokchang-ni site (Sohn 1978a), the lower level at Kulp'o-ri in North Hamgyong province (Kim JH 1978b), Billemot Cave on Cheju Island (Sohn 1974; Kim WY 1974), and Durubong Cave in the Taebaek range (Kim WY 1975a) are some examples of sites with flake tools. Rocks placed in a rectangular pattern 11.5 by 8 m at Kulp'o-ri represent the earliest man-made shelter yet reported in Korea, if the Middle Paleolithic Age claimed for it is correct (Kim JH 1978b).

Two other ^{14}C dates make the age of the Upper Paleolithic layer in Korea secure. A habitation floor at Sokchang-ni, a rectangular windbreak similar to that at Kulp'o-ri, has been dated at 20,830 ± 1880 B.P. (AERIK–8), and a lower layer has a date of 30,830 ± 1880 B.P. (AERIK–5). Pollen from the windbreak level included *Pinus, Lingustrum, Osmunda, Lilacea, Magnolia,* and *Alnus,* indicating a climate at least as warm as the present. Sohn (1973) suggests it may represent the final Würm interstadial. This is the best reported Upper Paleolithic site in Korea, and summaries in English are available in a number of places (Sohn 1973, 1975, 1978b).

Although published faunal charts from Korean cave sites give only presence or absence by depth (e.g., Sohn 1974:10), or less usefully only a list of fauna identified from the site, the present evidence points to the persistence of forest-adapted fauna throughout the Pleistocene and continuing into the Holocene, despite minor climatic fluctuations. Thus, deer (*Cervus*) are reported consistently, and other common animals are cave bear, tiger, and macaque. Not only did Korea escape major glaciations, but evidence from the Soviet Far East in the form of surviving Tertiary flora suggests that severe cold did not occur in this region (Derevianko 1978).

The only human remains reported from the Paleolithic are *Homo sapiens,* from a cave at Sungni-san in South Pyongan province (FLPH 1977).

A great deal of interdisciplinary study is needed to further our understanding of the Paleolithic period in Korea, but that which has taken place so far indicates the results will be well worth the effort.

NEOLITHIC

The Neolithic, or Chulmun, period in Korean archaeology has been comparatively neglected. This is a great pity, because there are many important questions to be answered from this cultural stage—how and why food production began, and what kind of social organization bound the villages together—as well as refining the temporal sequences about which far too little is known.

Two important discoveries have been made, however, both necessitating changes in relative regional and temporal sequences. The first of these was the confirmation of Sample's (1967) finding of pinched, appliqué, and undecorated pottery types in strata below incised wares. This was accomplished by means of further explorations in the same region on the southeast coast near Pusan. The second important event was the obtaining of two ^{14}C dates from Amsa-dong in central Korea going back to the sixth millennium B.C. To put these events in perspective, it is necessary to review briefly the history of Neolithic studies in Korea. Sites referred to in the text are shown in Figure 3.5, as well as the general pattern of Chulmun site locations.

History of Korean Neolithic Studies

The early Japanese archaeologists studying the Neolithic in Korea believed there were two distinct and mutually exclusive kinds of handmade pottery, and the first 50 years or so of study of the Neolithic were devoted to the questions of which kind of pottery came first, and where the two types originated. One ware, called Mumun (Plain Ware), is largely undecorated, and the buff-to-brown-colored pottery is thick, with coarse tempering. Vessels usually have small flat bases, and occasionally appendages are found. The other ware, known as Chulmun (Comb Ware), consists almost entirely of wide-mouthed pots with rounded or pointed bases, covered over the surface with various incised decorations. Appendages are absent. Chulmun means comb-marked, and is a Korean translation of *Kammkeramik,* because it was believed to be derived ultimately from Baltic pit and comb ware, by way of Siberia where conical incised pots are also found.

The two kinds of ceramic seemed to be unassociated, and in fact, the settlements were noted for their placement according to different locational strategies.

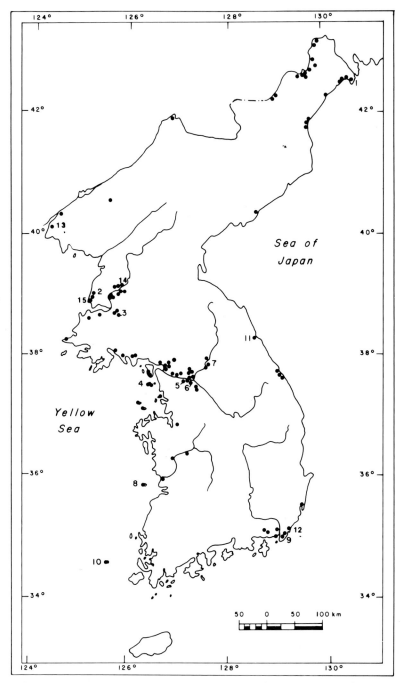

Figure 3.5 Neolithic sites in Korea; numbered sites are mentioned in the text: (1) Sop'ohang, Kulp'o; (2) Kungsan; (3) Chit'am-ni; (4) Si Do; (5) Amsa-dong; (6) Misa-ri; (7) Kyo-dong; (8) Sonyu Do; (9) Tongsam-dong; (10) Taehuksan Do; (11) Yongjil-li; (12) Cho Do; (13) Sinam-ni; (14) Chongho-ri; and (15) Yŏndo-ri.

Chulmun sites were found to occur exclusively on coasts and river banks, while Mumun sites were found on hillsides. These were interpreted as different "cultures," and the debate as to whether they were contemporary, or if not, which was earlier, occupied archaeologists for a considerable length of time. Stratigraphic tests (Sample 1967, 1974) at first failed to settle the controversy for a number of reasons, but the combination of radiocarbon dates and the firm association of Mumun with bronze artifacts has shown Chulmun to be earlier, given the choice of those two. The real answer is that not all undecorated pottery is Mumun, and some incised pottery is probably Early Bronze Age, so the picture is much more complex than was originally envisioned.

"Neolithic" proper, therefore, includes only Chulmun sites. However, this designation needs to be accepted in a very broad sense, as *Jomon* is used in Japan to cover all techniques of pottery decoration, not merely cordmarking, that appear from the beginning of the ceramic period to about 400 B.C. (Chard 1974:167), or perhaps 300 B.C. (Ikawa-Smith 1980:134) when a distinctive new pottery, Yayoi, begins to be found. Only a small proportion of Chulmum sherds are actually comb marked, although the majority of them have decorations that could fall under the general rubric of incised. Some sherds with pinched and appliqué decorations belong to this time period as well, and rarely cordmarking has been found.

Stratified sites with both Mumun and Chulmun are quite rare, due largely to the difference in locations. When Sample and Mohr excavated at Tongsamdong in 1964, it was with the explicit hope of elucidating the stratigraphic questions. Sample analyzed the ceramics in the method familiar to American archeologists, making intuitive types and then reporting these types in detail, with percentages by level (Sample 1967). The resulting picture was indeed complex, but overall showed a progression from pinched and/or appliqué sherds through incised sherds to undecorated types. Sample named the levels Chodo, Mokto, Pusan, Tudo, and Yongdo, from bottom to top. No date came from Sample's lowest level, the sparsely represented Chodo period, but a date of 5890 ± 140 B.P. (4745 B.C.)* (GX–0378) was a surprisingly early date for the Mokto period. The Pusan period was dated at 4945 ± 125 B.P. (3780 B.C.) (GX–0379), and Sample's Tudo period, which contains Chulmun pottery, was dated as late as 3400 ± 120 B.P. (1770 B.C.) (GX–0493). This is an identical date to that from the Yongdo period, which was generally recognized as "real" Mumun, although the date seemed rather early. Sample's results sparked further excavations at Tongsamdong and at other shell mounds near Pusan. Im (1968) found pinched pottery in a shell mound at Tongnae, and Chodo Island shell mound had undecorated pottery, called by Kim "Tongsamdong Plain" (Kim WY 1974), at the basal level. At the Sinam-ni site both "raised-band" decoration and incised ware were uncovered, although not at the same part of the site (Kim WY 1975a).

---

*All radiocarbon dates within the appropriate time range have been recalibrated according to Clark (1975). Thus, uncalibrated dates are represented by B.P., calibrated dates by B.C.

Subsequent excavations and ^{14}C dates at Tongsamdong by Korean archaeological teams have further confirmed Sample's stratigraphic results. In the lowest
level, called Tongsamdong I, dates of 5180 ± 125 B.P. (4020 B.C.) (N–1132) and
4880 ± 100 B.P. (3710 B.C.) (Lee 1977) were reported. A total of six Tongsamdong
II dates ranged from 4950 ± 100 B.P. (3785 B.C.) (Lee 1977) to 3880 ± 100 B.P.
(2430 B.C.) (AERIK–26). Of these, all but the earliest were associated with
Chulmun sherds. Tongsamdong III, the uppermost layer which contains plain
pottery, produced a date of 4170 ± 100 B.P. (2875 B.C.) (AERIK–22). These dates,
especially with the bristlecone pine calibration pushing them back still further,
are much earlier than expected. Figure 3.6 includes all Neolithic and Bronze Age
radiocarbon dates from Korea for comparison, and Tables 3.2 and 3.3 list the
dates.

Chulmun Sites and Artifacts

Before considering the implications of these dates further, and before discussing the still earlier central Korean Chulmun dates of 6230 ± 111 B.P. (5155 B.C.)
(KIM JB 1975a) and 6050 ± 105 B.P. (4975 B.C.) (N–2336) at Amsa-dong, it is

TABLE 3.2

[14]C Dates in Neolithic Sites[a]

Site	Date B.P.	Date B.C.	Lab	No. in FIG. 3.7
Si Do	2870 ± 60	1130	AERIK–12	1
Si Do	3040 ± 60	1370	AERIK–11	2
Si Do	3040 ± 60	1370	AERIK–14	3
Si Do	3100 ± 60	1440	AERIK–13	4
Amsa-dong	3420 ± 250	1810	Lee 1977	5
Amsa-dong	4950 ± 200	3785	Lee 1977	6
Amsa-dong	6050 ± 105	4975	N–2336	7
Amsa-dong	6230 ± 110	5155	Kim W.Y. 1975a	8
Taehuksan Do	3420 ± 120	1800	Pearson 1981	9
Sonyu Do	4812 ± 44	3650	Lee 1977	10
Cho Do	4190 ± 120	2900	Pearson 1981	11
Tongsamdong I	5180 ± 125	4020	N–1132	12
Tongsamdong I	4880 ± 100	3710	Lee 1977	13
Tongsamdong II	4950 ± 100	3785	Lee 1977	14
Tongsamdong II	4400 ± 80	3175	AERIK–27	15
Tongsamdong II	4020 ± 100	2625	AERIK–23	16
Tongsamdong II	3980 ± 100	2565	AERIK–24	17
Tongsamdong II	3930 ± 100	2495	AERIK–25	18
Tongsamdong II	3880 ± 100	2430	AERIK–26	19
Tongsamdong (Mokto)	5890 ± 140	4745	GX–0378	20
Tongsamdong (Pusan)	4945 ± 125	3780	GX–0379	21
Tongsamdong (Tudo)	3400 ± 120	1770	GX–0493	22

[a] Calibrated according to Clark 1975.

TABLE 3.3

¹⁴C Dates Associated with Mumun Pottery, Bronze, or Dolmens[a]

Site	Date B.P.	Date B.C.	Laboratory	No. in FIG. 3.6
Musan Pomuigusok (House 15)	2430 ± 120	560	Kim WY 1969	23
Musan Hoguk (House 14)	2430 ± 110	560	Kim JH 1978b	24
Si Do	2470 ± 60	710, 655, 635	AERIK–10	25
Susong-ni	2340 ± 120	445	Lee 1977	26
Susong-ni	2230 ± 280	395	Lee 1977	27
Sangjapo-ri	2170 ± 60	225, 320, 355	KAERI–91	28
Yanggul-li	2760 ± 70	985	AERIK–81	29
Yangsu-ri	3900 ± 200	2455	Lee 1977	30
Oksong-ni	2590 ± 105	830	GX–0554	31
Naepyong-ni	2290 ± 60	420	AERIK–28	32
Naepyong-ni	2590 ± 60	830	AERIK–30	33
Naepyong-ni	2930 ± 60	1220	AERIK–29	34
Hunam-ni (House 8)	2541 ± 150	770	KAERI–153	35
Hunam-ni	2520 ± 120	775	Kim et al. 1976	36
Hunam-ni	2620 ± 100	855	KAERI–169	37
Hunam-ni (House 8)	2666 ± 160	900	KAERI–154–2	38
Hunam-ni (House 8)	2696 ± 160	925	KAERI–151–1	39
Hunam-ni	2920 ± 70	1205	Kim et al. 1978	40
Hunam-ni	2980 ± 70	1295	Kim et al. 1978	41
Hunam-ni	3210 ± 70	1560	KAERI–170	42
Hwangsong-ni	2360 ± 370	460	GX–0555	43
Taegong-ni	2560 ± 120	810	KAERI–80	44
Tongnae	3469 ± 78	1860	AERIK–3	45
Tongmyong-ni	3578 ± 48	2005	AERIK–7	46
Kumgok-dong	3580 ± 75	2155	N–2135	47
Tongsamdong III	4170 ± 100	2875	AERIK–22	48
Tongsamdong III (Yongdo)	3400 ± 215	1770	GY–0492	49
Songwon-ni	2880 ± 120	1145	AERIK–16	[b]

[a] Calibrated according to Clark 1975.
[b] Inadvertently omitted from chart; on the Kum River, in the southwest.

necessary to review the overall pattern of Chulmun sites, and then the regional differences of the pottery.

Chulmun sites are found throughout the Korean peninsula, but they are not evenly spaced. Regional groups are noticeable both in terms of clustering of sites near major rivers and in terms of stylistic differences from region to region. As is the case for the Paleolithic, different kinds of information are available for various sites. Nevertheless, enough sites have been excavated to allow a general picture of Neolithic settlements.

Sites on the coasts are shell mounds, in which bone and antler artifacts have been preserved, whereas riverbank sites lack both shell and bone. Comparison of inland and coastal sites therefore seems to emphasize differences in utilization of bone for tools as well as animals for food, but this is very likely a reflection of the preservative aspect of shell mounds as opposed to the podzolic soil in which bone disintegrates quickly.

Throughout Korea, stone artifacts of the Chulmun period are more chipped than ground. Projectile points are small and triangular, with indented, notched, or flat bases. In the northeast and southeast where obsidian could be obtained locally, it was widely used. But this material was not traded to the interior or around the coast. Elsewhere the projectile points and other stone artifacts tend to be made of silicified shale. Net sinkers (or perhaps loom weights [Kent and Nelson 1976]) are made from thin natural pebbles with flakes removed from each end to make notches. Small flat celts were created in a similar fashion, selecting pebbles of appropriate shape and size and minimally chipping a broad, flat end for digging and a narrower end for hafting. Grinding stones and saddle querns have been found in abundance at most sites, and polished stone axes are also frequently reported.

Bone implements include needles, awls, fishhooks, spatulas, and "knitting needles" that presumably were used to make nets. Hoes and digging sticks made of antler have also been reported, as well as boar's tusk sickles at Kungsan-ni (Han YH 1978).

Ornaments are not common, although glycymeris shell bracelets were present in some abundance at Tongsamdong (Sample 1967), and jade beads have been reported from sites in the northeast (Kim JH 1978b). Ceremonial objects, in the form of crude figurines and carved bones, have been reported from Sop'ohang on the northeast coast (Henthorn 1968) and a few other sites.

Dwellings have not been excavated in many sites, but there is a clear pattern in the houses that have been excavated (Kim CK 1968, 1976). All are round or subrectangular with approximately equal sides, and range in size from 4 to 7 m in diameter. They are semisubterranean, usually less than 1 m below the original ground surface. Each has a central hearth, slightly depressed and outlined with upright slabs or river cobbles in a squarish shape. Northern sites have floors coated with clay, and in two sites large conical vessels were found embedded in the floor upside down, with the bottom removed. Other pits are rarely reported. Postholes along the wall are a common feature, although not universal. At Chitam-ni, entrances were noted on the southern or southeastern side. Elsewhere no doorways were located, and it is assumed that entry was through the roof (Kim CK 1976).

The question of the subsistence base has not yet been settled to the satisfaction of all workers in the field. It is is likely that the mix of subsistence strategies differed from region to region, but too few sites are reported in enough detail to make generalizations. At Sop'ohang in the northeast, a shell mound 40 by 100 m and 3 m thick was composed largely of oyster shells. Mammal bones identified include deer, boar, dog, bear, and whale. In addition to the oysters, clams and other bivalves, snails, and fish bones were also found (Henthorn 1968).

Kungsan, in the northwest, produced more than 100 fragments of antelope mandible (*Capreolus*), bones of two water buffalo (*Bubalus*), and other bones of deer and boar. Fish bones were found, and the shell mound consisted of clams, oysters, and cowrie (*Cypraea*) (Kim JH 1978b). Kim SK (1974) points out that deer are more common in the western plains sites, and carnivores in the mountainous area. Boar is also common. North Koreans believe that pig domestication took place in the beginning of the Neolithic (FLPH, 1977). Central Korean inland sites, lacking shell mounds, produce little food debris. Acorns and chestnuts have been identified, however, at Misa-ri (Chase 1960) and Amsa-dong (Kim JH 1978b), and one fragment of unidentifiable mammal bone was recovered from Amsa-dong (Lim Byung-tae, personal communication, 1971).

The only site from which stratigraphic information regarding bone and shell exists is Tongsam-dong, in the southeast. At this site, sea mammals and large fish are found in the lower shell lenses, while in upper layers the percentage of oyster shell increases and land animals become more prominent. Antler and tusk artifacts are confined to the upper layers, as are projectile points, grinding stones, and hoes. The appearance of hunted land animals coincides with the beginning of Chulmun pottery, whereas the sea mammals and large fish are associated with plain, pinched, and appliqué types (Sample 1967).

The usual conclusion is that a broad spectrum strategy of obtaining wild food resources was being pursued. Projectile points attest to hunting, and fish hooks, netting needles, and sinkers demonstrate fishing. Digging implements could have been used merely to excavate the dwelling areas, and grinding stones might have been used on wild grains or nuts, so neither can be said to indicate agriculture indisputably. The discovery of 1.2 liters of grain in a storage jar at Chitam-ni (Chard 1960) has modified this picture, but it is usually said that millet cultivation began toward the end of the Chulmun period (Han 1974; Kim WY 1977b; Kim JH 1978b). There is, however, no inherent reason to place Chitam-ni later than other Chulmun sites. (See following text.) The grains are generally accepted as *Panicum miliaceum* and *Setaria italica* (Kim JH 1978a), although no comparison of these grains with wild and domesticated forms has been published (Kim WY 1975b).

From the fact that very large jars (up to 50 cm in diameter) have been found, storage at least is certain, whether or not grains or vegetables were being cultivated. I have argued elsewhere (Nelson 1975b) that it is likely that some early form of *kimch'i*, a vegetable preserve eaten at nearly every meal in Korea, dates back to these early times. The dwellings were equipped with central hearths for warmth in winter, and therefore were in year-round settlements, because winter is the season in Korea when the fewest wild food resources would be available. Even with small populations, it is unlikely that the deciduous forest could supply sufficient excess nuts to last the entire winter, even if supplemented with game. Wild millet, unlike the wheat and barley reported in southwest Asia (Harlan 1967), does not grow in stands sufficient to support large populations. In the deciduous forest, the major habitat for grasses and herbs is along the riverbanks—the locations where inland Chulmun sites are in fact found, and where incipient agriculture would be expected (Sauer 1952).

In summary, the Neolithic period was a time of a broad spectrum subsistence pattern, including fishing, hunting, collecting, and probably some cultivation. Nuclear family houses in small groups along seacoasts and rivers imply little need for leadership, and indeed there is no evidence of any kind of rank differentiation. No burials have ever been found, perhaps indicating some means of disposal of the dead other than interment. A later Chinese source (*Hou Han Shu*, translated in Watson 1961) attributes the custom of keeping bones of lineage members in bone boxes to the Ok-ye tribes; perhaps this custom was preserved from much earlier times. Although the presence of many obsidian artifacts and waste flakes has caused the excavator of Nonp'o-dong in the northeast to postulate a manufacturing center (Kim JH 1968), obsidian is not found except in that region and in the far southeast. Marine shells are not found inland, jade beads are extremely rare, and there is no evidence of any sort of long distance trade among the sites or regions. The only evidence of intersite communication is similarity of pottery styles within regions, which may indicate self-conscious groups that might be labeled "tribes" (Nelson 1980).

Regional Styles of Pottery

Chulmun has been described in the past largely in terms of these regional stylistic differences in the pottery, without regard to time sequences. Indeed, since the pottery has been assumed to have come from Siberia, the northern sites have been presumed to be older, and evidence was deemed unnecessary (Figure 3.6).

Arimitsu (1962), in the first book-length synthesis of the Chulmun period, divided the sites into four regional groups: northeast, northwest, central, and south. Clusters of sites were known in each of these regions, with large gaps between them. Each area was found to have a distinctive style. Briefly, these are in the northeast, flat-bottomed and sometimes globular shapes decorated with hatched meanders; "maggotlike" impressions and saw-tooth designs with hatched lines in the northwest; conical bases with direct rims and overall incised designs in the central region; and in the south, appliqué and cord marking occur in addition to the typical incised patterns.

Gaps between the regions have been partly filled in as new sites have been discovered, but the regional distinctions remain valid. To what extent regional styles also reflect temporal differences is not yet thoroughly understood.

Temporal Models of Ceramic Change

Stylistic differences have been interpreted as temporal change by Kim JH (1968, 1978b), although not entirely convincingly. Kim Won-yong (1977b) was able to create a more sophisticated chronology based on many more ^{14}C dates, but the most recently published dates have forced a rearrangement of this sequence also.

The new dates, especially those from Amsa-dong, are important not merely in

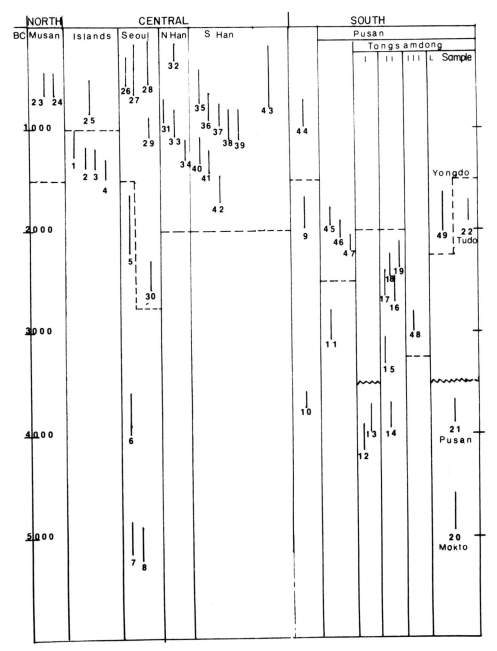

Figure 3.6 ^{14}C dates for Neolithic and Bronze Age sites. Above dashed lines are Bronze Age sites, below are Neolithic sites. Pinched pottery sites are below zigzag lines. For full citations, see Tables 3.2 and 3.3.

establishing the existence of permanent settlements with ceramics much earlier than was previously known, but in reestablishing Chulmun as the earliest ceramic ware known in Korea at present. It appears that Korea may have participated in the general East Asian early ceramic horizon. Some undated incised sherds from Szechuan appear identical to Amsa-dong sherds (Cheng 1967:213). Perhaps the earliest Korean sites are in fact submerged in the Yellow Sea, as suggested some time ago by Hewes (1947). In any case, the *Kammkeramik* connection has little remaining appeal.

With long temporal sequences now established at Amsadong and Tongsandong, and some Chulmun sites in the north also reported to have distinguishable levels within the Neolithic, finer chronological divisions may become possible, based firmly on stratigraphy and ^{14}C dates. Attempts made to sequence pottery types within a region have not yet been successful, however. Two such studies merely show that finer regional groupings can be made. One study compares central Han River sites, western island sites, and a site (Naepyong-ni) on the North Han River, and shows that these groupings can be distinguished statistically largely on the basis of decorative patterns (Nelson 1975a). Another study shows that similar groups can be created using paste and temper as the critical variables (Im 1977).

Han (1978) conducted the most extensive comparative study to date. Using sites in the Han River and Taedong River areas, Han compared details of dwellings and their contents; the pottery on the basis of temper and shape; rim, body, and base decorative patterns; grinding stone shapes; bone tools by type; unworked animal bone by specific animal; chipped stone; and net sinkers. The precise methodology is unstated, but the arrangement of sites is based on the presence or absence of traits in various categories, apparently on the same principle as a Guttman scale. Subcategories are scaled and then the various orderings joined into an overall seriation. The final result has four stages: (1) Chitam-ni I, Kungsan; (2) Chitam-ni II, Amsa-dong; (3) Kumtal-li I, Banwol-dong; and (4) Kumtal-li II, Chongho-ri, Oya-dong, Yondo-ri.

There are still problems to be solved, as can be seen from the fact that Amsadong, where the Chulmun occupation lasted for more than 2000 years, occupies only one slot in the chronology. It seems increasingly likely that regional and even site differences have more to do with traditions than with horizons.

BRONZE AGE

A number of important Bronze Age discoveries have been made in the 1970s. One of the most provocative was the identification of rice, sorghum, barley, and millet from a house context at Hunam-ni in central Korea near the Han River. Previously, the earliest known rice in Korea was from the Iron Age Kimhae shell mound, dated by a Wang Mang coin to the first few years of the first century A.D. Since the Hunam-ni discovery, rice has been found in two other Bronze Age sites. The implications of this will be discussed in following text.

Other finds of particular types of bronze weapons in situ, and a number of ^{14}C dates, have helped refine the chronology. There are increasing numbers of Korean archaeologists who accept a date of 1000 B.C. for the beginning of the Bronze Age, but there is evidence from radiocarbon dates (see Table 3.3) that Mumun pottery begins up to 1000 years earlier than that. If Mumun is equated with the Bronze Age, this is indeed unexpected. These dates require rethinking of the relationship with other bronze-using areas, especially Shang China and the Karasuk of Siberia (Figure 3.7 and Table 3.3).

The earliest entry regarding Korea recorded in Chinese annals is that Kija (Chi-tzu in Chinese), a relative of the last Shang king, went into exile in Choson, or Korea, with a retinue of 5000 people. This is generally not taken literally by historians (see, e.g., Gardiner 1969; Joe 1972), but it begins to seem possible, if not yet probable, in the light of the new dates. Interrelationships of East Asian bronze-using groups will be discussed further in the following.

The very existence of a Bronze Age, defined as a time before the introduction of iron when bronze artifacts were being used and made locally, has only been recently acknowledged in Korea. Several different burial styles, three kinds of pottery, and the association of elaborate polished stone daggers with bronze implements on the one hand, and the occasional occurrence of bronze and iron on the other, made the time period of the introduction of metal seem impossibly complex. Some of this complexity is being sorted out as temporal variation with the aid of radiocarbon dates and more careful excavation. To define what pro-

Figure 3.7 Chulmun sherds from central Korea: (a) Amsa-dong, (b) Tongmak, (c) Naepyong, (d) Misa-ri, and (e) Misa-ri.

portion of the rest is attributable to regional differences and/or functional variability is the next task in understanding the Korean Bronze Age. Figure 3.8 shows Bronze Age sites mentioned in the text.

Excavations of dwellings and burials have confirmed that the basic ceramic style associated with bronze is Mumun. Although Mumun occurs far more often without than with bronze artifacts, all occurrences of this pottery are now attributed to the Bronze Age, a stance that may require reevaluation in the light of the ^{14}C dates. The new pattern of sites, including different settlement locations, house styles, and stone artifacts as well as Mumun, bronze, and burials, is seen as intrusive. Some of these elements are intrusive without doubt, but others could be seen as modified from Chulmun. Before discussing some of these problems, the archaeological finds will be briefly reviewed.

Ceramic Variability

The three types of ceramic, mentioned previously, include Mumun in several regional styles, a burnished red ceramic, and polished black vessels. Red and black vessels and sherds are never found alone, but always in small numbers in association with Mumun, which is therefore seen as the "type fossil," and indeed is the most abundant artifact, of the Bronze Age in Korea.

Aside from the problematical ceramics with handles and unusual shapes from Kumtal-li and Misong-ni, which will be treated later, Mumun pottery seems to have two basic variants. In the northwest, especially in the Hwanghae Province, but also in South P'yong'an Province near the Taedong River, the Top-shaped pottery is found, so called because of its very narrow flat bases. Karak pottery, found predominantly on the Han River and further south, has a slightly wider base. Although Kim Jong-hak (1978b) believes that these two types represent a chronological succession, the regional differentiation is striking, and a change from Top-shaped to Karak is not apparent in any site. Furthermore, a series of ^{14}C dates near Pusan is much earlier than any in the northwest (Figure 3.8).

Mumun pottery from most sites takes on two basic shapes, about equally divided: a wide-mouthed pot and a jar with constricted neck. The wide-mouthed pot is different from the Chulmun in several ways, but is not a drastic departure. Flat bases are created by the addition of a small clay disc to the bottom of a round-based pot. The very large storage jars disappear, but Top-shaped vessels are similar in size to the smaller Chulmun jar. The typical wide-mouthed vessel from the Hwanghae region is about 22 cm high, 18 cm mouth diameter, and 2.5 cm diameter at the base. Rims are doubled over rather than direct, and decoration is reduced to a row of punctates, arced impressions, or short parallel lines.

The other common shape, the jar with constricted neck, slightly flaring mouth, and rounded body, also has a very small base. Frequently one or two holes, up to 1 cm in diameter, are pierced in the bottom. The purpose of this is not clear, but it has been suggested that it might be for steaming rice. Similar holes in Siberian pottery are said to be for making cheese (Okladnikov 1965). The

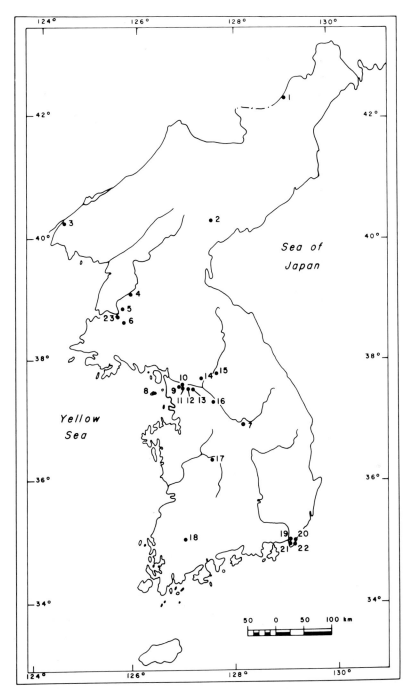

Figure 3.8 Bronze Age sites in Korea mentioned in the text: (1) Musan Pomueguisok, Hogokdong; (2) Taesong-ni; (3) Misong-ni; (4) Kumtal-li; (5) Simchol-li; (6) Sinhungdong; (7) Hwangsong-ni; (8) Si Do; (9) Sangjapo-ri; (10) Karakdong, Yoksamdong, Songamdong; (11) Susong-ni; (12) Yangsu-ri; (13) Yanggun-ni; (14) Oksong-ni; (15) Naep'yong-ni; (16) Hunam-ni; (17) Songwon-ni; (18) Taegong-ni; (19) Kumgok dong; (20) Tongnae; (21) Tokmyong-ni; (22) Tongsamdong; and (23) Soktal-li.

holes were pierced before the pottery was fired, so they are clearly part of the intended function of the vessels.

Karak pottery, found in central and southern Korea, also has a narrow base and the pottery looks unstable, but the bases are nevertheless wider than those of the northwest. Again the wide-mouthed pot has a doubled-over rim, with minimal incised decoration in many cases. A row of punctates below scalloped edges is found in some instances instead of the doubled rim. Some Han River pottery is sand tempered, but steatite temper also appears (Figure 3.9a,e).

In the south, in the vicinity of the Naktong River, Mumun wide-mouthed pots were used as burial urns, usually two placed with mouths together. Some of these burials have associated iron artifacts, or glass beads, which makes it clear that this pottery type persists for a long time in the southeast, as iron is not dated earlier than 400 B.C. in this region.

Mumun pottery sites have also been found in the Cholla provinces, in Kang-won, and in South Hamgyong. These partake in general of the Karak characteristics rather than the Hwangae Top-shaped type.

Red pottery is found very frequently in association with Mumun, both in dwelling sites and in burials. The typical shape is a small globular jar with flaring mouth, usually painted with iron oxide and burnished to a high gloss. The smaller size of the pottery and its comparative rarity suggest that it has either a ritual or a class function (Figure 3.9b).

Black pottery is frequently compared by Korean scholars to Lungshan pottery, but in fact has little in common with Lungshan other than its color. It nowhere has the eggshell thinness of Lungshan, and rarely has a high polish. Neither is it found in most of the typical complex Chinese shapes, such as various tripods, although very rarely pedestal cups have been unearthed. There is no concentration of black pottery in Korea—in fact, no site of which I am aware has more than one such vessel. It is so rare as to suggest a marker of extremely high rank, belonging to only one person, family, or lineage in one location (e.g., Susong-ni [Kim WY 1966, 1967]).

A few sites contain necked, flat-based pottery that fails to fit into any classification. Polychrome painted pottery from the far northeast is one such case. Others include incised pottery with constricted necks and handles on the widest part of the globular bodies, from Sinam-ni in North P'yong'an Province. Kim Jong-hak classifies this pottery with Chŭlmun because of the decoration, but the overall shape is more like Mumun. Associated artifacts, including spindle whorls and crescent knives, definitely demonstrate that this is a variety of Mumun, however aberrant. The Misong-ni Upper Cave ceramics have some of the same shapes, but are decorated more like standard Mumun (Henthorn 1966). Thus, Mumun has a number of variations, the meaning of which is as yet unknown.

Stone Artifacts

Artifacts associated with Mumun vary little from region to region and from site to site. The stone tools of daily use are all polished, and are frequently made of slate. Projectile points tend to be small, and occur in two shapes. One of these has a flattened hexagonal cross section and an indented base. The other has a diamond-shaped cross section and is provided with a tang for hafting. These two types co-occur frequently enough to suggest that the difference between them may be functional and not temporal. Larger points, diamond-shaped in cross section and tanged, are referred to as spearheads (Figure 3.9g).

The most common stone artifact, however, is the polished crescent-shaped stone knife with two holes drilled near the upper center. This is a reaping instrument, very commonly found in Chinese sites from the Lungshan and later times (Yangshao knives are a different shape [Watson 1971]). Its presence was used to infer grain cultivation, even before the actual evidence was found. In dwelling site excavations, nearly every house has several of these crescent knives (Figure 3.9f).

Assorted celts, axes, and adzes are other common artifacts. The stepped adze, meant to be hafted on the side opposite to the working edge, is typical of many Asian tools in use at present. The double-stepped adze is an unusual Korean manifestation, of unknown use. Very small adze-like stone tools may be chisels. Certainly extensive tree chopping and other woodworking were taking place.

Spoked maceheads in a variety of forms are found. Many look quite lethal, and must have been used in warfare as opposed to hunting. Some, however, have such thin spokes as to have been of questionable practical use. Large perforated stone discs have been called "stone money" by North Korean excava- tors. They are similar in form to Chinese weights for digging sticks, but perhaps are too large for that purpose. They could be unspoked battle axes, and are sometimes so described (Figure 3.9d).

Grinding stones are common in Mumun sites, and whetstones also appear. One site has a possible fire drill. Stone spindle whorls are common, but net sinkers are not common except in the Han River sites, where they occur in ceramic form. Some sites have spindle whorls made of potsherds.

One of the most prized stone items from Mumun sites, and therefore often pothunted, is the polished stone dagger. These daggers include handle and blade in one piece (unlike the bronze daggers), and range from quite simple, crude, and utilitarian shapes to ornate and unusable forms. Several scholars have suggested that they are copies of bronze prototypes, but they do not resemble closely any bronze dagger style, and must have evolved on their own. In the Soviet Maritime Region, some bone daggers have been found which could be seen as prototypes of the simplest stone daggers. Stone daggers have been found in house sites occasionally (Figure 3.9c), but the most elaborate ones are from burials.

Finally, mention must be made of the *magatama,* an ornament made of pol- ished stone in the shape of a comma. Possibly the original form was a fang or claw. By the time of the Silla dynasty the *magatama* is found in large numbers on crowns, earrings, and belts of the nobility. Some suggestion of special symbolic value of this shape, as well as the relationships between Japan and Korea, is that the *magatama,* along with the mirror and sword, is one of the Imperial properties in Japan. The earliest of these comma-shaped jewels found in Korea are made of

Figure 3.9 Artifacts from Hunam-ni: (a) Karak jar, (b) polished red jars, (c) polished stone daggers, (d) stone weights, (e) Karak jar, (f) crescent knife (left) and bone tool (right), and (g) polished stone knife or spearhead and projectile points.

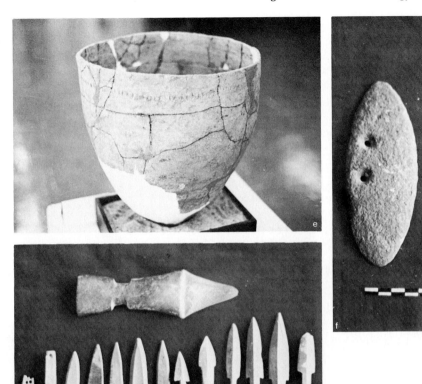

green nephrite and associated with bronze swords. Similar ornaments have been found in the Soviet Maritime Region (Okladnikov 1964), and in the Amur basin (Okladnikov 1964:38). *Magatama* have not been found in the Hwang Ho region of China.

Dwellings

Quite a few dwellings associated with Mumun pottery have been found, widely spread throughout the peninsula. While they are not identical, as a group they can be easily differentiated from Neolithic houses. The most common dwelling is a rectangle about 6 m by 4 m. Some long houses have been found in the Han River region, for instance a dwelling 16 by 3 m at Yoksamdong (Kim YS and Lim BT 1968). Long houses that have been excavated are usually the sole dwellings known at the site, whereas the smaller rectangular houses are grouped into villages. Circular houses excavated in southwestern Korea near Puyo (Kim WY 1974), and oval houses at Songam-dong near Seoul (Choi 1978), may represent continuance of Neolithic traditions into the Bronze Age. Round or oval semi-subterranean houses were still being used in the southwest in protohistoric times. Twelve houses have been excavated at Soktal-li, out of reported dozens, but it is unusual to have so much information about a single site. The dwelling floor is sometimes at ground level, but more frequently is shallowly excavated. Hearths lined with stones are uncommon, as are subfloor features. A row of small post holes, 10 cm or so in diameter, is frequently found around the entire inside perimeter. Whether village or single dwelling, the location is almost always on a hillside, rather than on riverbanks or coastlines as the Chulmun sites were. No structure has been found that seems to have a special function, such as a communal building, ceremonial center, or chief's house.

Burials and Dolmens

Features that point to a ranked society are burials and the associated artifacts. Several burial modes are found with Mumun ceramics: stone cist graves, pit graves, jar burials, stone cairns, and two styles of "dolmen." The first three burial types are subterranean, and may or may not be associated with a dolmen or cairn marking the burial above the ground. Present evidence indicates that stone cists are earlier than jar burials or pit graves, for both the latter sometimes have iron artifacts as well as bronze weapons and polished stone tools (Kim JB 1975). Jar burials tend to be regional as well as temporal markers, largely confined to the south. Only a few jar burial cemeteries contain Mumun jars; most of the burial urns are in Iron Age pottery styles. The two dolmen styles have been called *northern* and *southern*, the former being a true dolmen with a large heavy flat stone raised on four tall supporting slabs, and the latter often being any unworked boulder placed on a pile of cobbles over a grave. While partly regional, there is considerable overlap. It is generally thought that the northern style is earlier. Southern dolmens always cover a burial, and are often found grouped by the hundreds in enormous graveyards. Northern-style dolmens are frequently found alone, and may have been territorial markers more than burial monuments. At Simch'ol-li (Kim JH 1978b), many cobbles are found not just under each individual dolmen, but spread over the entire burial area. Stone cairns may be a development from this, without the dolmen capstone. Pit tombs tend to be associated with cairns.

Dolmens are known from several dozen of the more than 400 inhabited islands off the south and west coasts (Im 1966; Kim WY and Im HJ 1966, 1968). Few of these have been excavated, so details of these sites are unknown. It is evident, however, that most of the habitable space was being occupied, and that population had increased significantly since Chulmun times.

Lone-standing stones of the menhir type are infrequently found in Korea also. Many crudely carved standing Buddhas, called *miruks,* may have been transformed from menhirs with the advent of Buddhism. Most standing stones have local legends, and figure in shamanistic rituals.

Skeletal remains are exceedingly rare in Korean sites, so that little is known about the physical characteristics of the population. Stone cists range from 1.5 to 2 m in length, and are usually less than a meter wide. Multiple burials in the same cist are not known, but in a few cases the same lid or low dolmen may have been intended to cover two graves.

Bronze Artifacts

Bronze artifacts range from weapons, including daggers, spearheads, and halberds, to mirrors, bells, belt hooks, and horse trappings. Although practically all known bronzes are probably from tombs, most were looted, so the exact provenience is unknown. Tomb robbing is unhappily a lucrative pastime, and the artifacts more often find their way into the hands of collectors than into museums. Of those with known provenience, bronze artifacts are more commonly found in burials than in dwellings. If it can be surmised that most of the items of unknown provenience have actually been found in graves, the percentage of bronze in graves becomes even more striking.

Bronze items found in contexts other than tombs have all been found in the north so far. A bronze button was found on a house floor in Sinhungdong, Hwanghae, and bronze implements associated with house floors were found at Kumtal-li near P'yongyang (Kim JH 1978b). Other bronze items found in locations other than burials include buttons, axes, bells, arrowheads, and a ring-handled knife. Weapons are noticeably absent from this list, and utilitarian items are uncommon in any context.

Weapons of various kinds are the most common bronze artifacts. Bronze daggers, *ko* halberds, socketed spearheads, and arrowheads have been widely found. Mirrors with geometric decoration, bells in a variety of forms, horse trappings, and carriage fixings are also found throughout Korea. Bronze knives and axes are less common, and least frequent of all are implements for daily use. Bronze molds have been found in Korea, and two types of dagger as well as the geometric-pattern mirror are specifically Korean designs showing that manufacture of bronze was local, not brought in by trade. The use of bronze seems to have been almost entirely restricted to weapons and ornaments for an elite group, and the majority of bronze artifacts probably went to the grave with their owners.

Subsistence

The existence of true agriculture in the Korean Bronze Age was never in any doubt, but the finding of rice (*Oryza sativa*) in a site ^{14}C dated to the thirteenth century B.C. did come as a surprise. The Hunam-ni site, excavated by a crew from Seoul National University under the direction of Im Hyo-Jai, is an excellent example of the state-of-the-art techniques in use in Korea (Kim *et al.* 1973, 1974, 1976, 1978). Fourteen houses were excavated on the slope of a hill above the South Han River. They were not all contemporary, for some were cut into others, but they all contained Mumun pottery and are dated to the Bronze Age. All the dwellings were rectangular and less than 10 m in the longest direction. Several had white plaster floors, others hardened clay. The locations of all artifacts were plotted, and activity areas defined, with storage pits and large pots in the southwest and polished stone tools in the northeast. Water flotation of the contents of five vessels and eight other samples produced carbonized rice (*Oryza sativa L.*), barley (*Hordeum sativa, J.*), sorghum (*Andropogon sorghum B.*), and foxtail millet (*Setaria italica B.*) (Kim *et al.* 1978). Identical samples of rice and barley were sent to laboratories in Korea and Japan for ^{14}C dating (Im Hyo-Jai, personal communication, 1978), with the following results:

Sample 1, from Vessel 3, House 12, west side.
Korean: 3210 ± 70 B.P. (1560 B.C.)
Japanese: 2920 ± 70 B.P. (1205 B.C.)

Sample 2, from Vessel 2, House 12, west side.
Korean: 2620 ± 100 B.P. (855 B.C.)
Japanese: 2900 ± 70 B.P. (1295 B.C.)

It is evident that more confidence can be placed in the Japanese dating process. These dates, recalibrated, show mixed farming with an emphasis on rice, somewhat before the end of China's Shang Dynasty and the legendary arrival of Kija. A comparison of rice grain average sizes from Hunam-ni, Puyo, and Kyongju show a progressively increasing size from north to south (Kim *et al.* 1978:Table 2), which may reflect time as well as regional differences.

Reports of agricultural products from the north do not include rice. At Hogok-dong on the Tuman River, millet flour was found in several locations, and red beans and soybeans have also been reported (Kim JB 1974:20). Ho, who has researched the Chinese written works for references to agricultural products, reports that "in the works of the fourth and third centuries B.C., soybean and millet were regarded as the most important food crops in north China" (Ho 1975:78). This suggests a linkage of northern Korea with northern China, and southern Chinese influences affecting southern Korea.

Temporal Sequences

Various artifacts have been sequenced on the basis of their stylistic development, such as daggers, mirrors, and pottery. These styles have then been used to date sites to some extent, but no overall divisions of the Bronze Age have yet been entirely successful.

Bronze daggers are a case in point. The blades vary from very wide blades with bracket-shaped points in the center of the long sides, through gradually more slender forms, to a straight-sided grooved dagger. The wide daggers are variously called Liaoning daggers, after their first find spot at Shi-erh-tzu-ya in Liaoning, or *pipa*-shaped, referring to a Korean stringed instrument. The stylistic change from wide to slender blades has been seen as chronological (Kim JB 1975; Kim JH 1978b). Although there are insufficient ^{14}C dates associated with dagger blades to verify the sequence, it seems reasonable since only slender daggers are found in association with iron (Kim JB 1975). There is a sufficient quantity of daggers to demonstrate an entire sequence, from wide to slender, so it will be surprising if subsequent dates fail to verify the sequence. Dagger handles, which were cast separately from the blade, have also been interpreted as time markers, the "antenna" form being seen as late.

A stylistic sequence of the geometric-design mirrors also seems to be secure on the basis of associations. The earliest mirrors are rather crudely done, with hatched zigzag patterns. Later mirrors have increasingly fine-lined and more detailed decoration, without straying from the straight-line geometric designs that are so characteristic of the Korean Bronze Age (Kim WY 1977b).

Estimated dates have been based to some extent on supposed relationships with bronze artifacts in other areas. Nothing remotely resembling the ceremonial bronze vessels of Shang China has ever been found in Korea, but the curved knife with ring handle and the broad-bladed axe have been seen as derived from Shang forms. However, most of the bronze artifacts have clearer relationships to Manchuria and ultimately perhaps to Scytho–Siberian prototypes than they have to China. I will return to these relationships later.

The accumulating ^{14}C dates require a new approach to the chronology of the Bronze Age. The oldest group of dates is in the southeast (Table 3.3), and ranges around 2000 B.C. Central Korean dates range from the thirteenth to the fourth centuries B.C., and the smaller number of dates from outside this region also fit into this range. Bronze artifacts associated with dated sites are too varied yet to verify stylistic chronologies, but it is interesting to note that a bronze mirror with geometric design was dated to 810 B.C. (Taegong-ni, South Cholla), and a pottery mold for casting bronze dates to 985 B.C. (Yanggun-ni, Kyonggi), suggesting the contemporaneity of bronze and stone daggers, as several Korean archaeologists have inferred on other grounds (Kim JB 1975). The earliest dated rice is from central Korea, dated to the thirteenth century B.C. (Hunam-ni).

In terms of the twin questions of the source of the Korean Bronze Age and whether all the elements (rice agriculture, bronze, Mumun pottery, polished stone implements) arrived together, these dates pose new questions rather than offering solutions. The southeastern coast, which has the oldest dates for Mumun, is the least likely point of contact for bronze, and an unlikely contact point for rice. Southern dolmens have always been presumed to be later than the Northern style, and the diffusion has been seen as occurring from northwest to southeast, ending in Japan with the Yayoi. It seems that early Mumun pottery in this region precedes some of the other elements. West central Korea, which has several sites with pottery which might be said to be transitional between Chŭlmun and Mumun (Sinam-ni, Misong-ni, and Kyodong, for instance) is a reasonable area for contact from Shang China, because the distance from the Shantung peninsula is least in that region, and the technology to cross the Yellow Sea was certainly present. There are too few reported dates from the north to make any useful generalizations at this point. The official North Korean dating for the Bronze Age, however, begins "from the first half of the second millennium B.C." (FLPH 1977:6), which would suggest contemporaneity with the Pusan area sites.

Dating the beginning of the Korean Bronze Age to around 2000 B.C. is not impossible in the light of the Soviet Maritime Region dates. Okladnikov has reported a date of 4150 ± 60 B.P. (2850 B.C.) (LE–177) from Bronze Age pit houses at Kirovsko in the Soviet Maritime Region (Chard 1962:85; 1974). Another supporting date called "terminal Neolithic or Early Bronze Age" (Chard 1962:85) from Pukhusun Bay in the Maritime Territory is 4250 ± 60 B.P. (2970 B.C.) (LE–193).

In terms of relationships with China, plastered floors, the stepped adze, perforated stone disks, the crescent reaping knife, and *ko* halberds are seen as related to central China, although these can be found in Manchuria as well. The *ko*, according to Cheng (1973:207), was the "only military weapon in the Neolithic," and "the most conspicuous and common armament in metal in Shang and Chou times." Probably bronze daggers are the most common weapon in Korea, and they seem to have developed indigenously, if the Liaotung area can be seen as culturally related to the Korean peninsula in the Bronze Age (Lattimore 1932; Lee 1979; Kim JH 1978a). The polished stone dagger appears to be a local Korean development as well. Socketed bronze spearheads that appear in Korea are related to a fifth century B.C. Chinese type (Kim WY 1978), but socketed spearheads are found in Siberia in the Andronovo Period, 1500–1200 B.C. (Okladnikov 1964:43).

Despite these similarities, striking differences also can be found. Most conspicuous is the difference in vessels. No Bronze Age bronze vessels have been found in Korea, in contrast to the richness of Shang and Chou bronze vessel finds. Furthermore, no tripods, which are conspicuous in Chinese ceramic assemblages as far back as the Yangshao, occur in Korean sites. Tripod pottery vessels have been found in Liaoning and Kirin (Rudolph 1978:62), so it is particularly curious that such forms did not diffuse to Korea. Even at Shang-ma-shih off the Liaotung Peninsula, Chulmun-type sherds are overlain by a Lungshanoid layer with black tripod vessels (Arimitsu 1962). Cha-pi-ku, however, in the same vicinity, contained vessels shaped like those at Misong-ni (Okladnikov 1965).

Stone cist graves seem to link the Korean Bronze Age more closely with Siberia and Manchuria than with China. Watson refers to these as "slab graves," and believes they did not occur in Korea (Watson 1971:128). The major difference is that many of the northern slab graves project above the ground, whereas Korean stone cist graves are usually below dolmens. Otherwise the descriptions are identical. Similar artifacts in both further indicate the relationship. In the slab graves nearest Korea, the pottery is similar to Mumun in shape and temper, and associated stone tools are also similar in both kind and shape. Pig bones are very conspicuously associated with these graves as well (e.g., Hsi-t'uan Hill, Kirin, where the pottery shapes are identical to those at Misong-ni [Rudolph 1978:153]). Although few Korean sites have preserved bones where fauna can be identified, pigs are prominent, beginning with the Neolithic and increasing in the Bronze Age (Kim SK 1974), which suggests similarity in subsistence as well.

It is difficult to discuss the source of the Korean bronze usage, because the interrelationships of bronze metallurgy in China, Siberia, and the Soviet Maritime Region are not well known. Ho (1975) believes that Karasuk bronze culture of the Lake Baikal region comes from European Russia from the Seima culture (1600–1300 B.C.), but that Shang China also influenced Karasuk (1300–1000 B.C.). The Karasuk culture, however (if these dates hold), is too late to have influenced the Korean Bronze Age in its earliest forms. The occurrence of bronze around 2000 B.C. in the Soviet Maritime Region is also a puzzle. Chang (1977:275) reports that in China, "bronze metallurgy was already well started by 1850 B.C."

Bronze objects found in Korea are all of the type that could be made in simple two-piece molds, and in fact the molds found have been of this type. Perhaps this speaks of wide diffusion of relatively simple bronze techniques in the late third millennium B.C., throughout northeast Asia.

Copper sources are widespread, but tin is less easily found. The Soviet Maritime Region and parts of Korea, however, are in one of the Asian tin belts (de Jesus 1977). Chemical analyses of Korean bronze indicate a high zinc content, which is unlike the Chinese bronzes (Chon 1976). Although the number of bronzes analyzed so far is small, the results are consistent. However, recent analyses of very early Chinese bronzes also suggest a high zinc content (Chang 1980a:36). The import of this for Korean bronzes is not yet clear.

Most of the Bronze Age Korean artifact types are found in both Shang China and eastern Siberia. The geometric bronze mirror is found in the Shang (Chang 1977:372), but Kim Jong-hak (1978b:174) derives the Korean geometric mirrors from Siberian bronze buttons. The *ko* halberd began as a Shang weapon (Chang 1977:371). It does appear in Liaoning, in both Hsia-chia-tien Upper culture sites and with Liaotung daggers, in spite of the fact that not a single *ko* is listed beyond Pohai Bay in Barnard and Sato's (1975) extensive search. Furthermore, they indicate the earliest bronze anywhere near Korea in the Late Western Chou (Barnard and Sato 1975:Map 1b), and not until the Warring States period do any significant number of bronzes appear (Barnard and Sato 1975:Map 1d).

Bronze bells are reported from Shang China (Hirth 1911:71), and Eastern Siberia (Okladnikov 1964:73), but again none have been found in Manchuria (Barnard and Sato 1975:137). The bronze dagger, the most typical of Korean bronze artifacts, is not known in the Shang (Kim JB 1975), and in any case appears to be an indigenous invention, if the Liaotung area can be included with

Korea in the second millennium B.C.—for which there is documentary Chinese evidence as well as Korean tradition.

Kim Jong-hak (1978a) has recently refined his chronology based on artifact changes. He dates the Korean Bronze Age from around the eighth to ninth centuries B.C. to A.D. 1, on the basis of these relationships.

Lee (1979) has compared sites in Liaoning containing the broad-bladed Liaoning dagger to sites of the Upper Hsia-chia-tien culture. The distribution of sites overlaps only slightly, with both "cultures" present at Namsan-gun. Major differences include sword handle shapes, sword blade shapes, knife shapes, and most telling of all, trappings for riding horses in the Liaoning culture, and decorations for carriage horses and carriages in the Upper Hsia-chia-tien (Lee 1979:65).

The lower Hsia-chia-tien culture has ^{14}C dates of 2410 ± 140 B.C., 1890 ± 130 B.C., and 1690 ± 160 B.C. (Chang 1980b:294). Copper artifacts were found in these sites. Shang "inroads" were made into this territory (Chang 1980b:310), so perhaps strong Chou influence can be assumed by the time of the Upper Hsia-chia-tien. A Liaoning date calibrated to 850 ± 160 B.C. (Chang 1980b:372) fits in with the assumption that the Liaoning bronze dagger is contemporaneous with the Upper Hsia-chia-tien culture.

The roots of the Korean Bronze Age are clearly complex, and a single source for all the elements is not tenable. The derivation of various traits, and the precise order in which they were accepted in various parts of Korea, will be vital information in understanding the development of the state in Korea.

IRON AGE

The dating of the beginning of the Iron Age in Korea is also still uncertain. The Iron Age corresponds approximately to protohistoric times; by the Warring States period, when iron was in use throughout Korea, the Chinese were chronicling events in the north in some detail. The peninsular territory became ever more important in guarding China's northeastern flank, and the ever-widening influence of China's economy impinged more and more directly on Korea (Yu 1967). In 108 B.C., most of Korea north of the Han River became commanderies under Han Chinese control. With expanding and contracting boundaries, the Chinese rule lasted more than 400 years. Because of this connection, Chinese interest in the Korean region was heightened, although Korea, as Chao-hsien (Choson), and the Tong-I (Eastern Barbarians) had appeared in earlier Chinese works. Scattered "ethnographic" information of various kinds, including customs, language, dress, and folklore, are found in Chinese writings with reference to various Korean "tribes."

Discussions of the protohistoric period of Korea can be therefore divided into three classes: (1) those relying on exegesis of written records alone, (2) those attempting to relate archaeological finds to written materials, and (3) purely archaeological problems, such as the beginning of iron production or the direction of diffusion of particular traits.

Although I do not consider the written sources here in any detail, because there are too many thorny problems to discuss in this space (for an interesting discussion, see Kim JB 1975), some basic information contained in the writings is generally accepted, and can serve as a basis for understanding the archaeology. Sites mentioned in the text can be located in Figure 3.10.

Written Documents

In the south were the Han tribes (a different Chinese character from "Han" China), divided into three named groups: the Mahan in the west, the Pyonhan in the lower Naktong River area, and the Chinhan in the east. These later developed into the historic states of Paekche, Kaya, and Silla respectively. Each Han group was composed of a number of federated villages, of which Mahan was the largest, containing more villages than the other two combined. Along the narrow eastern coastal strip lived the Ye-maek tribe, and farther north by the Tumen River, the Okcho. The northwest was the territory of Choson, which under pressure from its western neighbors had already developed into a state. The Lolang Commandery took over the territory of Choson by defeating its armies, which put up a stiff resistance. Other tribes, or perhaps states (e.g., Puyo and Koguryo) considered to be of Korean language and culture, occupied areas to the north of present-day Korea. Several sources covering this period are available in English. Sohn *et al.* (1970), Choi (1971), Joe (1972), Han (1970), and Henthorn (1971) all touch on this time period with varying interpretations. Only Gardiner (1969) is both thoroughly documented and specifically focused on this time period, but the other histories, especially those by Koreans, add different dimensions in their interpretations of prehistory and protohistory.

The Archaeological "Cultures"

Archaeologically, the Iron Age is marked by pit burials and jar burials, the appearance of iron tools and weapons, and a new type of pottery called Kimhae, which is harder and better fired than the utility ware of Mumun. Some of these characteristics were retained long into the historic period, so that the sites that are definitively called Three Kingdoms are tombs, fortresses, and palaces. Without ^{14}C dates, it is often difficult to place other sites. However, few sites other than burials are known from the Iron Age. Almost nothing about daily life is known directly from excavations.

In fact, protohistoric sites are surprisingly few in number. In the southeast, several shell mounds have been found to date to this age, the "Able Site" in Kapyong in central Korea, a dwelling site uncovered secondarily to digging foxholes (MacCord 1958), a dwelling site in the far north at Musan, near Korea's largest iron mines, and some scattered pit burials covered by cairns.

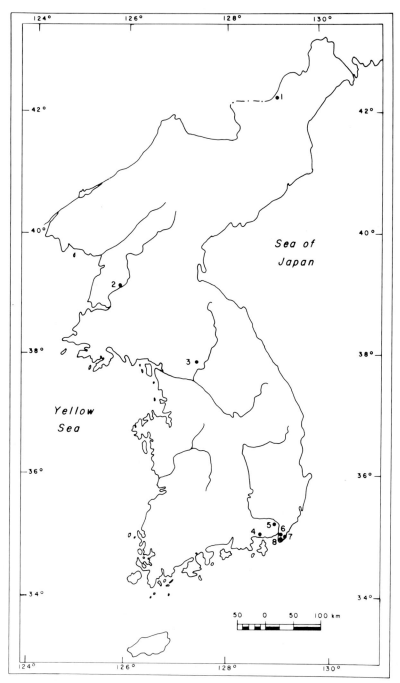

Figure 3.10 Iron Age sites in Korea mentioned in the text: (1) Musan; (2) O-dong, P'yongyang (site of Lolang capital); (3) Kap'yong; (4) Masan; (5) Yean-ni; (6) Kosong; (7) Koijong; and (8) Cho Do.

A common find in the northwest, from the Yalu River to the Taedong, is *myŏngdo* coins, or "knife money," minted in the northeastern Chinese state of Yen (Yang 1952:15). Yen is first mentioned in the late sixth century B.C. and was conquered in 222 B.C., which serves to give some time dimension to the sites at which the Yen coins were found. Yen trade with its "neighboring barbarians" was recorded by Ssu-ma Chien (Watson 1961:487). Coins from later Chinese states have been found elsewhere in Korea, but not in great numbers. In any case, there is no question that by the Iron Age, Korea was well within the sphere of Chinese merchants.

Apparently the *ondŏl* floor, a method of heating which is universal in traditional Korean houses, began in the Iron Age. Heat from the cooking stove is led through passages under the house, and ultimately released through a chimney on the other side. Han (1971:Fig. 1) includes a photograph of an excavated *ondŏl* floor, from North Hamgyong province. Wooden houses could now be constructed with the new iron tools, but being built at ground level rather than partly underground, more efficient heating was needed. Okladnikov (1964) mentions two excavations in Siberia where *ondŏl* floors have been uncovered. The semisubterranean house lasted longer in Mahan territory, according to Chinese writings.

Lolang

Archaeology of the Chinese commanderies, especially that of Lolang with its capital at the present site of Pyongyang, began with excavations of spectacular tombs of Chinese nobles by the Japanese in the earlier part of this century. These tombs revealed much about the splendor indulged in by the colonial Chinese, but little about the indigenous population. Most of the tomb furnishings were imported from China, including bronze mirrors and weapons, horse and chariot fittings, jade ceremonial objects, lacquerware from Szechuan, and even scraps of fabric from Szechuan or Shangtung (Gardiner 1969:18). One inscribed lacquer bowl contains the names of twelve artisans and supervisors who were responsible for its production—a fascinating insight into the manufacture of goods for the nobility (Umehara 1926). Paintings on tomb walls show the clothing and some activities of the nobility. The capital city itself has been partially excavated, revealing a walled city with paved streets and a drainage system (Joe 1972:32).

One tomb, according to a silver seal found inside it, was the burial of a native Korean official, Pujo Yegun. He was given a typical Chinese burial, with bronze and iron weapons, horse and chariot equipment, and ceramic vessels. Pujo seems to be the name of a city, identified with Hamhung in South Hamgyong Province. *Yegun* was a title given to the heads of smaller countries. Therefore, Kim Jong-hak identifies the seal as given to the head of the Ye tribe, before the time of the Han commanderies (Kim JH 1978b:143).

Another Korean official was buried, with his wife, 100 m to the east of Pujo Yegun. There are two silver seals, with the inscription "Pujo Chang." *Chang* was a title given to rulers of territory containing less than 10,000 houses (Kim JH 1978b:143). A black lacquered canopy pole contains an inscription dating the tomb to A.D. 14. Although the same kinds of artifacts are found in the Korean graves as in those of Chinese nobles, they are local Korean products, including the Korean slender bronze dagger, rather than imported Chinese items. The reason these Koreans were buried in the Chinese capital is unknown, but presumably they were sinicized enough to require a Chinese type of burial. Recently, some Koreans have questioned whether the Japanese interpretations, made earlier in this century, of the finds in the vicinity of P'yongyang, are entirely appropriate. One opinion seems to be that there was no Chinese commandery at Lolang (Yi and Chan 1975a,b,c, as explained in Pearson 1978). This is too extreme to be seriously considered, because the contemporary Chinese documents are too explicit and detailed to have been made up out of whole cloth. A more reasonable position is that of Kim JB (1978a,b), who believes that the pit tombs of the Lolang region are actually pre-Lolang, probably graves from Wiman's Choson, about which there is also much detail in Chinese documents. Other evidence that these are pre-Lolang includes the weapons with inscriptions dating them to 221 B.C. (Kim JB 1978a:43), more than 100 years before the Han conquests, and coins minted in 136 B.C. (Kayamoto 1962:117). The pit graves include horse and chariot trappings, and slender daggers of indigenous Korean style, which would be compatible with a state composed of both native Koreans and Koreanized, exiled Chinese.

Southern Korea

More mundane archaeology of this period has been taking place in the south. A shell mound on Chodo island, near Pusan, has produced hard reddish Kimhae pottery which is said to be "identical in paste, color, and shape" to Early Yayoi (Kim WY 1974). It was associated with Mumun pottery and a simple polished stone dagger. This has led Han Byong-sam (1974) to propose the date of 300 B.C. for the beginning of this stage. In the middle layer of the site an extended burial was found, with a necklace of tubular green beads and an iron dagger. The uppermost level contained early Three Kingdoms artifacts.

Kosong, another shell mound in the same region, produced iron blooms demonstrating iron production, along with stone knives, bronze spearheads and daggers, a bronze mirror of Han (Chinese) type, and carbonized grains. Stone cists were found nearby; and iron daggers were collected from the surface (Kim WY 1975a).

A fortified settlement associated with a shell mound was excavated near Masan on the south coast. The hilltop settlement was surrounded by a stone wall. The slope below had been used for iron smelting, apparently earlier than the settlement for it was surmounted by 2–3 m of shell deposits. Artifacts in the shell layer included both iron and bronze implements as well as stone and bone, and much pottery. A Han Chinese bronze coin helped date the site.

A number of pit burials also produced new information. At Yean-ni, Kimhae, pit burials in the subsoil beneath later stone tombs had hard grey pottery, transitional from the red Kimhae to late Silla pottery (Kim JH 1977). Also in southeastern Korea, 28 burials in small stone-lined pits were uncovered at Oryun-dae. Burial goods, poor in quantity and quality, included early Silla-type pottery, an iron arrowhead, an ax, and a sword (Kim JH and Chung CW 1973).

Some newly discovered jar burial cemeteries have also been excavated. Twelve such jar burials were found close to the earliest extended burials at Yean-ni. Five had skeletal remains of infants. Many, but not all, jar burials seem to be infants or children (Kim WY 1964). At Koijong, Pusan, five jar burials were excavated, of which two were attached to stone-lined tombs (Chung 1977). Many jars have no grave goods at all, but some have bronze and iron objects, and even glass beads.

The custom of jar burial lasted into the historic period in southwestern Korea (Kim WY 1964). The origin of this custom is unknown. Jar burials are rare in the north, and are apparently from Lolang times, directly related to the Chinese custom (Kim JB 1975). Jar burials are reported by Okladnikov in the Soviet Far East (Okladnikov 1964:87; 1965:157) and in a site on the Liaotung peninsula (Okladnikov 1965:148). The custom was transferred to Kyushu in the Yayoi period, with cemeteries similar to those in southern Korea (Kaneko 1966).

Dating

The date for the beginning of the Iron Age is still in dispute. North Koreans estimate the seventh century B.C., on the basis of the Musan finds, which include iron tools as well as iron weapons. One radiocarbon date from a dwelling at this site is 2430 B.P. (480 B.C.). Kim Jong-bae (1975) agrees with this early date, and suggests that iron working may have come originally from eastern Manchuria and the Soviet Maritime Region rather than directly from China. He believes the black pottery occasionally found in association with Mumun to be a mark of the Iron Age, and would include Susong-ni near Seoul, ^{14}C dated at 2340 ± 120 B.P. (440 B.C.) and 2230 ± 280 B.P. (390 B.C.) (Lee 1977; Kim WY 1966, 1967), as well as O-dong near P'yongyang and Chodo near Pusan (Kim JB 1975).

These claims are earlier than many investigators would make for China. Needham (1958:46) puts the beginning of cast iron "from the fourth century onwards at the latest," although metallic iron is mentioned as early as the sixth century B.C., and Ho (1975:83) also believes that iron implements on a significant scale did not begin before the fourth century B.C. Barnard and Sato's (1975) compendium of metal sites in China shows iron in various forms at 17 sites in Liaoning and 8 sites in the Kirin area during the Warring States period. One site had evidence of iron casting, and three included chariot parts and harness equipment. North Koreans date the Loushan tomb on the Liaotung peninsula, which contains iron objects, to the seventh to fifth centuries B.C. (FLPH 1977).

Hirth (1911), using written rather than archaeological materials, came to the conclusion that, in terms of weapons, the Iron Age began in China about 500 B.C. Before this there had been a "sporadic occurrence of iron swords, recorded as having been presented as tribute from abroad" (Hirth 1911:236). By the Han dynasty, iron had become a state monopoly in China (Gale 1931), which may partly explain the extensive evidence of iron foundries in Korea at this time. The early kings of Silla were said to belong to a blacksmith family, suggesting the power to be gained by control of iron technology (Sohn *et al.* 1970).

The date 400 B.C. is used as the approximate beginning of the Yayoi period in Japan, when a new complex of items appeared in Kyushu, including some artifacts and burial styles (Chard 1974:167) related to the Korean Bronze Age, and others related to newer developments in Korea such as jar burials and the use of iron. In any case, the Korean Iron Age must have been in full swing before the beginning of Yayoi. It does not seem unreasonable to date iron in the north a few centuries earlier.

THREE KINGDOMS

After the overthrow of the Chinese commanderies by Koguryo in the north, native Korean states flourished. Koguryo, previously centered north of the Yalu River, moved into the former Lolang territory and transferred its capital to the present P'yóngyang. The state of Paekche developed in west central Korea, originally centered near Seoul on the Han River, and later being pushed farther south to new capitals near the Kum River. Paekche had close connections with Japan, and introduced Buddhism to that area along with many arts and crafts. Silla developed from a coalition of six villages near the present Kyongju, protected by a row of hills from the east coast. The last of the three states to develop, Silla eventually became the most powerful, unifying most of the peninsula in alliance with T'ang China in A.D. 668 (Joe 1972:65). An area near the mouth of the Naktong River, called Kaya, had strong ties with Japan, and was not conquered by Silla until A.D. 562 (Joe 1972:56). Grayson (1977) has argued persuasively in favor of viewing this area as essentially Korean, however, and not Japanese.

The history of the Three Kingdoms is known from Korean sources written down at a much later date, from references in Chinese and Japanese writings, and from archaeology. The archaeological information is almost exclusively from tombs, from which magnificent gold and jewels have been extracted, especially in the Silla region (Figure 3.11). The splendor and intricacy of the gold crowns from these tombs has tended to overshadow all other Korean archaeology, and the antiquarian mentality has predominated in these excavations until recent years. A great deal is known about the kings and queens, and little about the daily lives of ordinary people.

Probably the most important group of tombs excavated in the last decade has been early Paekche tombs in and near Seoul. (Sites mentioned in the text are located in Figure 3.12). Three pyramidal tombs were excavated, in plan exactly like Koguryo tombs on the Yalu River. This lends much weight to the legends which linked the royal house of Paekche with that of Koguryo. Tomb 3 of Sokch'ondong, and a tomb at Yangp'yong, are similar. Both are constructed on a stone platform base, and the three-tiered pyramid is made from stones. The Sokch'ondong tomb is 4.6 m high, twice as large as that from Yangp'yong. Tomb 4 at Sokch'ondong had a clay core rather than a stone platform. It was 2.3 m high (Kim WY 1975a).

Other Paekche tombs excavated recently in the Seoul area have been mounded tombs. One at Karak-dong had a burnished black pot which is said to be related to both Koguryo and Lolang. A tomb at Koi-dong had a circular stone wall under the mound. The wall was 1.8 m high and 14.8 m in diameter. Inside the stone was a circle of burned postholes and some burned board, and the floor had the *ondol* stone structure for heating that is still used in Korea. A 2.7 m square shaft in the center, 2.3 m deep, contained only burned earth. Burial goods included iron implements: a plow shoe, three-tined cultivating tools, an ax, iron sickles, and spearheads. Pottery included a steamer with horn-like handles and an undecorated tall jar with long handles (Yun 1974).

Tombs at Bang'i-dong included one with a stone chamber and an entrance passage, a small stone-lined pit, and a rectangular stone chamber partitioned into two parts by a longitudinal wall. Pottery in Tomb 4 was footed, with lids, in Silla style. This was thought to be a Silla tomb until Japanese finds on Tsushima dated the pottery earlier (Oda 1977, cited in Kim WY 1978). Now it is known to be a Paekche tomb because of the date. A small tomb in Wonsong-gun, Pobch'on-ni, contained three gray pottery vessels and a celadon sheep. The sheep was "identical to a piece recovered from Tomb 7 at Xiangshan near Nan-king, dated to the fourth century A.D." (Kim WY 1974:12). The burial pit was small, rectangular, and lined with stones. Originally it had been covered with boards. One vessel is seen by Kim as related to Lolang pottery.

The most spectacular Paekche find of the decade, however, was the tomb of King Muryong and his queen in the Puyo region. This was the first unlooted Paekche burial to be professionally excavated. Muryong, the twenty-fifth King of Paekche, was buried in A.D. 526, in an arched tomb. The bricks which made up the tomb were patterned with lotus and geometric designs. The king and queen were buried in separate wooden coffins, each with a gold crown and bronze shoes. The king's casket included a bronze sword and a silver belt, while the queen's had gold and silver bracelets and beads. Five niches each contained a Chinese porcelain bowl, and a stone lion stood guard outside the burial cham-ber. Other items included inscribed slabs, coins, bronze bowls, gold earrings, gold filigree cups on curved jade ornaments, and a gold hairpin (Han 1971; Kim WY and R. Pearson 1977).

Kaya burials were unearthed at Koryong, the ancient Kaya capital. Two earth-mound tombs were generally similar in construction, with stone burial chambers including larger chambers in the center surrounded by smaller stone-lined pits.

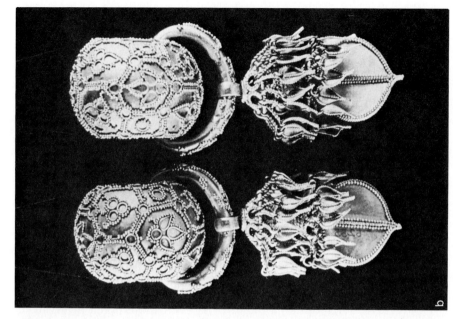

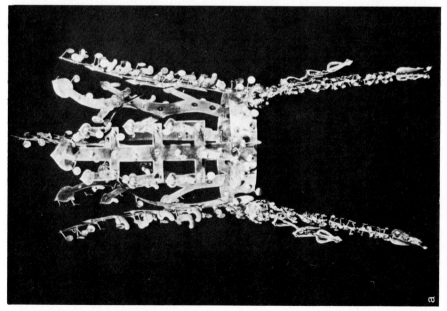

Figure 3.11 Gold artifacts from the Three Kingdoms period: (a) Silla gold crown, National Treasure No. 90; (b) Silla earrings, National Treasure No. 399; (c) Paekche gold crown ornament, King Munyong's tomb, National Treasure No. 54; and (d) Silla gold belt, National Treasure No. 88.

c

d

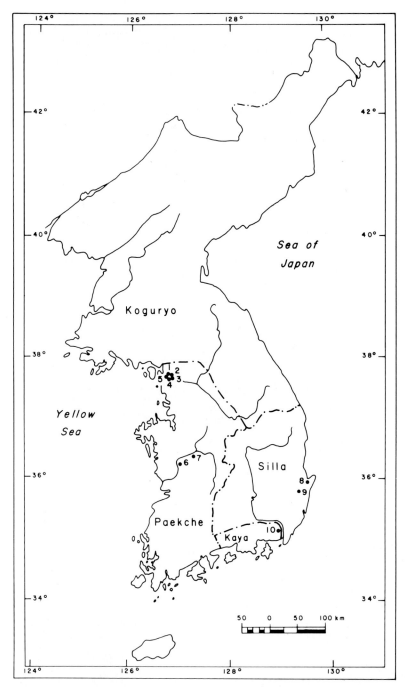

Figure 3.12 Three Kingdoms sites mentioned in the text: (1) Sokch'ong-dong, (2) Yangp'yong, (3) Karak, (4) Koi-dong, (5) Bangi-dong, (6) Tomb of King Munyong, (7) Pobchon-ni, (8) Koryong, (9) Kyongju, and (10) Chisan-dong.

Tomb 44 was 7 m high and 32 m in diameter. It contained three main burial chambers and 32 pits, some of which still had extended skeletons. One pit contained a female and a child, the others had only single skeletons. Tomb 45 had 2 main chambers and 11 pits under a smaller mound 3 m high and 23 m in diameter. The people in the smaller pits are believed to have been sacrificed slaves, as this practice is mentioned in historical documents. Tomb 44 is the largest such burial found so far in Korea (Kim WY 1978). Pit graves have been found increasingly in the Kaya region. Im HT (1978) believes them to be the earliest form of Kaya burial.

Probably over 100 Silla tombs have been excavated in the last decade. Most Silla tombs are easily recognized by their large mounds, and many in the vicinity of Kyongju are connected by folk memory to a particular person (Adams 1979). Even most of the early kings, considered by historians to be legendary, have their named mounds. The earliest excavated tombs, however, datable to the second and third centuries A.D., are small stone-lined pits, approximately 2 by 1 by 0.6 m, with no mounds. Grave goods include pots of the soft reddish ware that disappear by the time of the wooden chamber tomb. These are not lower-class burials, for gold earrings have been found in them. A tall Silla jar was also found, with three-dimensional figures on the shoulder (Kim WY 1974, 1978). Another type of early Silla burial contained up to 10 burial units within a single tomb. This has been interpreted as a family or lineage tomb (Kyung-hee University Museum 1974).

Tomb 98, in Kyongju, was a double mound with a female buried in the north part and a male in the south. The queen had a magnificent gold crown, with green curved jewels and golden heart-shaped dangles, of the typical Silla type. A small *tenmoku* bottle identified as originating in South China around A.D. 300 was the first piece of Chinese pottery discovered in a Silla tomb. Another spectacular find included a striped glass goblet probably made in Alexandria at about the same time. The south mound personage had only a gilt bronze crown and less impressive personal ornaments, although the burial was accompanied by a separate pit filled with about 2500 items, including a large number of iron weapons and pottery vessels (Kim WY and R. Pearson 1977). Two other glass vessels were also included, which probably also came from the Roman world (Kim WY 1975a, 1976). (See Chon 1976 on Korean glass.)

Tomb 155 in Kyongju was an entirely intact Silla tomb. It produced the first known Silla paintings, including an elegant white horse painted on a chariot mudguard, and a painted birchbark hat rim. This was a typical Silla tomb, with much gold interred with a single individual. The burial chamber, built of wood, was on the original ground surface rather than in an excavated pit. The chamber contained a coffin and a wooden chest (1 by 1.8 by 0.8 m) with burial gifts in it. Cobbles had been placed over the chamber and an earth mound over that (Kim WY 1974).

The supine extended body, head to the east, was wearing a gold crown, gold earrings, gold belt, gold bracelets, and gold rings on all fingers. Burial furnishings were piled in the accompanying chest in three layers. Pots and iron kettles were on the bottom with bronze vessels and decorated lacquer ware above. Four saddles and two sets of mudguards were included in the top layer (Kim WY and R. Pearson 1977).

Parts of palaces dating to United Silla, and some Buddhist temples, have also been excavated. Forts are recorded but not excavated. It is clear that a highly stratified society, with power to command builders, artisans, soldiers, and farmers, had taken its place among other world civilizations.

CONCLUSION

The progress in Korean archaeology in the 1970s has been nothing short of spectacular. New dates, associations of artifacts, and environmental material have broadened the understanding of all periods. The quantity of excavated material makes possible for the first time reasonable generalizations about subsistence and settlement patterns in Korean prehistory to be tested against future excavations.

Korean archaeology is a necessary link in deciphering the prehistory of East Asia. Although the basic temporal–spatial–morphological questions have not been answered entirely, the framework has been established and relationships with the rest of East Asia can be explored—on more than impressionistic grounds.

Finally, Korea is an interesting example of sociocultural evolution in its own right, and can now be used as an independent test of various theoretical models created on the basis of data sets in other regions of the world.

ACKNOWLEDGMENTS

I would like to thank Professors Kim Wŏn-yong, Im Hyo-jai, Sohn Pow-key, and Kim Jŏng-hak for discussing their recent research with me in March, 1978, which ultimately led to this paper, and the Institute for Shipboard Education, which made the trip to Korea possible. Thanks also to Julie Hoff who drafted the maps, to Maria Thornton who did the typing, to Helen Pustmueller and G. L. Barnhill for technical assistance, and to Greg Bowen for discussing with me his Paleolithic finds.

REFERENCES

Adams, Edward B.
    1979   *Kyongju guide: cultural spirit of Silla in Korea.* Seoul: International Tourist.
Arimitsu Kyoichi
    1962   The comb pattern pottery of Korea. *The Department of Archaeology Publication,* Vol. III.
            Kyoto University. (In Japanese with English Summary.)
Barnard, Noel, and Satō Tamotsu
    1975   *Metallurgical remains of ancient China.* Tokyo: Nichiōsha.

Bartz, Patricia M.
    1972   *South Korea: a descriptive geography*. Oxford: Oxford University Press.
Bowen, Greg
    1979   Report on stone tools from Chongok-ri. *Chintan Hakpo* **46–47**:48–55.
Chang Kwang-chih
    1977   *The archaeology of ancient China* (3rd ed.). New Haven: Yale University Press.
    1980a   The Chinese Bronze Age: a modern synthesis. In *The Great Bronze Age of China*, edited
            by Wen Fong. New York: Alfred A. Knopf. Pp. 35–50.
    1980b   *Shang civilization*. New Haven: Yale University Press.
Chard, Chester S.
    1960   Neolithic archaeology in North Korea. *Asian Perspectives* **4**:151–155.
    1962   First radiocarbon dates from the U.S.S.R. *Arctic Anthropology* **1**:84–86.
    1974   *Northeast Asia in prehistory*. Madison: The University of Wisconsin Press.
Chase, David W.
    1960   A limited archaeological survey of the Han River Valley in central Korea. *Asian Perspec-
            tives* **4**:141–149.
Cheng Te-kun
    1967   *Archaeological studies in Szechwan*. Cambridge: Cambridge University Press.
    1973   The beginning of Chinese civilization. *Antiquity* **42**:197–209.
Choi Hochin
    1971   *The economic history of Korea*. Seoul: The Freedom Library.
Choi Mong-young
    1978   Archaeological report of Songam-dong house site excavation, Kwang ju. *University of
            Korea Archaeological Studies*, No. 4. Pp. 53–73. (In Korean.)
Chŏn Sang-woon
    1976   Chemical technology in ancient Korea. *Korea Journal* **16**(11):34–40.
Chung Jing-won
    1977   Jar-burials at Koijong-dong, Pusan. *Kogohak*, No. 4:36–74. (In Korean.)
Clark, R. M.
    1975   A calibration curve for radiocarbon dates. *Antiquity* **49**(196):251–266.
de Jesus, Prentiss S.
    1977   Considerations of the occurrence and exploitation of tin sources in the ancient Near
            East. In *The search for ancient tin*, edited by A. D. Franklin, J. S. Olin, and T. A. Wertime.
            Washington, D.C.: Smithsonian Institution. Pp. 33–38.
Derevianko, A. P.
    1978   The problem of the Lower Paleolithic in the south of the Soviet Far East. In *Early
            Paleolithic in South and East Asia*, edited by F. Ikawa-Smith. The Hague: Mouton. Pp.
            303–315.
FLPH (Foreign Languages Publishing House)
    1977   *The outline of Korean history (until August 1945)*. Pyongyang, Korea.
Gale, Esson M.
    1931   Discourses on salt and iron: a debate on state control of commerce and industry in
            ancient China. *Sinica Leidensis*, Vol. II. Leyden.
Gardiner, K. J. H.
    1969   *The early history of Korea*. Honolulu: University of Hawaii Press.
Grayson, James H.
    1977   Mimana, a problem in Korean historiography. *Korea Journal* **7**(8):65–68.
Han Byŏng-sam
    1971   *Treasures from the tomb of King Muryong (r. 501–523) of the Paekche Dynasty*. Seoul: Na-
            tional Museum of Korea. (In Korean.)
    1974   Neolithic culture of Korea. *Korea Journal* **14**(4):12–17.
Han Young-hee
    1978   The neolithic culture of central-western Korea. *Hanguk Kogo Hakbo (Journal of Korean
            Archaeological Studies)*, No. 5:17–108. (In Korean.)

Han Woo-keun
    1970   *The history of Korea,* translated by Lee Kyung-shik. Seoul: Eul-yoo.
Harlan, Jack R.
    1967   A wild wheat harvest in Turkey. *Archaeology* **20**:197–201.
Henthorn, William E.
    1966   Recent archaeological activity in North Korea (I): The cave at Misong-ni. *Asian Perspectives* **9**:73–78.
    1968   Recent archaeological activity in North Korea (II): The shellmound at Sopohang. *Asian Perspectives* **11**:1–18.
    1971   *A history of Korea.* New York: The Free Press.
Ho Ping-ti
    1975   *The cradle of the East.* Chicago: The University of Chicago Press.
Hewes, Gordon
    1947   Archaeology of Korea: a selected bibliography. *Research Monographs on Korea,* Series F, No. 1. Ann Arbor, Michigan.
Hirth, Friedrich
    1911   *Ancient history of China to the end of the Chou Dynasty.* New York: Columbia University Press.
Ikawa-Smith, Fumiko
    1978   Introduction: The Early Paleolithic Tradition of East Asia. In *Early Paleolithic in South and East Asia,* edited by F. Ikawa-Smith. The Hague: Mouton. Pp. 1–10.
    1980   Current issues in Japanese archaeology. *American Scientist* **68**:134–145.
Im Hyo-jai
    1966   Dolmens in Kicha Island. *Korean Archaeology* **1**:5–18. (In Korean.)
    1968   The pottery with raised decoration found from Sŏsaeng-myon, Tongnae, near Pusan. *Kogohak* **1**:115–125. (In Korean.)
    1977   Similarities and differences among Neolithic Cultures of central Korea. *Hanguk Kogo Hakbo, (Journal of Korean Archaeological Studies),* No. 2. Pp. 19–39. (In Korean.)
Im Hyo-taek
    1978   A study on the pit grave of the Kaya on the lower Nakdong River. *Hanguk Kogo Hakbo, (Journal of Korean Archaeological Studies),* No. 4:75–120. (In Korean.)
Joe, Wanne J.
    1972   *Traditional Korea: a cultural history.* Seoul: Chung'ang University Press.
Kaneko, Erika
    1966   A review of Yayoi Period burial practices. *Asian Perspectives* **9**:1–26.
Kayamoto Togin
    1962   Han tombs of Lolang: their study by Japanese scholars. *Memoirs of the Research Department of the Toyo Bunko,* 21. Tokyo. (In Japanese with English summary.)
Kent, Kate P., and Sarah M. Nelson
    1976   Net sinkers or weft weights? *Current Archaeology* **17**(1):152.
Kim Chŏng-ki
    1968   Study on the dwelling sites in prehistoric Korea. *Kogohak,* No. 1:31–60. (In Korean.)
    1976   Dwelling sites from the Geometric Period, Korea. *Asian Perspectives* **18**(2):185–203.
Kim Jŏng-bae
    1974   Bronze Age culture in Korea. *Korea Journal* **14**(4):18–24.
    1975   Bronze artifacts in Korea and their cultural-historical significance. In *The traditional culture and society of Korea: prehistory,* edited by R. J. Pearson. Honolulu: The Center for Korean Studies, University of Hawaii. Pp. 130–191.
    1978a   The question of horse-riding people in Korea (I). *Korea Journal* **18**(9):39–50.
    1978b   The question of horse-riding people in Korea (II). *Korea Journal* **18**(11):41–52.
Kim Jŏng-hak
    1968   A study of geometric pattern pottery culture in Korea. *The Paek-San Hakbo,* No. 4. Pp. 1–100. (In Korean with English summary pp. 244–249.)

1977   Preliminary report on ancient tombs at Yean-ni. *Hanguk Kogo Hakbo (Journal of Korean Archaeological Studies)*, No. 2:7–18. (In Korean.)
1978a   The chronology of Bronze culture in Korea. *Hanguk Kogo Hakbo (Journal of Korean Archaeological Studies)*, No. 5:1–15. (In Korean.)
1978b   *The prehistory of Korea*. Honolulu: The University of Hawaii Press.
Kim Jŏng-hak and Chung Ching-won
1973   *Report of excavation of tombs at Oryundai*. Pusan: University Museum.
Kim Shin-kyu
1974   The mammal phase in primitive sites in our country (2), *Chosen Gakujutsu Tsuho* **9**(2):44–63. (In Japanese.)
Kim Wŏn-yong
1964   A jar-coffin cemetery at Shinch'angri, Southwestern Korea. *Seoul National University, Archaeological and Anthropological Papers*, No. 1, Seoul. (In Korean.)
1966   Excavation of a prehistoric dwelling site at Susongni near Seoul. *Misul Chanyo*. (In Korean.)
1967   A black pottery pot from Susokni. *Korean Archaeology*, No. 1. Seoul: Seoul National University. Pp. 1–4. (In Korean.)
1969   Carbon dates in Korean archaeology. *Kogohak*, No. 2:1–16. (In Korean.)
1974   *Archaeology in Korea 1973* (Vol. 1). The University Museum, Seoul National University.
1975a   *Archaeology in Korea 1974* (Vol. 2). The University Museum, Seoul National University.
1975b   The Neolithic culture of Korea. In *The traditional culture and society of Korea: prehistory*, edited by R. J. Pearson. Honolulu: The Center for Korean Studies, The University of Hawaii. Pp. 61–111.
1976   *Archaeology in Korea 1975* (Vol. 3). The University Museum, Seoul National University.
1977a   *Archaeology in Korea 1976* (Vol. 4). The University Museum, Seoul National University.
1977b   *Introduction to Korean archaeology* (2nd ed.). Seoul: Il Chi Sa. (In Korean.)
1978   *Archaeology in Korea 1977* (Vol. 5). The University Museum, Seoul National University.
Kim Wŏn-yong and Chung Young-hwa
1979   Note préliminaire sur l'industrie acheuléenne de Chongokni en Corée. *Chintan Hakpo* **46–47**:25–47.
Kim Wŏn-yong and Im Hyo-jai
1968   *Archaeological reconnaissance in the southern islands, Korea*. Seoul National University. (In Korean with English summary.)
Kim Wŏn-yong, Im Hyo-jai, Choi Mong-lyong, Yeo Jung-chool, and Kwak Sung-hun
1973   The Hunamri site—a prehistoric village site on the Han River: progress reports 1972–1973. *Archaeological and Anthropological Papers of Seoul National University* (Vol. 4). (In Korean with English summary.)
1974   The Hunamri site—a prehistoric village site on the Han River: progress reports 1974. *Archaeological and Anthropological Papers of Seoul National University* (Vol. 5). (In Korean with English summary.)
1976   The Hunamri site—a prehistoric village site on the Han River: progress reports 1975. *Archaeological and Anthropological Papers of Seoul National University* (Vol. 7). (In Korean with English summary.)
1978   The Hunamri site—a prehistoric village site on the Han River: progress reports 1976, 1977. *Archaeological and Anthropological Papers of Seoul National University* (Vol. 8). (In Korean with English abstract.)
Kim Wŏn-yong and Richard Pearson
1977   Three royal tombs: new discoveries in Korean archaeology. *Archaeology* **30**(5):302–313.
Kim Yang-sun and Lim Byung-tae
1968   Yoksamdong dwelling site excavation report. *Hanguk Sa Yongu (The Journal of Korean History)*, No. 20:1–51. (In Korean with English summary pp. 443–444.)
Kyung-hee University Museum
1974   Report of Tombs 19, 20 at Inwang-dong, Kyongju. *Kyung-hee University Museum Publication*, 1, Seoul. (In Korean.)

Lattimore, Owen
    1932   *Manchuria: cradle of conflict.* New York: Macmillan.
Lee Kang-sŭng
    1979   A study on Bronze Culture in Liaoming Bronze-dagger Culture and the Hsia-chia-tien
            Upper Culture through bronze artifacts. *Hangok Kogo Hakbo (Journal of Korean Archae-
            ological Studies,* No. 6:1–95. (In Korean.)
Lee Yung-jo
    1977   A new interpretation of the prehistoric chronology of Korea: the application of MASCA
            theory. *Hanguk Sa Yŏngu (The Journal of Korean History),* No. 15:3–43. (In Korean.)
MacCord, Howard A.
    1958   The Able site, Kapyong, Korea. *Asian Perspectives* 2(1):128–138.
McCune, Shannon
    1956   *Korea's heritage: a regional and social geography.* Rutland, Vermont: Charles E. Tuttle.
National Museum of Korea
    1970   *National Museum of Korea* (3rd ed.). Seoul, Korea.
Needham, Joseph
    1958   *The development of iron and steel technology in China.* London: Newcomen Society, The
            Science Museum.
Nelson, Sarah M.
    1975a   Han River Chulmuntogi. *Program in East Asian Studies Occasional Paper,* No. 9. Bell-
            ingham: Western Washington State College.
    1975b   The subsistence base of middle Han sites of the Chŭlmun period. *Asian Perspectives*
            18(1):5–14.
    1980   Tribes in Korea: an independent case. Paper presented at the 79th Annual Meeting of
            the American Anthropological Association, Washington, D.C.
Oda Fujio
    1977   Paekche type potteries from western Japan. *Paekche Munhwa,* No. 10:31–46. (In
            Korean.)
Okladnikov, A. P.
    1964   Ancient population of Siberia and its culture. In *The peoples of Siberia,* edited by M. B.
            Levin and L. P. Potapov, translated by S. Dunn. Chicago: The University of Chicago
            Press. Pp. 13–98.
    1965   The Soviet Far East in antiquity: An archaeological and historical study of the Maritime
            regions of the U.S.S.R. *Arctic Institute of North America, Anthropology of the North: Trans-
            lations from Russian Sources,* No. 6. University of Toronto Press.
Pearson, Richard J.
    1978   Lolang and the rise of Korean states and chiefdoms. *Journal of the Hong Kong Archaeologi-
            cal Society* 7(1976–1978):77–90.
    1981   The study of Korean archaeology. Draft copy of Ms. to appear in *Studies on Korea: a
            scholar's guide,* edited by Han Kyo-kim. Honolulu: University Press of Hawaii.
Rudolph, Richard C. (editor)
    1978   *Chinese archaeological abstracts, Monumenta Archaeologica* 6. Los Angles: The Institute of
            Archaeology, The University of California.
Sample, L. L.
    1967   *Culture history and chronology in South Korea's Neolithic.* Ann Arbor: University
            Microfilms.
    1974   Tongsamdong: A contribution to Korean Neolithic culture history. *Arctic Anthropology*
            11(2):1–125.
Sauer, C. O.
    1952   *Agricultural origins and dispersals.* New York: The American Geographical Society.
Serizawa Chosuke
    1978   The Early Paleolithic in Japan. In *Early Paleolithic in South and East Asia,* edited by F.
            Ikawa-Smith. The Hague: Mouton. Pp. 287–297.

1980 The Choen-kok-li site in Korea. Paper presented at the Annual Meeting of the Association of Asian Studies.

Sohn Pow-key
1972 Lower and Middle Paleolithic industries of the stratified Sokchang-ni cultures. *Hanguk Sa Yŏngu (The Journal of Korean History)*, No. 7:1–58. (In Korean.)
1973 The Upper Paleolithic habitation, Sŏkchang-ni, Korea. *Hanguk Sa Yŏngu (The Journal of Korean History)*, No. 9:15–57. (In Korean.)
1974 Paleolithic culture of Korea. *Korea Journal* **14**(4):4–11.
1975 Chejon Chŏmmal Cave preliminary report. *Hanguk Sa Yŏngu (Journal of Korean History)*, No. 11:9–53. (In Korean.)
1978a The Early Paleolithic industries of Sŏkchang-ni, Korea. In *Early Paleolithic in South and East Asia*, edited by F. Ikawa-Smith. The Hague: Mouton. Pp. 233–245.
1978b Korean Paleolithic culture: investigations at Chommal Cave, Chejon. *Hanguk Sa Yŏngu (Journal of Korean History)*, No. 19:1–18. (In Korean.)

Sohn Pow-key, Kim Chul-choon, and Hong Yi-sup
1970 *The history of Korea.* Seoul: Korean National Commission for UNESCO.

Umehara Sueji
1926 Deux grandes découvertes archéologiques en Corée. *Revue des Arts Asiatiques* **3**:24–33.

Watson, Burton
1961 *Records of the grand historian of China* (Vol. 2). New York: Columbia University Press.

Watson, William
1971 *Cultural frontiers in ancient East Asia.* Edinburgh: Edinburgh University Press.

Yang Lien-sheng
1952 *Money and credit in China: a short history.* Cambridge: Harvard University Press.

Yi Sun-jin and Chan Ju-yop
1975a The culture of Mahan (1). *Chosen Gakujutsu Tsuho* **12**(2):31–34.
1975b The culture of Mahan (2). *Chosen Gakujutsu Tsuho* **12**(3):44–55.
1975c The culture of Mahan (4). *Chosen Gakujutsu Tsuho* **12**(5,6):60–66.

Yu, Ying-shih
1967 *Trade and expansion in Han China.* Berkeley: University of California Press.

Yun Se-young
1974 Preliminary report of the excavations of Paekche tombs 1 and 2 at Karak-dong, Seoul. *Kogohak* No. 3:131–146. (In Korean.)

4

Cultural Change in Prehistoric Japan: Receptivity to Rice Agriculture in the Japanese Archipelago

TAKERU AKAZAWA

INTRODUCTION

This chapter is concerned with *how* and *why* the Japanese Jomon people, who had been characterized by a subsistence economy primarily based on hunting–gathering, responded to a settled life based on rice cultivation. Although there have been very few systematic investigations of Japanese prehistory of this kind, the Japanese archipelago is an attractive field for reviewing these subjects, in that Japanese history witnessed a radical shift from hunting–gathering to food production caused by innovation and/or stimulus derived from the continent.

Since the discovery of the Japanese Paleolithic at the Iwajuku site in A.D. 1949, hundreds of investigations have vastly improved our understanding of Japanese prehistory. It is well known that Japanese history originated in the Pleistocene epoch, but the question remains unanswered of when and from where the earliest Japanese immigrants came. For instance, there has been much debate about the beginning of the Japanese Paleolithic despite 30 years of progress since the Iwajuku excavation. As stated by Ikawa-Smith (1980:136), "some archaeologists believe that human occupation of the Japanese archipelago began over 100,000 years ago; others believe that it did not begin until about 30,000 years ago; and still others, including myself, feel that 50,000 is the reasonable figure."

Japanese prehistory shifted to the new chronological and cultural period known as Jomon over 10,000 years ago, and was followed by the Yayoi and Kofun periods (Table 4.1). The subsistence economy of the Jomon people was

151

characterized by hunting, gathering, and fishing associated with very sophisticated potteries and various polished stone tools. As well illustrated by Pearson
and Pearson (1978) and Ikawa-Smith (1980), in recent years some archaeologists
and botanical ecologists have raised the question of the possibility of early
cultivation during the Jomon period. Although some kind of incipient cultivation might have been introduced, the hypothesis that the majority of Jomon
subsistence was probably supported by wild plants and animals explains the
data reasonably well, including the nature of shell middens and associated
artifacts.

The succeeding Yayoi period witnessed the appearance of a settled life of
agriculture in a true sense. The initial appearance of rice cultivation in the
Japanese archipelago has been regarded as the product of diffusion. Although it
is certain that this diffusion was crucial in mediating the transition between
subsistence technologies, the problems remain unsolved of how and why the
former Jomon people reacted positively to a new way of life. There has been
much debate about what kind of preadjustment and readjustment occurred in
the Jomon hunting–gathering societies in the process of their transition to the
agricultural society of the Yayoi period.

In light of recent research on the cultural change from hunting–gathering to
rice agriculture in Japan, it has been found that different groups of Jomon people
followed divergent paths at variable rates in the transition to a settled life of
agriculture, and that this variability might be explained by the differences in
resource potentials within the archipelago during the Jomon period. That is to
say, subsistence activities diversified by area during the Jomon period, and,
further, in the coastal areas where people subsisted on fishing activities, agricultural innovation was resisted and/or accepted slowly (Akazawa 1981).

TABLE 4.1

Chronology of Japanese Cultural Periods[a]

Period	Temporal span
Historic	A.D. 600–present
Kofun	A.D. 300–A.D. 600
Yayoi	
Late	A.D. 100–A.D. 300
Middle	100 B.C.–A.D. 100
Early	300 B.C.–100 B.C.
Jomon	
Final	1000 B.C.–300 B.C.
Late	2500 B.C.–1000 B.C.
Middle	3600 B.C.–2500 B.C.
Early	5300 B.C.–3600 B.C.
Initial	7500 B.C.–5300 B.C.
Incipient	11,000 B.C.–7,500 B.C.
Paleolithic	before 11,000 B.C.

[a] Modified from Ikawa-Smith (1980: Table 1).

Sedentary population rather than the nonsedentary population can be readily initiated into agricultural experimentation. Sedentism derived mainly from intensive exploitation of resources within a small geographical area and the storing of resources to tide over lean seasons. Conditions of this kind flourished in fishing societies that relied heavily on marine resources. This general view has been stated by numerous scholars.

On comparing worldwide aboriginal cultures, Murdock discusses the problem of fishing societies and their relationship to early agriculture in the process of cultural evolution:

> Fishing (including shellfishing and the pursuit of aquatic animals) is the only relatively simple mode of subsistence that appears conducive to a settled way of life, and it is highly probable that prior to the first appearance of agriculture about 10,000 years ago the only sedentary population for many millennia were groups of fishermen. For hunters and gatherers to settle down to a settled life of agriculture a revolutionary readjustment of cultural habits is needed, but for fishermen the transition is vastly easier, and it is by no means improbable that fishing may have played a very important cultural–historical role in mediating the transition to early agriculture (Murdock 1969:144).

These statements may reveal a reasonable possibility that fishing societies occupied a kind of transitional stage from hunting–gathering to agriculture. But as far as Japan is concerned, we can propose another interpretation, since for Jomon shell-midden people, the transition to a new way of rice cultivation was not necessarily easy. These fishermen were well adapted to a small geographical area and became sedentary with increased population, as is commonly recognized in other fishing societies. These conditions could have predisposed the shell-midden people to accept rice agriculture, if Murdock's formula is correct. However, taking into account the entire process of rice cultivation in Japan, I think that Murdock places too much emphasis on fishing for the explanation of culture change to agriculture in human history.

Reed (1977:943) concludes, on reviewing the papers presented at the symposium on *Origins of Agriculture,* "the shift to agriculture by original innovators was not sudden, and it depended in large part upon the possession of preadaptive cultural artifacts and the practices of particular hunters/gatherers." This kind of preadaptation occurred among sedentary hunter–gatherers whose subsistence economy was specifically relevant to native plants (Caldwell 1977:81–82). They could develop an appropriate cultural milieu as one general condition for the receptivity of innovation. These statements are true for the explanation of the receptivity process of an agricultural way of life in Japan. In every case of the presence of outside stimuli, a cultural and ecological relationship can be established between the areas providing the stimulus and the area receiving it, a hypothesis that is discussed in the following.

This chapter is divided into four sections. I first consider a general environmental characteristic of the Japanese archipelago. This part focuses on the fact that ecological conditions are not consistent throughout the Japanese archipelago, and therefore there is the possibility of diversity in subsistence activities and associated technologies of the Jomon people. Second, I examine the beginning and diffusion of rice cultivation in Japan. This part focuses on the facts that different groups of Jomon people followed divergent paths and at variable rates in the transition to a settled life of agriculture, and that the Jomon groups in the coastal area of eastern Japan seemingly resisted accepting rice cultivation. Third, the analysis is concerned with the fishing adaptation of the Jomon people and increased efficiency in the performance of their intensive activities within a marine territory. This part focuses on the differences in fishing adaptations due to the potentials of the respective settled marine sites and on the tentative classification of fishing economy by area. The final section examines the characteristics specific to the cultural change from hunting–gathering to rice agriculture in Japan, and the problem of to what extent fishing societies played a cultural–historical role in facilitating the transition to early agriculture in Japan.

ENVIRONMENTAL BACKGROUND

A knowledge of the various biophysical environments of the Japanese archipelago is necessary to understand the cultural diversity and evolution during the prehistoric era. For our purposes, it is sufficient to point out some of the broad distinctions by vegetation area and landforms along the coastal areas.

The Japanese archipelago lies along the east coast of Asia, stretching for approximately 3000 km from north to south (Figure 4.1). Its latitude extends over 22°, and climatic conditions vary. An important argument recently put forth claims the existence of a number of distinctive vegetational zones on this elongated archipelago. According to Honda (1912) and Yasuda (1978), the natural vegetation of Japan may be broadly described as follows (Figure 4.2):

1. Broad-leafed evergreen forest (evergreen-oak forest): The major tree species consist of *Machilus thunbergii, Castanopsis cuspidata,* and *Castanopsis cuspidata* var. *sieboldii* in the coastal areas, and *Quercus glauca, Q. gilva, Q. salicina, Q. myrsinaefolia,* and *Q. acuta* in the inland regions. These species are common in western Japan.

2. Broad-leafed deciduous forest (beech forest): The major species are *Fagus crenata, Tilia japonica, Quercus mongolica* var. *grosseserrata, Acer mono, Aesculus turbinata, Acanthopanax sciadophylloides,* and *Viburunum furcatum.* These species are common in eastern Japan.

3. Alpine and subpolar forest (fir forest): *Picea jezoensis, Abies sachalinensis,* and *Picea glehnii* are dominant species. The eastern part of Hokkaido and the mountainous part of Honshu are covered by these species.

4. Alpine desert and glassland (areas above timber line): The alpine regions are covered by shrubs such as *Pinus pumila, Vaccinum vitis-idaea, Rubus pedatus,* and others.

These vegetation areas include a wide range of climate, terrain, and food resources with which the Jomon people could devise a variety of subsistence activities. The climatic oscillations and vegetational changes of the past millennia have been reconstructed by a number of geomorphologists and paleobotanists.

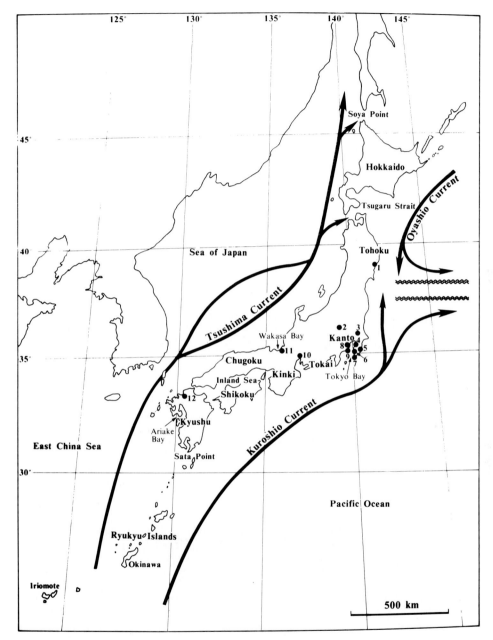

Figure 4.1 Map of Japan. Archaeological sites discussed in the text are shown by key numbers. (1) Miyano, (2) Iwajuku, (3) Kamitakatsu, (4) Saihiro, (5) Nittano, (6) Fujimidai, (7) Natagiri, (8) Kikuna, (9) Shomyoji, (10) Nishishiga, (11) Torihama, and (12) Itazuke.

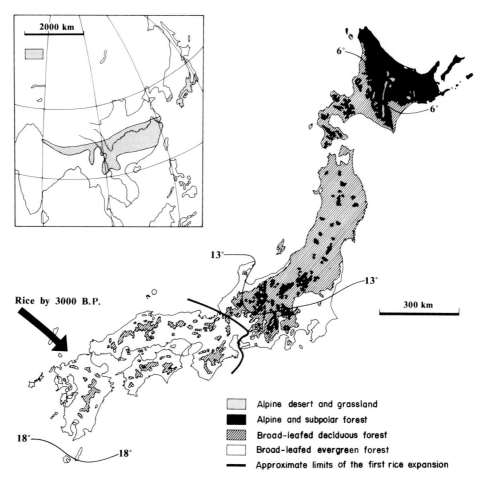

Figure 4.2 Map illustrating the major classification of natural forest zones and their relationship to rice expansion in Japan. (Compiled from Honda 1912; Sasaki 1971: Fig. 1; approximate limits of the first rice expansion used here are modified from Sugihara and Otsuka 1964: Fig. 2.)

The expansion of the laurel forest zone, consisting of broad-leafed evergreen species, into the lowlands covering most of western Japan (illustrated in Figure 4.2), occurred around 6500 B.P. (Yasuda 1978:202).

It is well known that the distribution of the Jomon sites is concentrated in eastern Japan; sites are scarce in western Japan. Koyama concluded from mathematical analysis of population distribution based upon the site numbers and sizes that

> the Jomon population was densest in the deciduous or evergreen–deciduous mixed forests of eastern Japan, but thin in the evergreen forest area of western Japan––matching the expected distribution of food resources. The population of the historic periods reverses this concentration due to better rice crops in the warm wet climate of the west (1978:60).

That is, Koyama proposed that the differing distribution and density of Jomon sites between western and eastern Japan should be attributed to the differences in the amount and nature of available foods between the two major areas.

Kondo's (1962) hypothesis concurs with Koyama's. He felt that the abundant food resources of eastern Japan enabled the Jomon people to specialize in the food-procuring activities of hunting, gathering, and fishing, thus resulting in a higher population density. Western Japan, however, was sparsely populated, because of scarce natural resources. As a result, a relatively simple mode of subsistence developed, and the people did not form specialized hunting–gathering societies.

Some botanical ecologists, such as Nakao (1966), Ueyama (1969), Ueyama *et al.* (1976), and Sasaki (1971), interpret cultural conditions of the western Jomon as indicative that a swidden type of agriculture had been practiced in western Japan during the later Jomon period. In the laurel forest zones of southeastern Asia, swidden-type agriculture, in which cereals and potatoes are cultivated, is widely distributed. The same type of agriculture could have been pursued by Jomon people living in the same laurel forest zones in western Japan (see Figure 4.2). The eastern Jomon people, on the other hand, would have adapted to the resource potentials in deciduous forest zones and further developed their hunting–gathering activities. Under these circumstances, the two major areas might have developed distinctive societies.

It becomes apparent from the foregoing that the works of botanical ecologists who have looked at the functional correlation between vegetation areas and human cultures should be synthesized. Another important fact is that maritime conditions provided a wide range of resource potentials on which prehistoric hunter–gatherers could have developed a specific variety of subsistence activities. As is well known, the adjacent seas of the Japanese archipelago are very productive in inshore and offshore fisheries. In particular, the Pacific coast of eastern Japan (Figure 4.1) is one of the most productive fishing grounds in the world, due to the junction of the two oceanic currents of Kuroshio and Oyashio (K. Yamaguchi 1964; Hiyama 1968; Hirasawa 1981). These conditions also existed in the Jomon period, as is evidenced by extensive shell middens of a great variety of fish species (see section on Fishing Adaptation of the Jomon People).

Insular and coastal environments are characterized by dramatic changes in landforms and ocean currents. Consequently, regional diversity in prehistoric maritime subsistence activities and associated technologies indicate different fishing adaptations due to the potentials of the settled sites.

RICE CULTIVATION IN JAPAN

It is generally accepted that the beginning of rice cultivation was first stimulated by influences from the continent. The problems of from where and over which route rice cultivation was diffused were very controversial in the study of Ja-

panese prehistory as seen by the suggested routes in Figure 4.3. However, in
light of recent research, it has been concluded that the most probable route was
from the lower reaches of the Yangtze River in southern China to northern
Kyushu in Japan via southern Korea (Route IIIa in Figure 4.3), and/or directly
(Route IIIb).

Ishige (1968a,b) concludes from his comparative studies of stone sickles in
Japan and its neighboring regions that sickles, a new lithic element of the Yayoi
period, had been diffused together with rice via Route III in Figure 4.3. In
proportion to the heavy concentration of the Japanese-type sickle blades found
in the lower reaches of the Yangtze River and the Korean Peninsula, those
excavated along diffusion Routes I and II, which was supported by some archae-

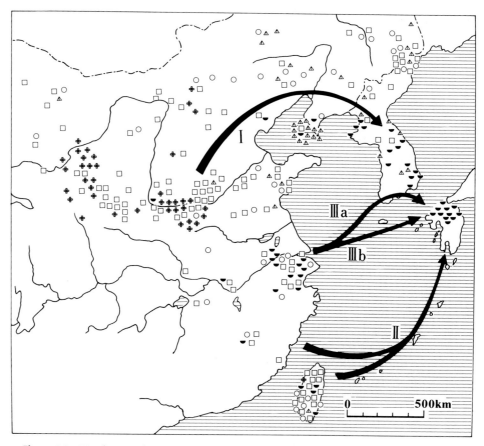

Figure 4.3 Distribution of stone sickles in China, Korea, and northern Kyushu in Japan, and the
suggested routes of rice diffusion to the Japanese archipelago. Sickle types: chipped (✤); polished with
rectangular outline (□); polished with spindle-shaped outline (△); polished with semicircular outline of
straight edge (○); polished with semicircular outline of convex edge (◗). (Compiled from Ishige
1968b:Fig. 5; Sasaki 1971:Fig. 21.)

ologists and folklorists referred to by Sasaki (1971:286–290), are rare and negligible.

Route III is, therefore, the most probable diffusion route over which the rice cultivation complex traveled to northern Kyushu in Japan. This is strengthened by a similar study on polished stone axes and adzes, which were also new lithic elements associated with the rice cultivation complex, as seen in Figure 4.4 (Matsubara 1971), and is compatible with the linguistic and agricultural data concerned with rice agriculture in eastern Asia. The problems of from where and

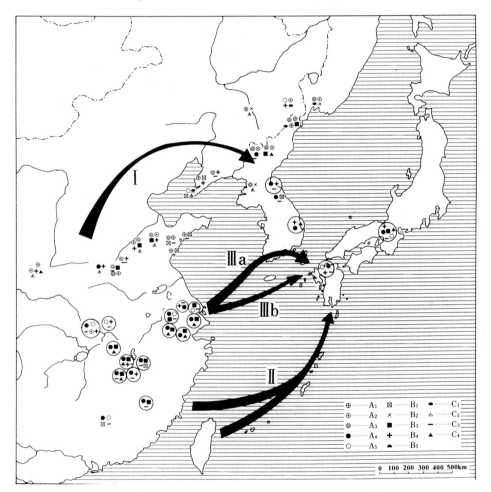

Figure 4.4 Distribution of polished stone axes and adzes in China, Korea, and Japan, and the suggested routes of rice diffusion to the Japanese archipelago. Letters indicate three major categorizations of axes and adzes: A, axe with thick butt and clamshell-shaped edge; B, adze with quadrangular polished edge and thick butt; C, adze of flat-edge type with rectangular cross section. Subscripts denote further morphological characteristics, such as outline. (Compiled from Matsubara 1971:Fig. 10; Sasaki 1971:Fig. 21.)

over which route rice agriculture traveled have thus been solved to a higher degree of reliability than before, although the debate over when this diffusion began and when rice agriculture established itself still continues.

The Beginning of Rice Cultivation

The earliest evidence of rice cultivation in Japan is found at a site in Itazuke in northern Kyushu, the type site for Itazuke-type pottery that represents the earliest phase of the Yayoi period. Evidence from this site indicates that rice cultivation was initiated in northern Kyushu around the final stage of the Jomon period. A number of elements (discussed in the following paragraph) were found that show radical technological innovation brought about by rice cultivation during the Yusu-type pottery stage, known as the Final Jomon in this region, together with carbonized grains of rice (Shimojo 1979). Furthermore, based upon the palynological studies of the sediments at this and other relevant sites, there can be no doubt that the occupants cultivated rice at the final stage of the Jomon period around 3000 B.P. (Nakamura 1979, 1980).

Figure 4.5 is a chronological table and schematic representation illustrating the

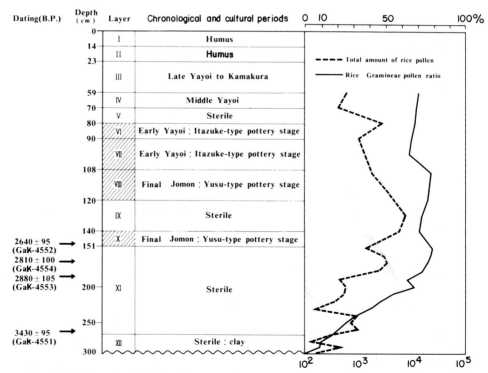

Figure 4.5 Chronological table illustrating schematic representation of rice cultivation during the Final Jomon and Yayoi periods at Itazuke site. (Compiled from Nakamura 1979; Fujiwara 1979:Fig. 1.)

frequency of rice (*Oryza sativa*) pollen during the Final Jomon and Yayoi periods at Itazuke site. At the 1978 excavation of this site, elements of the rice culture complex were found in layer X, together with Yusu-type pottery. These rice culture elements included irrigated paddy fields equipped with special devices, such as dams, and various agricultural equipment, such as harvesting stone sickles and wooden hoes (Shimojo 1979:137–139). According to Nakamura (1979), rice pollen at this site appears as deep as 290 cm below the surface, occurring increasingly in more recent deposits, and comprising over 60% in the total amount of Gramineae pollen above the 200-cm level. From this evidence, Nakamura states that rice cultivation had already begun in irrigated fields during Late to Final Jomon in the northern Kyushu area.

This assumption has been strengthened by a new research method based upon plant opal analysis. Fujiwara and colleagues (Fujiwara 1976a,b, 1979; Fujiwara and Sasaki 1978; Fujiwara *et al.* 1980) have utilized this technique, which detects silica body remains of motor cells of plants in stratified deposits of sites. From systematic studies on a sample from Itazuke, Fujiwara concludes that the high frequency of rice plant opal in layer X indicates that rice plants were cultivated in paddy fields around the site. This evidence, in addition to Nakamura's palynological work, is beginning to be accepted by Japanese archaeologists, who had firmly believed that rice cultivation first appeared in the Yayoi period around 200–300 B.C.

Following the initial introduction of rice cultivation was the Itazuke-type pottery stage, which began around 2500 B.P., as estimated from two radiocarbon datings of the Itazuke site—2560 ± 100 B.P. (GaK–2360) and 2400 ± 90 B.P. (GaK–2358). About this time, Yayoi agricultural societies, which had developed new agricultural technologies and knowledge, were established in northern Kyushu, although the former Yusu-type pottery stage might have been a prelude to a true settled life of rice agriculture (Shimojo 1979:144). Simultaneously, the Itazuke-type pottery culture spread eastward and southward.

Spread of Rice Cultivation

The first expansion of rice technology (Figure 4.6) is generally accepted to have occurred quite rapidly through Chugoku and Kinki districts up to around the western part of the Tokai district (e.g., Kondo 1962; Kanaseki and Sahara 1978; Shimojo 1979). This rapid diffusion is supported by the fact that the cultural complexes of the early Yayoi period are quite homogenous from Kyushu to the Tokai district (Kondo 1962; Kanaseki and Sahara 1978). In particular, all the sites of the early Yayoi period throughout the area produced a specific pottery that is known generally as Ongagawa-type pottery, its uniformity seen on the basis of similar technological and morphological features. Kanaseki and Sahara (1978:20) state that homogeneity of this kind is explained by the rapid spread of the cultural complex from its place of origin in northern Kyushu.

This assumption is strengthened by the radiocarbon dating of the early stage

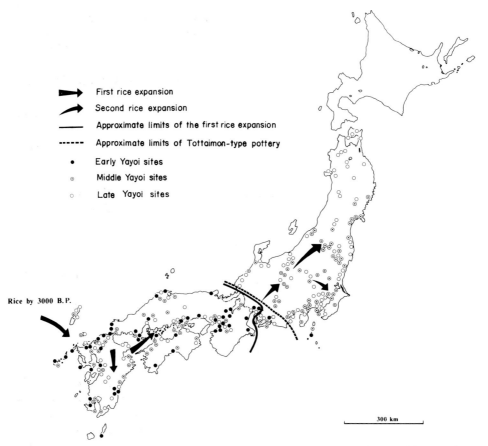

Figure 4.6 Map illustrating the probable route over which rice was diffused eastward from northern Kyushu to the Tokai district (first expansion), and its subsequent dispersal to eastern Japan. Distribution of Yayoi sites classifiable as three subperiods is modified from Egami (1976:inserted Map III); approximate limits of Tottaimon-type pottery used here are modified from Harunari (1979:Fig. 2).

of the Yayoi period from Nishishiga site in the Tokai district. The deposit at this site, which is associated with the earliest Yayoi pottery of this region, is dated at 2520 ± 140 B.P. (N–120), 2220 ± 120 B.P. (N–161–1), and 2440 ± 130 B.P. (N–161–2). These dates indicate that this site was formed during the first stage of rice expansion around the same age as the formation of the Itazuke site in Kyushu.

Recently, Nakamura (1981) has presented important evidence on the frequency of rice pollen identified in several localities producing Jomon and/or Yayoi deposits (see Figure 4.7). This figure indicates that a number of localities distributed in western Japan, approximately covering the areas influenced by the first stage of rice expansion, yielded a certain proportion of rice pollen around 2500 B.P. These facts might strengthen the hypothesis that the western Jomon

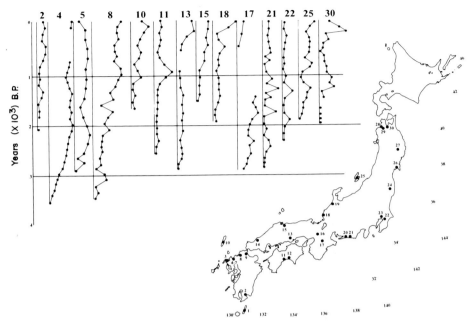

Figure 4.7 Comparison of the frequency distribution of rice pollen at localities in the Japanese archipelago. (From Nakamura 1981.)

people accepted rice agriculture around the same age of the formation of the Itazuke site, even if rice had not been cultivated intensively.

After passing through the Tokai district, rice cultivation spread farther eastward as the second stage of rice expansion. During the middle stage of the Yayoi period, the Jomon people of Chubu, Kanto, and the southern part of Tohoku continuously accepted a new way of life diffused from the west. By around A.D. 300, the beginning of the next cultural period known as Kofun, the Yayoi culture had spread over most of the Japanese islands except the Ryukyus and Hokkaido (Kanaseki and Sahara 1978:16). However, comparisons between the first and succeeding stages of rice expansion reveal a number of significant differences both in the process and the results of the expansion.

Differences in the Reception of Rice Cultivation

Diffusion Routes of Rice Expansions

Figure 4.6 compares the geographical distribution of Yayoi sites classified as three different periods: Early, 300–100 B.C.; Middle, 100 B.C. to A.D. 100; and Late, A.D. 100–300. Each period corresponds to the stages of rice expansion. As discussed earlier, the distribution of Early Yayoi sites resulting from the first rice expansion is, in the eastern extremity, adjacent to the western part of the Tokai district.

More important, however, is the fact that the geographical distributions of these sites were different by period, in particular, between the sites of the first and the succeeding periods. The Early Yayoi sites were concentrated along the lowlands along the Inland Sea and estuaries in western Japan, while the succeeding sites spread into inland as well as coastal zones. The point to be noted here is that large numbers of the Middle Yayoi sites corresponding to the second rice expansion were distributed along upper streams and inland lakes in the mountainous inland zones of eastern Japan. This evidence coincides with the diffusion routes of rice cultivation proposed by Japanese archaeologists.

> Soon after the Yayoi people settled in northern Kyushu, they moved along the coast looking for cultivated [arable] land. . . . It is curious that the first Yayoi culture in eastern Japan did not diffuse to the large southern Kanto plain, though it did spread from the basins in Yamanashi and Nagano prefectures to the northern Kanto by way of the base of the Asama mountains and then into Fukushima Prefecture. . . . It is interesting to trace the route through which Yayoi culture was diffused. In western Japan, Yayoi people moved mainly along the coast. On the other hand, in eastern Japan the route followed river valleys and mountain passes (Kanaseki and Sahara 1978:20–21).

In other words, the observed routes of the second stage of rice expansion were different from those of the first. Early Yayoi settlements were concentrated along lowlands through Kyushu to Tokai because the first rice expansion had followed these routes. The second rice expansion, however, spread into mountainous inland zones, and as a result, left its traces behind as habitation sites in inland regions, although it also continued to settle in the coastal regions.

Jomon Tradition in Yayoi Culture

A significant difference in the Jomon influence on western and eastern Yayoi cultures is found in pottery-making. All the sites of the Early Yayoi period throughout the area of the first stage of rice expansion yield the Ongagawa-type pottery. In contrast, the Yayoi pottery complex of eastern Japan was characterized by strong influences from the local Jomon traditions (Kondo 1962:141–142). For instance, the Yayoi pottery of the southern Kanto district was decorated by the same technique of cord-marking as that utilized in Jomon pottery. It lasted from the beginning up to the final stage of the Yayoi in this region, although certain gradual changes did take place (Kumano 1979).

Another Jomon influence can be seen in fishing gear. As reported by Kenmochi (1972) and Kanzawa (1979), a number of cave sites along the Pacific coast in the Kanto district were characterized by shell-midden deposits containing a large amount of fishing gear, such as fishhooks and harpoon heads. These tools were made by the same technological traditions as those of the preceding Jomon shell-midden people in this region.

Thus, the Yayoi people of this region retained a traditional life-style based upon the locally flourishing, preceding Jomon tradition, and a strong tendency toward cultural regionalism is found in contrast to the cultural uniformity observed in the early western Yayoi culture.

It can be postulated that the eastern Yayoi people retained, to some extent, the hunting–gathering economy of the preceding Jomon-type subsistence after adopting rice cultivation. Moreover, this assumption is supported by the analysis of the form and degree of the tooth attrition of the Yayoi people from a cave site in the Kanto district. Suzuki (1975) reported that their tooth attrition coincides entirely with that of the Jomon people but is quite different from the succeeding Kofun and later peoples. He concludes that "this type of attrition shows that the mode of life of the Sano Cave men was quite the same as that of the Jomon people, who are regarded as belonging to a hunter–gatherer culture" (Suzuki 1975:8).

Hypotheses for Diffusion Patterns

The reason for the difference of diffusion patterns between western and eastern Japan is a subject of continuing discussion in the field of Japanese prehistory. In order to explain these differences of culture change from Jomon to Yayoi by area, a number of working hypotheses have been offered so far.

As for geographical closeness to the donor area, it is hardly necessary to point out that western Japan was situated nearer to the avenue through which rice cultivation passed from the continent. Prior to the first appearance of rice cultivation, preadjustments of sociocultural habits may have taken place in western Japan, which was under constant stimuli from the continent (Kondo 1962:144–146, 152–155). In such a situation, it is probable that western Japan could easily accept a new cultural complex, even if a revolutionary readjustment of cultural habits had been needed. Nevertheless, differences in agricultural adaptation in different groups cannot be explained only from the case of "propinquity" (Haury 1962:116).

Some climatic difference between the two major areas has been observed. It is generally accepted that eastern Japan receives slightly less sunshine than western Japan (Kondo 1962:62). Kanaseki and Sahara (1978:20) describe the situation as follows: "The relatively small amount of sunshine in eastern Japan made rice cultivation difficult. Therefore the Yayoi people could not settle in the area until suitable types of rice were evolved." Nevertheless, the climatic setting is almost the same throughout the Japanese islands because of their location within the monsoon zone. Temperature and humidity for rice cultivation do not differ much from area to area except for northern Tohoku and Hokkaido. Moreover, lowlands had formed along the seacoasts and the lower reaches of rivers and estuaries with the regression of the sea during the later Jomon period, and these lowlands could have easily been used as paddy fields by early farmers. It might be quite possible to cultivate rice on a simple level without special water-control devices as speculated by Kanaseki and Sahara (1978:22). All these situations were comparable in western and eastern Japan, with only the amount of sunshine slightly differing between the two. In consequence, it is reasonable to believe that the second stage of rice expansion could have begun before new species of rice evolved.

Another diffusion pattern hypothesis worthy of discussion is the condition described as the "biogeographical setting" and "optimum cultural environment" (by Haury (1962:116). As described earlier, the distribution of Jomon sites is concentrated in eastern Japan; sites are scarcer in western Japan. Thus, Kondo (1962:149–150) proposes that the difference in population density had already appeared during the Jomon period. Further, he speculates that this should be attributed to differences in the amount and nature of food resources. As mentioned earlier, western Japan during the Jomon period was sparsely populated due to the paucity of natural resources. As a result, there developed a relatively simple mode of subsistence, and people did not become specialized hunter–gatherers. For the western hunter–gatherers to settle down to a new way of life, a revolutionary readjustment of sociocultural habits was not demanded, and the transition was easier. On the other hand, the eastern Jomon society specialized in hunting–gathering activities in an environment rich in natural resources, resulting in a higher population density. Thus, the eastern society could not readily change to a new way of life; even after shifting to it, the regional tradition of the Jomon period survived in the Yayoi culture (Kondo 1962:150–152).

Actually, Kondo's claim, which has been widely supported by Japanese archaeologists, does not refer to an "optimum cultural environment" of the western Jomon people for the acceptance of rice culture. He proposes that the western Jomon society readily accepted rice cultivation, since they depended on a relatively simple rather than specialized mode of subsistence. This view might be given considerable weight if the first rice expansion had been due to the conquest of large immigrant groups from the continent. However, recent research on human skeletal remains of the Yayoi period has not offered any substantial evidence for supporting this kind of working model (e.g., Naito 1971; Yamaguchi 1979).

For instance, Kanaseki (1966, 1976) proposed, from the analysis of human skeletal remains in Kyushu and Chugoku districts, a hypothesis that the Yayoi population in western Japan was composed of the descendants of the indigenous Jomon population and of immigrants from the continent, who brought rice culture into the Japanese archipelago. The Yayoi people found in the sites at Doigahama and Mitsu on which Kanaseki's studies were based were distinct from the preceding Jomon population in some physical characters. Nevertheless, the recent findings of the Yayoi people in northern Kyushu (Naito 1971) and Shikoku (Yamaguchi 1979) have indicated that their physical characters can be classified as Jomon type. That is, evidence that the first expansion of rice technology was due to the conquest of immigrant groups has not been obtained in the field of physical anthropology.

Another diffusion pattern viewpoint has been proposed by some botanical ecologists, on the basis that the two major areas are characterized by different forest zones (e.g., Honda 1912; Kira 1949; Yamanaka 1979). Western Japan is situated at the northern end of the laurel forest zones characterizing southeast Asia (see Figure 4.2), in which a swidden type of agriculture is widely distributed. Therefore, it is probable that the same type of agriculture could have diffused to western Japan during the Jomon period and been pursued by the inhabitants of this region (Nakao 1966; Ueyama 1969; Ueyama *et al.* 1976; Sasaki 1971). Furthermore, Sasaki has suggested that an appropriate cultural milieu resulting from dependence on a swidden subsistence economy played a crucial role in mediating the transition to rice cultivation in western Japan.

In order to support this hypothetical view, some problems remain to be solved. Among them is the fact that the swidden type of agriculture differs from rice cultivation in field preparation and related technologies, as referred to by Pearson and Pearson (1978:25). From the beginning, Japanese rice cultivation utilized a type of prepared paddy field (Sato 1971); thus, whether the transition to rice agriculture was vastly easier for swidden farmers than hunter–gatherers is questionable because both lacked experience with the proper technologies. Furthermore, this hypothetical approach cannot explain why the eastern Tokai and Kanto districts showed resistance even in the first stage of rice expansion though these regions are included in the same forest zones as western Japan (see Figure 4.2) and probably offered similar conditions for rice expansion.

In conclusion, the resistance to rice cultivation, which can be traced along the Pacific coast in eastern Japan, is not adequately explained by the circumstances that have been discussed in various spheres so far. That is to say, the conditions mentioned cannot provide substantial evidence for the explanation of the cultural dichotomy between the area where rice spread rapidly and the area where it was resisted. Therefore, further examination is required of the earliest Yayoi people and their relation to the preceding Jomon societies around the bordering area of the Tokai district at the time when the first rice expansion arrived.

Jomon Shell-Midden People's Resistance to Rice

As described earlier, the first stage of rice expansion stops at the western part of the Tokai district. Thus, for several decades the Yayoi and Jomon peoples seemingly coexisted on both sides of this line, although both groups enjoyed contact through trade as suggested by Kanaseki and Sahara (1978:21).

In examining archaeological data before the first stage of rice expansion, it is generally accepted that the final Jomon sites of both regions, where rice spread smoothly and where it was resisted, yielded a specific pottery that is generally known as Tottaimon type, its uniformity seen on the basis of similar features distributed throughout the area from Kyushu to Tokai districts (e.g., Kondo 1962; Kanaseki and Sahara 1978; Harunari 1979) (see also Figure 4.6). From this evidence, one view has been presented that the Tottaimon pottery stage played an important role in spreading the rice cultivation eastward.

Another important point to be noted here is that the easternmost part of the distribution of this type of pottery does not entirely coincide with that of the area characterized by accepting the first stage of rice expansion as stated by Komura (1963, 1980) and Harunari (1979:109–112). This shows that different groups of the Tottaimon in the Tokai district followed divergent paths at variable rates in the transition to rice cultivation. That is to say, the western Tokai Tottaimon group quickly reacted to the rice cultivation and produced Yayoi pottery of the Ongagawa type as represented by Nishishiga site occupants, while the eastern Tokai Jomon people still produced Jomon pottery of the preceding Tottaimon type, not accepting the Ongagawa type of pottery making.

The next important feature is that the sites of the eastern Tokai district, where the first rice expansion was resisted and which coexisted adjacent to the first rice farmers, are often characterized by extensive shell middens along the coastal regions and rivers (e.g., Hisanaga 1976; Komura 1980). Moreover, the number of sites increased exceedingly along the coastal regions and rivers of this region at the beginning of the Final Jomon period (Hisanaga 1976:32). Figure 4.8 shows the comparison of population density of the Final Jomon period by area, computed by Koyama (in press). The Tokai district shows a population density of .42, which is high when compared with other areas, particularly with western Japan. From an archaeological viewpoint, the high population density of the Tokai district can be explained by the increase in the number of shell-midden sites of this period.

In conclusion, evidence indicates that the resistance to rice cultivation, which can be traced along the eastern part of the Tokai district, is adequately explained

Figure 4.8 Regional differences in population density per square kilometer during the Final Jomon period, except Hokkaido. (Modified from Koyama, in press:Fig. 6.)

by the circumstances that supported existing flourishing fishing societies. The shell-midden people resisted rice cultivation since their societies were not an "optimum cultural environment" for the acceptance of rice. The rapid increase of Final Jomon sites in this region, mentioned previously, may well be explained by the possibility that groups of the Jomon people unwilling to accept rice cultivation immigrated there in meeting a new wave of cultural stimuli from the west. Because the second stage of rice expansion also met with resistance from the shell-midden people along the coastal regions of eastern Japan, it did not follow the coastal route of the first rice expansion but spread first to inland regions.

These same circumstances can be determined along the Pacific coast of eastern Japan where a greater emphasis on fishing had been placed (Akazawa 1980, 1981). Hence, this analysis is concerned with the possibility that the regions where the first rice expansion did not penetrate are characterized by fishing adaptations.

FISHING ADAPTATION OF THE JOMON PEOPLE

Prehistoric sites of the Jomon period in the coastal region are characterized by extensive shell middens. Although shell middens were made throughout the period, the most outstanding in size and density occurred during the later Jomon period. Furthermore, this development is concentrated along the Pacific coast of eastern Japan, that is, from the Tokai to Tohoku districts. Watanabe states, from his extensive studies on the Jomon shell middens and associated remains, as follows:

> The sites containing the fish-hooks are concentrated along the Pacific coast of central and northeast Honshu, and are very rare in the prefectures bordering the Japan Sea and in southern Honshu and Hokkaido. It is noteworthy that the areas of heaviest concentration of the sites from which the first fish-hooks have been recovered correspond to the areas where the Jomon culture most flourished (1966a:46).

Fishing became a well-established subsistence activity during Early Jomon around 6000 B.P. as is deduced from the increase in the number of shell middens of this period (Oikawa *et al.* 1980). This date coincides with the maximum stage of the early Holocene Jomon Transgression in Japan, as referred to by many Japanese geomorphologists (e.g., Iseki 1975, 1978; Maeda 1976; Ota *et al.* 1978; Okada 1978; Endo 1979). At that time, the sea flooded into the coastal lowlands of the Japanese archipelago, and, as the transgression spread, embayment conditions were formed in many places along the coast. In such a situation, it is highly probable that a cultural tradition of hunting–gathering was replaced by one of maritime orientation, occupying a region with a much larger coastline. However, the nature of the fishing adaptation differed from area to area.

Before beginning the actual description of the material analyzed from this deposit, a few comments about the analytical model and techniques of midden deposits in general are necessary. First, I consider the "exploitation territory" of the site, that is, the area assumed to be exploited regularly by the shell-midden people. Second, I review the research techniques used in analyzing fish remains from midden deposits.

Territorial Model for the Jomon Site

The *exploitation territory* of a site has been defined as "the territory surrounding the site which is exploited habitually by the inhabitants of the site" (Vita-Finzi and Higgs 1970:7). The site territory is different from the site catchment, which is defined as the total area from which the contents of a site were derived (Higgs 1975:IX). These concepts have been used as "analytic devices" for examining sites, the inhabitants of the sites, and their relationship to the environment as referred to by Roper (1979).

The exploitation territory of groups of hunter–gatherers differed in shape, size, and location. Methods of determining the site territory by means of a 10-km radius and 2-hour walking distance for nonagricultural sites, which were exemplified by Vita-Finzi and Higgs (1970), have been used by a number of European scholars (e.g., Barker 1975; Jarman and Webley 1975), but it is not certain that application of these methods to the Jomon case is effective. Nevertheless, this method does explain the relationship of the Jomon shell midden with its local environment (Akazawa 1980), and hence is used in this chapter.

Fish Remains in Shell Middens

The faunal remains found in shell middens most often were originally from the local faunal assemblage. They therefore provide some of the basic data needed to reconstruct the local prehistoric environment and to understand patterns in the exploitation of available food resources. In order to understand these aspects of the past, the faunal remains must be classified, followed by examination of the relative frequencies of the species and their size–age frequency distributions.

Relative Frequency of Shell-Midden Fish Species

Table 4.2 shows the relative frequencies of fish (*Lateolabrax japonicus, Acanthopagrus schlegeli,* and *Chrysophrys major*) found at eight shell middens in the Kanto district. Two different methods were used to estimate the relative frequencies of the three species, because the estimation of the number of individuals from the number of skeletal elements always becomes a subject of argument in quantitative analyses. One method estimated the maximum number of individuals (Max.) from the total number of premaxillary and dentary bones; the other estimated the minimum number of individuals (Min.) from the largest

TABLE 4.2

Comparison of the Frequency Distributions of *Lateolabrax japonicus*, *Acanthopagrus schlegeli*, and *Chrysophrys major* at Shell Middens in the Kanto District[a]

Shell midden	Jomon period	Estimated number of individuals	*Lateolabrax japonicus*		*Acanthopagrus schlegeli*		*Chrysophrys major*		Total		Reference
			N	%	N	%	N	%	N	%	
1. Terawaki	Late	Max.	6	1.35	30	6.77	407	91.87	443	99.99	Watanabe (1966b)
		Min.	5	3.94	11	8.66	111	87.40	127	100.00	
2. Tsunatori	Late	Max.	6	4.20	30	20.98	107	74.83	143	100.01	Kaneko et al. (1968)
		Min.	5	10.64	11	23.40	31	65.96	47	100.00	
3. Ohata	Middle	Max.	5	6.67	17	22.67	53	70.67	75	100.01	Kaneko et al. (1975)
		Min.	3	10.34	10	34.48	16	55.17	29	99.99	
4. Natagiri	Late	Max.	2	0.50	13	3.24	386	96.26	401	100.00	Kaneko (1958)
		Min.	2	1.56	5	3.91	121	94.53	128	100.00	
5. Fujimidai	Late	Max.	15	7.89	16	8.42	159	83.68	190	99.99	Kaneko (1964)
		Min.	9	7.14	10	7.94	107	84.92	126	100.00	
6. Saihiro	Late to Final	Max.	17	6.54	240	92.31	3	1.15	260	100.00	Kaneko et al. (1977)
		Min.	12	12.12	85	85.86	2	2.02	99	100.00	
7. Miyanohara	Middle	Max.	54	22.04	185	75.51	6	2.45	245	100.00	Kaneko (1972)
		Min.	28	29.79	64	68.09	2	2.13	94	100.01	
8. Nittano	Middle	Max.	122	65.59	60	32.26	4	2.15	186	100.00	Ogawa et al. (1975)
		Min.	46	64.29	23	32.86	2	2.86	70	100.01	
8. Nittano	Early	Max.	551	60.68	336	37.00	21	2.31	908	99.99	Ogawa et al. (1975)
		Min.	198	62.94	111	33.55	11	3.51	313	100.00	

[a] The locations of these shell middens are shown in Figure 4.9.

number of right or left premaxillary or right or left dentary bones. The two methods consistently show the same trend in the relative frequencies of the species.

From these data, the sites can be separated into three groups according to the dominant species: (*a*) Terawaki, Tsunatori, Ohata, Natagiri, and Fujimidai; (*b*) Saihiro and Miyanohara; and (*c*) Nittano Middle and Early. *C. major* characterizes the Terawaki-Fujimidai group, *A. schlegeli* the Saihiro-Miyanohara group, and *L. japonicus* the Nittano group. These three species are equally representative of coastal fish, but their habitats are different (Matsubara and Ochiai 1965:702–720, 892–901, 903–910; Kuwatani 1962). *C. major* inhabits the rocky shore facing the open sea and dislikes the brackish-water to freshwater environments. Contrarily, the other two species like the brackish-water environment of the tidal and littoral zones in bays.

Figure 4.9 shows the geographical distribution of the eight shell middens studied here. Each site is enclosed by a circle with a radius of 10 km, an area assumed to be the subsistence activity territory of the site for the purposes of the present studies. The sites characterized by *C. major* are distributed along the present coast facing the open sea, in localities with rocky-shore zones and no direct influence from freshwater. A marine territory of this kind should be highly productive of *C. major*, as far as the ecological habitat of the living species is concerned (e.g., Kajiyama 1937; Tanaka 1958; Matsubara and Ochiai 1965:704–709).

In contrast, the three sites in the other two groups are located inland, about 10 km from the present coastline. Moreover, the sites of Saihiro and Miyanohara are situated near Tokyo Bay. It can be seen in Figure 4.9 that the shell middens are distributed perpendicular rather than parallel to the present coastline, and that most of them are more than 10 km inland from the present seashore. This unusual distribution of shell middens has been explained by showing that they are arranged along the shoreline of the Jomon Marine Transgression in this region (e.g., Toki 1926a,b; Esaka 1943, 1954, 1971; Endo 1979). At the peak of the Jomon Transgression about 6000 B.P., lowlands less than about 10 m above the present sea level were flooded, and embayment conditions were widely formed throughout the Kanto district. These bays had brackish-water environments of tidal and littoral zones that were influenced by the rivers flowing into them but were not directly influenced by the ocean. These environments should provide agreeable surroundings for the feeding and breeding of *A. schlegeli* and *L. japonicus*, according to their habitats of the living species (Kuwatani 1962; Matsubara and Ochiai 1965:683–687, 702–704; Kawana 1968). Accordingly, it is reasonable that these sites are characterized by a high frequency of these two species.

In other words, the relative frequencies of the three species examined here depend mostly on the potential of the marine territory of the site in which they are found.

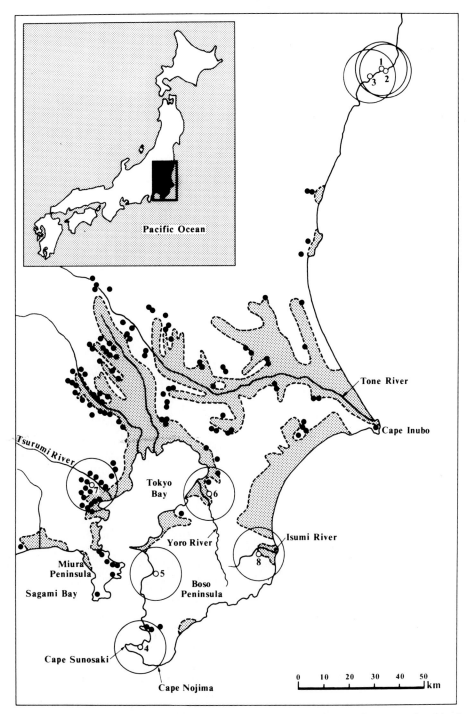

Figure 4.9 Distribution of Jomon shell-midden sites in the Kanto district. The sites enclosed by the circles (10-km radius) are (1) Terawaki, (2) Tsunatori, (3) Ohata, (4) Natagiri, (5) Fujimidai, (6) Saihiro, (7) Miyanohara, and (8) Nittano. The dotted site shows the distribution of early Jomon (about 6000 B.P.) shell middens in the Kanto district, and the stippled portions show the approximate expanse of the maximum transgression at that time. (Compiled from Toki 1926a:Fig. 3; Endo 1979:Fig. 2.)

Size–Age Frequency of Shell-Midden Fish Species

Figure 4.10 compares the size frequency distribution of *C. major*, based upon the results of body size estimated from the premaxillary and dentary bone fragments collected from the two shell middens of Miyano and Shomyoji. It is apparent that their respective size populations differed; the Miyano sample includes only adult groups, and the Shomyoji sample includes both young and adult groups, as seen in two size classes above and below 300 mm in body length (Kajiyama 1937; Tanaka 1958; Matsubara and Ochiai 1965:706–707). Also from these data, it might be possible to state a strong correlation between the marine territory and the behavioral pattern of shell-midden people.

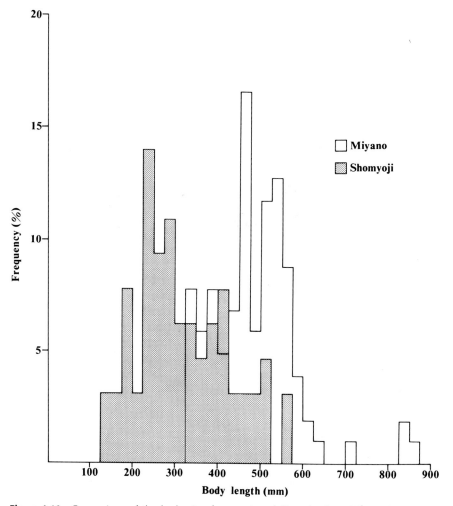

Figure 4.10 Comparison of the body size frequencies of *C. major* from Miyano (*N* = 102) and Shomyoji (*N* = 64).

Both sites, dating to approximately the same period of the Late Jomon around 4000 B.P., show a marked difference in the proportion and nature of marine territory. The marine territory of the Miyano site is characterized by rocky to ria-type sandy flats facing the Pacific Ocean. The Shomyoji site is located along the present coast facing Tokyo Bay, and has rocky-shore zones with some direct influence from fresh water.

C. major move inshore and offshore to some extent. With the rising water temperature in spring, they move shoreward to breed and feed along the coast and/or in bays; but with the lowering water temperature in fall, they migrate to the open sea or to deeper water in the bays for the winter (Kajiyama 1937; Tanaka 1958; Matsubara and Ochiai 1965:707–708). The important characteristic of this species is that the routes and degree of its migrations alter according to the growth of the individual members.

Hayashi (1968:25) has provided the data for a detailed examination of the relationship between the growth and habitat of this species (Figure 4.11). Yearlings, which are spawned in the Zostera areas during spring, stay in rocky-shore zones of bays and then migrate to the rocky-shore zones along the open sea. In other words, the non-adults of this species, 10–15 cm in body length, are found in the shallow water along the rocky shores of bays and open sea. But the adults

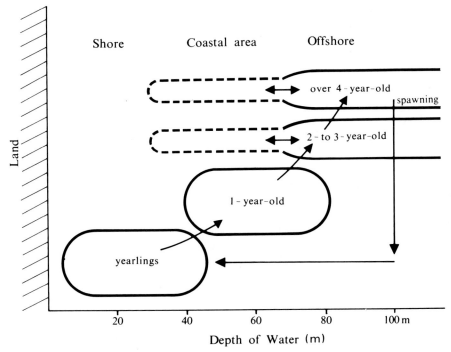

Figure 4.11 Schematic representation of the annual variations of the habitat of *C. major*. (Compiled from Tsukahara 1968:Fig. 2.)

of this species move offshore during winter to deep water (90–100 m) in the open sea, and then migrate and stay in the rocky-shore zones for breeding during spring when the water temperature rises.

From the habits of C. *major* summarized in the preceding, it might be possible to state that discrepancies in the size frequency distributions of these two shell middens indicate differences in the natural population of this species at the marine territory. Obviously, criticism can be made of results based on such indirect evidence. For instance, the size-age frequencies of the catch are influenced by a number of selection factors due to the nature of fishing gear utilized (e.g., McCracken 1963).

Figure 4.12 shows comparison of size frequency of cod catches with different sizes of hooks. As explained by McCracken (1963:152), the selection of cod by hooks follows a regular progression from smaller to larger hooks. That is to say, each succeeding larger hook caught fewer small cod and the maximum size at which fish escaped increased, although both large and small hooks took similar quantities of large fish. Accordingly, it cannot be denied that the possibility that selections of C. *major* taken from Miyano and Shomyoji assemblages resulted in the different size frequencies between the two seen in Figure 4.10. Nevertheless, it might be possible that the natural population of the species differed, at least during the fishing season, since the nature of the marine territory of the sites was markedly different; therefore, the size composition of the catch would indicate these discrepancies.

Taking into account the above data, it is found that the shell-midden people were well adapted to their local environment. In the process of adaptation, they

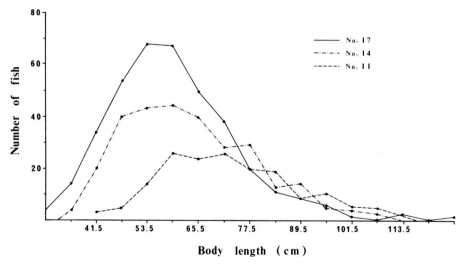

Figure 4.12 Size frequency of cod catches with different hook sizes (No. 17 is the Mustad hook 17 with a maximum width of 17 mm; No. 14 is the Mustad hook 14 with a maximum width of 23 mm; and No. 11 is the Mustad hook 11 with a maximum width of 33 mm). (Modified from McCracken 1963:Fig. 4.)

tended to work a certain area surrounding a site, which is generally known as the site territory. Although it is not easy to estimate the extent of a prehistoric site territory, the site territory of the shell-midden people—at least the marine territory—may be considered smaller than that of other gatherers and hunters.

The exploitation patterns of the shell-midden people were basically characterized by sea-oriented and/or freshwater-oriented systems centered on the area on the immediate proximity of the site. Furthermore, although other auxiliary food resources should not be overlooked, those systems can be mostly defined by the most basic fish available, as is shown in the previous example, and is well known in the case of site catchment analysis of the Jomon shell-midden sites (Akazawa 1980). However, it is important that the assumption of a functional correlation between the shell-midden people and the exploitation territory is also supported by the data from the analysis of the artifactual remains collected from the shell middens. Therefore, the regional specialization of fishing adaptation will hereafter be examined by additional analysis of fishing equipment of the Jomon people.

Craft Specialization in Fishing Equipment of the Jomon People

Kroeber and Barrett have drawn ethnographic generalizations from the fishing activities of California Indians:

> Different environmental conditions rule the cycles of these [fish] species, controlled the methods by which each might be taken, and gave rise to the different devices: weirs, nets, traps, spears, harpoons, gaffs, and other inventions of the primitive fishermen (1960:8).

Regional differences in technological specialization should also be examined, since it is highly reasonable to believe that craft specialization in fishing equipment was promoted by a series of interactions between fishermen and the nature of their exploitation territory, as illustrated in California Indians.

As indicated by Kono (1942), Jomon fishing activities can be broadly classified into two types: inner-bay and ocean fishing. This idea has been strengthened by further discussion based on Watanabe's data (1966a, 1968, 1973). In summary, Jomon fishing developed into two major types through the Late Jomon period: one concentrated on inner-bay fishing equipped with gaffs and nets, and the other on ocean fishing with harpoons and fishhooks. The inner-bay fishing flourished in the sites where marine territory included shallow bays at the time when the sea flooded the nearby lowlands during the postglacial marine transgression. The emphasis on ocean fishing continued on the northern Pacific coast, in particular, along the rocky-shore zones.

Among these differentiations, a functional correlation between the type of marine environment in the site territory and craft specialization in fishing equipments should be emphasized here, as deduced from Kroeber and Barrett's previously mentioned work. The next analysis will concern the examination of the context of the Jomon fishing gear assemblages and the significance of their inter-assemblage variability.

The materials utilized in this paper consist of 45 assemblages found in Jomon shell-midden sites (Figure 4.13). The sites were approximately contemporaneous, that is, Late to Final Jomon. Because the associated fishing gears were fully studied by Watanabe (1973), we can assume a set of entirely standardized data.

The original data were derived from Watanabe (1973:Tables 1, 5, and 11). Unfortunately, it is not easy to establish with certainty a mutual relationship between assemblages reported under Watanabe's nomenclature, because his classification system is rather complex. For instance, one-piece hooks are classified into six types: (*a*) non-barbed, (*b*) out-barbed, (*c*) in-barbed, (*d*) both-barbed, (*e*) stem-barbed, and (*f*) anchor-type (Watanabe 1966a, 1973). This classification system shows a number of typological and chronological factors concerning

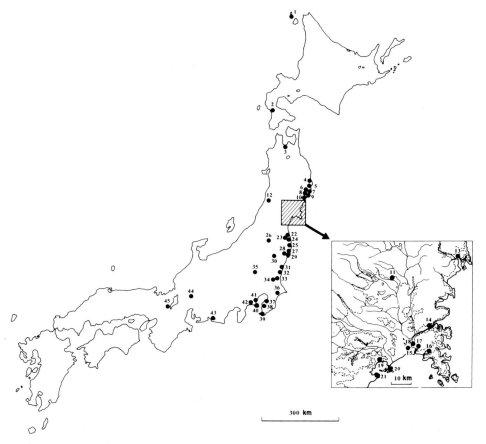

Figure 4.13 Distribution of 45 sites utilized for clustering Jomon sites in terms of their subsistence system.

fishing gear which flourished in the Jomon period, but it is also reasonable to believe that other important evidences might be overlooked since the nomenclature was devised according to minute morphological features. Accordingly, the original data, the frequency of fishing gear types, were modified according to the following classification system.

1. Watanabe's six types of harpoon heads were categorized into two groups: toggle harpoon heads of open socket type and of closed socket type.
2. Watanabe's eight types of fishhooks were categorized into three groups: one-piece, anchor, and composite.
3. Watanabe's 29 types of netsinkers into 4 groups: reused potsherd, notched stone, grooved pottery, and grooved stone.

The methods employed were factor and distance analyses, selected for the purpose of clustering the selected Jomon sites. These computations were processed by the HITAC system of the University of Tokyo Computer Center using the Biomedical Computer Programs-P, BMDP2M for the clustering analysis, and BMDP4M for the factor analysis.

Combination of Fishing Gear

The data analyzed here were composed of the relative frequency of fishing gear, classified under the nine type-groups outlined above. Tables 4.3 and 4.4 show the basic data tabulation and the intervariable correlations in the present sample.

The result of the factor analysis is shown in Table 4.5, which gives the correlations between variables as they occur in each factor. The table is divided into four major groupings of variables, exhibiting higher correlations as they occur in each factor. Three fishing gears—closed socket toggle harpoon heads, one-piece fishhooks, and reused pottery netsinkers—were selected as diagnostic of Factor

TABLE 4.3

Basic Statistics of Nine Groups of the Jomon Fishing Gear in the Selected Assemblages[a]

Nine groups of variables	N	Mean	Standard deviation	Coefficient of variation
H1: open socket toggle harpoon head	20	3.67	14.9267	4.05
H2: closed socket toggle harpoon head	429	15.30	25.2227	1.64
F1: one-piece fishhook	527	25.31	28.4919	1.12
F2: one-piece fishhook of anchor type	20	1.53	5.6308	3.67
F3: composite fishhook	53	1.51	5.8887	3.88
N1: reused potsherd netsinker	1059	26.11	41.0171	1.57
N2: notched stone netsinker	136	9.70	26.4983	2.73
N3: grooved pottery netsinker	156	11.21	26.6995	2.38
N4: grooved stone netsinker	86	5.61	16.3028	2.90

[a] From Watanabe (1973).

TABLE 4.4

Correlation Matrix of Nine Groups of the Jomon Fishing Gear in the Selected Assemblages

	H1	H2	F1	F2	F3	N1	N2	N3	N4
H1	—								
H2	−.153	—							
F1	−.021	.300	—						
F2	−.069	.070	.306	—					
F3	.539	−.047	.014	−.072	—				
N1	−.160	−.395	−.415	−.177	−.168	—			
N2	−.092	−.227	−.325	−.102	−.095	−.217	—		
N3	−.106	−.223	−.279	−.116	−.078	−.240	−.082	—	
N4	−.087	−.212	−.277	−.096	−.077	−.166	.129	.097	—

1. Among these variables, the first two show positive values while the last one has higher negative values. In the case of Factor 2, the open socket toggle harpoon heads and anchor-type fishhooks were taken as diagnostic of this factor. Diagnostic variables to Factors 3 and 4 consist of notched stone netsinkers and grooved pottery netsinkers, respectively. Both these show higher positive values.

In addition, using the first and second factor loadings, a two-dimensional scattergram can be drawn (Figure 4.14). Although, in this case, only about 40% of the total variance is provided by these two factors (Table 4.6), four clusters can be separated on the basis of the two-dimensional expression of the group constellation. These four clusters are composed of the following: (a) the closed socket toggle harpoon head—one-piece and anchor-type fishhooks cluster, (b) the open socket toggle harpoon head—composite fishhook cluster, (c) the notched stone—grooved pottery and stone netsinker cluster, and (d) the reused

TABLE 4.5

Pattern of Rotated Factor Loadings of Nine Groups of the Jomon Fishing Gear[a]

Nine groups of variables	Factors			
	1	2	3	4
H1	−.089	.875	−.043	−.056
H2	.694	−.094	−.133	−.050
F1	.780	.063	−.265	−.137
F2	.491	−.119	−.048	−.130
F3	−.022	.864	−.057	−.016
N1	−.717	−.288	−.458	−.421
N2	−.147	−.063	.872	−.222
N3	−.180	−.079	−.036	.925
N4	−.181	−.081	.540	.326

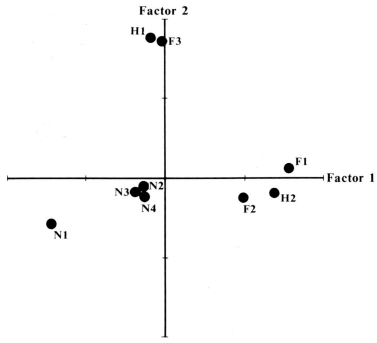

Figure 4.14   Constellation of the Jomon fishing gear plotted with respect to the first and second factor loadings calculated by factor analysis of the sites (groups of variables are as defined in Table 4.3).

potsherd netsinker cluster. In comparing these separations with the factor loading pattern shown in Table 4.5, it is evident that those four major clusterings can be considered diagnostic of the factors mentioned previously. As a result, it was found that a combination of fishing gear can be used as diagnostic of each factor.

From these well-defined clusters, we can postulate the possibility that certain sets of fishing gear were developed in certain groups of sites, at least in the sites

TABLE 4.6

Eigenvalues for the Calculated Factors and Cumulative Proportion in Total Variance

Factor	Eigenvalue	Cumulative proportion
1	2.053	.228
2	1.620	.408
3	1.407	.564
4	1.085	.685
5	.959	.792
6	.828	.884
7	.591	.949
8	.456	1.000

analyzed here. Further, it might be possible that a certain group of sites characterized by the same pattern of fishing equipment had a similar kind of fishing
adaptation as sites of the same type of exploitation territory, at least in the case
of marine territory. Therefore, we will examine the clustering of the Jomon sites
based upon associated fishing gear.

Clustering the Jomon Sites

Taking the same data used in the previous section, factor and clustering
analyses were performed by pairing 45 Jomon sites. Figure 4.15 shows the
distances between the analyzed sites delineated by the factor scores calculated
for each site assemblage on the basis of factor analysis. First we can see, in
general, the formation of three major clusters. On closer examination of these

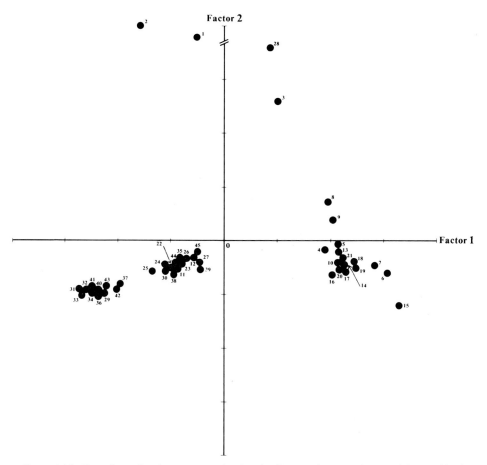

Figure 4.15 Two-dimensional scattergram showing the distances between the sites delineated by the
first and second factor scores on the basis of factor analysis.

clusters, through the original data used in the present study, each cluster can be explained according to diagnostic variables.

The 16 sites clustered on the right along the x axis are all characterized by high-to-moderate frequencies of closed socket toggle harpoon heads and fishhooks of one-piece and anchor types, and low-to-negligible quantities of various netsinkers. The lefthand group represents sites characterized by high frequencies of various types of netsinkers as their main gear constituent. The four sites forming another cluster broadly located in the upper part along the y axis are generally characterized by high quantities of open socket toggle harpoon heads and/or composite-type fishhooks.

Next, the large cluster located on the left-hand side of the y axis was further separated into smaller clusters, although the distance between the clusters is not so clear. This separation is due to the different combination of netsinkers of the four designated groups. In particular, the different frequencies of the reused potsherd netsinkers and other types of netsinkers can be understood to separate these sites into two clusters. These general features of the major separation into clusters and their relation to diagnostic variables agree well with the separation of fishing gear into clusters by the factor analysis previously described. The results obtained are further examined by the following clustering analysis with more identical patterns.

Taking the same data used in factor analysis, average-linkage cluster analysis with the Euclidean distance measure was calculated by pairing the sites. Figure 4.16 is the cluster diagram of the total sites analyzed. This dendrogram shows clear evidence of shell-midden clustering. In comparing these separations with the results obtained in factor analysis, the overall pattern of separation is more positive than that of factor analysis.

The shell-midden sites can be separated into four clusterings, designated as A to D in Figure 4.16, at the cophenetic value of 3.0. Each cluster can be explained by distinctive diagnostic variables through examination of the original data studied here. The site group of cluster A was selected as diagnostic of notched stone netsinkers; the diagnostic variables for cluster B consist of netsinkers of various types, in particular, of grooved pottery netsinkers. Although the diagnostic variables for the cluster C are somewhat variable, the reused potsherd netsinkers can be considered the most important diagnostic of this cluster. Also, in this case, the high quantities of one-piece fishhooks were selected as diagnostic of a number of sites of this cluster. In cluster D, the two variables consisting of closed socket toggle harpoon heads and one-piece fishhooks are diagnostic.

On further examination of the observed separation into the four clusters, it is found that the results obtained here match wholly with certain groups of sites on the basis of their geographical distribution (see Fig. 4.13). The sites clustered in B and D are located in the coastal regions facing the open sea, as seen in sites 22–25 and 27 for B, and 4–10, 13, 14, and 16–21 for D. Of these, the marine territory of the sites of cluster D is characterized by rocky to sandy flats of the ria type, and also by high frequencies of rocky-shore and large-migratory species due to the

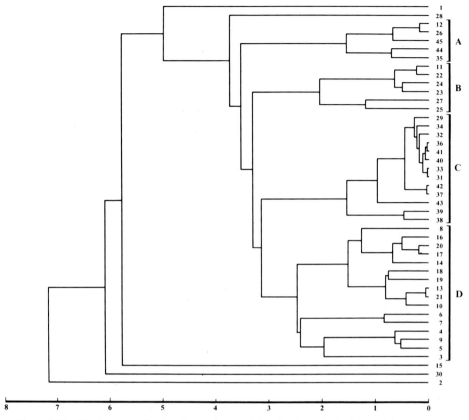

Figure 4.16 Dendrograms showing the result of applying cluster analysis of the weighted average pair method to a matrix of correlations of the sites. Four major clusters (A–D) can be detected at the cophenetic value of 3.0.

junction of the Kuroshio and Oyashio. The sites of cluster C were similarly located inland, that is, these sites were oriented to the embayment conditions formed during the marine transgression of Jomon period. Also included in this group were sites oriented to the littoral regions, as seen with site 39.

In contrast to the sites of these three clusters, which are all characterized by extensive midden deposits distributed in the coastal regions, the sites clustered in A are situated inland along rivers and nearby inland lakes, as seen in sites 12, 26, 35, 44, and 45. These sites are quite different from other groups of sites in their nature of craft specialization indicated by earlier research. That is, cluster A sites were selected by a simple combination of fishing gear as diagnostic of notched netsinkers, while other groups of sites were selected as diagnostic variables.

Thus, the variability observed in the types of fishing adaptation of the Jomon people is greatly reflected in the craft specialization in fishing equipment. Again, from these analytical data, we can postulate a functional correlation between hunter–gatherers and their adaptation to environments. In compiling the results described above, we can classify the fishing adaptation of the Jomon people into four types: (*a*) oceanic, (*b*) littoral, (*c*) embayment, and (*d*) lake to riverine.

In order to define the types of fishing adaptation, four Jomon sites (Miyano, Natagiri, Nittano, and Torihama) will be examined in detail. All these sites are among the few at which systematic sampling techniques were used to recover all the material from the excavated areas and where the identified fish species were described both qualitatively and quantitatively.

Oceanic Type Fishing adaptation of this type can be represented by the sites grouped as cluster D in the clustering analysis. The Miyano site is described here as an example of this cluster type.

The Miyano site (Figure 4.17) is a coastal shell midden located along the Pacific Ocean in the Tohoku district (141°48′E, 39°03′N). The marine territory of the site is characterized by rocky to ria-type sandy flats directly facing the open sea. These flats are strongly influenced by the Kuroshio and the Oyashio currents along the Pacific coast of Japan; they are not influenced by freshwater. Furthermore, the marine territory of this type was only slightly influenced by early Holocene Jomon Transgression. As a result, the marine environment—its proportion to the total territory, salinity, depth, and bottom sediments—has not changed from the time when the site was occupied until today. This assumption can be supported by data from the analysis of the faunal remains from the midden deposit.

The Miyano fish assemblage is characterized by high frequencies of rocky-shore species, such as *C. major* and the families Scorpaenidae and Hexagrammidae (Suzuki 1977). These species are equally common coastal fish which widely inhabit the rocky-shore zones facing the open sea (Matsubara and Ochiai 1965:892–901, 903–910). Another feature is the high proportion of other oceanic species, such as the family Scombridae including the genera *Thunnus, Katsuwonus,* and *Scomber.* These are all large-scale migratory species that seasonally migrate to the Japanese archipelago (Matsubara and Ochiai 1965:763–862). These frequency figures on fish species identified are not different from the nature of the potential marine resources available under the present conditions.

Other remains of mollusks will be summarized from findings of related sites in this region since the molluscan collection has not been analyzed at Miyano. The molluscan assemblage is also characterized by high frequencies of rocky to sandy flat species, although the relative quantities of the species are highly variable by site (Kaneko 1965, 1980). Nevertheless, the most common species consist of *Mytilus coruscus, Lunella coronata, Meretrix lamarcki, Umbonium (Suchium) giganteum,* and *Tapes (Amygdala) philippinarum.* All of these species inhabit rocky to sandy flats facing the open sea.

The associated fishing gear are characterized by the development of toggle harpoon heads of closed socket type and one-piece fishhooks. Figure 4.18 shows the distribution of sites producing fishhooks and also indicates frequency dis-

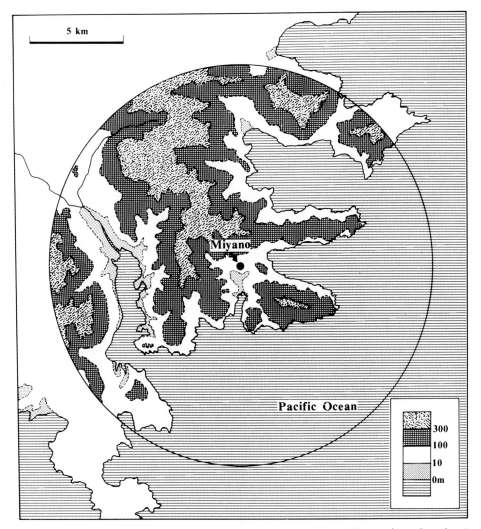

Figure 4.17 Hypothetical exploitation territory of Miyano site delimited by a 10-km radius, showing topographical conditions based on altitudinal zones.

tribution by region of these fishhooks. They are evidently concentrated on sites located on the seashore including the Pacific coast of the Tohoku district. It is also well known that the frequency of toggle harpoon heads of closed socket type is very high in coastal sites along the same coast of the Tohoku district (Otsuka 1966; Watanabe 1973).

In conclusion, this type of fishing adaptation is characterized by the ocean-oriented subsistence system that was developed in the coastal regions influenced by the Kuroshio and Oyashio currents.

Littoral Type   This type of fishing adaptation is well defined by the charac-

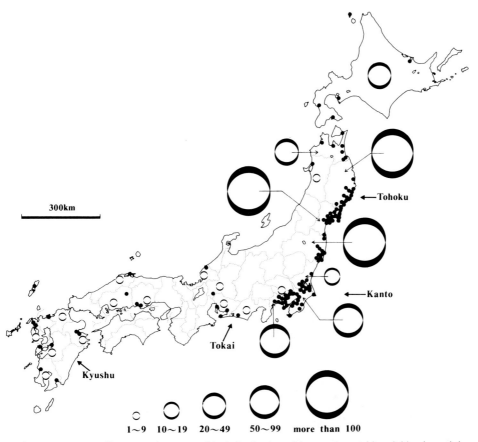

Figure 4.18 Map illustrating the geographical distribution of Jomon sites yielding fishhooks and the relative frequencies of the fishhooks by area. (Compiled from Watanabe 1973:Figs. 38, 39, 41, 42, 45, 47, 49, 52, 56, and 61.)

teristic features of Natagiri site. This site falls into the embayment type by cluster analysis on the basis of the fishing gear assemblage. However, the overall features of the site, including the nature of the marine territory, evidently coincide with those observed in the sites characterized by the littoral type. This contradiction may be due to variable features used in the cluster analysis.

Natagiri site (Figure 4.19) is a cave producing a large amount of midden deposit, located at the southern extremity of Boso Peninsula in the Kanto district (139°48′E, 34°58′N). The marine territory of this site is also characterized by rocky to sandy flats directly facing the open sea. These flats are influenced by the Kuroshio but are not influenced by freshwater. Furthermore, the marine territory of the site was hardly influenced by early Holocene Jomon Transgression. The sea may have flooded the coastal lowlands to some extent within the territory during the maximum stage of the Jomon Transgression as shown in Figure 4.19.

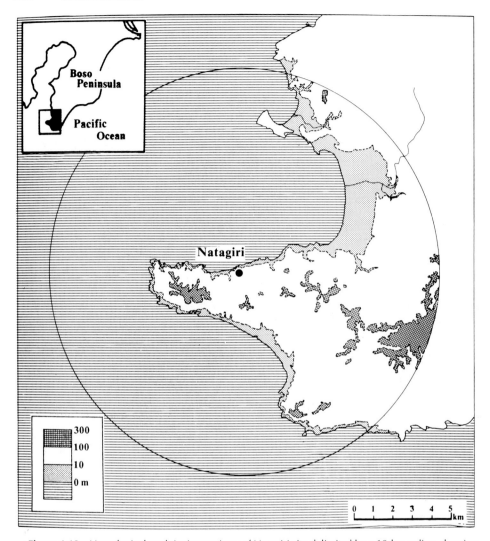

Figure 4.19 Hypothetical exploitation territory of Natagiri site delimited by a 10-km radius, showing topographical conditions based on altitudinal zones.

But the sea had probably receded to the present shoreline by the time of later Jomon when the site was occupied, according to geomorphological studies on the Kanto district (e.g., Kaizuka 1976; Endo 1979).

Forty-seven varieties of fish, including genera and/or families, were identified and described in the original report of the Natagiri site (Kaneko 1958). Almost all of the species identified are found in the rocky-shore environments of littoral zones in the open sea. In particular, the dominant species, *C. major, Gymnothorax kidako, Epinephelus septemfasciatus, Leptoscarus japonicus,* and *Calliodon ovifrons,* and the family Labridae, inhabit littoral zones along the rocky shore facing the open sea. In these littoral zones, the ocean water directly affects the environment, as determined by study of the ecological habits of the living species (e.g., Matsubara and Ochiai 1965).

The same general characteristics are observed in the molluscan assemblage of the site. Kaneko (1958) identified 40 species of gastropods and 28 species of pelecypods (both including genera and/or families). It is not clear whether or not all these species were transported by people. In particular, some of the species of very low frequencies might be derived from natural agencies. The species of gastropoda, *Batillus cornutus*, *Cellana nigrolineata*, *Thais (Mancinella) clavigera*, *Thais bronni*, and *L. coronata*, and the family Haliotidae, occupy the major portion of the assemblage. These were brought to the site from the rocky-shore flats of tidal to littoral zones facing the open sea, according to their habitat as classified by Japanese malacologists (e.g., Kira 1969; Habe and Kosuge 1967).

Cluster analysis shows that fishing gear characterizing this type of fishing adaptation basically consists of netsinkers of various types, particularly the grooved pottery type, but the actual features vary by area. For instance, the Natagiri assemblage is characterized by high frequencies of one-piece fishhooks and reused potsherd netsinkers. The most distinct difference from the oceanic-type adaptation is the absence or low incidence of toggle harpoon heads, although the frequency of fishhooks shows the same pattern between the two, as illustrated in Figure 4.18.

In conclusion, this type of fishing adaptation is characterized by a littoral-oriented subsistence system which generally flourished in the coastal regions along the Pacific Coast of eastern Japan. The potential prehistoric resources for this type of adaptation are dominated by nonmigratory, rocky-shore and open-sea species inhabiting the coastal zones influenced by the Kuroshio Current, and do not include large-scale migratory species, which were the major constituents of the ocean-oriented subsistence system.

Embayment Type   The embayment type, representative of Cluster C, is observable at the Nittano site. This site (Figure 4.20) is located over 5 km inland from the present coastline (140°20′E, 35°17′N). But Nittano was not an inland shell midden, because the prehistoric environment around the site at the time of the Jomon occupation was markedly different from that of today.

After examining the topography around the site from the paleogeomorphological viewpoint, it seems quite possible that an embayment once existed along the coast between Capes Taito and Hachiman, stretching inland along the lower reaches of the Isumi River (Akazawa 1980). The stippled portions in Figure 4.20 show the area less than 10 m above the present sea level; this suggests the maximum extent of the Jomon Transgression along the Isumi River about 6000 B.P. This dating for the maximum transgression in the early Holocene agrees well with the fact that the Early Jomon Hanazumi-type pottery stage is the first evidence of human habitation at this site.

If we assume that embayments of this kind existed in the territory of the site,

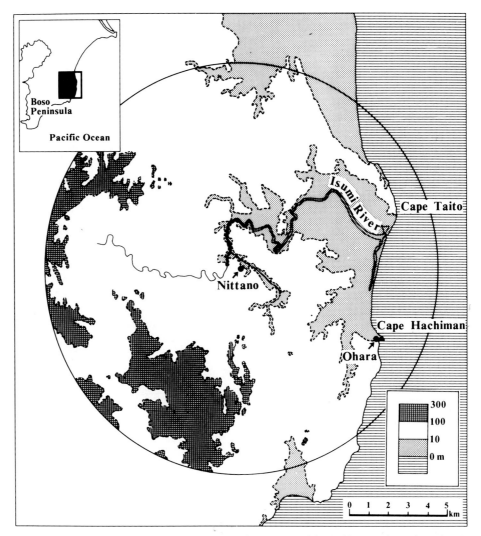

Figure 4.20 Hypothetical exploitation territory of Nittano site delimited by a 10-km radius, showing topographical conditions based on altitudinal zones.

the potential prehistoric marine resources had to be considerably different from those presently available. Data provided by the fishermen's union at Ohara, a fishing port near Cape Hachiman, show that the majority of the catch obtained by inshore fishing from Ohara consists of rocky-shore and open-sea species, such as the mollusks *B. cornutus* and *Haliotis gigantea,* and the fish *Seriola quinqueradiata* and *C. major.* These figures are completely different from the relative frequencies of molluscan and fish species identified in the Jomon deposits at

Nittano site. The Nittano assemblage was characterized by high frequencies of brackish-water species from tidal and sublittoral zones in bays.

Common fish species of the Nittano assemblage are *Mugil cephalus*, *L. japonicus*, *A. schlegeli,* and *Platycephalus indicus* (Ogawa *et al.* 1975). All these species are found in the brackish-water environments of tidal to sublittoral zones in bays during their breeding and feeding seasons. In particular, the two most abundant species, *L. japonicus* and *M. cephalus,* migrate to the brackish-water environment of riverine zones for certain periods of feeding. Another feature of the fish assemblage identified here is the high proportion of freshwater and brackish-water species from riverine and tidal zones in bays—such as the families Anguillidae and Tetraodontidae; the genera *Carassius* and *Hemiramphus;* and *Engraulis japonica, Cyprinus carpio,* and *Acanthogobius flavimanus,* as shown in the Kamitakatsu assemblage (Komiya 1980).

The molluscan assemblage of Nittano site shows the same characteristic features as seen in the fish assemblage. The dominant species identified consist of *Cyclina sinensis* and *Corbicula japona;* their total frequency is over 90%. The molluscan assemblages vary in species sample and proportion by site. Nevertheless, the dominant species of this type of site consist of those from muddy to sandy mud flats of estuaries and tidal zones in bays, such as *Meretrix lusoria, Crassostrea gigas, Tegillarca granosa,* and *Umbonium (Suchium) moniliferum* (Komiya 1980).

The fishing gear of these sites is rather simple compared with those of the preceding oceanic-type and littoral-type assemblages, and the reused potsherd netsinker characterized this type of fishing adaptation. The use and function of this type of netsinker is controversial, although it is designated as sinker for inner-bay net fishing by Watanabe (1973). Nevertheless, these are the most noteworthy remains distributed throughout most embayment-type shell-midden sites, and particularly concentrated on the later Jomon sites in the Kanto district.

Another major gear found in these sites is gaff heads. This type of gear is excluded from the multivariate analyses mentioned earlier, since quantitative data could not be obtained in the sites analyzed here. Table 4.7 shows the frequency distributions of three major types of fishing gear including gaff heads at the sites. The embayment-oriented sites show a simple assemblage of fishing gear consisting of largely gaff heads, in contrast to a great variety of assemblages from the oceanic-type to littoral-type sites.

The marine territory of the site already mentioned was formed in many places along the coastal lowlands, as the marine transgression spread (see Figure 4.9). Since the peak of the Jomon Transgression around 6000 B.P., embayment conditions increased in the coastal lowlands, advancing a new type of subsistence system—a bay-oriented exploitation system. During the later Jomon period around 6000–4000 B.P., this kind of occupational specialization was established along the Pacific coast, particularly in the Kanto district.

Lake to Riverine Type This type of fishing adaptation can be defined by the

TABLE 4.7

Comparison of the Frequency Distributions of the Three Major Types of Jomon Fishing Gear at Shell Middens[a]

Shell midden	Jomon period	Harpoon heads	Fishhooks	Gaff heads	Excavated area (m²)	Marine territory type
Nishinohama	Late	38	43	10	274	Oceanic
Natagiri	Late	2	20	28	?	Littoral
Yoyama	Late	22	22	43	128	Littoral
Fujimidai	Late	4	7	9	24	Littoral
Shomyoji	Late	12	6	16	70	Littoral
Okuraminami	Late	0	2	54	21	Embayment
Onigoe	Late	0	0	22	16.6	Embayment
Kamitakatsu	Late	0	1	23	27.2	Embayment
Shiizuka	Late	1?	2	40	16	Embayment
Hirohata	Late	0	3	30	16	Embayment
Shijimizuka	Late to Final	0	0	148	?	Lake to riverine
Torihama	Late	0	0	>50	?	Lake to riverine

[a]The frequencies are from Kaneko (1958) at Natagiri; Morikawa (1979) at Torihama; and the others from Kaneko (1971: Table 1).

sites clustered in A by clustering analysis based upon associated fishing gear. When compared with the preceding three types of adaptations, there is less quantitative and qualitative archaeological evidence available for the evaluation of this kind of adaptation. Here, discussion on type A fishing activity will be centered on the data of Torihama site.

Torihama site is situated inland (Figure 4.21), about 5 km from the present coastline of Wakasa Bay in western Japan (135°54'E, 35°33'N). Occupational deposits of the site indicate that it was occupied at the same time as the Nittano site, that is, around 6000 B.P. The stippled portion in Figure 4.21 represents the area less than 10 m above the present sea level. This 10-m elevation represents the maximum extent of the Jomon Transgression around the Wakasa Bay, as in the case of the Nittano site. In comparing the exploitation territory of these two sites from paleotopographical viewpoints, a marked difference is seen between the two although some general similarities are observed.

The circle in Figure 4.21 encloses an area within 10-km and 5-km radii of the site, the area assumed to be the exploitation territory. The large circle includes a large amount of open-sea environment characterized by rocky to sandy flats directly facing the open sea. These flats are influenced by an oceanic current running along the coast of the Sea of Japan. The potential prehistoric marine resources in the flats were most likely characterized by oceanic species, but excavations have shown contrary results, that is, the site is characterized by freshwater to brackish-water species.

The relative frequencies are greatest for fish and molluscan species living in freshwater to brackish-water environments with riverine to lake conditions

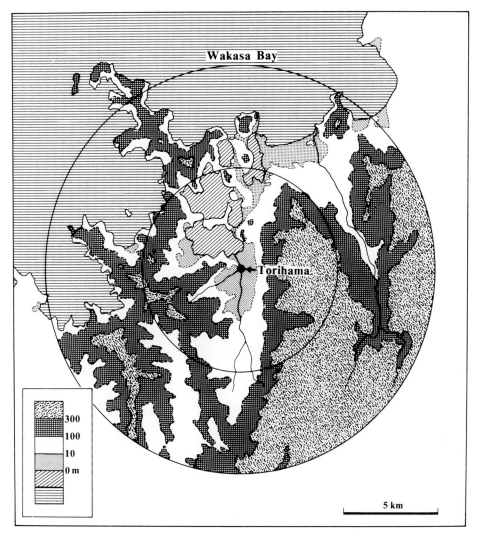

Figure 4.21   Hypothetical exploitation territory of Torihama site delimited by 10-km and 5-km radii, showing topographical conditions based on altitudinal zones.

(Nishida 1980). For instance, most dominant fish identified are freshwater species of the genera *Carassius* and *Cyprinus*. Fish species such as *L. japonicus, A. schlegeli,* and *C. major* are common in eastern shell middens of littoral-oriented to embayment-oriented types. Hence, they might be expected to be the major potential marine resources in a 10-km exploitation territory of the site; yet, these fish species show very low frequencies in the Torihama assemblages.

The living species of *C. japonica,* the most frequent species of molluscan remains identified, lives in freshwater to brackish-water environments, such as the lower reaches of streams and estuaries. The next most common mollusks identified are also freshwater to brackish-water species, including *Lanceolaria cuspidata, Unio douglasiae nipponensis,* and *Inversidens japanensis* (Fujii and Takayama 1979:167). The mollusks of oceanic and rocky species, such as *B. cornutus* and *T. bronni,* have very low frequencies, and some species are found in almost negligible proportions.

Thus, the relative frequencies of rocky and sandy flat species in the open sea are almost negligible at Torihama. The dominant species of fish and mollusks are found in freshwater to brackish-water environments, such as lakes, the lower reaches of streams, and estuaries. The species found in the highest frequencies are restricted to those closest to the site which lived in the enlarged lake and riverine environment formed by the Early Jomon Transgression. An exploitation territory enclosed by a circle with a 10-km radius is too large for the site, at least for the marine exploitation activities: The area habitually exploited by the Torihama people was the lakes and rivers within the 5-km radius. The high caloric values of molluscan and fish species, as shown in Table 4.8, are obtained from these freshwater to brackish-water species exploited with the marine territory of the site (Nishida 1980).

As discussed earlier, this type of fishing adaptation is characterized by a high frequency of notched-stone netsinkers. The same tendency is also observed in the Torihama assemblage (Tanabe *et al.* 1979). In addition, gaff heads are very common in this assemblage (see Table 4.7). That is, the combination pattern of fishing gear is generally the same as that of the embayment-type sites, although the typological features of netsinkers differ between the two, as seen in the reused potsherd netsinkers for the embayment type.

In conclusion, this type of fishing adaptation is generally characterized by a freshwater-oriented subsistence system which was developed in inland lakes and riverine regions. Their fishing activities, including shellfishing, concentrated on freshwater species with rather simple equipment.

MARITIME HUNTER–GATHERERS IN JAPAN AND THEIR RESPONSE TO RICE AGRICULTURE

The four types of fishing adaptation can be discerned among the occupational specializations of the Jomon people. Obviously, criticism can be made of results based upon regional archaeological data differing in quantity and quality. Nevertheless, the hypothesis that the Jomon sites can probably be categorized into these four groups explains the data analyzed here reasonably well. However, for further evaluation of this kind, more descriptive information is needed on paleotopography around the sites and faunal and artifactual remains. We therefore cannot conclude that the fishing adaptation was limited to only these four types. But the evidence presented gives some support for further discussion on the reason of the receptivity differences of the Jomon people for rice agriculture.

TABLE 4.8

Percentage Comparison of the Caloric Values of the Major Food Residues at Torihama Site, Calculated on the Two Core Samples[a]

Component	Shellfish		Fish		Mammals		Walnuts		Water chestnuts		Chestnuts		Acorns		Total	
	IE	IM	IE	IM	IE	IM	IE	IM	IE	IM	IE	IM	IE	IM	IE	IM
Whole residue	70.6	89.7	4.4	1.6	5.1	.6	12.6	7.7	3.7	.3	1.2	+[b]	3.6	1.7	100.1	100.1
Edible portion	12.7	36.7	47.4	39.0	18.2	5.5	4.6	7.0	3.8	.9	3.4	+	10.0	10.8	100.1	100.1
Caloric value	8.5	24.8	31.9	26.3	17.5	5.3	16.1	24.8	4.4	1.1	5.5	+	16.0	17.7	99.9	100.0

[a] Total weight of residue of 8.8 kg for IE and 5.3 kg for IM core samples. (From Nishida 1980: Table II).
[b] Unprocessed.

It is a fact that the most conspicuous features of the Jomon shell middens are observed in the coastal regions of the Pacific coast in eastern Japan, as stressed earlier. Most noteworthy, however, are the data presented here concerning regional differentiation of fishing adaptation resulting from the functional correlation between the Jomon people, and their exploitation territory and its resource potentials. Examining these types and their relationship to the actual diffusion pattern of rice cultivation shows that different sites classifiable into these types showed distinct patterns in their transition to a settled life of agriculture. First, the distribution of sites classifiable as oceanic-oriented and littoral-oriented types generally overlaps with the area characterized by resistance to the first stage of rice expansion and by continued reliance on fishing in the Yayoi culture even after adapting to a rice culture. Second, the sites classified as the lake-oriented to riverine-oriented type generally occur in the area where rice cultivation was smoothly accepted in the first and second stages of rice expansion. However, the final group of sites, classified as the embayment-oriented type, showed another case in the final stage of the Jomon period, discussed in the following section.

Embayment-Oriented Subsistence System

The embayment-oriented subsistence system developed in the coastal lowlands from the Early Jomon period when postglacial marine transgression began. In particular, it should be pointed out that in the Kanto Plain, a large quantity of shell middens and settlements was formed, occupying a region with a much longer coastline during the Jomon Transgression as seen in Figure 4.9. However, sites of shell-midden type decreased in number and were reduced in scale during the Final Jomon period in the Kanto Plain (e.g., Kanaseki and Sahara 1978:21; Oikawa et al. 1980). Oikawa et al. (1980:464–468) describe these phenomena in terms of the decline of carrying capacity due to the deterioration in biophysical conditions during this period.

A more reasonable explanation is the paleoenvironmental changes that took place in the marine territory of these sites. The embayment conditions which had yielded the major part of the marine resources used by these shell-midden people were reduced in area and also were moving away from the site during the period of the post-maximum sea regression. These environmental changes quite possibly brought about changes in the potential marine resources that could be exploited by the shell-midden people. The fish and molluscan assemblages certainly were influenced directly by these environmental changes. That is, it is possible that the embayment-oriented subsistence system tended to concentrate population and maintain an enlarged and sedentary community during this period, but it also might have been easily affected by environmental changes.

Another important point to be noted here is the nature of the hinterland zones of these sites. The areas adjacent to these sites are essentially flat. In examining the topography within the site territory of Nittano site (see Figure 4.20), over 80% of the total land is less than 100 m above the present sea level. To the west and south, there is a slight gain in altitude toward the edge of the territory. These geomorphological features around the site might indicate high potential for marine resources due to a widespread transgression of the sea and large formation of embayment and coastal marsh conditions during the Early Jomon Transgression. However, the embayment subsistence system that developed in the lowland regions might not have survived in adapting to the new environmental conditions which occurred after the reduction and/or disappearance of the embayment.

Shell-midden sites of this type not only decreased in number, but the midden deposits changed in character during the Final Jomon period (Suzuki 1968). Suzuki points out that some Final Jomon sites of the Kanto district were characterized by exceedingly large quantities of bone fragments of such land animals as deer and boar, in contrast to the large deposits of molluscan and fish remains of the preceding Jomon shell middens, and he concludes that the possibility of overexploiting these land resources does exist. From these phenomena, as well as the decrease in the number of sites, it might be shown that these embayment-oriented people changed their production system in the Final Jomon to a land-oriented system in order to adapt to the new circumstances resulting from the sea regression, and/or migrated to another suitable place in order to retain their traditional fishing habits.

As explained in earlier sections, the first rice cultivation did not penetrate in the southern Kanto Plain, which is characterized by a high density in the embayment-oriented subsistence system during the later Jomon period. From this evidence we may infer that the areas where an embayment-oriented subsistence system thrived were not suitable for rice cultivation, at least at the beginning of the diffusion, because the life-style of the first rice farmers had to be supported by auxiliary wild food resources until rice became established as a staple.

Oceanic- and Littoral-Oriented Subsistence Systems

Oceanic-oriented and littoral-oriented societies distributed in the coastal regions were only slightly influenced by marine transgression. That is, these kinds of fishing societies became increasingly important along the eastern Pacific Coast during the Final Jomon period. This contrasts with the decline of the embayment fishing societies during the same period. These groups were well adapted to the marine territory and its resource potential. Furthermore, these systems might have been promoted by other basic subsistence activities, such as salmon fishing.

Salmon fishing of the Jomon people has been a controversial question since bone remains of this species have been found only in negligible proportions in middens (e.g., Watanabe 1967; Obayashi 1971; Takayama 1974). However, in recent research made in the Tohoku district, a large quantity of salmon bone fragments has been found in some midden deposits (e.g., Matsui and Yamada 1981; personal communication from Fujiwara and Komiya 1981). Although the evidence is still not sufficient, these findings enable us to predict the possibility of the salmon fishing. Nevertheless, we need not place too much emphasis on salmon fishing for the explanation of the fishing adaptation of these kinds, as described by Jochim:

> No group can or does rely solely on this resource [salmon]. Even in years of good runs, a variety of other resources are available and utilized. Consequently, in dealing with prehistoric salmon fishing, an entire set of alternatives must be considered—in salmon abundance, harvesting efficiency, storage ability, and use of other resources (1979:223).

That is to say, we may define these two types of fishing adaptation according to a combination of salmon fishing and catching oceanic and seawater species. If this is the case, the fishing adaptation of eastern Jomon people might have been much more stable than has been presumed.

From all this evidence, occupational specialization of the oceanic-oriented and littoral-oriented subsistence systems was basically different from other types of subsistence systems defined here. These circumstances can be generally observed along the Pacific coast from Tokai to Tohoku districts where resistance was seemingly made against the first stage of rice expansion. As stressed earlier, the Yayoi people of this region retained their traditional life based upon the preceding local Jomon tradition, and showed a strong tendency toward cultural regionalism. These phenomena also can be explained by the fact that this area was characterized by the oceanic-oriented and littoral-oriented subsistence systems with heavy emphasis on fishing during several thousand years of the Jomon period.

As a result, these regions were not an "optimum cultural environment" for the acceptance of rice. The shell-midden people living there were not willing to accept rice cultivation and, further, would not make the revolutionary readjustment of their cultural habits needed in the transition from a hunting–gathering emphasis on fishing to agriculture.

Lake-Oriented to Riverine-Oriented Subsistence System

Finally, why did the rice cultivation spread rapidly in western Japan and to inland regions of eastern Japan? It is reasonable to believe that comparisons between the marine adaptation of the Jomon people in western and eastern Japan reveal a significant difference. It seems that the western Jomon people were engaged in a lake-oriented to riverine-oriented subsistence system. Fishing activities at Torihama were concentrated in an enlarged lake and riverine environment closest to the site. They did not go on fishing excursions to the seacoast to collect the oceanic and seawater species that were so common in eastern Japan.

According to Watanabe, the Jomon people of western Japan appear to have concentrated their efforts on freshwater species. Comparative studies of the relationship between western Jomon sites and the associated faunal remains show that the distribution of western Jomon sites was along rivers and lakes, not along seacoasts, and their exploitation pattern was lake-oriented and river-oriented for the pursuit of the freshwater species (Watanabe 1968:16–18). This kind of fishing adaptation is characterized by craft equipment and collecting habits. Fishing of the genera *Carasius* and *Cyprinus,* which are the dominant species identified in these sites (Watanabe 1968:18), is not so much regulated by their ecological habits as in the case of the oceanic and seawater species. This circumstance is quite different from the oceanic-fishing and littoral-fishing societies which depended on the regularity of the ecological habits of the basic species of available fish.

Another important fact to be noted here is a high potentiality for land resource use due to the site territory composed of a variety of ecotones. For instance, the site territory of Torihama contains a mountainous environment providing a great variety of food resources. In fact, the Torihama site report identified and described 26 species of plants plus 11 genera and/or families (Nishida 1979), and 10 species of mammals plus 2 genera and/or families. Based upon the caloric levels in the main food resources of the Torihama people, calculated by Nishida (see Table 4.8), they obtained a high proportion of their calories from native plants such as *Juglans mandshurica, Castanea crenata,* and the genus *Trapa,* and from land mammals, such as *Sus scrofa* and *Cervus nippon.* It is evident that the Torihama people had a balanced diet, as Torihama is located at the junction of different zones referred to by Vita-Finzi and Higgs (1970:5). The most important zone was the mountainous region in the hinterlands of the sites.

In the Torihama sites, various acorns and nuts comprised the major portion of plant remains in the total frequencies identified (Nishida 1979, 1980). In addition, some cultivated plant species of *Phaseolus radiatus* and *Lagenaria leucantha* were identified; their frequencies were very low but not negligible (Nishida 1979, 1980; Matsumoto 1979). The Torihama people obtained a high proportion of their calories from these plants (see Table 4.8). In the site were found a large number of axes, adzes, and wooden handles (Tanabe *et al.* 1979; Morikawa and Yamada 1979), which might have been harvesting tools for plants.

Recently, Makabe (1979:238) reported that western Jomon settlement sites are frequently associated with a number of storage pits containing plant remains such as various acorns and nuts. In particular, during the later Jomon period of this region, the number of pits increased drastically. From this evidence, in addition to the Torihama data, it is easy to argue that the western people of the Japanese archipelago gained a greater degree of botanical experience and innovation during the Jomon period than the eastern shell-midden people. These arguments are strengthened by recent research on lithic artifacts of the later Jomon people.

Akazawa (in press) has found that differing combinations of lithic tools were extracted at western and eastern Jomon sites: chipped axes and adzes, various querns and grindstones were found in western Jomon settlements, whereas chipped arrowheads and various scrapers and awls were found in eastern Jomon settlements. If distinctive combinations of tools reflect differences in activities or adaptations to different environments, the western Jomon people might have developed an appropriate cultural milieu as one general condition for the receptivity to agricultural innovation, since these lithic combinations might be concerned with harvesting and processing of plants (Kobayashi 1975).

It can be further postulated that the inland Jomon people of eastern Japan were also engaged in intensive plant collecting and/or incipient plant cultivation of native species in maintaining a cultural tradition of hunting and fishing in the mountainous regions. Although the evidence is still insufficient, it appears that this hypothesis explains reasonably well the fact that the second rice diffusion first traveled inland and not along the coastal regions.

FINAL CONSIDERATIONS

Differences in the receptivity of a settled life based on rice cultivation can be adequately explained by the fact that the subsistence systems of the former Jomon inhabitants varied between areas. The entire process of transition from hunting–gathering to food production agrees with the working model of "broad spectrum" revolution in the origins of early domestication in human history. Flannery proposed, from the comparative data of early Near Eastern domestica-tion, an exploitation system of hunter–gatherers changed from "narrow spec-trum" to "broad spectrum."

> The trend is rather from exploiting a more "narrow spectrum" of environmental resources to a more "broad spectrum" of edible wild products. This "broad spectrum" collecting pattern characterized all subsequent cultures up to about 6,000 B.C., and I would argue that it is only in such a context that the first domestication could take place. It is a pattern in which everything from land snails (*Helix* sp.) to very small crabs (*Potamon* sp.), and perhaps even cereal grasses, was viewed as potential food. It was also accompanied by a number of "pre-adaptations" for early cultivation (Flannery 1969:77).

The same model can be applied to the culture change from Jomon hunting–gathering to Yayoi rice agriculture and its diffusion patterns. The area where rice cultivation spread rapidly expanded its subsistence base to promote pro-gressively a lake-oriented to river-oriented subsistence system possibly includ-ing some incipient plant cultivation. On the other hand, the Jomon people in eastern Japan along the Pacific coast did not react positively to a new way of life since they had developed the exploitation system of a more "narrow spectrum." We can conclude, from the whole discussion presented here, that the differ-entiation between "narrow spectrum" and "broad spectrum" subsistence pat-terns basically originated in the Jomon people's relation to their exploitation territory and its resource potentiality.

Table 4.9 shows the proportional differences of territorial area calculated ac-

TABLE 4.9

Comparison of Altitudinal Zones at Shell Middens, Excluding Riverine Areas[a]

Shell midden	Radius (km)	Total territory Area (km²)	Below 0 m Area (km²)	%	0–10 m Area (km²)	%	10–100 m Area (km²)	%	100–300 m Area (km²)	%	Above 300 m Area (km²)	%
Miyano	5	78.54	21.90	27.9	2.10	2.6	18.75	23.9	25.74	32.8	10.05	12.8
	10	314.16	142.35	45.3	8.40	2.7	49.85	15.3	74.16	23.6	39.30	12.5
Natagiri	5	78.54	45.49	57.9	5.42	6.9	24.72	31.5	2.91	3.7	0	0
	10	314.16	199.70	63.6	21.20	6.7	84.13	26.8	9.13	2.9	0	0
Nittano	5	78.54	0	0	13.32	17.0	63.32	80.6	1.90	2.4	0	0
	10	314.16	30.41	9.7	46.97	14.9	195.94	62.4	40.84	13.0	0	0
Torihama	5	78.54	10.20[b] / 0	13.0 / 0	8.70	11.1	24.30	30.9	16.74	21.3	18.60	23.7
	10	314.16	13.95[b] / 61.20	4.4 / 19.5	16.65	5.3	51.96	16.5	89.85	28.6	80.55	25.7

[a] Topographical feature of each site is shown in Figures 4.17 and 4.19–4.21.
[b] Inland water.

cording to altitudinal zones at the sites which were selected for designating the four types of fishing adaptations (see also Figures 4.17 and 4.19–4.21). Two different methods (i.e., using 10-km and 5-km radii) were used to estimate the area, as the extent of the exploitation territory of the sites has not yet been well established. The two methods consistently show the same trend in the proportion of altitudinal zones. Greater variety of zones including high proportion of marine water characterize the Miyano site–oceanic type; wider range of marine territory, the Natagiri site–littoral type; wider range of rather flat landform, the Nittano site–embayment type; and greater variety of zones including moderate proportion of inland water, but low proportion of marine water, the Torihama site–lake-to-riverine type.

Comparing regional differences in the prosperity and decline of sites classifiable into these four types through time, it is reasonable to apply to Japanese prehistory the statement by Rhoades (1978:609): "High species diversity and density in ecotonal areas may have been conducive to increased sedentism and population expansion." The most outstanding feature concerned with this hypothesis is the history of the embayment-oriented subsistence system. This kind of subsistence system had no power to resist the environmental deterioration which occurred in the later Jomon period, since it had been developed by "narrow spectrum" populations adapted to limited ecotonal zones.

Other examples of exploitative use of ecotones are more varied. Among them, the lake-oriented to riverine-oriented subsistence system like the Torihama case is a more "broad spectrum" economic pattern developed in "transition zones or ecotones between major ecosystems, especially forest- and woodland-edge situations" referred to by Harris (1972:184). Thus, the response to rice cultivation was vastly easier in the lake-oriented to riverine-oriented subsistence system than in other systems. In other words, Caldwell's hypothesis (1977:81) that "if there has been enough time to elaborate hunting–gathering efficiency to a point where domestication would seem redundant, agricultural innovation would be resisted" can be applied to the case of eastern Japan where the oceanic-oriented and littoral-oriented subsistence systems were well developed.

Rice culture spread over most of the Japanese islands by the end of the Yayoi culture, around A.D. 300, but the cultural dichotomy which occurred during the Jomon period continued to exist through the Yayoi to Kofun periods. In order to trace this idea archaeologically, we will make a brief consideration of bronze material which was a new element in the Yayoi period.

Kobayashi (1972) referred to the interesting fact that the distribution of bronze material generally overlapped the area of the first stage of rice expansion (Figure 4.22). It is usually considered that these bronze objects were tangible remains concerned with the religion and/or authority of the contemporary people, and forms of socioreligious and/or sociopolitical leadership may be inferred from these materials. A kind of centralized authority was probably initiated in western Japan, but again in this case, the people in eastern Japan were not willing to receive such material from the west. In eastern Japan a tendency toward cultural

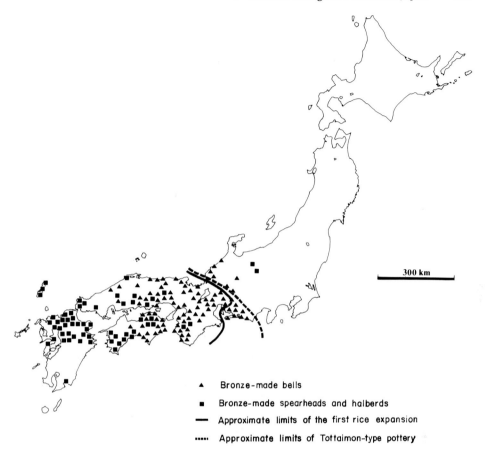

Figure 4.22 Distribution of bronze objects of Yayoi and Kofun periods. (From Kidder 1959:Map 4.)

regionalism, which was derived largely from fishing adaptations, survived into later times in repelling stimuli from the west (Figure 4.23).

The purpose of this chapter has been to show cultural dichotomization in Japan that occurred during the Jomon period and survived into later times, possibly to the present, and to explain these phenomena from the adaptation processes of different groups of Jomon people. This process leads us to a better understanding of man's relationship to his environment and of the cultural change from a hunting–gathering subsistence system to one based on agriculture. Moreover, the entire process of the cultural change from hunting–gathering to rice cultivation in Japan has proved that the cultural change, at least from food procuring to food production, did not originate under circumstances like demographic stress claimed by Binford (1968) and others, but was seen as a series of interactions between food procurers and food producers.

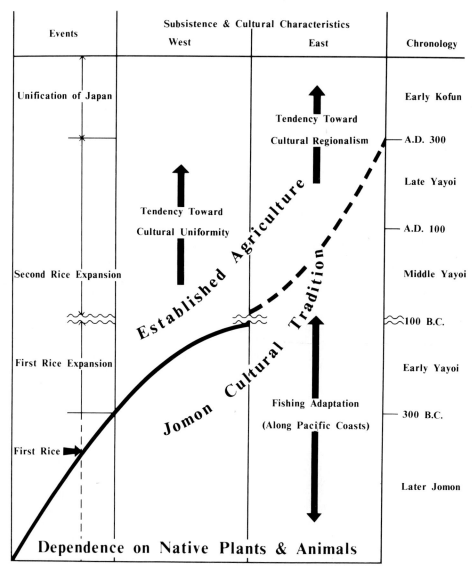

Figure 4.23 Chronological table and synoptic chart illustrating the major economic changes taking place during the later Jomon and Yayoi periods.

ACKNOWLEDGMENTS

I should like to thank Richard Pearson and Shuzo Koyama with whom I have discussed Japanese prehistory, in particular, new research methods in Japanese archaeology. I have received valuable suggestions from many discussions with them. About the new finding of salmon remains from Tohoku shell-midden deposits presented here, I have benefitted from the kind advice of Kunihiko Fujinuma and Hajime Komiya.

REFERENCES

Akazawa, T.
    1980   Fishing adaptation of prehistoric hunter–gatherers at the Nittano site, Japan. *Journal of Archaeological Science* **7**:325–344.
    1981   Maritime adaptation of prehistoric hunter–gatherers and their transition to agriculture in Japan. In *The affluent foragers: Pacific coasts east & west*, Senri Ethnological Studies No. 9, edited by S. Koyama and D. H. Thomas. Osaka: National Museum of Ethnology. Pp. 191–236.
    in press Jomon people subsistence and settlements: Discriminatory analysis of the later Jomon settlements. *Journal of Anthropological Society of Nippon* (Supplement).
Barker, G. W. W.
    1975   Prehistoric territories and economies in central Italy. In *Palaeoeconomy*, edited by E. S. Higgs. London: Cambridge University Press. Pp. 111–175.
Binford, L. R.
    1968   Post-Pleistocene adaptations. In *New perspectives in archeology*, edited by S. R. Binford and L. R. Binford. Chicago: Aldine. Pp. 313–341.
Caldwell, J. R.
    1977   Cultural evolution in the old world and the new, leading to the beginnings and spread of agriculture. In *Origins of agriculture*, edited by C. A. Reed. Paris: Mouton. Pp. 77–88.
Egami, N. (editor)
    1976   *Archaeological seminar*. Tokyo: Yamakawa Shuppan. (In Japanese.)
Endo, K.
    1979   Geomorphological study of the distribution of Jomon sites and their relation to Holocene sea-level change. *Natural Science and Museums* **46**:151–156. (In Japanese.)
Esaka, T.
    1943   Transgression and regression in the Kantoh plain during the alluvial epoch, estimated from distribution of shell middens. *Cultura Antiqua* **14**:133–135. (In Japanese.)
    1954   Movement of shoreline estimated from the distribution of stone age sites in Japan. *Kagaku-Asahi* **163**(1):75–76. (In Japanese.)
    1971   Geographical distribution of sites and the transition of the coastline in ancient Japan. *Marine Science Monthly* **3**:14–21. (In Japanese.)
Flannery, K. V.
    1969   Origins and ecological effects of early domestication in Iran and the Near East. In *The domestication and exploitation of plants and animals*, edited by P. J. Ucko and G. W. Dimbleby. London: Duckworth. Pp. 73–100.
Fujii, S., and S. Takayama
    1979   Molluscan remains. In *Torihama shell-midden site*, edited by Education Committee of Fukui Prefecture. Pp. 167–169. (In Japanese.)
Fujiwara, H.
    1976a   Investigation on the remains of crops in ancient times by plant opal analysis. *Journal of the Archaeological Society of Nippon* **62**:148–156. (In Japanese.)

1976b   Fundamental studies of plant opal analysis (1). *Archaeology and Physical Science* No. 9:15–29. (In Japanese.)

1979   Fundamental studies of plant opal analysis (3): estimation of the yield of rice in ancient paddy fields through quantitative analysis of plant opal. *Archaeology and Physical Science* No. 12:29–42. (In Japanese.)

Fujiwara, H., and A. Sasaki

1978   Fundamental studies of plant opal analysis (2). *Archaeology and Physical Science* No. 11:9–20. (In Japanese.)

Fujiwara, H., A. Matsutani, K. Umemoto, and A. Sasaki

1980   Palaeobotanical studies by means of plant opal and spodographic analyses. In *Studies on archaeological sites and remains by means of physical sciences*, edited by Commission for the Joint Studies of Archaeology and Physical Science. Pp. 214–221. (In Japanese.)

Habe, T., and T. Kosuge

1967   *Mollusks.* Osaka: Hoikusha. (In Japanese.)

Harris, D. R.

1972   The origins of agriculture in the tropics. *American Scientist* **60:**180–193.

Harunari, S.

1979   Terminal stage of Jomon culture. *Rekishi Koron* **5**(2):105–115. (In Japanese.)

Haury, E. W.

1962   The greater American southwest. In *Courses toward urban life*, edited by R. Braidwood and G. Willey. New York: Aldine. Pp. 106–131.

Hayashi, T.

1968   Studies on the management of fisheries in the shore and coastal areas. Paper presented at the Symposium on Porgy of the Japanese Society of Scientific Fisheries. (In Japanese.)

Higgs, E. S. (editor)

1975   *Palaeoeconomy.* London: Cambridge University Press.

Hirasawa, Y.

1981   *Japanese fisheries.* NHK (Nippon Hoso Kyokai) Book No. 383. Tokyo: Japan Broadcasting Corporation. (In Japanese.)

Hisanaga, H.

1976   Primitive community of the Final Jomon in the Tokai district. *Dorumen* No. 8:32–42. (In Japanese.)

Hiyama, Y.

1968   *Textbook of scientific fisheries.* Tokyo: University of Tokyo Press. (In Japanese.)

Honda, S.

1912   *A treatise on Japanese forest zones.* Tokyo: Miura Shoten. (In Japanese.)

Ikawa-Smith, F.

1980   Current issues in Japanese archaeology. *American Scientist* **68:**134–145.

Iseki, H.

1975   The sea-level changes in the late Holocene and the topographical environment of archaeological sites in Japan. *Archaeology and Physical Science* No. 8:39–52. (In Japanese.)

1978   Review of studies on sea-level changes in Japan. *Geographical Review of Japan* **51:**188–196. (Special issue on Holocene sea-level change. In Japanese.)

Ishige, N.

1968a   Genealogy of Japanese rice cultivation (1). *Shirin,* **51**(5):130–150. (In Japanese.)

1968b   Genealogy of Japanese rice cultivation (2). *Shirin* **51**(6):96–127. (In Japanese.)

Jarman, M. R., and D. Webley

1975   Settlement and land use in Capitanata, Italy. In *Palaeoeconomy*, edited by E. S. Higgs. London: Cambridge University Press. Pp. 177–221.

Jochim, M. A.

1979   Catches and catches: ethnographic alternatives for prehistory. In *Ethnoarchaeology*, edited by C. Kramer. New York: Columbia University Press. Pp. 219–246.

Kaizuka, S.
　1976　*Natural history of Tokyo* (2nd ed.). Tokyo: Kinokuniya Shoten. (In Japanese.)
Kajiyama, E.
　1937　*Studies on porgy.* Tokyo: Sugiyama Shoten. (In Japanese.)
Kanaseki, T.
　1966　Yayoi people. In *Japanese archaeology* (Vol. 3), edited by S. Wajima. Tokyo: Kawade Shobo. Pp. 460–471. (In Japanese.)
　1976　*Origin of Japanese people.* Tokyo: Hosei University Press. (In Japanese.)
Kanaseki, H., and M. Sahara
　1978　The Yayoi Period. *Asian Perspectives* **19**(1):15–26.
Kaneko, H.
　1958　Faunal remains of the Natagiri Cave. In *Natagiri Cave,* edited by H. Kaneko Education Committee of Chiba Prefecture. Pp. 75–123. (In Japanese.)
　1964　Shell mound of Fujimidai, Kimitsu, Chiba Prefecture. *Journal of the archaeological society of Waseda* Nos. 42–43:1–64. (In Japanese.)
　1965　Shell middens and food resources. In *Japanese Archaeology* (Vol. 2), edited by Y. Kamaki. Tokyo: Kawade Shobo. Pp. 372–398. (In Japanese.)
　1971　Fishing activities of the Jomon period in lower reaches of the Tone River. In *The Tone River: nature, culture, and society,* edited by Joint Expedition to the Tone River. Tokyo: Kobundo. Pp. 113–132. (In Japanese.)
　1972　Outline of the faunal remains from Miyanohara site. In *Miyanohara shell-midden site,* edited by Archaeological Society of Musashino Art University. Pp. 36–45. (In Japanese.)
　1980　Fishing activities of Jomon people seen from shell middens. *Shizen* **35**(2):38–46. (In Japanese.)
Kaneko, H., and Y. Ushizawa
　1975　Vertebrate remains from Ohata site. In *The Shellmound Site of Ohata,* edited by Education Committee of Iwaki City. Pp. 443–530. (In Japanese.)
　1977　Faunal remains from the Saihiro shell midden site. In *Saihiro shell-midden site,* edited by Expedition to Kazusa Kokubunji site. Education Committee of Ichikawa City. Pp. 443–530. (In Japanese.)
Kaneko, H., and T. Wada
　1968　Excavation of Locality C of Tsunatori shell-midden site. In *Onahama,* edited by Education Committee of Iwaki City. Pp. 79–124. (In Japanese.)
Kanzawa, Y.
　1979　Mortuary system of the Yayoi period in the southern Kanto district. *Dorumen* No. 23:35–47. (In Japanese.)
Kawana, T.
　1968　Notes on offshore migration of black sea bream, *A. schlegeli. Rakusui* No. 656:1–6. (In Japanese.)
Kenmochi, T.
　1972　On the fishing of Yayoi period in Miura Peninsula. *Material Culture* No. 19:11–22. (In Japanese.)
Kidder, J. E.
　1959　*Japan before Buddhism.* London: Thames and Hudson.
Kira, T.
　1949　*Forest zones in Japan.* Tokyo: Japanese Association of Forestry. (In Japanese.)
Kira, T.
　1969　*Illustrated book of the Japanese mollusc.* Tokyo: Hoikusha. (In Japanese.)
Kobayashi, Y.
　1972　*Origins of Japanese population:* Tokyo: Hanawa Shobo. (In Japanese.)
Kobayashi, Y.
　1975　Subsistence activities of the Jomon period based on the lithic assemblage of the Early to Middle Jomon in Chubu district (1). *Shinano* **25**(1):59–69. (In Japanese.)

Komiya, H.
1980　Identification and consideration on shells and fish remains from Kamitakatsu shell mound, Tsuchiura City. *The Quaternary Research* **19**(4):1–16. (In Japanese.)

Komura, H.
1963　*Archaeological sites of the Tokai District.* Nagoya: Nagoya Tetsudo Company. (In Japanese.)
1980　*Developmental studies of the Yayoi culture based upon the sites in the Aichi Prefecture.* Gifu: Komura. (In Japanese.)

Kondo, Y.
1962　Yayoi culture. In *Japanese history* (Vol. 1). Tokyo: Iwanami Shoten. Pp. 139–188. (In Japanese.)

Kono, I.
1942　Fishhooks of Prehistoric Japan. *Kodaibunka,* No. 13:136–142. (In Japanese.)

Koyama, S.
1978　Jomon subsistence and population. *Senri Ethnological Studies* **2**:1–65.
in press Nonagriculture to agriculture: population dynamics in Japan. In *Comparative studies of origins of Japanese population and their culture,* edited by K. Sasaki. Tokyo: Japan Broadcasting Corporation. (In Japanese.)

Kroeber, A. L., and S. A. Barrett
1960　Fishing among the Indians of northwestern California. *University of California Publications, Anthropological Records* **21**(1).

Kumano, M.
1979　Characteristics of Yayoi culture in the southern Kanto district. *Dorumen* No. **23**:6–18. (In Japanese.)

Kuwatani, Y.
1962　Studies on the Fish Bank for *Lateolabrax japonicus. Scientific Reports of the Fisheries Research Laboratory of Kyoto-fu* No. 8. (In Japanese.)

Maeda, Y.
1976　The sea-level changes of Osaka Bay from 12,000 B.P. to 6,000 B.P. *Archaeology and Physical Science* No. 9:31–41. (In Japanese.)

Makabe, Y.
1979　Prehistoric diet. In *Japanese archaeology* (Vol. 2), edited by H. Otsuka, M. Tozawa, and M. Sahara. Tokyo: Yuhikaku. Pp. 231–253. (In Japanese.)

Matsubara, K., and A. Ochiai
1965　*Ichthyology.* Tokyo: Koseisha-Koseikaku. (In Japanese.)

Matsubara, M.
1971　Hypothetical view on genealogy of Yayoi culture in terms of experimental studies of polished stone axes and adzes. *Quarterly Anthropology* **2**(2):144–192. (In Japanese.)

Matsui, A., and I. Yamada
1981　Report on the fish remains of the Yunosato site, Shiriuchi, Hokkaido. *Archaeology Study* **28**(3):97–105. (In Japanese.)

Matsumoto, T.
1979　Remains of green grams. In *Torihama shell-midden site,* edited by Education Committee of Fukui Prefecture. Pp. 162–163. (In Japanese.)

McCracken, F. D.
1963　Selection by coded meshes and hooks on cod, haddock, flatfish, and redfish. *Proceedings of the Joint Scientific Meeting of ICNAF/ICES/FAO on the Selectivity of Fishing Gear* (Vol. 2). Dartmouth: International Commission for the Northwest Atlantic Fisheries. Pp. 131–155.

Morikawa, M.
1979　Bone and antler artifacts from the Torihama site. In *Torihama shell-midden site,* edited by Education Committee of Fukui Prefecture. Pp. 146–150. (In Japanese.)

Morikawa, M., and M. Yamada
    1979   Wooden artifacts from the Torihama Site. In *Torihama shell-midden site,* edited by Educa-
            tion Committee of Fukui Prefecture. Pp. 85–142. (In Japanese.)
Murdock, G. P.
    1969   Correlations of exploitative and settlement patterns. In *Contributions to anthropology:
            ecological essays,* edited by D. Damas. National Museums of Canada, Bulletin No. 230.
            Pp. 129–146.
Naito, Y.
    1971   On the human skeletons of Yayoi period excavated at sites in northwestern Kyushu.
            Journal of the Anthropological Society of Nippon 79:236–248. (In Japanese.)
Nakamura, J.
    1979   Some palynological aspects of rice cultivation in northern Kyushu, Japan. *Ethnos* No.
            12:46–49. (In Japanese.)
    1980   History of rice cultivation in Japan reconstructed from palynological analysis. In
            Studies on archaeological sites and remains by means of physical sciences, edited by Commis-
            sion for the Joint Studies of Archaeology and Physical Science. Pp. 185–204. (In
            Japanese.)
    1981   Palynological studies on rice cultivation in Japan. Paper presented at the Symposium
            on Origins of Early Domestication in Japan, Tokyo. Sponsored by the Japanese Minis-
            try of Education, Science and Culture. (In Japanese.)
Nakao, S.
    1966   *Cultivated plants and origin of agriculture.* Tokyo: Iwanami Shoten. (In Japanese.)
Nishida, M.
    1979   Floral remains. In *Torihama shell-midden site,* edited by Education Committee of Fukui
            Prefecture. Pp. 158–161. (In Japanese.)
    1980   Food resources and subsistence activities during the Jomon period. *Quarterly Anthropol-
            ogy* 11(3):3–56. (In Japanese.)
Ogawa, N., H. Sano, and Y. Shimotori
    1975   Vertebrate remains of the Nittano shell-midden site. In *Report of the excavation of the
            Nittano shell-midden site,* edited by Archeological Society of Rikkyo University. Pp.
            52–61. (In Japanese.)
Oikawa, A., S. Miyamoto, and S. Koyama
    1980   A Jomon shellmound database: its compilation and application. *Bulletin of the National
            Museum of Ethnology* 5(2):439–470. (In Japanese.)
Okada, A.
    1978   Sea-level change and geomorphic development since the last glacial age in the Wakasa
            Bay region, central west of the Japan Sea coast. *Geographical Review of Japan* 51:131–146.
            (Special issue on Holocene sea-level change; in Japanese.)
Ota, Y., H. Machida, N. Hori, K. Konishi, and A. Omura
    1978   Holocene raised coral reefs of Kikai-jima (Ryukyu Islands): an approach to Holocene
            sea-level study. *Geographical Review of Japan* 51:109–130. (Special issue on Holocene sea-
            level change; in Japanese.)
Otsuka, K.
    1966   Toggle harpoon heads of open socket type. *Material Culture* No. 7:33–46. (In Japanese.)
Pearson, R., and K. Pearson
    1978   Some problems in the study of Jomon subsistence. *Antiquity* 52:21–27.
Reed, C. A.
    1977   Origins of agriculture: discussion and some conclusions. In *Origins of agriculture,* edited
            by C. A. Reed. Paris: Mouton. Pp. 879–953.
Rhoades, R. E.
    1978   Archaeological use and abuse of ecological concepts and studies: the ecotone example.
            American Antiquity 43:608–614.

Roper, D. C.
1979   The method and theory of site catchment analysis: a review. In *Advances in archaeological method and theory* (Vol. 2), edited by M. B. Schiffer. New York: Academic Press. Pp. 119–140.

Sasaki, K.
1971   *Before rice cultivation.* NHK (Nippon Hoso Kyokai) Book No. 147. Tokyo: Japan Broadcasting Corporation. (In Japanese.)

Sato, T.
1971   *Ancient rice in Japan.* Tokyo: Yuzankaku. (In Japanese.)

Shimojo, N.
1979   Agricultural development during the Yayoi period. In *Japanese archaeology* (Vol. 2), edited by H. Otsuka, M. Tozawa, and M. Sahara. Tokyo: Yuhikaku. Pp. 137–155. (In Japanese.)

Sugihara, S., and H. Otsuka (editors)
1964   *Yayoi type pottery.* Tokyo: Kodansha. (In Japanese.)

Suzuki, H.
1975   A case of microcephaly in an aeneolithic Yayoi period population in Japan. *Bulletin of the National Science Museum, Series D (Anthropology)* **1:**1–10.

Suzuki, K.
1968   An outline of the Final Jomon culture in Kanto district. *Rekishi Kyoiku* **16**(4):62–73. (In Japanese.)
1977   Fish remains in archaeology: Comparison of methods for reconstruction of prehistoric fish assemblages. Annual report presented at the Symposium on Archaeology and Physical Sciences, Tokyo. (In Japanese.)

Takayama, J.
1974   Salmon and Jomon people. *Quarterly Anthropology* **5**(1):3–56. (In Japanese.)

Tanabe, T., E. Yamaguchi, K. Hatanaka, M. Yamada, and H. Omori
1979   Stone artifacts from the Torihama site. In *Torihama shell-midden site,* edited by Education Committee of Fukui Prefecture. Pp. 61–84. (In Japanese.)

Tanaka, K.
1958   A study on the ecology of porgy (*Pagrosomus major*). *Scientific Reports of the Kagawa Prefectural Fisheries Research Laboratory* No. 12. (In Japanese.)

Toki, R.
1926a   Geomorphological study of the distribution of shell middens. *Journal of the Anthropological Society of Nippon* **41:**746–773. (In Japanese.)
1926b   The ancient shoreline in the lowlands of the Kantoh districts, estimated from the distribution of shell middens. *Geographical Review of Japan* **2:**597–607. (In Japanese.)

Tsukahara, H.
1968   Studies on the management of offshore fisheries. Paper presented at the Symposium on Porgy of the Japanese Society of Scientific Fisheries. (In Japanese.)

Ueyama, S. (editor)
1969   *Laurel forest culture* (Vol. 1). Tokyo: Chuokoronsha. (In Japanese.)

Ueyama, S., K. Sasaki, and S. Nakao
1976   *Laurel forest culture* (Vol. 2). Tokyo: Chuokoronsha. (In Japanese.)

Vita-Finzi, C., and E. S. Higgs
1970   Prehistoric economy in the Mount Carmel area of Palestine. Site catchment analysis. *Proceedings of the Prehistoric Society* **36:**1–37.

Watanabe, M.
1966a   A study of fishhooks in the Jomon culture. *Journal of Archaeological Society of Nippon* **74:**19–46. (In Japanese.)
1966b   Faunal remains from Terawaki site. In *Terawaki shell-midden site,* edited by Education Committee of Iwaki City. Pp. 25–44. (In Japanese.)

1967   Controversial point on salmon fishing in prehistoric Japan. *Cultura Antiqua* **18**(2):33–36. (In Japanese.)

1968   On the use of the fishing net of the Jomon period in western Japan. *Material Culture* No. 12:14–19. (In Japanese.)

1973   *Fishing during the Jomon period.* Tokyo: Yuzankaku. (In Japanese.)

Yamaguchi, B.
1979   A human skeletal remains of Yayoi period from Shakameyama site, Ehime Prefecture, Shikoku. *Bulletin of the National Science Museum, Series D (Anthropology)* **5**:13–30.

Yamaguchi, K.
1964   *History of the Japanese fisheries* (2nd ed.). Tokyo: University of Tokyo Press. (In Japanese.)

Yamanaka, T.
1979   *Forest and vegetationary zones in Japan.* Tokyo: Tsukiji Shokan. (In Japanese.)

Yasuda, Y.
1978   Prehistoric environment in Japan: palynological approach. *Science Reports of the Tohoku University, 7th Series (Geography)* **29**(2):117–281.

5

The Indian Bronze Age Cultures and Their Metal Technology

D. P. AGRAWAL

INTRODUCTION

In this chapter I summarize the latest archaeological evidence now available for the period from approximately 3000 to 1000 B.C., with special emphasis on copper technology but also including the latest archaeological discoveries, relevant paleoecological data, and radiocarbon and thermoluminescence dates. In the Indian subcontinent, this period was characterized by the use of copper, although stone blades continued to be used. The subcontinent did not have a unified, unilineal, socioeconomic development during this period, and some of the cultural terms have special connotations in Indian archaeology.

The Harappan, the Chalcolithic, and the Copper Hoards cultures were the three main copper-using cultures. The Harappa culture was a fully urbanized culture and is generally excluded from the Chalcolithic group. The latter group includes exclusively nonurban cultures whose economy was akin to the non-metal-using Neolithic cultures of the South. The third group is called the Copper Hoards culture, so named because most of the finds were in hoards.

INDUS CIVILIZATION

The Indus civilization or Harappa culture (named after the first discovered site, Harappa) is well known for its uniformity and standardization in weights, measures, ceramics, architecture, town planning, and in other arts and crafts. This uniformity appears all the more imposing when one considers that the culture

213

extended over more than a million square kilometers, an area larger than that of Pakistan today. It spread in the west to Sutkagendor (Makran), in the east to Alamgirpur (Uttar Pradesh), to Rupar in the north, and to Bhagatrav in the south (Gujarat) (Figure 5.1). Whether this uniformity indicates an empire or a trading zone can only be guessed. Such uniformity, at times amounting to monotony, in a third millennium B.C. context is puzzling, even though recent discoveries have brought out some regional variation as well (Possehl 1978).

Wheeler (1968) attempted to define the Harappa culture by the alternative or accumulative presence of: (a) Indus seals; (b) Indus script; (c) motifs like intersecting circles; (d) ceramic forms like goblets with pointed base, cylindrical pots with multiple perforations, jars with an S-shaped profile and dishes-on-stand (Figure 5.2); (e) triangular terracotta cakes; (f) kidney-shaped inlays of shells or faience; and (g) certain beads, notably discoid with tubular holes. To these one may add gridiron town planning and standardized brick dimensions in the ratio of 1:2:4.

There is some regional variation in the Harappan tradition. For example, the mother goddess figurines and phalli of the Sind are absent in Rajasthan and Gujarat; and the fire altars at Lothal (Gujarat) are different from those of Kalibangan (Rajasthan). It appears that, although uniform standards were perhaps imposed over artifacts for mass consumption and trade, local differences in culture and religion continued to exist.

Despite its very sudden appearance, the Harappa culture in fact derived a great deal from the antecedent cultures, so much so that Mughal (1970) terms the so-called Pre-Harappan cultures as *Early Harappan*. Fortification of towns, stone blade technology, copper metallurgy, steatite beads, standardized brick sizes, several ceramic motifs, terracotta cakes, bullock carts, and so forth are all contributions of the Pre-Harappans to the Indus civilization. It should also be emphasized that the fortified sites of the Pre-Harappan cultures are almost as impressive as the Harappan ones (Mughal 1970). The Pre-Harappan people had fairly permanent settlements in the riverine environment, indicating that they possessed the technology to exploit such ecology, and some centers were sufficiently organized to be capable of carrying out the large-scale, communal work of elaborate fortifications.

In fact, *Pre-Harappan* is a much misused term. It appears quite likely that the so-called Pre-Harappan cultures were actually a substratum contemporaneous with the Harappan urbanization. This would explain the continuity of the Pre-Harappan cultures in Late Harappan contexts in the peripheral regions, and could also explain the stark contrast between the delicacy and diversity of the regional expressions of the Pre-Harappan cultures and the commercialized uniformity of the Harappan industries. I have elsewhere tried to account for the partial contemporaneity of the Pre-Harappan and Harappan cultures by proposing that the Harappa culture was an urban, artificially standardized, selectively "Indianized" form, which derived from, and yet continued to be coeval with, the so-called Pre-Harappan cultures. The two cultures seem to have coexisted in

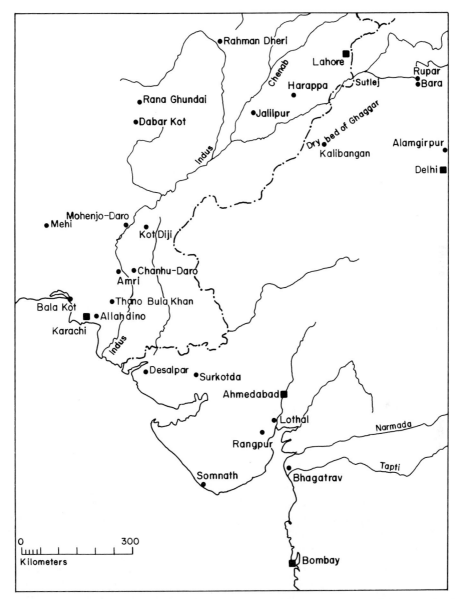

Figure 5.1 Distribution zone of the Indus civilization. Main archaeological sites (●) mentioned in the text are marked, as are modern towns (■).

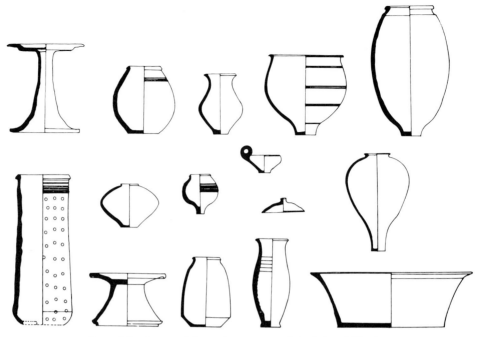

Figure 5.2   Representative red ware types of the Indus civilization.

the same way as the present day planned city of Chandigarh exists in the matrix of rural Punjab. The Pre-Harappan and the Harappa cultures are not two different entities but urban and rural aspects of the same cultural phenomenon, and the Harappa culture did not supplant the Pre-Harappan cultures (except where cities were built) but had a bilateral relationship with them (Agrawal, 1972–1973: 37–44).

Arts and Crafts

On the whole, the art of the Harappans does not compare favorably with contemporary Egyptian or Mesopotamian artifacts, but a few surviving examples do show their mastery of plastic art. Narrow eyes, stylized ears and hair, shaven upper lip, inlaid eyes, and a hieratic rendering characterize a number of the statues. Two such pieces were discovered in a building suspected to be a temple at Mohenjo-Daro (Wheeler 1968:52). The plastic rendering of the Kalibangan terracotta head is more lifelike than that of Mohenjo-Daro statues, but the modeling of the two male, stone torsos from Harappa is very naturalistic, almost sensuous. One of these may have been ithyphallic (with erect penis) and was probably connected with Siva, the Hindu god. The dancing girl in bronze from Mohenjo-Daro is a very delicate representation in the round of a female nude (Figure 5.3). The ease of her stance, the graceful way of resting one hand

Figure 5.3 Bronze female figurine 11 cm high from Mohenjo-Daro.

218   D. P. Agrawal

on the hip, and the slight tilt of the head enhance her voluptuous appeal. The rendering of animals, especially bulls and rhinoceroses, in the steatite seals is also naturalistic. Massiveness of form and the fury and movement of the charge are eloquently expressed in the terracotta bull from Kalibangan (Lal 1979:91).

Bead factories have been discovered at Chanhudaro (Mackay 1943) and Lothal (Rao 1973a). Beads were made of agate, carnelian, faience, shell, terracotta, gold, silver, and steatite; beads with inlay work and etchings were probably exported.

A highly standardized system of weights and measures was evolved by the Harappans. Two systems of measurement were used: cubits and a long foot. A cubit was about 52 cm (52.5–52.8 cm) and the long foot was 33.5 cm. Graduated scales with decimal graduations (up to 1.7 mm) have been reported. The cubical, stone weights followed a binary system (1, 2, ⅓ × 8, 4, 8, 16, 32 up to 12800) in the lower denominations, and the traditional Indian sexagesimal ratio of 1:16 (1 rupee is equal to 16 annas) may derive from this. The unit weighs 13.625 gm. Higher weights follow a decimal system with fractional weights in thirds. The accuracy of these weights throughout the Harappan territory is quite remarkable.

The Harappa culture is distinguished by its town planning, although fortifications and some degree of planning are also evident both at Kot Diji and Kalibangan in Pre-Harappan contexts. To protect against floods, the citadels and the lower town buildings were built over raised mud-brick platforms. The settlement was divided into a citadel, which was on a higher ground located in the west, and the lower town towards the east. The citadel was always fortified, and often so was the lower town. Kalibangan, Harappa, and Mohenjo-Daro have remarkably similar plans, with fortified citadels west of the lower town. At Kalibangan the lower town also had a fortification, and at Lothal and Surkotda both the citadel and the lower town are enclosed by a common wall. At Surkotda the two are separated by a further wall. At Lothal there is no wall between the lower town and the acropolis, and the latter is situated on the southeast, a unique location. Houses were provided with wells, drains, and latrines.

Trade

International trade of the Harappans is minimized by Fairservis (1971) and Lamberg-Karlovsky (1972), though Rao (1973a) lays great emphasis on it. During-Caspers (1972) and Kohl (1978) have written critical surveys of trade in the third millennium B.C., and Mughal (1970) has pointed out that there is considerable evidence of trade contact from the Early Dynastic III period. This means that international trade began in Pre-Harappan times and was not confined to the Harappan period only.

There are many references in the Mesopotamian texts, mostly from the Early Dynastic to Isin-Larsa periods, to Dilmun, Magan, and Meluhha, with which Mesopotamia had frequent commercial intercourse. Dilmun was located on the "Lower Sea" (i.e., where the Arabian Sea and Persian Gulf meet), and is now usually identified with the region comprising Turant, Bahrain, and Kuwait. Dilmun produced only pearls and dates, but it served as an entrepôt port for carnelian, semiprecious stones, ivory artifacts, timber, silver, lapis lazuli, red gold, white corals, and eye paint. There is much evidence for contact between Dilmun and Mesopotamia and the Indus. For example, the weight system followed there is the same as that of the Harappans, and a Persian Gulf seal, typical of the Dilmun region, has been reported from Lothal.

Magan has been identified variously with Umm-an-Nar near Abu Dhabi; with the area around Minab or Tiz (Chah Bazar); and even with the inland region comprising Shahr-i-Sokhta and Tepe-Yahya in Iran. Textual references mention reeds, onions, diorite, carnelian, red ocher, copper and ivory as the products received from Magan. Steatite vessels, probably produced at Tepe-Yahya (Lamberg-Karlovsky 1972) and exported west and east, may support identification of Magan with the Tepe-Yahya region, but evidence for overland trade is lacking at the moment. Lamberg-Karlovsky (1972), however, emphasizes the role of sites like Tepe-Yahya in the Indus-Mesopotamian, indirect, land-route trade, and believes that there was an established dialectic between these (Iranian) resource-rich areas and resource-poor Mesopotamia on the one hand and the Indus on the other (Tosi 1979:149–172), which brought about a mutually dependent, parallel, and contemporary process towards urbanization. Shahr-i-Sokhta was a large manufacturing and export center for lapis lazuli objects (Tosi 1979:149–172).

In the later part of the second millennium B.C., Magan and Meluhha denoted Egypt and Nubia, respectively, but they may previously have been regions to the southeast. According to the texts, Meluhha exported a variety of timbers, copper, gold dust, lapis lazuli, carnelian and other stones, ivory figurines of birds and monkeys, etc. Most of these items were available from India, except perhaps lapis lazuli. At Chanhudaro, however, there is evidence for the manufacture of lapis beads; the nearest source for lapis would be Badkshan in Afghanistan. Timber, growing in Panch Mahal hills in Gujarat and also reported from Lothal, has traditionally been exported from the western Indian ports. Baluchistan, Afghanistan, Oman, and Rajasthan all have copper mines. Sixteen copper furnaces from Harappa, the copper workshops in Lothal, and the large quantities of copper-oxide ore from a brick-lined pit at Mohenjo-Daro all suggest that copper metallurgy was a developed craft in the Indus civilization. Placer gold is found in the streams of Punjab and Kashmir and may have been the source of the gold dust. Carnelian was obtained from the Rajpipla mines of Gujarat and was manufactured into beads at Lothal and Chanhudaro. Etched carnelian beads have been reported from most of the Harappan sites and, in Mesopotamia, from Ur, Kish, Al-Hiba, and Tell Asmar. Sumerian and Harappan ornaments show similarities in gold caps for stone beads, discoid beads with axial tubes, and spherical beads joined together. The Mesopotamian texts mention ivory objects like combs, figurines, boxes and inlay pieces, and ivory artifacts have been reported from Surkotda, Lothal, Mohenjo-Daro, and

Chanhudaro. It is therefore likely that Meluhha may represent the northwest part of the Indian subcontinent.

The Ur texts mention that the commodities exported to the east were barley, flour, oils, wool and woollen goods, and silver; unfortunately, most of these items are perishable and have left no material record.

Religion

The Indus seals seem to have served both religious and secular functions. Their discovery in Lothal warehouses clearly suggests that they were used to seal grains or merchandise, but a majority depict scenes that can be interpreted only as religious. A well-known seal, depicting a seated, three-faced, horned, and ithyphallic figure surrounded by a number of animals, recalls the *pasupata* (animal loving) nature of Siva (Figure 5.4). A terracotta cake from Kalibangan shows a standing human figure with horned headdress and, on the reverse, a man carrying a goat or bovine tied with a rope; the horned deity may represent Siva and the animal may be for sacrifice. In the religious sector of the citadel at Kalibangan, bovine and antler bones and ash were discovered in a pit, probably indicating a sacrifice (Thapar 1973). The discovery of several naturalistic phallic stones and terracottas and perforated stones (perhaps depicting female organs) from the Harappan sites in Pakistan may take the present *sivalinga* and *yoni* worship back to the Harappan times. A nude male stone torso from Harappa also appears to be ithyphallic, recalling the *yogisvara* (master of senses) aspect of Siva; even in later historical sculptures he is quite often depicted as ithyphallic. Another male statue from Harappa shows a nude male in a dancing pose reminiscent of Siva's cosmic dance. Such traits may indicate that the elements of the latter day Hindu god, Siva, were already present in the Harappa culture. Indeed, we can trace the roots of the Indian culture deep into the Indus civilization.

The elaborate provision of drains on the Kalibangan platforms and the Great Bath of Mohenjo-Daro may mark the beginning of the ablutionary rituals that form a vital part of Hindu religious practices today. A number of seals and pots depict *pipal (Ficus religiosa)* (Figure 5.5), considered sacred both in Hinduism and Buddhism. The bull is associated with Siva as his *vahana* (mount) and is worshipped even today. The depiction of bulls on several seals and terracottas, and a scene on a seal where one is carried on the shoulders in a procession, perhaps underline its religious significance: finally, quite a few small terracotta human figurines from Harappa show various postures identified as yogic exercises.

Seals also deal with other themes. On one what is perhaps a deity is shown with a supplicating figure and what is possibly a sacrificial goat. In the lower row are seven standing figures, perhaps devotees. Another seal shows an upside-down woman with legs spread apart and a plant emerging from her vagina; on the reverse side are a man holding a scimitar and a seated figure with dishevelled hair; this has been interpreted as a human sacrifice to a tree spirit. Other

Figure 5.4 Steatite seal with a three-faced, three-horned seated male figure in an ithyphallic pose, suggestive of the latter-day Siva. He is surrounded by animals. On the top is a legend in the Harappan script. Size: 3.5 cm wide.

depictions recall the Sumerian mythology of Enkidu and Gilgamesh (Wheeler 1968), showing a bull-headed man attacking a tiger, or two tigers being lifted up by a horned person.

The naked, female, terracotta figurines with their elaborate headdresses may indicate a mother goddess cult. Such cults seem to be widespread from Turkey to Iran from Neolithic times onwards, and they continue in India even to this day.

21

Figure 5.5 A typical red ware jar of the Indus civilization, painted in black with intersecting circles, pipal leaf, and peacock motifs.

Surprisingly, figurines are lacking both at Kalibangan and at Lothal, despite very extensive excavations at these sites. On the other hand, seven fire altars in a row were found on the citadel at Kalibangan, associated with a sacrificial pit containing animal bones. A small structure outside the settlement housed five such altars (Figure 5.6), and each house also seems to have had such an altar (Lal 1979:79). Several slightly different fire altars are reported from Lothal also, but none has been reported from the main Indus sites. One can perhaps infer that some sort of fire worship (*yajna*), rather than iconic worship, was predominant in Rajasthan and Gujarat, while the converse is true of the Harappan sites of Pakistan.

Burials

The most common Harappan custom for burial was inhumation in an unlined pit with the head toward the north; there are only a few exceptions, such as at Rupar where the direction is northwest. Usually about 20 pots were put in as funerary goods, and ornaments like rings, earrings, necklaces, anklets, bangles

Figure 5.6 A mud-brick structure; outside the city wall of Kalibangan, a Harappan site in Rajasthan. Several fire altars can be seen inside the structure.

and, at times, copper mirrors have been found with burials; the dead were also provided with meat and drink for the afterlife. The Harappan graves, however, stand no comparison to the macabre splendor of the Ur graves.

Graves were rarely lined with bricks; only one such example is known from each of Harappa, Lothal, and Kalibangan, and the Nal graves of southern Baluchistan are similarly lined. A unique example from the Harappan R-37 cemetery has a coffin of rosewood with a lid of *Cedrus deodara,* which must have been imported from the Himalayas, several hundred kilometers away. The woman thus buried was provided with 37 pots, but the grave was otherwise unremarkable (Wheeler 1968:66–68).

Kalibangan has provided other varieties of burial besides inhumation. Urns were found inside circular or oval pits in an area north of the inhumations, and there was one subrectangular pit, with the longer axis oriented north–south, containing only pots; no skeletal remains were found in either type of burial. All grave goods are typically Harappan (Lal 1979:86). The sociological significance of such variety in funerary customs is unknown.

It is worth noting that the urban Harappan cemeteries were located away from the settlements, unlike the Chalcolithic cultures of Central India and Deccan where burials were below house floors, as they had been also in the Neolithic.

Indus Script

The Harappans used a pictographic script, comprising some 400 signs, in which no evolution is discernible. Obviously such a large number of signs precludes the possibility of it being a purely alphabetic script, but Rao has discovered that there were only 52 basic signs, and therefore believes that it was a syllabic-cum-alphabetic script, which developed into an alphabetic one around 1500 B.C. (Rao 1973b:323). The Harappan script does not seem to bear any resemblance either to contemporaneous scripts elsewhere or to the historical scripts of India.

Lal has proved that the Indus script was boustrophedon in character (the first line written from right to left and the second line from left to right) (Lal 1966:52–55). The decipherment of the script is, however, problematical, since there are no long inscriptions (Figure 5.4), where recurrent formations could be studied, nor any bilingual inscriptions. Claims of decipherment fall into two main groups: one proposing that the Indus script is proto-Dravidian (Gurov 1970; Parpola 1975), and the other, Indo-Aryan (Rao 1979:13–18). These claims have been critically discussed (and rejected) by Lal (1977).

Chronology

Wheeler's (1968) time bracket of approximately 2500–1500 B.C. for the Harappa culture was based upon the discovery of Harappan objects in Western Asian archaeological contexts and of Mesopotamian artifacts in Harappan sites. Fairservis (1967) found it hard to accept a millennium-long monotony for the Harappa culture and preferred a range of about 2000–1500 B.C. Allchin and Allchin (1968) proposed that around 2150–1750 B.C. would better fit the evidence. We, however, have suggested periods of 2300–2000 B.C. for the nuclear regions and 2200–1700 B.C. for the peripheral zone of the Harappa culture (Agrawal and Kusumgar 1974).

The archaeological evidence from the older Mesopotamian excavations is not reliable and has created much confusion. It should also be emphasized that trade had already begun in Pre-Harappan times and, therefore, that not all contacts with Mesopotamia necessarily pertain to the Harappan period. The evidence of carnelian beads and steatite vases belongs to the Early Dynastic III period and may refer to the Pre-Harappan phase, an inference supported by the discovery of a carved steatite vase fragment from the Pre-Harappan levels of Mohenjo-Daro (House 5, D.K. Area, 8.7 m depth).

There is, however, more definite evidence for contacts between Mesopotamia and the Indus during the Sargon of Agade (around 2350 B.C.) and Isin-Larsa periods (about 1900–2000 B.C.). A circular steatite seal (Gadd No. 15) with a scorpion and a crowded inscription and a similar seal (Gadd No. 16) with a bull motif were found in Sargonic association. (Gadd numbers for seals follow the system given in Gadd 1932). A square seal with Indus script was found at Kish below the pavement of Samsuiluna, datable to about 1900 B.C., and a seal with a Harappan legend came from Telloh's Larsa levels. The "Persian Gulf Seals" belong mainly to the Bahrain (Dilmun) area and date around 2000 B.C. These are round, steatite seals (comparable to Gadd Nos. 2–5, 8–16), sometimes bearing Indus characters (Bibby 1958). They are associated with the long-distance trade between the Indus and Mesopotamia through the entrepôt of Bahrain, and occur in the Failaka and Bahrain regions, as well as in the Mesopotamian and the Indus sites. One such seal has been reported from the surface at Lothal (Gujarat). It is probable that etched carnelian beads were produced in the Indus region from the Pre-Harappan onwards. Frankfort (1939) has reported such beads from houses of the Sargonic period at Tell Asmar, and from Early Dynastic levels elsewhere. Disk-shaped beads of gold and silver with axial tubes have been reported from Akkadian and Troy II levels.

Analyzing the data on contacts between Mesopotamia and the Indus, Buchanan concluded: "The Mesopotamian evidence, therefore, does not require a date for the mature Indus civilization much, if at all, before the 23rd century B.C. It would be surprising if it lasted more than 300 years. We think that this is a fairly balanced conclusion from the archaeological evidence" (1967:107).

A fairly large number of radiocarbon dates is now available for Harappan sites (Agrawal and Kusumgar 1974), and there are also ^{14}C dated sites like Balakot, Damb Sadaat, and Kot Diji with both pre-Harappan and Harappan deposits (Table 5.1). Harappa itself has no ^{14}C dates nor do we have any dates for the lower levels of Mohenjo-Daro. It should be emphasized again that the so-called Pre-Harappan cultures ("Early Harappan" of Mughal) overlapped in time with

TABLE 5.1

¹⁴C Dates of Harappan and Pre-Harappan Sites

Sites (state)	Cultural association	Lab no.	^{14}C dates (uncorrected) in years B.C. based on half-life = 5730 yr
Allahdino (W. Pakistan)	Harappan	P-2237,	2005 ± 62
		P-2295-A,	1923 ± 72
		P-2296,	2098 ± 51
Amri (W. Pakistan)	Pre-Harappan	TF-863,	2665 ± 110
		TF-864,	2900 ± 115
Balakot (W. Pakistan)	Pre-Harappan	UCLA-1923A,	3406 ± 137
		UCLA-1923B,	3334 ± 77
		UCLA-1923C,	3061 ± 82
		UCLA-1924D,	2386 ± 82
Banawali (Haryana)	Harappan	PRL-204,	1400 ± 130
		PRL-203,	1960 ± 160
		PRL-205,	1980 ± 190
		PRL-207,	1240 ± 110
Bara (Punjab)	Harappan(?)	TF-1204,	1845 ± 155
		TF-1205,	1890 ± 95
		TF-1207,	1645 ± 90
Damb Sadaat (W. Pakistan)	Pre-Harappan	UW-60,	2200 ± 165
		P-523,	2200 ± 75
		L-180E,	2200 ± 360
Damb Sadaat (W. Pakistan)	Pre-Harappan	L-180C,	2220 ± 410
		P-522,	2550 ± 200
		L-180B,	2320 ± 360
		UW-59,	2510 ± 70
Ghalighai (W. Pakistan)	Harappan	R-378a,	1923 ± 55
Gumla (W. Pakistan)	Pre-Harappan	P-1812,	2248 ± 74
		P-1882,	2382 ± 151
Hathala (W. Pakistan)	Pre-Harappan	P-1813,	2214 ± 62
Kalibangan Pd. I (Rajasthan)	Pre-Harappan	TF-154,	1820 ± 115
		TF-156,	1900 ± 110
		TF-165,	1965 ± 105
		TF-161,	2095 ± 105
TF-240,	1765 ± 115	TF-240,	1765 ± 115
TF-162,	2105 ± 105	TF-162,	2105 ± 105
TF-241,	2251 ± 95	TF-241,	2251 ± 95
TF-157,	2290 ± 120	TF-157,	2290 ± 120
		TF-155,	2370 ± 120
Kalibangan Pd. II (Rajasthan)	Harappan	TF-143,	1665 ± 110
		TF-946,	1765 ± 105
		TF-149,	1830 ± 145
		TF-150,	1900 ± 105
		TF-605,	1975 ± 110
		P-481,	2050 ± 75

TABLE 5.1—*Continued*

Sites (state)	Cultural association	Lab no.	^{14}C dates (uncorrected) in years B.C. based on half-life = 5730 yr
		TF-153,	2075 ± 110
		TF-25,	2090 ± 115
		TF-942,	2225 ± 115
		TF-152,	1770 ± 90
		TF-142,	1790 ± 105
		TF-141,	1860 ± 115
		TF-139,	1930 ± 105
		TF-151,	1960 ± 105
		TF-948,	1980 ± 100
		TF-147,	2030 ± 105
		TF-145,	2060 ± 105
		TF-608,	2075 ± 110
		TF-947,	1925 ± 90
		TF-163,	2080 ± 105
		TF-607,	2090 ± 125
		TF-160,	2230 ± 105
Kot-Diji Pd. I (W. Pakistan)	Pre-Harappan	P-195,	2100 ± 140
		P-180,	2250 ± 140
		P-179,	2330 ± 155
		P-196,	2600 ± 145
Lothal (Gujarat)	Harappan	TF-19,	1800 ± 140
		TF-23,	1865 ± 110
		TF-29,	1895 ± 115
		TF-26,	2000 ± 125
		TF-27,	2000 ± 115
		TF-22,	2010 ± 115
		TF-133,	1895 ± 115
		TF-136,	2080 ± 135
Mitathal (Uttar Pradesh)	Harappan(?)	PRL-290,	1980 ± 140
		PRL-292,	2380 ± 220
		PRL-291,	1760 ± 110
Mohenjo-Daro (W. Pakistan)	Harappan	TF-75,	1755 ± 115
		P-1182A,	1865 ± 65
		P-1176,	1965 ± 60
		P-1178A,	1965 ± 60
		P-1180,	1995 ± 65
		P-1179,	2085 ± 65
		P-1177,	2155 ± 65
Mundigak (Afghanistan)	Pre-Harappan	TF-1129,	3145 ± 110
		TF-1132,	2995 ± 105
		TF-1131,	2755 ± 105
Nindovari Damb (W. Pakistan)	Pre-Harappan	TF-862,	2065 ± 110
Rojdi (Gujarat)	Harappan	TF-199,	1745 ± 105
		TF-200,	1970 ± 115

(continued)

TABLE 5.1—*Continued*

Sites (state)	Cultural association	Lab no.	^{14}C dates (uncorrected) in years B.C. based on half-life = 5730 yr
Sanghol (Punjab)	Late-Harappan	PRL-509,	1730 ± 160
		PRL-510,	1700 ± 150
		PRL-511,	1900 ± 160
		PRL-512,	1490 ± 110
		PRL-513,	1690 ± 160
Surkotada (Gujarat)	Harappan	TF-1304 & -1309,	1805 ± 90
		TF-1301,	2000 ± 135
		TF-1305,	2055 ± 100
		PRL-85,	2315 ± 135
		TF-1295,	1940 ± 100
		TF-1297,	1790 ± 95
		TF-1294,	1780 ± 100
		TF-1307,	1660 ± 110
		TF-1311,	1780 ± 90

the Harappan. They began earlier but continued in the form of the rural cultures, contemporaneous with the Harappan.

In the main Indus Valley, there are no radiocarbon dates for the early levels of the Harappa culture, and we must, therefore, extrapolate its beginnings from the dated sites of Damb Sadaat and Kot Diji. The three dates from Damb Sadaat II are consistent, with P-523 (4150 ± 75 B.P.) having the smallest error. This would suggest a date of about 4225 B.P. for the anterior limit of the Harappa culture. The uppermost levels at Kot Diji (Period I) are dated to 4050 ± 140 B.P. Six dates from the uppermost levels of Mohenjo-Daro give a mean date of around 3950 B.P. Radiocarbon dates in the main Indus region, therefore, show a spread of about 4250–3950 B.P., which agrees well with the archaeological evidence from Mesopotamia.

In the peripheral zone, Kalibangan in Rajasthan has been exhaustively dated. Considering only those samples that were protected from more recent contamination by a good soil cover, we find that TF-607 and TF-608 date the beginning of the Harappa culture at that site around 4150 B.P. and that TF-143, TF-149, and TF-946 date the upper levels to around 3700 B.P. Lothal provides a quite consistent set of dates giving a minimum spread of 4050–3750 B.P., or a maximum spread of 4150–3650 B.P. (obtained by adding one standard deviation on either side). In view of the thinness of the occupational deposit at Lothal, compared to the other Harappan sites, we prefer the minimum time spread of

around 4050–3750 B.P. This bracket is further confirmed by the radiocarbon
dates from Surkotada, also in Gujarat, where a bracket of 4150–3750 B.P. covers
the total Harappan occupation and is in conformity with the dates from Rojdi.
Thus, a comprehensive bracket of 4250–3650 B.P. covers both the nuclear (main
Indus) and the peripheral Harappan timespreads (Figure 5.7).

What Caused the End?

Sahni (1956) was the first to suggest the impounding of the River Indus to
explain the end of Mohenjo-Daro. Raikes (1964) and Dales (1966) later revived
this theory and proposed that a tectonically caused, large mud extrusion im-
pounded the river, giving rise to colossal silting that eventually engulfed
Mohenjo-Daro. The barrier was thought to be permeable, so that only the silt
level rose, not the water level.

This theory was widely accepted at the time, but flaws are now apparent.
Lambrick (1967) has pointed out that such a barrier would cause deposition of

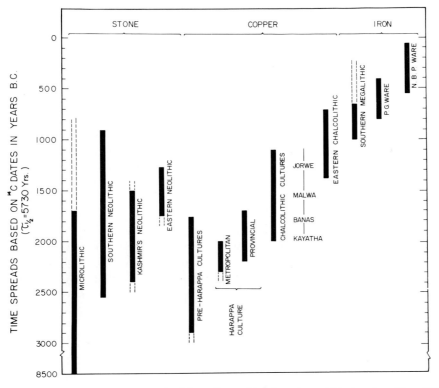

Figure 5.7 Radiocarbon time-spreads of the Indian prehistoric and protohistoric culture ($T_{1/2}=5730$;
uncorrected for $^{14}C/^{12}C$ variations).

the river's silt load far upstream and not on the inner side of the proposed dam. He also suggested that such a permeable barrier could not have withstood the enormous impact of water arriving at the rate of 2,270,000 liters per second; the Allahbund, a similar mud extrusion caused by the 1819 earthquake, was washed away by the first flood to come down the Nara in 1826 (Lambrick 1967). According to Possehl (1967), it would have required a dam 250 km in length to engulf Mohenjo-Daro, but he could not find the traces of such a bund anywhere. He also argued that the lake would have flooded vast areas, including the Lake Manchar region, but the discovery of several Harappan sites there precludes such a possibility (Possehl 1967). I, too, have expressed doubts (Agrawal 1971). If there was such a vast, engulfing lake, how could crops have grown and provided the surplus needed to sustain a city? Waterlogging would kill the gallery forests and drive away the game; few fish could have survived in the shallow waters of a mud lake. How could carts ply on muddy roads? How could the drains function at all, and what would have happened to sanitary arrangements? Such extreme conditions would have killed the people en masse before any mud lake engulfed them. A developed civilization needs some optimal ecological conditions for its florescence, and a people fighting for sheer survival could never usher in such a grand urbanization.

It should, however, be emphasized that the River Indus did affect the fortunes of the Harappans. The flood level of the Indus was rising continuously, and the ubiquitous raised platforms and massive bunds indicate the severity of the problem. The rise in the water table could itself destabilize buildings, cause salinity, and render vast tracts useless for agriculture. By periodic changes in its course, the River Indus could also leave Mohenjo-Daro and other cities high and dry.

One must also consider the geomorphological, palynological, and archaeological evidence from Rajasthan, which indicates wet and dry fluctuations (Figure 5.8) (Agrawal and Pande 1977; Singh *et al.* 1974). Increasing aridity may have aggravated the stress on the Harappan people, already exhausted by their incessant fight against floods, and evidence of progressive degeneration is found in the successive levels of Mohenjo-Daro.

Furthermore, the sea level at about 5000 B.P. was some 5 m higher than at present and then fell. The Harappan ports of Sutkagendor, Lothal, etc., are inland today, but must have been connected with the sea in their time and perhaps fell out of use because of the fall in sea level. At Amri in the Pre-Harappan period 90% of the mollusks were marine, but riverine species tended to increase with the advent of the Harappans, attaining a parity with the marine species by the end of the Harappan period.

The Aryans also have been accused of giving the coup de grace to the Harappans. Wheeler (1968) cites the finding of six groups of skeletons (mostly from the late levels of Mohenjo-Daro) showing signs of violent death. Four skeletons on the staircase of a well room in D.K. area; thirteen skeletons of adults and children, indicating simultaneous death from H.R. area; and the discovery by Dales in 1964 of the sprawling skeletons of three men, one woman, and a child, all

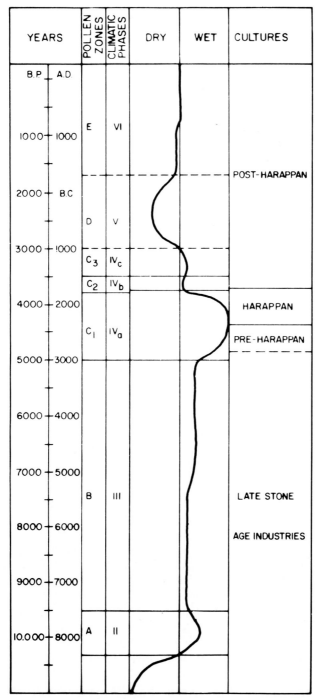

Figure 5.8 Dry and wet periods as inferred from the pollen analyses of the sediments of the northern salt lakes of Rajasthan. The ecological amelioration coincides with the flourishing of human cultures (After Singh *et al.* 1974).

tend to support Wheeler's accusation (Wheeler 1968). The ancient Hindu book, *Rigveda* (from possibly around 1500 B.C.), describes several types of forts or ramparts (*pur*) which are known from the Harappan period, and the Aryan war god, Indra, has been called the devastator of forts (*puraindara*), who destroyed 90 of them for his ally, Divodasa (Wheeler 1968). The recent discovery of several fortified sites in Kutch (Surkotada, Kotdi, Desalpar, etc.), Judier-jo-daro, and Ali Murad in Sind, Rakhigarhi in Haryana, Lurewala-Ther and Trekoi on the Hakra, and a host of other sites, besides the well-known Harappan cities, may raise the number of Harappan forts to 90 (Mughal 1970). Wheeler (1968) has also referred to the possibility of identifying Harappa with Hari-Yupiya mentioned in the Rigveda where Abhayavartin Cayamana, an Aryan warrior, defeated Vrichivan-tas, probably of non-Aryan origin. The remains of the Aryans themselves have been identified with the flimsy post-Harappan occupations represented by the Jhangar and the Cemetery H cultures.

Rao (1973a), however, would like to equate the Indus civilization itself with the Aryans. Allchin and Allchin (1968) seem to support him and to associate the Harappan beginnings with the movement of the Aryans around 2200 B.C. both to Greece and Asia. The consensus of opinion, however, considers the Indus civilization as of a non-Aryan origin.

In any case, the Harappa culture had lost its identity by around 1700 B.C. and was transformed and transmuted into the later cultures of adjoining areas. It seems likely that not one, but several, causes contributed towards its decline and disappearance.

Metal Technology of the Harappans

Before we discuss copper artifacts and their technology, it will be useful to mention the types of ores and their main locations in India. The main Indian copper minerals are (*a*) chalcopyrite ($CuS \cdot Fe_2S_3$), (*b*) chalcocite (Cu_2S), (*c*) malachite ($CuCO_3 \cdot Cu(OH)_2$), and (*d*) azurite ($2 CuCO_3 \cdot Cu(OH)_2$). The major copper mines are located in the 80-km long Khetri belt in Rajasthan and the Singhbhum copper belt in Bihar, which is 130 km in length. Other important deposits occur in the districts of Guntur, Arcot, and Kumaon (Brown and Dey 1955; Agrawal 1971). Sources in Baluchistan, such as Shah Maksud and Kalih Zeri, have also been mentioned as probable mines for Harappan copper (Sana Ullah 1931).

Pre-Harappan contexts are generally poor in copper; from the Pre-Harappan levels of Kalibangan, for example, we have three artifacts, including a *parasu* (hatchet), similar to one found at Khurdi. Only from Nal, in Quetta, is there a richer repertoire composed of knives, bangles, and axes.

The Harappans were far richer in copper and also in copper tool types, al-though they continued to use chert blades (Figure 5.9). They had flat celts, knives, arrowheads, spearheads, chisels, razors, fishhooks, saws, drills, etc. (Figure 5.10), in addition to vessels and metal figurines. It may be noted here

Figure 5.9 Typical chert blades of the Indus civilization from Mohenjo-Daro. The longest blade in the plate measures about 15 cm.

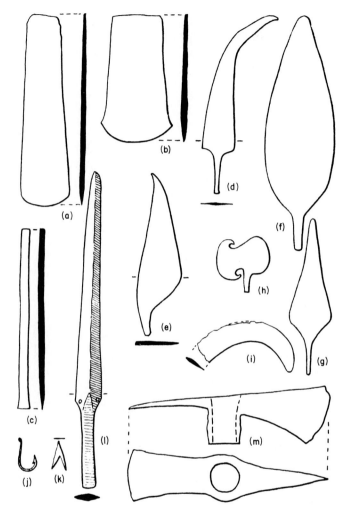

Figure 5.10 Typical Indus civilization copper tool types from Mohenjo-Daro. The sword (l) measures about 40 cm in length. Socketed axes (m) are quite rare in the Indus civilization.

that tubular drills, true saws, and needles with eyes at the pointed ends are contributions of the Harappans to the world of instruments.

The Harappans were the only people in India who used metal lavishly for vessels, including a variety of vases (Figure 5.11). Most of them seem to have been made in two parts, the bottom and the top, and then joined together. For vessel fabrication they used *sinking, raising,* and *lapping,* and for joining metal, they used *running on* and rivetting techniques. (Soldering was used only for noble metals.) Metallographic examination shows that they resorted to open and closed casting, slow cooling of casting, annealing, and cold work (Agrawal 1971; Agrawal *et al.* 1978b).

Small animal and female figurines (for an example, see Figure 5.3) were cast by the *cire perdue* (lost wax) process, although none of the Harappan moulds is as ornate as the Chinese nor as intricate as the Mesopotamian examples. A number of axes from Chanhudaro and Mohenjo-Daro show puckered surfaces, indicating that they did not always use *green poling* in open moulds; the use of green branches for poling in molten copper releases hydrocarbons that reduce the oxides, thus avoiding blowholes.

Pure copper is not a hard metal, but it can be made harder through beating (cold work). Too much cold work, however, makes the edge brittle and it then requires heating (annealing) to make it ductile again. Alloying copper with arsenic or tin increases its hardness considerably, and today we know that copper should be alloyed with up to 5% arsenic and 8–12% tin for maximal ductility and hardness. We have now more than 200 analyses of Harappan artifacts (Agrawal *et al.* 1978b), which indicate that only 23% were alloyed with tin, 12% with arsenic, 8% with lead, besides a smaller percentage with an admixture of these elements (Figure 5.12). It should be noted that the Harappans used both tin and arsenic, but the Copper Hoards culture used exclusively arsenic alloying and the Chalcolithic cultures exclusively tin alloying.

In an effort to locate the copper sources used by the Harappans, a large number of ancient copper workings have been radiocarbon dated (Agrawal *et al.*

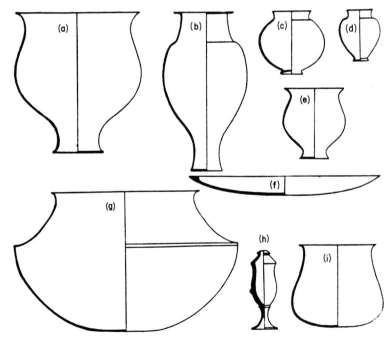

Figure 5.11   Typical Indus civilization copper vessels from Mohenjo-Daro. Jar (b) is about 18 cm high.

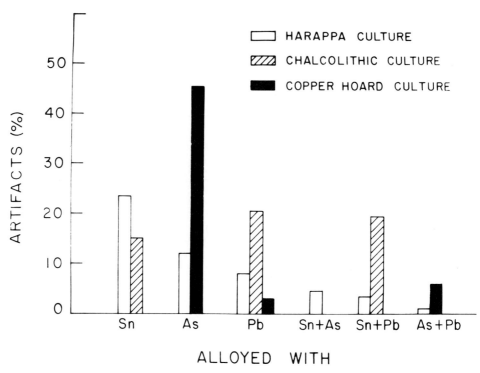

Figure 5.12 Histogram showing arsenic, tin, and lead alloying of copper by the Harappa, the Chalcolithic, and the Copper Hoard cultures. More than 1% addition is considered as deliberate alloying. It is interesting to note that more than 45% of the artifacts of the Copper Hoard culture are alloyed with arsenic, but there was no tin alloying whatsoever.

1976), but none of the dates so far is older than 3150 B.P. With further work, older workings are expected to be found. We have also tried to use comparisons of trace-impurity patterns between ores and artifacts. In both the Khetri (Rajasthan) ores and Harappan artifacts, gold is absent, but a number of other trace elements (silver, iron, arsenic, antimony, lead, bismuth, tin, nickel zinc, manganese, cobalt, aluminum, copper, molybdenum, titanium, magnesium, and vanadium) are present, suggesting the use of the Khetri ores by the Harappans. This method is not foolproof, and it is therefore hoped that results can be refined by the use of lead isotope ratio comparison between ores and artifacts and also by the techniques used by Chernykh and Tarakhova (personal communication). Circumstantially, Khetri mines of Rajasthan are likely to have been exploited by the Harappans, because they are found in roughly the same area.

CHALCOLITHIC CULTURES

The so-called *Chalcolithic* cultures are characterized by the use of stone and copper artifacts, but metal is rare, and the cultures are nonurban. Traditionally, the non-Harappan cultures of the second millennium B.C. are included in this category. I discuss here the main cultures belonging to this group, starting from southeastern Rajasthan and covering Central India and Maharashtra. The Ocher-Colored Pottery cultures and the Copper Hoard culture of the Gangetic valley are discussed in the last section. During the second millennium B.C. the rest of the subcontinent was occupied either by Neolithic cultures, or by the Indus or Indus-related cultures.

The Banas Culture

More than fifty sites of the Banas culture are known from the valleys of the Rivers Banas and Berach in southeastern Rajasthan, but the only excavated sites are Ahar and Gilund in Rajasthan and Kayatha in Madhya Pradesh (Figure 5.13). The available ^{14}C dates (Table 5.2) suggest a bracket of about 3950–3350 B.P. for this culture (Agrawal and Kusumgar 1974).

In contrast to the arid and flat western region where the only relief is provided by extensive sand dunes, Rajasthan is greener and more hilly in its eastern part, and the Banas and the Chambal are almost perennial rivers in this area. Udaipur and its environs form a large basin, enclosed by hills, with a single broad opening on the northwestern side. Ahar, the type site of the Banas culture, is located in this basin, which has good soil, fair rainfall, and plentiful game even today. There are schist and quartz outcrops, which the Aharians used in house building, and copper ores for their tools.

The mound of Ahar covers an area of 500 by 270 m and was anciently known as Tambavati (a city of copper), indicating its association with copper mines. The 13-m-deep deposit at the site has been divided by the excavators into two periods (I and II), each further subdivided into three phases (a, b, and c) (Sankalia *et al.* 1969). The Banasians (or Aharians) cultivated *jawari* (a millet) and long-grained rice in Period II, as is evident from the impressions on potsherds. No other evidence of grains has been found. Bones of turtle, fish, goat, sheep, deer, pig, and cattle were plentiful, with bovine bone predominant.

The houses have mud or mud brick walls built over plinths of schist and decorated with quartz cobbles. They are usually oriented north–south. The longest house discovered was more than 10 m long, although more typical sizes are 7 by 5 m and 3 by 3 m. Timber was used minimally, perhaps for the central post to support a thatched roof, and the floors were made either of burnt clay or of clay mixed with river gravels. Larger houses were partitioned and *chulahs* (hearths) were a common feature of the kitchen. Quartzite saddle querns formed part of the kitchen equipment.

It is curious that at Ahar only copper was used and no stone blades, while the Banas culture had a developed blade industry at Gilund, a mere 80 km away, and also at Kayatha in Madhya Pradesh. Even copper, however, is not abundant, as only five axes, one knife blade, one sheet, a bangle, and two rings have been reported from Ahar.

There are seven major, ceramic wares associated with the Banas culture,

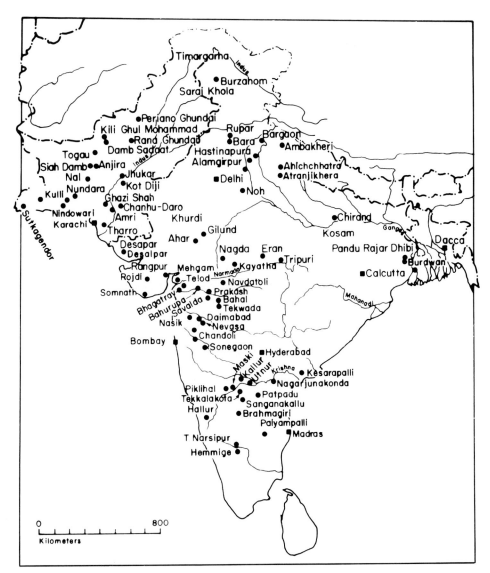

Figure 5.13 The main Chalcolithic and early Iron Age sites of the subcontinent. The main archaeological sites (●) mentioned in the text are marked. Modern towns are indicated by ■.

TABLE 5.2

[14]C Dates of Chalcolithic Sites

Sites	Cultural association[a]	Lab no.	[14]C dates (uncorrected) in years B.C. based on half-life = 5730 yr
Ahar	Banas Culture	TF-31,	1270 ± 110
(Rajasthan)		TF-32,	1550 ± 110
		TF-34,	1725 ± 140
		TF-37,	1305 ± 115
		V-56,	1875 ± 100
		V-55,	1990 ± 125
		V-54,	2000 ± 100
		V-58,	2055 ± 105
		V-57,	2145 ± 100
Bagor	Chalcolithic	TF-1005 &	
(Rajasthan)		-1006,	2110 ± 90
		TF-1009,	2765 ± 105
Barkhera	Chalcolithic	PRL-111,	1315 ± 110
(Madhya Pradesh)			
Bharatpur	Chalcolithic	PRL-15,	1435 ± 140
(W. Bengal)		PRL-188A,	900 ± 150
Chandoli	Jorwe Culture	TF-43,	1040 ± 105
(Maharashtra)		TF-42,	1170 ± 120
		P-474,	1240 ± 190
		P-472,	1300 ± 70
		P-473,	1330 ± 70
Daimabad	Chalcolithic	PRL-411,	1370 ± 100
(Madhya Pradesh)		PRL-412,	1390 ± 120
		PRL-419,	1120 ± 110
		PRL-420,	A.D. 500 ± 140
		PRL-426,	1760 ± 150
		PRL-428,	1550 ± 110
		PRL-429,	1540 ± 160
Eran	Chalcolithic	TF-326,	1040 ± 110
(Madhya Pradesh)		TF-324,	1270 ± 110
		P-525,	1340 ± 70
		P-528,	1050 ± 65
		P-526,	1280 ± 70
		TF-330,	1365 ± 100
		TF-327,	1425 ± 105
		TF-329,	1445 ± 110
		TF-331,	1500 ± 95
Inamgaon	Chalcolithic	TF-1085,	1440 ± 110
(Maharashtra)		TF-1086,	1535 ± 155
		TF-1001,	1565 ± 95
		TF-77,	1450 ± 115
Inamgaon	Chalcolithic	PRL-59,	1350 ± 110
(Maharashtra)		PRL-133,	1370 ± 110
		TF-923,	1025 ± 170

(continued)

TABLE 5.2—*Continued*

Sites	Cultural association[a]	Lab no.	[14]C dates (uncorrected) in years B.C. based on half-life = 5730 yr
		TF-996,	1070 ± 185
		TF-922,	1345 ± 100
		TF-924,	1370 ± 200
		TF-1087,	1405 ± 105
		TF-1000,	1375 ± 85
		PRL-93,	1160 ± 105
		PRL-94,	1155 ± 120
		PRL-57,	1190 ± 110
		TF-1330,	1225 ± 105
		TF-1235,	1275 ± 95
		PRL-78,	870 ± 115
		PRL-76,	1355 ± 100
Jodhpura	OCP	PRL-278,	2230 ± 180
(Rajasthan)		PRL-275,	2530 ± 160
Kayatha	Chalcolithic	TF-776,	1605 ± 115
(Madhya Pradesh)		TF-974,	1635 ± 100
		TF-778,	1705 ± 95
		TF-777,	1780 ± 100
		TF-780,	1835 ± 100
		TF-779,	1840 ± 110
		TF-781,	1880 ± 105
		TF-679,	1300 ± 135
		TF-676,	1305 ± 105
		TF-401,	1335 ± 105
		TF-402,	1380 ± 100
		TF-405,	1465 ± 100
		TF-397,	1500 ± 100
		TF-398,	1675 ± 100
		TF-678,	1685 ± 100
		TF-399,	1675 ± 100
		TF-396,	1730 ± 100
		TF-680,	2015 ± 110
Khed	Jorwe Culture	PRL-220,	1030 ± 160
(Maharashtra)		PRL-221,	1180 ± 90
Mahishadal	BRW	TF-390,	855 ± 100
(W. Bengal)		TF-391,	1380 ± 105
		TF-392,	1085 ± 110
Malvan Gujarat	Late Harappan	TF-1084,	800 ± 95
Navdatoli	Malwa	P-205,	1445 ± 130
(Madhya Pradesh)		TF-59,	1525 ± 100
		P-204,	1600 ± 130
		P-200,	1610 ± 130
		P-475,	1610 ± 70

TABLE 5.2—*Continued*

Sites	Cultural association[a]	Lab no.	^{14}C dates (uncorrected) in years B.C. based on half-life = 5730 yr
		P-201,	1645 ± 130
		P-202,	1660 ± 130
		P-476,	2300 ± 70
Nevasa	Jorwe Culture	TF-40,	1250 ± 110
(Maharashtra)		P-181,	1250 ± 125
Pandu Rajar Dhibi	BRW	?	1012 ± 120
(W. Bengal)			
Prabhas Patan	Prabhas Culture	TF-1287,	2455 ± 110
		PRL-90,	2410 ± 115
		TF-1284,	1615 ± 100
		TF-1286,	1755 ± 95
Prabhas Patan	Prabhas Culture	PRL-92,	1990 ± 100
(Gujarat)		PRL-91,	2020 ± 170
		PRL-20,	1485 ± 110
Sohgaura	BRW (painted)	PRL-178,	1330 ± 110
(Uttar Pradesh)		PRL-179,	1230 ± 110
Sonegaon	Jorwe Culture	TF-379,	1290 ± 95
(Maharashtra)		TF-383,	1330 ± 100
		TF-382,	1340 ± 100
		TF-380,	1375 ± 110
		TF-384,	1565 ± 100

[a] OCP is Ocher-colored pottery; BRW is Black and Red Ware.

which led Sankalia (1974) to wonder if this ceramic variety might reflect some ethnic diversity. The typical Banasian pottery is Black and Red Ware, externally painted in white (Figure 5.14a, d). Thin incised lines on the necks of bowls are very characteristic of the Banasian pottery at Kayatha, although this feature is less frequent at Ahar itself. The common shapes are bowls and dishes, and the pottery was made on a potter's wheel. The second important type is Red Slipped Ware, which is made on a potter's wheel with the slip ranging from tan, to orange, to chocolate. Vases with corrugated shoulders and long necks are important, although bowls, *lotas*, and ribbed vessels are more common. Some of the dishes-on-stands are so well made as to suggest the use of wooden tables (Figure 5.14b). There are also handmade, coarse, red and gray storage jars with appliqué decoration, basins, etc., associated with the Red Slipped Ware, and a buff or cream slipped ware, made of kaolin mixed with clay.

A large number of terracotta bulls, both naturalistic and stylized, were discovered in the Banasian levels at Kayatha, although there were few at the type site of Ahar. The stylized animal figurines emphasize the horns and the hump,

242   D. P. Agrawal

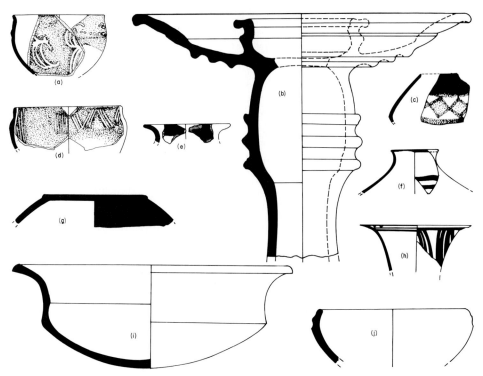

Figure 5.14   The Banasian and the Kayathan wares. (a, d) White painted Black and Red Ware; (b) dish-on-stand; (c) Red and Buff Ware, Kayatha Period I; (e–i) Kayathan Ware; (j) Combed Ware, Kayatha Period I.

but the rump is more like a pedestal. Decoration is not evident on these figurines, except for occasional fingernail impressions.

Sankalia cites parallelism between the Banasian animal handles, vessels with appliqué, and punctured decoration and those from the Iranian sites of Sah Tepe, Geoy Tepe, and Hissar. He also finds close parallels in the incised patterns on beads from Anatolia and Ahar, and concludes

> Some pottery forms from Ahar, for example the animal-headed handles and the hollow-stemmed bowl in Grey Ware, do recall similar types at Shah Tepe and Geoy Tepe and Hissar. So it would not be quite strange if some folk movement from Western Asia, starting in about 2000 B.C., had reached south-eastern Rajasthan. (Sankalia *et al.* 1969:223)

The Kayatha Culture

In Madhya Pradesh, the fertile Malwa region is drained by the River Narbada and its affluents, the Tapti and the Mahi, which debouch into the Arabian Sea. The Rivers Chambal and Betwa also drain this tract and join the River Yamuna in the north. Annual rainfall averages about 105 cm, and nights are cool even during the summer. Chalcolithic man seems to have confined himself to the narrow, alluvial areas of the rivers, since his meager copper implements were not adequate to plough the sticky black soil. This may have imposed ecological constraints on surplus food production, so that the Chalcolithic cultures never developed urbanism, despite their copper technology.

The Kayatha culture, discovered by Wakankar at Kayatha (Figure 5.13) on the River Kalisindh, a tributary of the Chambal, is the earliest Chalcolithic culture in Central India and is radiocarbon dated between 3950 and 3750 B.P. (Table 5.2). This culture is mainly confined to the Chambal Valley, but, out of approximately 40 known sites, only Kayatha has been excavated (Ansari and Dhavalikar 1975).

The Kayatha culture is characterized by three types of pottery. The predominant variety is a thick, sturdy, Brown Slipped Ware painted in violet or deep red (Figure 5.14:e,f,g,h,i,j) and made of a fine, pinkish, well-levigated clay. Decorative motifs are generally linear and painted on the rim. The main shapes are bowls and basins, and globular jars with concave necks; storage jars are also found. Most of the pots have a ring base, but it does not appear functional as the base protrudes beyond the ring, recalling the Pre-Harappan Sothi types. Deep bowls with beaded rims and the globular jars are common to the Sothi and the Kayatha cultures, and the fabrics and surface treatment of these two wares show striking resemblances. Some affinity with the Harappan ceramics has also been claimed, although it appears very tenuous (Ansari and Dhavalikar 1975).

The Kayathan Buff-Painted Red Ware (Figure 5.14c) is thin and has a fine fabric. After a buff wash, pots were painted in red with geometric designs, such as loops, festoons, latticed diamonds, and oblique lines. The main shapes of this ware are concave-necked jars, basins, and *lotas* (small vessels with carinated bodies, bulbous bottoms, and flaring rims). The last shape is worthy of note as it marks the first appearance of this form, which was eventually adopted throughout India and has changed little with the passage of time. Because of resemblances in shape and fabric, Dhavalikar traces the origin of Malwa Ware from the Buff-Painted Red Ware of Kayatha.

Combed Ware, another important component of the Kayatha culture, is a red ware, generally without a slip, and is represented by bowls and basins. The incised decorations, mainly chevrons and zigzags, recall those of the Sothi culture.

The Kayathans seem to have been rich in copper; 28 copper bangles were recovered from a single pot. The two copper axes with sharp cutting edge and a lenticular section are the finest examples in the Bronze Age of India; they were cast in a mold, unlike the later Chalcolithic artifacts, which were merely hammered out of sheets. A chisel is also reported from Kayatha.

As the term *Chalcolithic* implies, most of these cultures used both copper and stone; even the Harappans, despite the abundance of copper artifacts, used long chert blades (Figure 5.9). The blades used by Chalcolithic cultures like the Kayathans, the Banasians, and the Navdatolians, however, are shorter than the Harappan examples, perhaps because of the smaller size of the available chalcedony nodules. The Kayathans had a developed blade industry, including lunates, penknives, and parallel-sided blades. These were made of chalcedony, which was locally available in the form of veins. Semiprecious stones like carnelian, agate, and steatite were used for ornaments. Two necklaces of long barrel, short bicone, and oblate beads of carnelian and agate (160–170 beads each) were found in a ceramic vessel; a similar find was made at Mohenjo-Daro. Forth thousand microbeads of steatite, all threaded, were found in another vessel.

No clear evidence for structures has been unearthed, but postholes indicate the use of circular and rectangular huts. No burials have been reported.

The Kayathan ceramics have some affinity with the red ware storage jars of the Harappans. The evidence of copper bangles and bead necklaces from pots both at Kayatha and Mohenjo-Daro has been used to support a Harappan affinity. The similarities of the Kayathan with the Sothi or the Pre-Harappan culture, however, seem to be more convincing: for example, the Combed Ware and the Red Slipped Ware of Sothi and Kayatha have quite specific affinities. Sankalia, therefore, identifies the Kayathans as the Pre-Harappans who were pushed out from Rajasthan by the Harappans. It seems significant that the name Kalisindh, on whose banks Kayatha is located, recalls Sind (the Indus), the original homeland of the Pre-Harappans.

The evidence of precious finds like bangles and beads in pots may indicate a sudden desertion of the site, probably under attack. As there is a sterile layer between the Kayathan and the succeeding Banasian layers at the site, it seems that the site was not reoccupied by the invaders.

The Malwa Culture

The Malwa culture is characterized by Malwa Ware (a buff- or orange-slipped pottery painted in black), by copper or stone artifacts, and by small settlements of wattle-and-daub huts. It was spread over the Malwa region (as were also the Kayatha culture and, to some extent, even the Banas culture), and also extends into Maharashtra. The excavated sites of Eran, Nagda, and Navdatoli are in Madhya Pradesh, and Inamgaon is in Maharashtra (see Figure 5.13). The Malwa culture has a radiocarbon range of around 3650–3350 B.P. (Table 5.2).

Navdatoli is not only the site par excellence of this culture but is also well published (Sankalia et al. 1958,1971). In the local dialect, Navdatoli means "village of the boatmen," and the site is situated on the southern bank of the River Narbada; the twin site of Maheshwar, also with extensive traces of settlement, is situated on the opposite bank. The site presents a beautiful panorama of the tall Vindhyas in the north, the low Satpuda hills in the south, and the wide expanse of the Narbada in between with considerable alluvial deposits on either side of the river. The selection of the site clearly shows that the Chalcolithic technology was adequate only for fresh alluvium and was not capable of dealing with the black cotton soil.

The Chalcolithic occupation of Navdatoli includes four distinct phases: Phase I is marked by the Banasian type of Black and Red Ware; Phase II by Cream-Slipped Ware; in Phase III appears Black on Red Ware; and Phase IV is characterized by a coarse red ware in association with Lustrous Red Ware, similar to that of the post-Harappan Gujarat cultures. Malwa Ware (Figure 5.15) occurs throughout the occupation, and there are no significant changes in the non-ceramic material culture.

Navdatoli does not appear to have been fortified (unlike Eran and Nagda), nor was the settlement "planned." The huts were either circular, with a diameter of about 3 m, or rectangular, averaging 3.5 by 2.5 m. Split bamboo screens plastered with mud were used as partition walls (there is no evidence of mud bricks), and floors were made of cobbles or gravels rammed with hard compact clay and coated with lime. The arrangement of the wooden posts suggests conical roofs. One- or two-mouthed *chulahs* (hearths) were used, storage jars

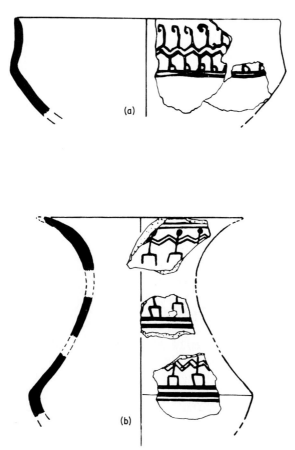

(a)

(b)

Figure 5.15 Malwa Ware bowl and *lota*. Note the hand-linked, dancing, human figures on (b).

were placed along the walls of the huts, and pottery vessels on terracotta stands occur in the centers. The purpose of these is unknown.

Charred grains of wheat (*Triticum vulgare compactum*), barley, and rice (*Oryza sativa* L.) were found in Phases II and IV. Other plant remains include black gram, green gram, lentil (*Lens culinaris* Medicus), grass pea (*Lathyrus sativus* L.), linseed, *ber* (*Zizyphus jujuba* Lamk), and *amla* (*Phyllanthus embelia*). The faunal remains indicate that beef, venison, and pork were eaten.

It has been claimed that Navdatoli has the richest repertoire of ceramic designs of all Chalcolithic cultures, including the Harappans. The main form is, of course, Malwa Ware (Figure 5.15), which constitutes one-third of all the pottery recovered at the site. Malwa Ware was painted in black or brown over a buff or orange slip, and has a thick fabric due to the use of chopped husk. A thinner variety of this ware, the Eran fabric, is dominant at Eran but also occurs at Navdatoli. The Malwa Ware types are *lotas* (Figure 5.15b), channeled spouts, and pedestaled goblets. More than 600 decorative motifs are known, both geometric and naturalistic, including black buck, dog, bull, deer, peacock, pig, panther, fox, tortoise, crocodile, insects, human figures (Figure 5.15), and lozenges and triangles (hatched, solid, or empty). The Cream-Slipped Ware has some different shapes, such as the medium-sized storage vessels and bowls, but *lotas* and goblets are held in common with Malwa Ware. The Black and Red Ware has the same shapes as Malwa Ware.

Each household made its own stone tools of a milky chalcedony, and the crested-ridge technique was used for obtaining blades. Of the 23,000 artifacts recovered from Navdatoli, penknife, blunted backed, serrated and parallel-sided blades, trapezes, and lunates were the main types. A single ground-stone axe is also reported found at the surface.

The use of copper is evidenced by flat celts with convex cutting edges, arrowheads, spearheads, chisels, and a mid-ribbed sword, which was cast; all other artifacts were probably hammered to shape. Copper beads, bangles, and rings are also found.

Some ceramic motifs are probably religious in character. A huge jar is decorated with appliqué figurines of what appear to be a female worshipper and a lizard flanking a shrine; in later Hindu iconography, the lizard is associated with the goddess Durga, the consort of Siva. Another motif depicts a shrine with a tortoise, an incarnation of Vishnu, and tortoise amulets were also worn. It therefore seems possible that the perforated stone disks with similar shrines and animal motifs, reported from 600 B.C. onwards from other sites, may represent a Chalcolithic religious tradition (Dhavalikar 1979a). Terracotta female figurines (perhaps a mother goddess) and a channel-spouted vessel with a painted male figure with dishevelled hair holding a spear also appear ritualistic. A squarish pit (2.5 by 2 by 1.2 m) with a plastered bottom and a charred log at each corner has been identified as a *vedi* (fire altar).

In the absence of skeletal remains, it is difficult to determine who were the originators of the Malwa culture. It has been suggested that they could have been a people of Iranian origin; or aborigines who merged with the Aryan society; or an indigenous people who developed this culture out of interaction with Western Asians. Similarities between the Malwa culture and those in Western Asia are numerous. Channeled spouts have close parallels with those of Tepe Sialk (about 1800 B.C.), and goblets with those of Sialk, Giyan, and Hissar II (around 3000 B.C.). Even the mother goddess cult has been traced to Western Asia (Sankalia 1974). Sankalia, however, believes that the Malwa people were not actual immigrants, but, rather, were acquainted with the way of life of Iran and Western Asia. However, the Malwa culture seems to have arrived at Navdatoli already fully developed, which would suggest that these people were colonists; Dhavalikar (1979a) associates them with the Vedic Aryans.

The important site of Eran, in District Sagar, is strategically located (Singh 1967). A horseshoe meander of the River Bina surrounds Eran on three sides; the fourth side was protected by a 47-m-wide mud rampart and a moat. This rampart has been assigned to Phase II of the Chalcolithic period (Period I). No house plans are discernible, but the floors were rammed with *kankar*, a feature peculiar to this site. The *chulahs* (hearths) have three arms, unlike the two-armed ones of Navdatoli (Singh 1967).

Among the ceramic types, black-painted red and gray wares, and white-painted black-and-red wares occur throughout the three phases of Period I. The gray ware forms are the same as those of Malwa Ware. In Phase II appears a deep red ware with a shiny surface and painted, geometric designs. Phase III is marked by channel-spouted vases in both red and black-and-red wares.

Nagda, located on the Chambal in District Ujjain, has a 7-m thick Chalcolithic deposit, with black-and-cream (Period I) and black-on-red (Period II) wares. The common decorative motifs are gazelles, antlers, and the sun. Sankalia (1974) would include the main Nagda ceramics within Malwa Ware but suspects that there might also be a Kayathan element in the lower levels. The use of copper was limited, and the chalcedony blade industry was well developed. Mud bricks were used in the construction of houses, and there is also evidence of a mud brick fortification.

The nuclear region of the Malwa culture seems to be within Madhya Pradesh, in the valleys of the Narbada and the Chambal. The Malwa people did not cross the barrier of the Vindhya Mountains to the north but moved southwards into the Deccan plateau, to the valley of the River Tapti. Daimabad and Inamgaon are the main sites of the Deccan, where they came in contact with the Neolithic culture.

Inamgaon is located on a terrace of the River Ghod, 80 km east of Poona. The site has been scientifically excavated and has yielded more information about the Chalcolithic way of life than any other site in India. The deposits are divisible into the Malwa culture (Period I), the Early Jorwe culture (Period II), and the Late Jorwe (Period III) (Dhavalikar 1977).

In addition to wattle-and-daub huts, Inamgaon has some unique pit dwellings. The pits are about 2 m wide and 50 cm deep, and usually nine poles were fixed along the periphery to support the roof. One of the biggest houses had a pit (with steps) 3 m in diameter and 1.2 m deep. A twin urn burial was discovered underneath the floor of one of the pit houses. A large (6.6 by 4.4 m), rectangular, wattle-and-daub house had a circular mud platform in one corner (perhaps for storage bins); a rectangular *chulah* (hearth); a storage jar; four clay bowls; a variety of other pots and pans; bone points; blades; beads; and faunal and floral remains (*Hordeum vulgare, Lens esculenta, Dolichos biflorus*). The house was so cluttered that there was room for only four or five people to have lived in it.

Prakesh is located at the junction of the Rivers Tapti and Gomai. It is a rather large mound into which Thapar (1967) dug only a small vertical trench. The main finds are terracotta bulls, shell bangles, stone blades, and beads of shell, paste, and semiprecious stone. Period I is marked by Malwa Ware, although the typical goblets and bowls of Navdatoli-type are absent. The excavators have reported both Jorwe and Lustrous Red Ware influences from Period I. The recovery of *Tectona grandis (sag), Anogeissus latifolia (damoda), Terminalia tomentosa, Dalbergis,* and *Dendrocalalamus* (bamboo) indicates a dry, deciduous type of forest cover.

Sawalda is also located on the River Tapti and was excavated by Sali. The material culture is distinguished by a red pottery painted in black, with highly stylized motifs. At the moment, the Sawalda culture seems unique, and it is difficult to find cultural affiliations for it. Sali has identified a Sawalda level at Daimabad also.

Further south, on the Godavari-Pravara system, is Daimabad, which was originally excavated by Deshpande in 1958, and was recently reopened by Sali. The discovery of a sherd with what is perhaps Indus script may be the first evidence of contact between the Indus civilization and the Chalcolithic cultures of the south. The Daimabad sequence starts with a Sawalda level, followed by Late Harappan, then Malwa, and is topped by the Jorwe culture.

A thick, coarse, gray ware with rims of bowls and lids painted with red ocher, recalling the Brahmagiri Neolithic style, occurs in Phase I of the site, and a buff jar with a jungle scene in two compartments is ascribed to Phase I, although not found in situ. Phase II is characterized by Malwa Ware and Phase III by Jorwe Ware. Phases I and II yielded extended inhumations, aligned north–south and without any funerary goods. On the other hand, a skeleton, probably of an important person, appears to have "lain in state" over a clay floor, covered by a canopy supported by 14 poles. Children were buried in urns (Dhavalikar 1979b:247–263).

A hoard of massive copper animal figures of a rhinoceros, an elephant, a buffalo, and a bull chariot driven by a man, all mounted on wheeled platforms, was accidentally discovered near Daimabad and has been ascribed by some to the Chalcolithic phase. Each object, however, weighs several kilograms and to use such a quantity of metal for nonutilitarian artifacts seems unlikely for a Chalcolithic phase.

The Jorwe Culture

Maharashtra, the home of the Jorwe culture, is composed mostly of the Deccan plateau, and only the river valleys have open plains with rich soil cover. Annual rainfall is in the range of 50–100 cm, but it varies greatly from year to year and droughts are frequent. The vegetation is xerophytic (examples include acacia, tamarind, and *caparis*). The vast alluvial stretches in the Pravara-Godavari basins have more than 3 m of fertile soil, and the main Jorwe culture sites are located on these alluvial flats. Smaller Jorwe sites seem to be concentrated around major centers. The former usually have only a few huts and an area of 2–3 ha whereas a major center, such as Prakash in the Tapti Valley, Inamgaon in the Bhima Valley, and Daimabad in the Godavari Basin, may cover 20 ha. Excavated Jorwe sites (Figure 5.13) include Inamgaon, Theur, Songaon, and Chandoli in Poona District; Bahal in Jalgaon District; Prakash in Dhulia District; and Jorwe and Nevasa in Ahmednagar District (Dhavalikar 1979b).

The Jorwe people at Inamgaon cultivated barley, wheat, lentil (*Lens esculenta*), *kulith* (*Dolichos biflorus*), grass pea (*Lathyrus sativus* L.), and occasionally rice. Wheat could not be grown by the Jorwe people elsewhere because of the paucity of the winter rain, but at Inamgaon it may have been possible by irrigation. Rice could have been grown only through irrigation. Fruits like *ber* (*Zizyphus jujuba*), *jamun* (*Syzigium cumini* L.), and *beheda* (*Terminalia belerica* Roxb) were also grown. A massive embankment, about 240 m long, 2.2 m wide and perhaps equally high, was probably used to divert flood water through a channel, which was 200 m long, 4 m wide and 3.5 m deep. This large channel seems to have been used for the storage of water for irrigating the fields. The embankment, built in the early Jorwe period, may indicate a higher rainfall and frequent floods. Earthen pans may have been used to bake *chapatis* (a thin bread), large saddle querns were probably used to make wheat and barley flour, and the perforated stone disks may have been used for digging sticks.

Five large pits were used to roast animals, including dog, elephant, horse, pig, cattle, and goat. Camel bones occur and may have been of a domesticated or of a wild variety. The wild species represented are black buck (*Antilope cervicapra*), nilgai (*Boselaphus tragocamelus*), wild buffalo (*Bubalus bubalis* L.), chital (*Axis axis*), sambhar (*Cervus unicolour*), and barasingh (*Cervus duvauceli* Cuvier).

Jorwe Ware has a fine fabric and is well baked. The surface is red or orange matt painted with geometric designs in black (Figure 5.16). The main vessel forms are the spouted jar with a flaring mouth, the carinated bowl, and the high-necked jar with a globular profile. Heavy-duty pots, like storage jars, platters, dough plates, and even lamps, were handmade in coarse red or gray ware. A few pots are theriomorphic.

A unique kiln, built on stone foundations, is in the form of a huge trough of clay about 1.7 m in diameter. It had a number of oval clay cushions with holes in their centers and grooves on the sides. These were placed over the fire chamber

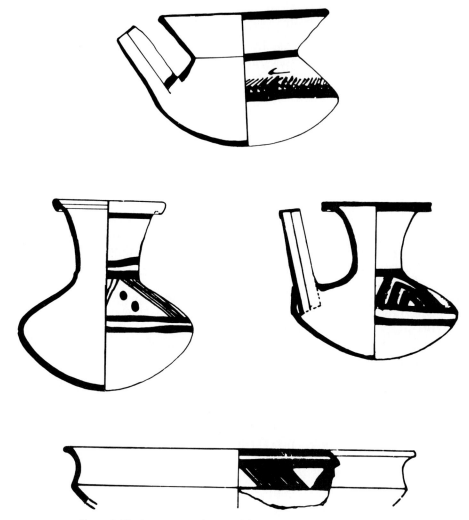

Figure 5.16 Jorwe Ware *lotas* and bowl. Some *lotas* are spouted.

at a depth of 60 cm to provide outlets for the hot gases. Air ducts radiated from the center of the kiln. The Inamgaon furnace is a little different in design and material from the Harappan kilns.

A variety of materials like agate, carnelian, jasper, chalcedony, gold, copper, and ivory were used for making ornamental beads; copper anklets and gold ear ornaments have also been reported. A pair of tongs and a crucible indicate local gold working, although the gold itself may have been imported from Kolar. Copper was also used to make axes, chisels, knives, fishhooks, beads, and bangles. A smelting kiln has been identified at Inamgaon.

The Jorwe culture people buried their dead with the head facing north. Adults were buried in extended positions with the feet chopped off below the ankles, perhaps to immobilize their ghosts. Children were buried in coarse handmade urns, some three to five urns being joined together to accommodate the bodies of older children. Spouted jars and bowls in the graves suggest that the dead were provided with food and drink for the afterlife. A unique, four-legged, unbaked urn burial (80 by 50 cm), containing a sitting adult skeleton, was also recovered. It is interesting to note that one of the sides of the urn is shaped like a female belly and that the skeleton was in an embryonic position. Another four-legged urn, with funerary jars and a bowl but no skeletal remains, was found in the largest house (five rooms) of the Early Jorwe period. If this was a chief's burial, he may have died in war so that his skeleton could not be recovered.

Terracotta female figurines, with or without heads, both baked and unbaked, are reported from Nevasa, Inamgaon, and elsewhere. The pendulous breasts on these figurines perhaps emphasize the fertility aspect. One of them was found in the central (elite) area of Inamgaon in a clay receptacle, which indicates its religious importance.

It is interesting to note that at Inamgaon, the craftsmen's quarters were located to the left of the entrance of the settlement, on its western periphery, a practice which is followed even today in the central Maharashtra villages. The craftsmen represented at Inamgaon are potters, ivory-carvers, goldsmiths, and lime makers. (Lime was used to paint floors and pits, perhaps as an insecticide). Pit silos dug into the house floors in this quarter were probably used to store coarse grains like barley and *kulith* (as is the practice today). Perhaps the craftsmen were paid in kind for their services, hence the need for storage space; today it is usual to pay the *bulutedars* (cobbler, potter, smith, carpenter, etc.) in kind in the form of coarse grains at the time of the harvest, a tradition which may go back to Jorwe times.

The center of the Inamgaon settlement was probably occupied by the elite, as is suggested by the presence of the largest houses here with five rooms in an area of 25 by 10 m. The skeleton of a male, 1.83 m tall and with his ankles and feet intact, was found in the largest house. Both the fact that his legs were not mutilated and the size of the house indicate that he may have been a chief. Unlike the silos of the peripheral area, in the central area there were only four-legged jars for storage; these were perhaps for wheat, which must be stored above ground. The granary is also located in the central part of the settlement, so taxes may have been paid to the chief in kind. The granary (10.5 by 9 m) had both pit silos and round mud platforms for storage bins. There were also large fire pits with round clay lumps in the center, of which the function is unknown.

At Theur, in Poona District, a number of stone circles 18–28 m in diameter were found to be the circular huts of the Chalcolithic people, fortified by one or two concentric rings of stone boulders. Here, black-and-red pottery constituted 40% of all ceramics. There was also a coarse red ware painted in black, chocolate, or pink. At Sastevadi, opposite Theur, on the River Mula-Mutha, Rao reported an abundance of gray, burnished, handmade ware of the southern Neolithic type, along with a sprinkling of Malwa Ware in Period I. Period II is marked by Jorwe Ware (Sankalia 1974).

Around the close of the first millennium B.C., increased aridity in Maharashtra may have resulted in large-scale desertion of sites in the northern Deccan plateau and migration to the Krishna and Kavery valleys in the south. Decline and degeneration seem to be reflected in the Late Jorwe period at Inamgaon by coarser paintings and pottery, and smaller rounded huts in contrast to the large rectangular houses of the previous period. Towards the close of the Late Jorwe period, the Megalithic black-and-red ware brings this culture to the threshold of the early historical period. The radiocarbon dates ascribe a time bracket of about 3350–3050 B.P. to the Jorwe culture at Inamgaon (Table 5.2).

As mentioned previously, Sankalia sees marked Western Asiatic influence on the Chalcolithic cultures, but Chakrabarti strongly disagrees:

> Almost all of the suggested analogies are too general to be of any use in a valid and meaningful archaeological comparison. For instance, one fails to understand how an archaeological study of cross-cultural relationship in widely separate geographical areas can be based on vague similarities in items like simple geometric, virtually ageless, terracotta types, painted stylized human and animal figures etc. Some of the analogies cited are positively misleading. To take only one example, there is no conceivable similarity between the Sialk 'tea-pots' and Navdatoli channel spouts, not even in any vague identity of form. Besides, the Navdatoli bowls are considerably earlier. The suggested West Asiatic analogies do not belong to any single cultural assemblage or even different assemblages of any specific period. One has only to remember that Catal Huyuk VI-A and Sialk Necropole B, two of the many horizons cited, belong to the sixth millennium B.C. and the first half of the first millennium B.C. respectively. Finally, it should be pointed out that not a single demonstrably West Asiatic type fossil occurs in the cited Indian assemblages. For instance, one may wonder why there is not a single sherd of typical Nuzi Ware in this Indian context, if Nuzi has really anything to do with the origin of this context. Moreover, the basic character of these Indian assemblages is very different from that of their supposedly parent (in Sankalia's hypothesis they are parent sites) West Asiatic sites, a difference which should be obvious to anybody who studies these assemblages without primarily looking for similarities (Chakrabarti 1977:25–38).

Chalcolithic Metal Technology

The Chalcolithic cultures depended on stone artifacts rather than on copper, to a greater extent than either the Harappans or the Copper Hoards people. On the whole, about 17% of Chalcolithic artifacts show tin alloying (see Figure 5.12), but the range varies considerably: at Ahar, only pure copper was used; a Jorwe axe has only 1.7% tin; a Nevasa chisel has 2.7% tin; at Navdatoli, the range of tin alloying is 3–5%; the highest tin (12.8%) recorded was in an axe from Somnath. Unlike the Harappan and Copper Hoard cultures, Chalcolithic groups did not alloy with arsenic. For better fusibility, lead alloying was more common; 20% of the artifacts contain lead.

A few artifacts have been examined metallographically (Agrawal et al. 1978b; Pathak and Medhekar 1955). An axe from Chandoli shows casting fins all over the surface. Although equiaxial grains and the absence of coring indicate a slow cooling of the cast, yet the holes on the surface show that the molten metal was not "green poled." An axe from Somnath shows evidence of cold work and annealing, and specimens from Navdatoli and Ahar indicate a knowledge of casting and annealing. The report of "glassy" slag at Ahar indicates local smelting.

Hegde (1965) has spectroscopically examined several Chalcolithic artifacts and compared their trace impurities with those of the Khetri copper ore. He finds a close similarity between the two, thus indicating the possibility of the Khetri ores having been used by the Chalcolithic cultures. The Khetri mines are quite close to Ahar.

The most beautiful examples of the Chalcolithic craft are the cast axes from Kayatha. Most Chalcolithic metal artifacts, however, are of simple, nondiagnostic types. The main forms are beads, nails, rods, wires, fishhooks, rings, flat celts, and daggers. The Chandoli dagger has been compared with the antennae-hilted sword from Fatehgarh, but we consider that there are very important technological differences between the two. The total length-to-blade ratio in the Chandoli dagger is only 1.6, compared to 5 in the Fatehgarh example; the tang was cut with a chisel and the incipient antennae so produced do not compare at all with the 10–15 cm long, cast antennae of the Copper Hoards types.

THE OCHER-COLORED POTTERY
AND THE COPPER HOARDS CULTURES

The third important group of copper-using cultures is the Copper Hoards culture, and there is some circumstantial evidence to associate it with the Ocher-Colored Pottery (OCP). However, as we shall see in the following, neither the OCP, nor perhaps the Copper Hoards, is one unified culture.

The Ocher-Colored Pottery Culture

The distribution zone of the OCP is primarily the Gangetic doab, an alluvial plain between the Himalayas and the Central massif, which was originally a trough but is now filled with alluvium, in places 5000 m deep, brought by the River Ganga and its affluents. Rainfall in the doab ranges from 60–100 cm and increases toward the east. The primaeval doab was probably a tangled forest with swampy valleys, which, obviously, did not provide optimal ecological conditions for the advent of cities. In fact, urbanization of the valley had to await the appearance of iron.

The sediments associated with the OCP sites are a few meters thick, brown in color, sandy and silty in texture, and bear a detrital appearance very different from a normal habitational deposit (Dikshit 1979). It has been proposed that the sediment was deposited either by a huge flood that engulfed the doab, or by prolonged aeolian activity. Our recent sedimentological and scanning electron microscopic analyses (SEM) indicate that these sediments were originally derived from glacial environments and subsequently redeposited in the valley by floods. The sediments do not show any of the characteristics of wind-borne deposition (Agrawal et al. 1978a).

The OCP was first discovered below the Painted Grey Ware levels at Hastinapur. On being rubbed, the potsherds left an ocherous color on the fingers, hence the name (Lal 1954–1955). This may have been a purely local effect, due to waterlogging or ill firing or both, but the name has remained. It is now known that the pottery originally had a slip and was painted black.

Bahadurabad, in Saharanpur District, was the first site where the Copper Hoards were discovered; subsequently, the OCP was reported from many other sites in Uttar Pradesh, such as Nasirpur and Jhinjhana, although the two are never together. The association of the OCP and the Copper Hoards is thus very circumstantial. Atranjikhera (Etah District) and Lal Qila (Bulandsahr District) have revealed different varieties of the OCP, which raises a number of questions: is there one OCP or several OCPs, was the OCP a Harappan-related ware or a local ceramic, and if there are several OCPs, which one, if any, was really the part of the Copper Hoards assemblage?

Dikshit (1971–1972) and Suraj Bhan (1975) suggested that there are two broad categories of the OCP: the Zone A or western type, including central and eastern Rajasthan, Haryana, Western Uttar Pradesh, and the Zone B or eastern type, including central and eastern Uttar Pradesh. The excavated sites in Zone A are Jodhpura, Siswal, Mitathal, Bara, Ambkheri, and Bargaon; in Zone B, Lal Qila, Atranjikhera, and Saipai. No detailed reports are, however, yet published. Basins with beaded rim; vases with out-curved flaring or flanged rims; dishes-on-stands; channel spouts; loop-handled vases; tubular spouts; and ring-footed bowls constitute the Zone A types, which seem to combine Late Harappan, Cemetery H, and also some local ceramic traits. The Zone B OCP lacks the basin with beaded rim, the dish-on-stand and the flask. Huxtable et al. (1972) reported some thermoluminescence (TL) dates on the OCP from Nasirpur, Jhinjhana, and elsewhere showing a scatter from around 2600 to 1100 B.C. TL dates for Sringverpura (Ayodhya District), however, place the OCP at that site at about 1000 B.C. (Table 5.3, and Agrawal et al. n.d.) The radiocarbon dates from Jodhpura range between about 4450 and 4250 B.P. If these few dates can be relied upon, the Zone A OCP would seem to be significantly older than the eastern (Zone B) OCP.

In Zone A, Mitathal Period II B appears to be a mixture of Pre-Harappan, Harappan, and Cemetery H ceramic traits. Jodhpura, in Jaipur District, has recently been excavated by Agrawal and Vijay Kumar (personal communication). The OCP occurs here in a 1.1-m thick deposit, below a pre-Painted Gray Ware and black-and-red ware level, which yielded bone points, stone beads, wattle-and-daub structures, sun-dried bricks, and houses 4 by 3.5 m in size, but no copper objects. The OCP yielded a red-slipped ware, with incised designs and occasional parallel bands in blue and a variety of shapes. Bowls, dishes, vases, knobbed lids, dishes-on-stands, and vases with flared rims are the main ceramic forms. The Harappan influence is obvious.

TABLE 5.3

Thermoluminescence dates from Various Ocher-Colored Ware Sites

Site	Sherd no.	TL age (years B.C.)
Atranjikhera	11164	1610[a]
	11165	1170[a]
	C1	2280[a]
	C2	1250[a]
	C3	2130[a]
Lal Qila	11291	1730[a]
	92	2030[a]
Jhinjhana	11392	1990[a]
	B1	1570[a]
	B2	2650[a]
Nasirpur	11491	1500[a]
	92	1180[a]
Sringaverapura	PRL-21	2660 ± 280[b]
	PRL-24(1)	2769 ± 400[b]
	PRL-24(2)	2690 ± 280[b]
	PRL-29	2743 ± 300[b]
	PRL-33(1)	2900 ± 380[b]
	PRL-33(2)	2855 ± 270[b]
	PRL-38(1)	3015 ± 280[b]

[a] TL dates from Research Laboratory for Archaeology and the History of Art, Oxford, United Kingdom.
[b] TL dates from Physical Research Laboratory, Ahmedabad, India.

At Lal Qila (Bulandsahar District) in Zone B are reported floors paved with rammed potsherds, mud bricks, postholes, burnt pieces of reed, and bamboo-marked plasters and even a burnt brick, although most of the floors and houses were badly damaged. The Lal Qila OCP includes a red ware painted in black or with incised designs. The ceramics have a distinct slip and do not look like the water-rolled OCP of Hastinapura or Bahadurabad. The vessel forms are storage jars, vases, basins, bowls, lids, miniature pots, and what appears to be dishes-on-stands. Gaur (1973:154–162) reports a great deal of similarity in the OCP (Zone B) of Saipai, Atranjikhera, and Lal Qila. The last two are both characterized by handled pots.

At Saipai the OCP sherds included those giving off ocherous color on rubbing, those with an intact red slip and some with black, painted designs or incised decoration. The major forms are jars with flaring rims, and bowls and basins sometimes with spouts and handles; the presence of dishes-on-stands and a ring base is also inferred but the evidence is not conclusive. The site also yielded rubbers, querns, a chert and a chalcedony blade, a burnt brickbat, chunks of burnt clay with reed impressions, bones of *Bos indicus,* a copper harpoon, and a hooked spearhead (Lal 1972).

Believing that a flood deposited the detrital-seeming sediments of the OCP, Lal postulated that potsherds must have floated, while the heavier copper implements sank (Lal 1968). It is difficult, however, to believe in the association of the Copper Hoard implements with the pottery at Saipai, and, with its spouted, handled and black-painted vessels and chert blades, Saipai appears to be quite unique. Moreover, the Copper Hoard artifacts have generally been found in caches rather than individually, so that the occurrence of only stray tools at Saipai raises doubts. I therefore feel that at present the association of the OCP and the Copper Hoard should be treated only as provisional.

The Copper Hoard Culture

Most of the tools of the Copper Hoard culture have been found in hoards or caches, mainly from Uttar Pradesh, Bihar, and Madhya Pradesh. Since most of the artifacts were chance finds, there was no control of a definite associated assemblage. As a result, finds from such far-flung sites as Shalozan in north-western Pakistan, Bhagrapir in Orissa, and Kallur in the south have been included in the Copper Hoard culture zone. A wide variety of types of tools was included in this amorphous collection: rings, a variety of celts, trunnion axes, anthropomorphs, harpoons, swords, double-edged and socketed axes, and so on.

Naturally, such an odd assortment of tools has given rise to a plethora of hypotheses, and it fell to Lal to bring some order to the Copper Hoards. In a brilliant analysis, he showed that a number of types (such as the Fort Monroe sword, axe-adze, socketed axes, and trunnion axes) were confined to the north-western part of the subcontinent (now Pakistan) and never occurred in the Gangetic doab. Other types of artifacts (such as antennae-hilted swords, anthropomorphs, harpoons, and barcelets) were concentrated mainly in the Gangetic doab. Lal also showed the significant technological differences between the Koban examples (compared by Heine Geldern to prove his Aryan equation) and the antennae swords (Lal 1951:20).

Following Lal, the distinctive types (Figure 5.15) that can be included under the Copper Hoard category are: flat and shouldered celts, antennae swords, harpoons, anthropomorphs, hooked swords, and double-edged axes. The last type has been reported from Bhagrapir (Orissa), where, although they are up to 40 cm wide, their thickness is less than 3 mm; they could not therefore have been used as tools. Their association with the main Copper Hoard types is, in any case, doubtful. The hooked swords seem to have parallels elsewhere, but closer examination reveals the distinctive features of the Copper-Hoard-associated hooked sword: in the apparently similar Harappan examples, a hole is provided for hafting and not a hook; in the Chalcolithic example from Navdatoli, there is hardly any median ridge, nor any hook. Moreover, the hooked sword has been found in association with such distinctive Copper Hoard types as anthropomorphs, antennae swords, and harpoons from Bahadurabad, Sarthauli, Fatehgarh, and Niori (all in Uttar Pradesh).

Anthropomorphs have been identified as ritual objects. We examined several specimens and have found three main features: externally sharpened and in-curved forearms, plain hindlimbs, and a thickened head (Figure 5.17b). We have proposed their possible use as missiles to kill birds: the sharp arms could cut the bird; the thick head could stun it; and the incurved arms could entangle and bring it down. When thrown, a replica of an anthropomorph traveled in a whirling fashion and followed a trajectory not unlike that of a boomerang (Agrawal 1969). Sankalia (1974) has objected to this hypothesis on the grounds that such a device would be too complicated to have been used by a primitive people. The boomerang, however, was not invented by a civilized people.

Rao (1973a) discovered a fragmentary copper piece with a convex end and two broken side lugs in the Harappan levels of Lothal, and compared it with the anthropomorphs from the doab. If it had had longer arms like those of the Copper Hoard examples, however, it would not be mechanically feasible for it to break so near the body (Agrawal 1971:192). It should also be noted that, in the whole range of the Harappan artifacts, this piece alone has alleged resemblances to the anthropomorphs.

Like the mid-ribbed sword, the harpoon has backward-pointing barbs and holes at the ends of the barbs. Two varieties of harpoons are known: one cut from a thick sheet, and the other cast in a double mould. Such harpoons could have been used either for killing fish or big game, as depicted in a rock shelter in Mirzapur (Figure 5.18) (Lal 1951).

The antennae sword type (Figure 5.17a) is confined to the doab zone. Its total

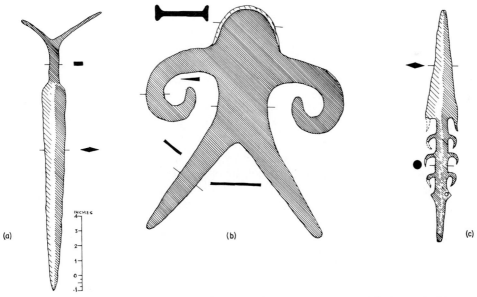

(a)   (b)   (c)

Figure 5.17 The main Copper Hoard culture tool types. (a) Antennae-hilted sword; (b) an-thropomorph; (c) harpoon.

Figure 5.18   Rhinoceros hunt, on a rock-painting near Mirzapur. Note the harpoon-mounted spears.

length varies from 42 to 75 cm and the antennae projections on the hilt end are more than 10 cm in length. I feel that such long antennae would be definite handicaps in using these artifacts as swords and have proposed that they could have been better used to kill wild game by fixing the swords upright in pits, with the antennae sitting in slits across green logs. If game were stampeded into the pits, the swords would pierce them without buckling, since the green logs (with branches) would serve as shock absorbers. Admittedly, this hypothesis would be difficult to test, except, perhaps, by examining use marks on a large number of such artifacts.

From the foregoing discussion it is obvious that the essential core of the Copper Hoards consists only of the anthropomorph, the harpoon, the hooked sword, and the antennae sword (Figure 5.17a). These types are found together: for example, at Bisauli, harpoons and anthropomorphs occur together; at Bithur, antennae swords and harpoons are associated; antennae swords and anthropomorphs were found together at Fatehgarh; and the hooked sword was associated with the other three types at Fatehgarh, Sarthauli, Bahadurabad, and Niori (Agrawal 1971).

We would divide the Copper Hoards into two zones: the main doab (Uttar Pradesh) types are specialized tools: the anthropomorph, the antennae sword, the harpoon, and the hooked sword; the main eastern (Bihar) type is the barcelt.

Flat and shouldered celts are common to both zones. The barcelt, from sites in copper-rich Bihar, is about 60 cm long with a beveled edge and a thick body. Its sturdiness and length suggests its use as crowbar for digging copper ores, and the use marks on barcelts do indicate their use against hard surfaces. The barcelt is the only specialized type in the eastern group; if typology is any clue, the simpler types of Bihar may have preceded the more specialized types of Uttar Pradesh. Except for a reported harpoon from Mitathal, no doab types have been discovered from Haryana or Rajasthan. The *parasu* seems to be a type of this area and has been reported from Mitathal (Suraj Bhan 1975) and Kurada (Figure 5.19) in Rajasthan (Agrawala 1980).

The distribution of the Copper Hoard types is therefore mainly confined to Uttar Pradesh, Bihar, and Madhya Pradesh. It is beyond doubt that the Copper Hoards have an individuality of their own and were not influenced by either the Harappan or the Chalcolithic cultures. This is further supported by the exclusive arsenic alloying of the Copper Hoards.

As regards the authorship of the Copper Hoards, there is considerable controversy and seems to be no objective solution. Heine Geldern (1936) identified them with the Aryans, Piggott (1950) with the Harappan refugees; Lal (1951) and Gupta (1963) with the Mundari-speaking Australoid tribes of the primaeval doab; and Sankalia (1974), as usual, finds Western Asiatic affinities for the OCP, and therefore for the Copper Hoards.

Copper Hoards Metal Technology

Because most of the Copper Hoards have been found in caches, they give an impression of abundance of metal. For example, at Gungeria, 424 artifacts with a total weight of more than 400 kg were discovered. Until we find these implements in regular excavations or habitation sites, however, it will be difficult to infer the real abundance of metal in an archaeological context.

An examination of the Copper Hoards artifacts shows that they were made both by hammering and cutting metal sheets, as well as by closed casting. A small percentage of the artifacts (Figure 5.12) show lead alloying, probably for better fusibility. Metallographic examination of the artifacts indicates slow cooling, cold work, and annealing.

We have few data on the trace impurity pattern of the Copper Hoards, but circumstantial evidence points to the use of Bihar mines. The exclusive occurrence of barcelts in the eastern region may also indicate their use for crowbar-like operations in mining.

More interesting is the evidence of arsenic alloying. Out of the 46 artifacts analyzed by us, 50% show more than 1% arsenic. None of the artifacts, however, has any tin (Figure 5.12). It is thus obvious that the Copper Hoards technological tradition is different from that of the other cultures. We may recall here that in the earliest phases, both in the Near and Middle East, only arsenic alloying was used (Eaton and McKerell 1976); tin replaces arsenic only in the third millennium B.C. in Western Asia. At Tepe Yahya, they used arsenic copper

Figure 5.19 Copper Hoards from Kurada (Khurdi), Rajasthan. From top to bottom, flat celt, chisel, four hatchets, and bangles.

ores, which made arsenic alloying easier for them, but there are no significant sources of arsenic in India, although small out-crops are known from Rajasthan, Kashmir, and Bihar. Nal in Pakistan, yielded lollingite ($FeAS_2$). Both of these features, exclusive arsenic alloying and characteristic tool-types, indicate the possibility of the Copper Hoards being an autochthonous, and perhaps the oldest, metallurgical tradition in India.

Before I conclude the discussion on the Copper Hoards, we should take note of some remarkable discoveries made recently in Rajasthan (Agrawala 1979:159–160; Agrawala 1980:89–92). Sixty copper flat celts and some arrowheads were discovered from Ganeshwar, in Sikar District of Rajasthan. Two points deserve notice: first, the arrowheads are of Harappan types; second, the site is only 60 km from the rich Khetri mines. Although we cannot technically include them with the Copper Hoards, they do indicate a factory site.

The Khurdi Hoard was reported earlier by Sankalia, but Agrawala (1980:89) reports that the site is actually Kurada, in Nagaur District of Rajasthan. The original hoard consisted of 103 artifacts, but only 10 now remain in the Jodhpur museum. None of the types is typical of the Copper Hoards artifacts; in fact, the channel-spouted bowl has affinities with the Malwa channel-spout and the hatchets with those found at Kalibangan.

Although there is a distinct possibility that some of these sites served as factory centers for the Harappan and Pre-Harappan towns, contacts with the Copper Hoards do not appear likely.

ACKNOWLEDGMENTS

For extensive discussions and assistance I thank the following friends: Dilip Chakrabarti, S. P. Gupta, Sheela Kusumgar, Virendra Misra, Rajendra Pant, and Vibha Tripathi. For help in connection with the illustrations, I thank the Archaeological Survey of India, the Cambridge University Press, Dr. R. C. Agrawala, Dr. V. N. Misra, and Prof. H. D. Sankalia.

REFERENCES

Agrawal, D. P.
      1969   The Copper Hoards problem: a technological angle. *Asian Perspectives* **12**:113–119.
      1971   *The Copper Bronze Age in India*. Delhi: Munshiram Manohorlal.
      1972–
      1973   Genesis of Harappa Culture. *Puratattva* **6**:37–44.
Agrawal, D. P., N. Bhandari, B. B. Lal, and A. K. Singhvi
      n.d.   Thermoluminescence dating of pottery from Sringaverapura—a Ramayana site. *Proceedings of the Indian Academy of Sciences*, in press.
Agrawal, D. P., M. N. Deshpande, S. N. Rajaguru, and B. Roy
      1978a   The ambient environment of the Gangetic sediments of Chalcolithic period. *Proceedings of the Indian Academy of Sciences* **87A**(3):22–28.
Agrawal, D. P., R. V. Krishnamurthy, and Sheela Kusumgar
      1978b   The early metallurgy in India and its origins. Paper presented at the Symposium on origins of agriculture and metallurgy, Moesgaard.

Agrawal, D. P., and Sheela Kusumgar
    1974   *Prehistoric chronology and radiocarbon dating in India.* Delhi: Munshiram Manoharlal.
Agrawal, D. P., C. Margabandhu, and N. C. Sekar
    1976   Ancient copper workings: some new ^{14}C dates. *Indian Journal of History of Sciences* **11**(2):133–136.
Agrawal, D. P., and B. M. Pande (editors)
    1977   *Archaeology and ecology of western India.* New Delhi: Concept.
Agrawala, R. C.
    1979   Three copper objects from Ganeshwar, Rajasthan. *Journal of the Oriental Institute* **28**(3–4):159–160.
    1980   Khurdi Copper Hoard from Rajasthan. *Man and Environment* **4**:89–92.
Allchin, R., and B. Allchin
    1968   *The birth of Indian civilization.* Harmondsworth: Penguin.
Ansari, Z. A., and M. K. Dhavalikar
    1975   *Excavations at Kayatha.* Poona: Deccan College.
Bibby, G.
    1958   The ancient Indian style seals from Behrain. *Antiquity* **32**:243–294.
Brown, J. C., and A. K. Dey
    1955   *India's mineral wealth.* London: Oxford University Press.
Buchanan, B. A.
    1967   A dated seal impression connecting Babylonia with ancient India. *Archaeology* **20**:104–107.
Chakrabarti, D. K.
    1977   India and West Asia: An alternative approach. *Man and Environment* **1**:25–38.
Dales, G. F.
    1966   The decline of the Harappans. *Scientific American* **214**(5):93–100.
Dhavalikar, M. K.
    1977   Inamgaon: the pattern of settlement. *Man and Environment* **1**:46–51.
    1979a   Early farming cultures of Central India. In *Essays in Indian protohistory,* edited by D. P. Agrawal and D. K. Chakrabarti. Delhi: B. R. Publishers. Pp. 229–245.
    1979b   Early farming cultures of Deccan. In *Essays in Indian protohistory,* edited by D. P. Agrawal and D. K. Chakrabarti. Delhi: B. R. Publishers. Pp. 247–265.
Dikshit, K. N.
    1971–
    1972   Comments on the OCP. *Puratattva* **5**:8–9.
    1979   The OCP settlements in Ganga-Yamuna doab. In *Essays in Indian protohistory,* edited by D. P. Agrawal and D. K. Chakrabarti. Delhi: B. R. Publishers. Pp. 285–299.
During-Caspers, F. C. L.
    1972   Harappan trade in the Arabian Gulf in the third millennium B.C. *Mesopotamia* **7**:167–191.
Eaton, E. R., and N. McKerell
    1976   Near-eastern alloying and some textual evidence for the early use of arsenical copper. *World Archaeology* **8**(2):169–197.
Fairservis, W. A.
    1967   The origin, character and decline of an early civilization. *American Museum Novitates No. 2302.* New York: The American Museum of Natural History.
    1971   *The roots of ancient India.* London: Macmillan.
Frankfort, H.
    1939   *Cylinder seals.* London: Macmillan.
Gadd, C. J.
    1932   Seals of ancient Indian style found at Ur. *Proceedings of the British Academy* **18**:1–22.
Gaur, R. C.
    1973   Lal Qila excavations and the OCP problem. In *Radiocarbon and the Indian archaeology,*

edited by D. P. Agrawal and A. Ghosh. Bombay: Tata Institute of Fundamental Research. Pp. 154–162.

Gupta, S. P.
1963   Indian Copper Hoards: The problems of homogeneity, development, origin, authorship and dating. *The Journal of Bihar Research Society* **49**:147–166.

Gurov, N. V.
1970   Towards the linguistic interpretation of the proto-Indian texts. *Journal of Tamil Studies*
2(1):53–58.

Hegde, K. T. M.
1965   Technical studies in Chalcolithic Period Copper Metallurgy in India. Ph.D. dissertation, M.S. University, Baroda.

Heine Geldern, R.
1936   Archaeological traces of Vedic Aryans. *Journal of the Indian Society of Oriental Art*
4:87–88.

Huxtable, J. H., D. W. Zimmerman, S. N. Hassan, and R. C. Gaur
1972   Thermoluminescence dates for OCP from India. *Antiquity* **56**(181):62–63.

Kohl, P. L.
1978   The balance of trade in southwestern Asia in the mid-third millennium B.C. *Current
Anthropology* **19**(3):463–492.

Lal, B. B.
1951   Further Copper Hoards from the Gangetic basin and a review of the problem. *Ancient
India* **7**:20–39.
1954–
1955   Excavations at Hastinapura and other explorations in the Upper Ganga and Satluj
basins. *Ancient India* **10–11**:5–151.
1966   The direction of writing in the Harappan script. *Antiquity* **40**(157):52–55.
1968   A deluge? Which deluge? Yet another facet of the problem of Copper Hoard culture.
American Anthropologist **70**(5):857–863.
1972   The Copper Hoard Culture of the Ganga Valley. *Antiquity* **56**:282–297.
1977   *Has the Indus Script been deciphered?* Simla: Indian Institute of Advanced Study.
1979   Kalibangan and Indus Civilization. In *Essays in Indian protohistory*, edited by D. P.
Agrawal and D. K. Chakrabarti. Delhi: B. R. Publishing. Pp. 65–97.

Lamberg-Karlovsky, C. C.
1972   Trade mechanism in Indus-Mesopotamian interrelations. *Journal of American Oriental
Society* **92**:222–229.

Lambrick, H. T.
1967   The Indus flood plain and the Indus civilization. *The Geographical Journal* **133**(4):483.

Mackay, E. J. H.
1943   *Chanhudaro Excavations 1935–36.* Boston: American Oriental Society.

Mughal, M. R.
1970   *The Early Harappan Period in the Greater Indus Valley.* Ann Arbor: University Microfilms.

Parpola, A.
1975   Tasks, methods and results in the study of the Indus script. *Journal of the Royal Asiatic
Society* **2**:178–209.

Pathak, B. R., and M. K. Medhekar
1955   Report on copper celt and bangle. In *Report on the Excavations at Nasik and Jorwe:
1950–51*, by S. B. Deo and H. D. Sankalia. Poona: Deccan College. Pp. 159–160.

Piggot, S.
1950   *Prehistoric India to 1000 B.C.* Harmondsworth: Pelican.

Possehl, G. L.
1967   The Mohenjodaro floods: a reply. *American Anthropologist* **69**(1):32–40.

Possehl, G. L. (editor)
1978   *Ancient cities of the Indus.* New Delhi: Vikas.

Raikes, R. L.
  1964   The end of the ancient cities of the Indus. *American Anthropologist* **66**(2):284–289.
Rao, S. R.
  1973a   *Lothal and Indian civilization.* Bombay: Asia.
  1973b   The Indus script methodology and language. In *Radiocarbon and Indian archaeology,* edited by D. P. Agrawal and A. Ghosh. Bombay: Tata Institute of Fundamental Research. Pp. 323–340.
  1979   Deciphering the Indus script. *Indian and Foreign Review* **17**(3):13–18.
Sahni, M. R.
  1956   Biogeological evidence bearing on the decline of the Indus civilization. *Journal of Palaeontological Society of India* **1**(1):101–107.
Sana Ullah, M.
  1931   Copper and bronze utensils and other objects. In *Mohenjo-Daro and the Indus civilization,* edited by J. Marshall. London: A. Probsthain. Pp. 481–488.
Sankalia, H. D.
  1974   *Prehistory and protohistory of India and Pakistan.* Poona: Deccan College.
Sankalia, H. D., B. Subbarao, and S. B. Deo
  1958   *The excavations at Maheshwar and Navdatoli.* Poona: Deccan College.
Sankalia, H. D., S. B. Deo, and Z. D. Ansari
  1969   *Excavations at Ahar.* Poona: Deccan College.
  1971   *Chalcolithic Navdatoli.* Poona: Deccan College.
Singh, G., R. D. Joshi, S. K. Chopra, and A. B. Singh
  1974   Late Quaternary history of vegetation and climate of Rajasthan desert. *Philosophical Transactions of the Royal Society of London* **267**(889):476–501.
Singh, U. V.
  1967   Eran—A Chalcolithic settlement. *Bulletin of Ancient History and Archaeology* **1**:29–38.
Suraj Bhan
  1975   *Excavation at Mitathal and other explorations.* Kurukshetra: Kurukshetra University.
Thapar, B. K.
  1967   Prakash 1955: A Chalcolithic settlement in the Tapti valley. *Ancient India,* **20–21**:1–67.
  1973   Synthesis of multiple data as obtained from Kalibangan. In *Radiocarbon and Indian archaeology,* edited by D. P. Agrawal and A. Ghosh. Bombay: Tata Institute of Fundamental Research. Pp. 264–271.
Tosi, M.
  1979   The proto-urban cultures of eastern Iran and the Indus civilization. In *South Asian Archaeology: 1977,* edited by M. Taddei. Naples: Inst. Univ. Orientale. Pp. 149–172.
Wheeler, R. E. M.
  1968   *The Indus civilization* (3rd ed.). Cambridge: Cambridge University Press.

6

The Bronze Age in Northwestern Europe: Problems and Advances

J. M. COLES

The Bronze Age was the central element of the Three Age system (Stone, Bronze, and Iron) devised in the nineteenth century to provide an order for the artifacts of the prehistoric period in northern Europe. Although this provided a popular way of dividing the prehistoric past, in recent years archaeologists of the later episodes of European prehistory have become increasingly dissatisfied with the concept of an "Age" based on a single material and lacking clearly defined characteristics. Before the development of radiocarbon chronologies, the Bronze Age could be thought of as a long and important episode in the development of prehistoric European societies, providing a link between the basic subsistence-orientated Neolithic and the highly organized Iron Age communities of Europe. The advent of radiocarbon dating has done little to give precision to the Bronze Age, as we shall see, but it did provide unequivocal indications that the Neolithic of Europe, in all its stages, occupied an unsuspectedly long period of time far in excess of the Bronze Age.

As the Bronze Age was defined on the basis of its metal, the realization that preceding the traditional Bronze Age there had existed a long period when gold and copper were in regular use, suggested to many archaeologists that the concept of the Bronze Age should be abandoned. To them, it was merely a short and rather undistinguished episode in European prehistory, and in no way important enough to deserve to retain its original designation. This view has many supporters today but I am not to be counted among them. Inertia still counts for much in prehistoric studies, and to propose any fundamental change in nomenclature is not really worth the effort; there is enough confusion in European prehistoric terminology as it is. The advantage of retaining and ac-

265

knowledging the existence of "the Bronze Age" is that it encourages consideration of the episode as a significant part in the overall development and evolution
of European society.

Such a generalistic approach is valuable in searching for evolutionary trends.
Some European prehistorians look beyond such apparently minor affairs as the
Bronze Age, beyond its minor characteristics and features. They try to gaze
through and overlook the imperfections and irregularities in human behavior
toward the evolutionary and developmental tendencies of ancient societies. In
doing this, any particular episode is merely an event, a small part of the large
whole, and can hardly be appreciated outside its position in the concept of the
development of European society. However, the defect in such an approach is
readily seen, and its antithesis provides the basis for almost all research in
European prehistory; only by particularizing from our data are we able to comprehend their place and their significance in the overall development of ancient
societies. Hence although it may be argued that 1,000 years of later European
prehistory is only a small episode when viewed over the 40,000 years of continuous human presence, the place of that millennium was important, as its contrasts with preceding and succeeding millennia can demonstrate. The point is
emphasized, that in the development of European society, and perhaps therefore of world society, a certain episode categorized by tradition and for convenience as the Bronze Age can be seen to be important not because it was "the
Bronze Age" but because it saw the emergence of certain characteristics that
helped create the European societies of historic times. Recent advances in archaeological thought have begun to examine these characteristics in detail, as we
shall see.

BASIC SOURCES OF EVIDENCE

The European area first to be categorized and dignified by the Three Age system
was northern Europe, eventually followed by parts of western Europe. It is
appropriate therefore to consider how Bronze Age studies have responded to
this original and persuasive direction. The history of the discipline in northwestern Europe unfortunately often demonstrates the rigidity of approach that
was imposed through overenthusiastic adoption of the system, and it is only in
the past decade that the stranglehold has been broken. Nonetheless, the reasons
for the original proposition, and its longevity, are strong and persuasive. To
understand these we should look briefly at the basic sources of evidence for the
Bronze Age of the north and west.

Traditionally, the concept of the Bronze Age was based upon artifacts of
bronze and gold, burial mounds, and funerary pottery. These were recoverable
from hoards of objects buried in the ground, or from the tombs themselves.
Because the latter were so abundant on the ground, easily recognizable, easily
explored, and rewardingly furnished, they were plundered in their thousands

during the eighteenth, nineteenth, and twentieth centuries. The plunderers were often the local landed gentry, or the religious leaders of the community, or outright tomb-robbers; more recently, they have been archaeologists working under various guises and excuses. The result of all this endeavor has been the total destruction over a mere 200 years of the work of numberless Bronze Age communities whose identification and perception is now almost totally lost to us and to our successors. We are not talking here of hundreds of tombs, but of tens of thousands. Even so, there exist records of many hundreds of such monuments, and these provide important evidence for current investigations.

The second traditional and hereditary source of information about the Bronze Age of northwestern Europe was the artifact in its narrow definition. Objects of metal (Figure 6.1), generally bronze but sometimes gold, objects of stone and bone, and clay vessels, provided the inspiration for the Three Age system. Pioneers of the Bronze Age such as Oscar Montelius in the north soon constructed an elaborate "chest-of-drawers" in which objects could be placed according to their characteristic features. Evolutionary tendencies were important and from artistic, technological, and functional elements a series of mutually related, successively evolving, groups of materials was devised. Inspirational ideas from foreign Bronze Age industries of central Germany and the south were constantly sought and therefore found, and cross-correlations thereby developed for chronological purposes. In time, a neat set of cameos was devised, each exclusive yet demonstrably related to its neighbors. For the north, a sixfold system was produced and astonishingly is still exhibited in more than one major museum in Scandinavia, not as an historic documentation but as a working chronology. Over the decades since the system was devised, many refinements have been attempted and achieved, but the system clearly still has a secure place for students of the Bronze Age. It has inspired, if that is the word, a whole series of comparable schemes for the Bronze Age of other regions of northern and western Europe. In western France, due to the quite appalling condition of the evidence, there is little else that can be attempted. In Britain and Ireland, where the evidence for the Bronze Age is extensive and varied, typological ordering is also a well-practiced art and performs a relatively small and increasingly smaller role in our understanding of the Bronze Age.

Beside these two main sources of evidence, tombs and small artifacts, the rest of the available information is secondary in quantity, but of primary importance today. Studies of rock carvings and other artistic manifestations, and typological studies of stone-built monuments provide many archaeologists with rather intractable material, and their investigations have tended to be inconclusive or untestable. Of far greater moment are the studies now underway on Bronze Age settlements, field systems and land use; in these studies the revolution in the approach to the Bronze Age has occurred. Only a decade ago, almost no Bronze Age settlements or fields were known in northwestern Europe outside the British Isles, and the few became type-fossils for the Bronze Age. Today, hundreds of settlements are known, sometimes directly associated with field systems; in

Figure 6.1 A richly furnished burial in a tree-trunk coffin from Wardböhmen, northern Germany. The body is shown partly reconstituted; the ornaments, all of bronze, are exceptionally varied and abundant. (From Piesker 1958:Pl. 65.)

some areas, very extensive land divisions and boundaries have been identified and related to their contemporary settlements. All of this has provided archaeologists with totally new insights into Bronze Age societies, and, equally important, has demonstrated firmly that metallurgy (despite the name "Bronze Age") was not the basis of society and was neither the reason for its existence, nor necessarily the major impetus for social change.

The evidence for the Bronze Age of northwestern Europe is therefore surprisingly varied and abundant. Although serious gaps exist in certain aspects, such as food subsistence practices, it begins to be possible to write a prehistory of the time and region rather than a series of disconnected essays about particular aspects in isolation. The aim of this chapter, however, is not a prehistory, but an outline of the state of knowledge, and a comment on the current studies that are advancing that knowledge along both traditional and new fronts. As always, views and developments outstrip publication, and while this may be excusable for conceptual studies, for many modern excavations of important settlements, the lack of adequate publication is disgraceful. The subject can only advance with free and full access to all data, and it is disturbing to find that a number of crucial sites remain obstinately unpublished. Often these Bronze Age sites are publicized in "interim reports," and our failure to find subsequent full documentation in accredited journals leads many to suspect that preliminary notifications were exaggeratedly optimistic about the quality and character of the site or that the investigators lack the archaeological determination to fulfill their obligations.

Nonetheless, many important sites and studies are now available and allow us to perceive the new directions in which archaeology of the Bronze Age is moving. To appreciate these new developments, a glance at the state of knowledge is essential. There are a number of general surveys of much of the evidence (Burgess 1980; Butler 1969; Coles and Harding 1979; de Laet 1974; Gaucher 1981; Giot et al. 1979; Guilaine 1976; Herity and Eogan 1977; Megaw and Simpson 1979; Thrane 1973). These and many others provide the general reader with a view, an impression, of the Bronze Age of the north and west, but only the specialist will appreciate the quantity of evidence. Thousands upon thousands of bronze objects, pottery vessels, burial mounds, decorated rock surfaces, and vast areas with surviving land boundaries are the recognizable remnants of Bronze Age communities. Less tangible but no less important are increasingly numerous traces of settlements, of coastlands quite unlike those of today, and of previous environments deduced from the battery of natural scientific disciplines. Among the last we may list radiocarbon determinations, which promised much for our understanding of the Bronze Age but have done little to clarify matters.

The Bronze Age of northwestern Europe is inextricably bound up with the interplay of land and sea (Figure 6.2). Landforms' altering by marine erosion and deposition, continuing isostatic recovery of the northern lands, and an essentially maritime environment on the western edges of the European landmass, all encouraged particular responses in subsistence, industry, travel, and the structure of Bronze Age societies. In addition, the uneven distribution of raw mate-

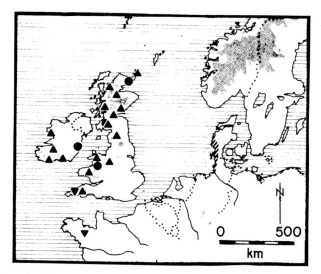

Figure 6.2   Map of northwestern Europe with major sources of copper (▲), tin (▼), gold (●), and amber (hatched areas) shown. The amber source in the southeastern Baltic Sea is off the map. Note the absence of all nonferrous metals from northern continental Europe. (From Coles and Harding 1979:Fig. 3.)

rials encouraged exchange, transport, and communication along the long Atlantic coastlands and beyond. Stone suitable for heavy equipment was widely available, and flint of high quality was also not uncommon, with supplies from quarries and mines in southern Britain, the Low Countries, northern France, and southwestern Scandinavia. Copper and gold were obtainable from highland Britain and Ireland, tin from Brittany and southwestern England, and silver from Brittany. Atlantic Europe was well endowed with materials, but the North lacked any supplies of copper, tin, or gold suitable for Bronze Age exploitation. Every piece of metal from the enormous numbers of hoards and graves and single finds in southern Scandinavia, the Low Countries and northwestern Germany was imported either as raw metal, or scrap, or finished product. The quantities are such that deliberate organization must be involved, exchange commodities offered, and security of supplies attempted; the implications of this are discussed in the following sections. The amber of Jutland and the southern Baltic shores is the only surviving commodity apparently offered in the exchange or whatever arrangement existed, but it and the metals can hardly have been the sole substances that passed from community to community and linked even in the most ephemeral way the northern lands with those of central Europe and the Atlantic west.

CHRONOLOGY

The chronology of these events is traditionally bound to the typological developments deduced from the artifacts of the north and west as they can be seen to relate to those of central Europe, and of the latter as they in turn relate to objects from southern Europe in historically dated contexts. The foundations upon which this edifice was constructed have never been totally undermined either by methodological arguments or by refined chronologies, but they are shaky, and until recently it was suspected that radiocarbon dating would permit the establishment of independent chronologies. In northern Europe, the schemes of Montelius, refined by many prehistorians, continue to persist and provide a rather gross series of episodes to which certain artifacts can be related. The philosophical problems of such an approach have been fully aired (Gräslund 1974, 1976; Kristiansen 1978b). Even so, the gross periodization allows us to point to a period when the new metals were being introduced into the north, then their full adoption and the development of the first major industry in the north, followed by other periods. Correlations with central Europe provide rough chronological guides for the ordering of this scheme (Harding 1980), and a few radiocarbon determinations indicate that the developed Early Bronze Age existed 1500–1200 B.C., within a final Late Bronze Age 900–600 B.C. This is well as far as it goes, but it has not provided the precision required for understanding the rates of change in the Bronze Age of the north. Beside it, unencumbered by periodization, the schemes for the Low Countries, based on multiple radiocarbon dates and archaeologically distinct assemblages, seem far more useful and independent of outside influences and connections (Brongers and Woltering 1973; Rijksdienst voor het Oudheidkundig Bodemonderzoek 1965–1966).

In the west, periodization and typology, those Bronze Age bugbears, emerged early and persist today in ever-increasing complexity. Few will doubt the care with which such multiphase episodes of the Bronze Age have been devised by Burgess (1974, 1980), Eogan (Herity and Eogan 1977), Briard (Giot *et al.* 1979) for Britain, Ireland, and Atlantic France, respectively, but their relevance to the most pressing problems of the Bronze Age remains to be asserted. Such schemes are based upon metal objects, less often on pottery, and rarely if ever on settlement and economy; it is of little surprise that those archaeologists engaged in the recognition and interpretation of land organization and use ignore the typological ordering of material that does not figure among their evidence. Yet such typologies do have their uses in the determination of supply-and-demand economies of the Bronze Age, as we shall see. Radiocarbon dates have failed to make much progress in refining the chronology of the Atlantic Bronze Age except in the cases of settlements where the materials suitable for periodization studies are totally absent. One major concern of British Bronze Age studies is the relationship, if any, of the "Wessex Culture" to Mycenae and the Aegean, and to central Europe (Gerloff 1975); here radiocarbon dates have proved equivocal.

We must conclude that the periodization of the Bronze Age in the north and west has not encouraged views of the Bronze Age as a dynamic episode in European prehistory, nor has it achieved the precision that is needed to test, refine, or upset the traditional chronologies. Even were these possible, the neglect with which archaeologists have selected samples for dating does not augur well for future needs; tree-trunk coffins, heavy timbers from ramparts, and charcoal from cremation pyres, all require thought before blind acceptance as potential dating materials for what is a rather short set of episodes in the second and early first millennia B.C. (Coles and Morgan 1975). When allied to the current problems with dendrochronological calibrations of the notoriously oscillatory second millennium radiocarbon dates, it is not difficult to be pessimistic about the future of Bronze Age chronologies. What is required is some method by which we could speak of half-centuries rather than the three or two centuries that we can estimate through a combination of typology and radiocarbon analyses; such a gross chronology will not allow us to speak with confidence about the quality and the rate of social and economic developments.

ORIGINS

The origins of the Bronze Age in northwestern Europe are no longer the puzzle or the source of argument that they once were. Evidence for the later Neolithic and Chalcolithic periods is now extensive, and with the current desire to seek internal explanations rather than external "influences," it can be demonstrated that the transition to the Bronze Age was an imperceptible one, to which quite obviously the indigenous people were unconscious.

Northwestern Europe in the centuries around 2000 B.C. was extensively occupied and exploited. Forest clearances were abundant, and wide areas were prepared and cultivated. Woodland managements were practiced, and hunting and gathering yielded a variety of foods to supplement the established domestic herds and flocks. Settlements were small but community monuments could be impressive in terms of material and manpower requirements. Fine-grained rock was regularly quarried, flaked, and ground; copper was extracted and gold was panned. Collective burial in megalithic tombs and single-grave burial were traditions practiced by various groups, and it would seem that all the ingredients for further development existed. In terms of metallurgy, many sources and technologies were present and known. For increased food supplies, equipment for clearance and cultivation was sufficient. For travel and transport, wheeled wagons, boats, and trackways were available. For major public works, manpower, incentive, and control were at hand. Upon this presumably stable society there was imposed no imported leader, no charismatic innovator, no exotic materials or products, no external incentives to expand; instead, naturally increased demands, efficiency and exploitation of resources yielded in due time a number of technological improvements, product enhancements, and transport expansions, all allied most importantly to that basic foundation of society: assured, reliable, and innovative food subsistence practices which helped bind the community together.

The Bronze Age as such is not marked by dramatic beginnings, but merely by a gradual and inevitable quickening of responses to the opportunities offered by the knowledge and stability of the originating and ancestral groups of the late third millennium. What is certain is that:

> during the Bronze Age a number of important changes took place—changes that lend the period its characteristic appearance and distinguish it from anything that had gone before. Many of these changes were in settlement and material culture. . . . Others were of a more general nature. Perhaps the most obvious of these is the rise of the privileged. In most parts of Europe one finds—in distinction to Neolithic practice—rich graves and poor graves side by side. The rich graves vary in richness, but the richest are remarkable not only for their splendour but also for the amount of potential wealth encapsulated in them and thus lost to the society that produced them. It is hard to think of this process in terms other than those of aggrandisement of the few, the rise of the elite, and the start of social stratification. Once acquired, this habit was never lost: it persists to the present day (Coles and Harding, 1979:535).

The current task of archaeologists is to examine statements such as this in an effort to discover the reasons why such social stratification might have developed, if indeed it did develop along the ways we propose. These problems will be examined later but it is certainly arguable that archaeologists have tended to assume that only one of several factors was responsible for the aggrandizement of a segment of Bronze Age society (Milisauskas 1978). This single factor is claimed to be metallurgy, and it can hardly be any other in archaeological terms for the simple reason that propositions of wealth, pricing of commodities, and ranking of artifacts, always place metal high in the scale—the argument is circular and unquestioned by most. There are, however, other factors as well, and we must distinguish between the reasons for and the manifestations of aggrandizement in Bronze Age societies—they need not be the same. It must not be forgotten that in the search for the explanations of social ordering in the Bronze Age we can ill-afford to neglect other related aspects of Bronze Age existence. For too long these remained as separate studies.

It is a commonplace in archaeological literature that the Bronze Age of Europe is an episode characterized by (a) extensive metalworking industries, many products of which were thrown into lakes and rivers; (b) merchants and smiths who regularly buried their stock in the ground and abandoned it; and (c) a people whose living places and habits are unknown, but whose disposal of the dead seems to have gone on continuously. The overall picture conjured by this is bizarre to say the least. The picture is of course inaccurate, but the historical development of the subject unfairly encouraged such an opinion, with impressive metal products displayed in museums, elaborate typological arguments constructed to demonstrate links between regions, and the grave goods and rituals singled out for particular emphasis. If there is one aspect of current research which redresses the balance, at least in part, it is the effort made by archaeologists to investigate the organization of the land in the second millennium B.C. As a result of this approach, the identification of hundreds of settlements has become possible and the reconstruction begun of Bronze Age landscapes and land use.

LANDSCAPE AND LAND USE

For northwestern Europe, the recognition in 1960 of a Bronze Age farmstead at Elp in Drenthe, Holland, marked the start of a phase of intensive investigation for further settlements (Waterbolk 1964). The site was in fact discovered only through the widening of an excavation of a burial mound, a widening that revealed postholes unrelated to the mound construction. The extraordinary ground plan eventually revealed by excavation revolutionized our knowledge of Bronze Age domestic arrangements and economic practices (Figure 6.3).

Over several centuries, a small farmstead had existed consisting of a long house with ancillary barn and sheds, each set rebuilt from time to time, with a population of perhaps 10–20 persons in permanent occupation. Each long house, 25–36 m in length, provided a dwelling at the west end and a cattle stall at the east (Waterbolk 1975). The domestic debris of pottery, stone, flint, and wood did not include any metal objects, a salutary example to many Bronze Age specialists. Allied to this and subsequent work was a continuing series of environmental programs that included the analysis of pollens in soils buried beneath burial monuments. These studies began to demonstrate the preferences of Bronze Age agriculturalists in the Low Countries for heavy fertile land in the valleys of the south, and the lighter sands of the west, until in the later Bronze Age many upland areas were brought into use, perhaps as a reflection of deteriorating climatic conditions (Groenman-van Waateringe 1977).

The Elp excavations and the long-term interest of prehistorians in biological

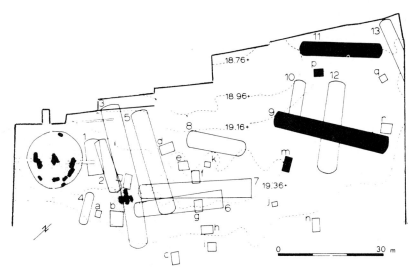

Figure 6.3 Plan of the Bronze Age settlement at Elp, Drenthe, Holland. The burial mound lies at left with its graves and pits. The houses and sheds marked in black represent the first settlement; outlined buildings are subsequent phases of the site. Contours are in meters above sea level. (From Waterbolk 1964.)

archaeology may fairly be said to have inspired the many important programs of research into Bronze Age environments and economies in the Low Countries (e.g., Brongers 1976; van Mensch and Ijzereef 1975); one of the advances is the recognition of part of a Bronze Age landscape, with settlements, burial mounds, and ditched fields at Hoogkarspel in west Friesland (Bakker *et al.* 1977). This evidence became known only through a lengthy period of aerial reconnaissance, field survey, soil studies, and excavations; the full publication of the animal remains should tell us much about Bronze Age stockbreeding practices. Almost any reasonable quality of evidence about Bronze Age food subsistence is urgently required for northern Europe, as our knowledge is extremely scanty, whether it be of agriculture, stockbreeding, hunting, gathering, or fishing; for example, studies of Baltic island economies have demonstrated seasonal exploitation of marine resources (Forstén 1977).

Outside the Low Countries, evidence for settlements and fields in the northern Bronze Age has been elusive. This picture, too, is undergoing revision through the sudden recognition and realization that at least in the later Bronze Age of southern Scandinavia a characteristic house type could be identified, namely and to no one's surprise a post-built structure resembling in many features the common house form of the Iron Age (Becker 1972, 1980); with this, many such houses have now been recovered by excavation (Figure 6.4), and villages of up to 30 houses have been acknowledged if not fully published (Thrane 1980). Considering the relative scarcity of domestic debris associated with many similar houses in the north, their automatic attribution to the Iron Age may need reconsideration. Even so, the problems of studying Bronze Age settlements in northern Europe are only now becoming apparent and there are not many outstanding well-preserved settlements such as Hallunda, near Stockholm, where a permanent hamlet with a workshop for metallurgy and an adjoining cemetery has been excavated (Jaanusson 1971, 1981). On the other hand, cultural material from well over 200 occupation sites in Sweden and Denmark alone is now acknowledged, and continuing research may well begin to yield enough information to allow firmer predictions about the nature of such settlements. The material so far recovered from these sites generally consists of potshards and stone artifacts, but mold fragments and metal objects occur on occasion, and structural features of houses and sheds have also been noted. The elucidation of these settlements remains an outstanding problem for the future.

In the interim, and because of the relative rarity of such sites, Scandinavian archaeologists in particular have devised and developed a set of regional surveys (e.g., Strömberg 1975), heavily reliant on pollen analyses, which have permitted the drawing of general pictures of land use through time in various areas of the north. In an area of Västmanland in Sweden, for example, a series of pollen analyses combined to make an "influence diagram" that shows the sum of human influence on the landscape, clearances, drainage, cultivation, maintenance of pasture, abandonment, and similar generalized activities (Welinder 1975). For the second millennium, a rather low level of activity was recorded, but

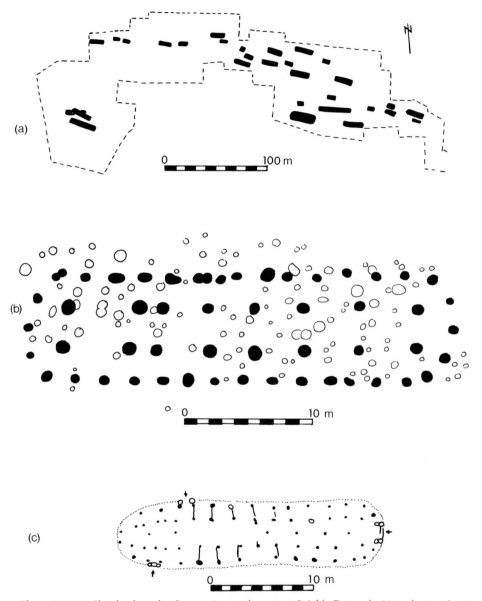

Figure 6.4 (a) Sketch plan of a Bronze Age settlement at Spjald, Denmark. Note the consistent orientation of the houses. The site also had been occupied in the Neolithic, and in the Iron Age. (Based on Becker 1972:Fig. 3.) (b) Plan of a Bronze Age house at Bjerg, Denmark, with major structural postholes marked in black. (From Becker 1972:Fig. 9.) (c) Plan of a Bronze Age house at Emmerhout, Holland, with cattle stalls in the central part of the house marked by narrow foundation trenches. The width of these stalls suggests that they may have held two animals, positioned to face the walls. (From Waterbolk 1975:Fig. 1.)

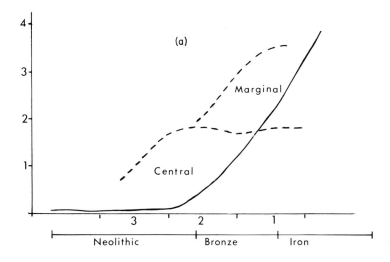

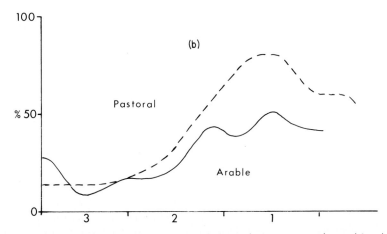

Figure 6.5 (a) Density of population and its growth during the Bronze Age of central Sweden (—) and expansion of agrarian activity in southern Sweden from the central area into marginal lands (---); see Figure 6.30. The degrees of magnitude are approximate; the millennia B.C. are marked along the base line. (Based on Welinder 1975, 1977.) (b) An attempt to compare the magnitude of arable and pastoral ratios in the Bronze Age of central Sweden (---) with those of southern Britain (—). The Swedish information is based on ratios of Cerealia and *Plantago lanceolata* pollen, with the latter percentage doubled. The British information is based on clearance horizons visible in radiocarbon-dated pollen diagrams. (Based on Welinder 1975 and Bradley 1978.)

late in the millennium a considerable expansion took place (Figure 6.5); most of this is ascribed to a sudden emphasis on cereal production, which must have involved wider and more careful clearances, maintained for longer periods, to the benefit of a growing population particularly in the Lake Mälaren plain.

As a result, it is postulated that all of the research area, 1200 km², was exploited from permanent settlements with a variable number of field systems involving ard cultivation (the ard is a type of scratch plow that does not turn a furrow), grassland grazing, and lengthy periods of fallow. The individual settlements appear to have been independent, that is, self-sufficient in almost all activities both economic and social. Much of this picture must be conjectural, of course, due to the continuing absence of stratified settlement sites and generally poor preservation of organic materials. In parts of Denmark, more dramatic problems have been illuminated by studies of pollen and soils. A generalized picture of light forest, arable fields, scrub and grassland pasture in Jutland and Zeeland masks the essential contrasts in soil type and exploitation patterns in the regions. In western Jutland, for example, the lighter and more easily exhausted soils were soon converted from arable to pasture, overgrazed by cattle or sheep, and abandoned, to be sealed in places by the construction of burial mounds. In eastern Jutland, in contrast, heavier soils probably retained fertility, and in parts the heavy forest was not cleared, or was allowed to regenerate.

Intensification of food production such as appears to be documented during the Bronze Age in the North must have been related to the growing needs of the population, and here the existing evidence tends to be too generalized for precision. The factors involved included climate, vegetational development, soil distribution and deterioration, and changes in the land and drainage through isostatic recovery (Figure 6.6). Trends can be distinguished that point to the gradual onset of a more Atlantic climate, the decline of climax forest, and the emergence of new land combined with a reduction of coastlands in the territory under observation. The plotting of these last factors through Bronze Age distributions and dated geographical features would seem to be crucial. It will not have escaped attention that this work does not rely upon the uneven and variable preservation of archaeological sites and materials, and the Swedish work has not escaped criticism for its generalities and lack of particularization (Larsson 1978). Nevertheless it seems to combine a modeling approach with sufficient data to present at the very least a version of population growth, movement, and activity during the Bronze Age. A more elaborate and controversial investigation of southern Sweden, using the same model but introducing many more factors, is noted hereafter. Comparisons with this economic approach, however, are most easily made with studies in Britain.

Settlements and fields of the south British Bronze Age have been known for many years, and many exemplary excavations have been conducted (Figure 6.7). These settlements previously performed a subsidiary role in the thoughts of archaeologists who were more concerned to examine and arrange the museum artifacts of the period, bronzes and pots in bewildering varieties. The transfor-

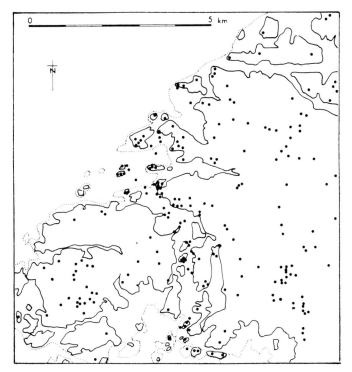

Figure 6.6 Map of burial cairns and stone settings near Göteborg, Sweden, showing the coastal positions of sites at Bronze Age sea level (—), which was 10 m above that of the present coastline (·····). Note the presumed existence of a strait beside which many cairns were placed. Sites off the Bronze Age coastline represent activity after land emergence, but small islands are obscured on this map by the black dots. (From Coles and Harding 1979:Fig. 101; based on Kaelas 1973.)

mation of interest on the part of many archaeologists today, just as in northern Europe, is well illustrated in the pages and bibliographies of recent works, both general and particular investigations (Barrett and Bradley 1980; Bowen and Fowler 1978; Ellison and Harriss 1972; Mercer 1981); the few exceptions are noted later. Pollen and other environmental indicators demonstrate a climate in southern Britain, and in northwestern France, slightly warmer and less wet than that of today, and in marginal upland areas such relatively minor fluctuations would have had a profound impact. The Bronze Age strategies adopted for these circumstances were until recently considered to be completely predictable and wholly unexciting, namely a series of apparently unrelated small self-contained farmsteads with grouped fields around, scattered at random over a landscape of southern England that was thought to be heavily destructive of such ancient settlements through soil erosion and hillwash, and ploughing. Through a combination of several factors this picture has been dramatically changed in both lowland and upland Britain.

The factors primarily responsible for this alteration included a reactionary

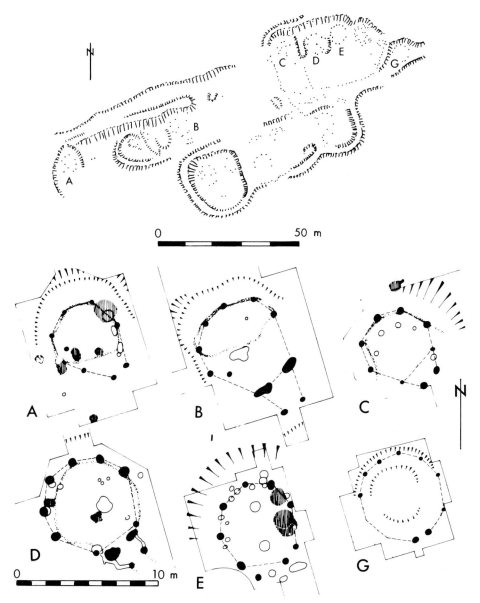

Figure 6.7 Plan of the Bronze Age settlement at Itford Hill, Sussex, England, in a small embanked enclosure, with six of the round houses indicated and planned below. Main postholes are shown in black, and shallower pits are hatched. Note the larger entrance postholes and slots. (Based on Megaw and Simpson 1979:Fig. 6.11, and Musson 1970:268.)

attitude on the part of British scholars, just as in Scandinavia, against the traditional views of the Bronze Age, heavily dependent on museum artifacts and burial monuments in a static landscape. As a result, attention was directed towards very intensive aerial surveys and more restricted field surveys over southern England, which in the space of a very few years yielded information of a quite astonishing extent. Basically, the landscape of parts of lowland southern England could be seen to contain the traces of vast arrangements of boundaries and fields (Figure 6.8), dividing the countryside and incorporating both ridges and valleys in a complex network of land divisions dated in part by sufficient stratigraphical evidence to the later second millennium and early first millennium B.C. (Bowen 1975). This demonstrated beyond question that woodland clearances had been extensive and maintained, and pollen analyses show that previously untouched forests were now being felled. The organization of the land into field systems also indicates that ard cultivation had continued with sufficient duration to create the lynchet systems surviving today; such lynchets, banks of earth occasionally several meters in height, formed against and over an original uncut turf boundary at the lower edges of the fields through gradual soil drift carried by cultivation and erosion. The rectangular fields were often arranged to hang from linear boundaries that could be natural or artificial features, and the existence of these therefore presupposes land arrangements devised and agreed by populations rather than by individual farmers. A system at Chaldon Herring in Dorset, for example, contained over 300 ha of fields and banks and small settlements. Another, at Winterbourne Steepleton, encompassed 200 ha of land with settlements of 4–5 huts linked to banked enclosures by sunken drove-roads. These systems remain unique in the European Bronze Age by their apparent completeness; arable fields, hoe plots, stock corrals, roadways, and farmsteads all combine to present an unduplicated opportunity to interpret Bronze Age communities in action. Surprisingly, no one has yet begun to do more than generalize about these sites, and environmental sciences have only begun to be employed to particularize the information. Nonetheless, continuing interest and activity on the part of archaeologists working in this area can hardly do other than create new insights into the functioning of Bronze Age societies.

The same can now be confidently said for another region of southern Britain, and also for more northerly parts of Britain where dating evidence is slight and conditions not so suitable for the recognition of ancient land use features (Barker 1981; Riley 1980). In southwestern England the long stone banks, called reaves, that systematically divide up the landscape of south Dartmoor have become the focus of intensive archaeological fieldwork and excavation. Previously, only the numerous hut circles, irregular plots, and small fields, all marked by stone heaps and alignments, were considered to mark prehistoric occupation in the Bronze Age (Figure 6.9). Because deteriorating climatic conditions forced the abandonment of the uplands, these structures have survived virtually untouched, although the severe environmental processes of decay have destroyed all organic matter and much inorganic debris as well. Even so, the existence of settlements of 20–30 small round houses, with associated fields, placed on the slopes of Dartmoor, implied a sizable population working land that must have required regeneration by manuring or an extensive fallow system in order to remain appropriate for settlement. The concept of an infield–outfield management seems appropriate, with some areas worked regularly by ard or spade, larger areas within a fallow sequence, and pastureland beyond the controlled land.

Some settlements on Dartmoor and Bodmin Moor consisted of more than 20 hut circles, with strip fields near at hand, hoe plots, and cattle enclosures; conditions for the preservation of anything but stone and some pottery generally

Figure 6.8 Field boundaries and alignments in central Dorset, England. The boundary banks are arranged on a northwest to southeast axis, crossing both ridge and valley, and demonstrate purposeful division of the landscape in the Bronze Age. (From Bowen 1975.)

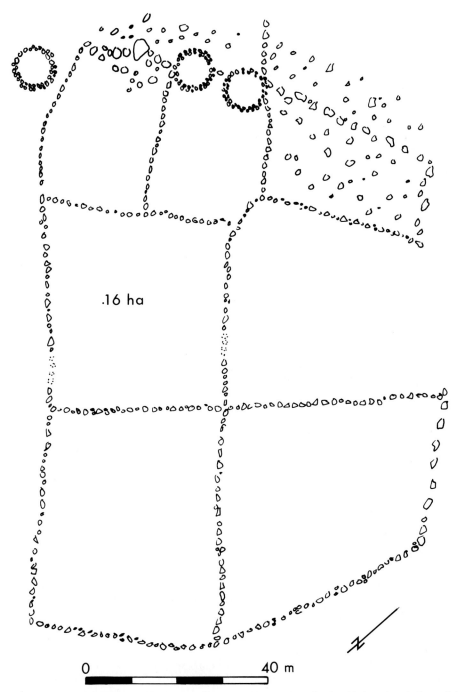

0   40 m

.16 ha

Figure 6.9   Plan of farming settlement at Blissmoor, Dartmoor, England, with three hut circles and six fields marked by stone banks and alignments. (Based on Fox 1954:20.)

restricts further detail, but excavations on Shaugh Moor, Dartmoor, promise much in the particularizing detail we now require (Smith *et al.* 1981). Here, a set of enclosures, houses, and a field system have been examined with the battery of scientific disciplines we now expect of all major projects. The identification of wooden post-built houses as well as stone-built houses within one enclosure immediately casts uncertainty upon all previous population estimates.

Although many of these settlements were themselves impressive as showing much of the organization of Bronze Age farmsteads, they too, as in lowland England, were apparently concerned with an inward-looking population, self-sufficient, with fields laboriously carved from a hitherto untouched woodland-covered land. Nothing could be inferred about choice, organization, and cooperation of Bronze Age society as a whole, and here is where the current advances in knowledge about land divisions are so important. On south Dartmoor the discovery that the reaves were extensive, preserved, and of prehistoric date has permitted archaeologists to view for the first time in any upland situation a functioning Bronze Age landscape (Fleming 1978, 1979).

The reaves exist as sets of parallel stone banks as well as single and longer reaves, and together they form a coherent pattern in the landscape (Figure 6.10). The long reaves occupy and demarcate valley systems which may therefore be regarded as some form of territories, often 150–200 ha in extent. Each territory also possessed access to the higher land with a boundary reave following a contour around the upper moor; one such reave is 10 km long. Hence a community would have had three environmental zones under its visible control: the upper moor, a lower valley catchment, and a large area divided by parallel reaves. Common grazing on the upper moor, with potential mixing of stock between several communities, would involve some form of seasonal separation facility. Below, and on the edge of the moor, lay the central part of the settlement, with the parallel reave systems forming fields at least in part under cereal cultivation; lynchets, querns, and pollen all indicate this use. Below this lay lower moor and valleys, perhaps retained for particular grazing rights but also containing walled enclosures with huts and houses. The parallel reave areas contain fewer and more isolated enclosures and huts. Each system, containing this variety of land, was divided from the next by a watershed reave that closely followed the natural boundary and that was the first to be laid out by the settlers.

This evidence poses many questions and answers some. It is clear that in the second millennium, the whole area of south Dartmoor was surveyed, inspected, perhaps haggled over, until divisions were agreed or selected on some obscure basis. Land boundaries were established, with watershed reaves; common grazing land was acknowledged on the uplands, and separated from the field systems by contour reaves with gates and enclosures for the movement and gathering of stock. Near the settlements was more restricted and controlled pastureland. Yet before we accept that the area was strictly divided, tightly controlled, and densely populated, other factors and evidence must be consid-

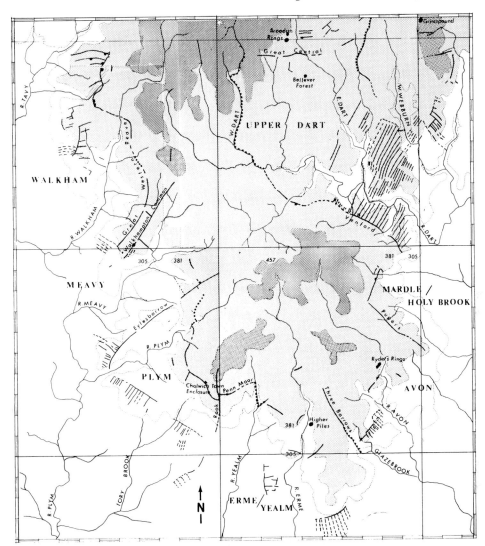

Figure 6.10 Map of south Dartmoor, England, with reave boundaries of territories (territories marked in capitals), contour reaves and parallel reaves (shown schematically). Contours are marked at approximately 300, 400, and 450 m. Squares have sides of 10 km. (From Fleming 1978:Fig. 2.)

ered. Unfinished reaves, reaves ending in marshland or continued as streams, and walled enclosed settlements, all pose questions of precise function, degree of protection, demarcation of ownership or tenure, herdsmanship, stock control and guardianship, contact and transportation, defense and access, and central control. The evidence is accumulating for some of these questions but not all.

A central or main settlement may be discernible for some of the 6–10 territories, with a particularly massive enclosure and numerous huts and houses placed where the "owned" valley could be observed. Were these groups there-fore mutually distrustful, or collectively united, and for what reasons might either condition have changed? Were areas individually or collectively owned? On what basis might an individual have assumed, and retained, possession? The careful stratigraphical observations being made along the reaves and their enclosures suggest a period of construction and use of several centuries, with sufficient confidence in social, economic, and perhaps political structures to devote time and power for their production and maintenance. That such situa-tions were not peculiar to Dartmoor, or to lowland England (Figure 6.11) is now becoming apparent through other work of survey and excavation in other parts of Britain (Burgess and Miket 1976; Pryor 1980). Besides this quality of evidence, the continuing yield of simple house plans, settlements even, seems of less value than it might have been even a decade ago. Yet we should not forget that only a decade or so ago, studies of the Bronze Age were still very firmly based on its original concept, on the basis of its metal products; because of their quantity

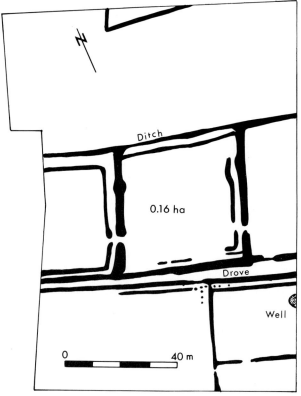

Figure 6.11   Plan of ditched fields from the Bronze Age settlement at Fengate, England. The ditches are shown in black, with a ditched drove and staggered entries into the fields. (Based on Pryor 1980; and Bowen and Fowler 1978.)

and quality they have continued to interest many prehistorians. This interest is not always well directed, as we shall see, but there can be no dispute that the bronze and gold artifacts of northwestern Europe in particular create many opportunities for modern studies and interpretations. Among these, contemporary interests appear to lie with technology rather than with typology, with circulation time rather than with precise function, and with redistribution and social roles rather than with the simple economics of trade.

METALLURGY

The metal industries of northwestern Europe had the advantage in many areas of seemingly abundant supplies of raw materials: copper, tin, lead and gold. These supplies were available to many communities of the second millennium in Britain and Ireland, and in Brittany, but few if any sources were readily at hand to the inhabitants of the Low Countries or Scandinavia. It is one of the phenomena of the European Bronze Age that such abundant quantities of metal were somehow made available to the north, and that the north European industries achieved such high standards of production with their imported supplies of copper, tin, and gold. From early in the second millennium, a series of metalworking industries was established throughout the northwest European area (Ryan 1980). Archaeologists can identify the products of many of these workshops through careful typological identification of specific features, and sometimes through spectrographic analyses of the trace elements in the original copper ores.

Spectrographic analysis should be able to determine if a metal is a deliberate alloy, of copper and tin for example, and should also be capable of identifying and measuring the metal impurities. In theory, the ore body itself should yield a pattern or patterns of impurities that relate to the products made from that particular source. In practice, it does not, except in circumstances where archaeological evidence is itself already very strongly in support of the link; ores from the Bronze Age mines of Austria, for example, can clearly be related to copper smelting areas near at hand, and to copper products also within a limited area. For northwestern Europe, however, there are few unambiguous facts concerning the relationship between ore bodies and metal products, although a very ambitious program of analyses has been underway for many years (Junghans *et al.* 1968). Still to be tested are the variations in the composition of the ore bodies themselves, variations introduced by the different production processes, and even variations yielded by different analytical techniques. The achievements are small; among them are the identification of a Scottish–Irish type of metal with high arsenic content used for the production of many axes in the Early Bronze Age. For gold, the identification of Irish Wicklow sources with patently Irish gold ornaments is unsurprising to say the least (Hartmann 1970). Spectrographic analysis of the metal products of the European Bronze Age is perhaps the most monumental disaster of all of the contemporary studies, because it promised and claimed to hold the answers to problems of long-standing questions about sources of material, methods of work, and identification of distribution networks. It has provided a few answers in restricted areas of inquiry, and created mass confusion in others.

Metallurgy was the growth industry of the second millennium. Besides its achievements, other Bronze Age industries appear to have remained static or even declined. For northwestern Europe, the manufacture of pottery in the Bronze Age seems to represent in most cases a response only to immediate and local needs, with characteristic styles, of course, but with little sign of real craftsmanship or artistry in either technique or decoration. Stoneworking and flint technology remained important for heavy equipment and for cutting implements, and in certain areas the manufacture of fine-grained stone artifacts was a laborious task and the products suitably impressive. Most archaeologists would not, however, argue that these and other industries were as important to Bronze Age society as the acquisition and working of metal.

Nevertheless, the recognition of many Bronze Age settlements in northwestern Europe over the past two decades has pointed to a contrary view, that for a majority of Bronze Age people the primary materials in regular use were those required for the provision of shelter, clothing, and food, and metals hardly figure in this range of equipment. The scarcity of metal artifacts on many small settlements also suggests that metal was restricted in its distribution and perhaps had a role outside the ordinary, at least in part. To this we will return after a brief excursion into progress, such as it is, on studies of this material.

Advances in the study of Bronze Age artifacts have not been abundant if we exclude the many efforts to devise and refine yet more subjective typologies. Nonetheless, a few of the latter make useful contributions to the literature, and a very few of the more objective studies are outstanding. The Bronze Age is characterized in many archaeological minds by thoughts of hoards, and indeed hordes, of bronzes cramming museum cases and drawers, periodically extracted and lovingly drawn by specialists who thereafter produce in interminable length and fusty detail a new classification destined almost at once for oblivion by all save their unfortunate students or followers. The continuing mammoth series of corpus publications of bronze types under the editorship of H. Müller-Karpe is the prime example of an effort to catalog all the prehistoric bronzes of Europe; with dozens of volumes published and many more in preparation, this series will, by the twenty-first century, open the floodgates to a new generation and breed of typologists able to computerize and print typologies by the minute until the point is reached when typologies outnumber artifacts. Then peace will descend. The point has only rarely been acknowledged that what we need for the continuing fruitful study of Bronze Age artifacts is not subjective assessments but objective documentation of the evidence. It is not at all realized how inadequate are the records of discoveries, the illustrations and measured details of individual objects, the reliance on uncertain associations and contexts of the artifacts. Nonetheless, there are very promising signs that studies of Bronze Age products are entering a new phase, and a few corpus-type of publications have already appeared, several of outstanding merit (Aner and Kersten 1978; Gaucher 1981; Oldeberg 1974; Taylor 1980).

In addition to the continuing work on the collection of data concerning bronze artifact-types, particular attention has been paid to associations of objects in hoards (Kristiansen 1974; Burgess and Coombs 1979; Briard 1965). For certain periods of the Bronze Age, metalwork represents only one of the major sources of information, and care must be exercized not to permit it to be used alone as an indicator of anything more than industrial organization. Even so, advances have been made along these lines, none more so than in the recent studies of metalwork of the later second millennium in southern Britain (Rowlands 1976). Here, typological assessments permitted the identification of several centers and subcenters of industry, and plots of distributions could determine the area of general circulation of each type of product. The very restricted ranges, and the number of varieties and variants, suggested that metalworking must have been carried out at a very localized level, and by smiths resident within these localities working presumably as part-time metalworkers. Suggestions of long-distance merchants, or itinerant smiths, seem unlikely in the face of this evidence, although the nature of the work must also mean the existence of fixed workshops where the precision required for economical productions could be assured. Furthermore, the existence of hoards of products, some in a semifinished state, suggests that the workshops were in operation for only restricted periods, perhaps seasonally, when sufficient supplies could be most economically made. Where such hoards were only rarely encountered, and where the evidence consisted of single and worn finds of bronzes, the explanation is different, a pattern of work whereby tools were produced as a single event, on demand, by a part-time resident smith or one who could be summoned from a catchment area only slightly larger than the local environment. However, until archaeologists begin seriously to question the reasons behind the deposition of such hoards, we shall probably not advance in our real understanding of Bronze Age economic and social organization; conspicuous consumption, for example, is only one of the possible explanations which have never been fully explored. It will not have escaped attention that the interpretation of metalworking industries along these lines is dependent upon the two main thrusts of contemporary studies, the compilation of accurate documentation of the evidence, and the construction of elaborate typologies which permit the distinction of very small but nonetheless significant variations in products. The approaches are complementary.

Of the industries themselves, there seems little need to provide descriptions; the enormous literature of the Bronze Age is crammed with illustrations and commentary on bronze products. What will be clear is that from early in the second millennium B.C. a vigorous and active industry, or set of industries, developed in many parts of northwestern Europe. The mechanisms involved

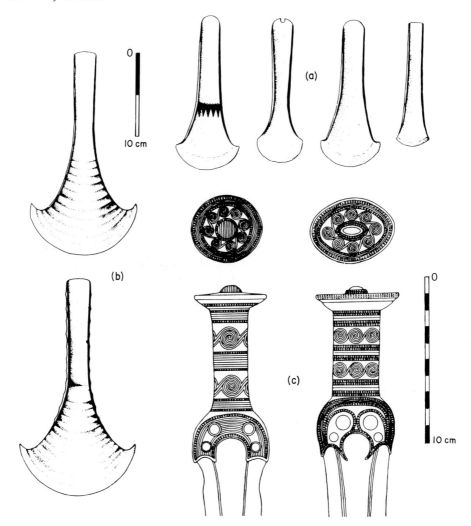

Figure 6.12 North European metalwork of the Bronze Age. Metal axes from two hoards at (a) Fjälkinge and (b) Lilla Bedinge, Sweden. These axes represent the earliest products of the Bronze Age in the north. (c) The metal hilts of swords from Bustrup and Rugbjerg, Denmark, represent a developed stage of the Bronze Age in the north. (a–b from Hachmann 1957:Tafel 22; c from Ottenjann, 1969:Tafel 5.)

were not inconsiderable. Supplies of copper and tin, as well as gold, had to be discovered and exploited, and the ways by which a knowledge of metallurgy was transmitted, exchanged, or withheld, are totally beyond our comprehension at this time. It is also clear that this knowledge was quite rapidly diffused, so that within a period of two centuries there came into existence a large number of workshops, seasonally or sporadically active, from which poured an ever-increasing quantity of metal products. These products include flat, flanged, and socketed axes; palstaves and battle-axes; daggers, dirk, rapiers, and swords; javelinheads and spearheads; a variety of tools; ornaments in profusion, necklets, armlets, bracelets, anklets, brooches and belt–discs, pins, rings, and studs; and toiletry articles including razors and tweezers. In addition to this, a panoply of golden ornaments was produced, and a wide range of beaten sheet bronze vessels and shields. The craftsmanship involved shows every sign of being experienced and ambitious, and the quality of metalwork is unsurpassed by any known metalworking tradition in the prehistoric Old or New Worlds; this last point is not one that is often recognized. When tied to an area, northern Europe, where no indigenous supplies of raw materials were available or worked, the products must represent a considerable undertaking and commitment on the part of the society to ensure the transmission of supplies into the northern workshops (Figure 6.12). The distribution of metalwork demonstrates the existence of routes along which raw metal as well as finished products were carried; central European sources as well as west European sources seem to be represented, and the precise mechanisms of supply and demand remain a subject for continuing debate (Thrane 1975). In general terms of European prehistory, the establishment of metallurgy in northern Europe was the first time that a major European industry was practiced in an area devoid of the natural substance used in that industry; this must mark an important shift or alteration in the concepts of exchange and transportation.

TRANSPORT

The problems of Bronze Age travel and transport have never been tackled by consistent and exhaustive research. Many natural ridgeways in northwestern Europe have been identified, through rather gross distributions, as providing the obvious routes for movement, avoiding the clogged valley bottoms and marshlands. Sand ridges, and chalk and limestone outcrops, often contain the abundant traces of prehistoric activity along their courses; such traces generally consist of burial monuments as well as stray finds of artifacts, and these do not exactly provide confidence in their identification as objects related to transport and travel. The whole subject of Bronze Age movements is one that persuades many to indulge in conjectures unencumbered by the need to adhere to observable evidence, for the simple reason that there is hardly any observable evidence that clearly relates to the subject. Distributions of artifacts may help suggest contacts and communication, and lead to consideration of natural land routes as well as of artificial roads and paths, and if sea travel is envisaged then landing places as well as boats must be involved. There are traces of all of these from the area and period in question.

Perhaps the greatest problem in this inquiry is the variety of ways by which we think material equipment of the Bronze Age could have come to be deposited, discarded, or lost (Figure 6.13). A distribution map of artifact find-spots

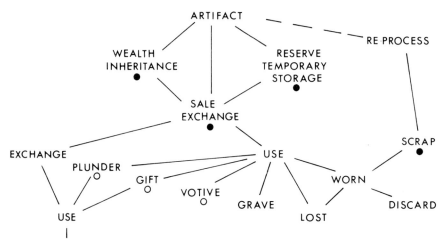

Figure 6.13 Flow diagram of Bronze Age metal artifacts, to demonstrate the variety of hoards (●) and uses assumed by archaeologists. The white dots mark other cases where hoard association of artifacts may occur. Archaeological distinctions between some of these hoards, and between some artifact uses, are not likely to be clear-cut, and distribution maps tend to mask the differences.

Figure 6.14 (a) Part of a Bronze Age wooden trackway made of coppiced hazel woven into hurdles and laid end to end on a marshy surface, Somerset, England. The contemporary settlement lies on the "island" in the background. (b) Variety of Bronze Age planks, boards, and stakes, the debris from a dismantled structure and used here as packing during the building of a wooden road through boggy ground, Somerset, England. (Photographs by J. M. Coles, Somerset Levels Project.)

may well include the incomplete evidence of a number of activities totally unrelated to one another, and therefore any pattern emerging from the map may be misleading. The tendency on the part of Bronze Age specialists to place large spots on small maps consistently masks or distorts the reality of the situation and discourages thought on the movement of materials and humans (Stjernquist 1967; Coles 1982).

Granted these problems, we can still perhaps point to distributions of artifacts of particular types or even specific composition and attempt to deduce the natural or artificial routes employed by their carriers and users. Ridgeways in Britain and Scandinavia have been identified and proposed as the great natural routes for travel, requiring no maintenance, providing wide views for direction

and protection, and allowing free passage of both men and goods. The Icknield Way in southern England is one of the more likely natural routes because of its position and the distribution of artifacts along and beside it. The old drove roads of Denmark are other candidates for prehistoric use again through the distribution of monuments and also because on occasion, where the ridges were truncated by streams and valleys, the rutted way descends to single crossings where artificial pavings of stone or wood were laid. Preserved in places by peat formation, some of these crossings are certainly prehistoric and may extend back into the Bronze Age. More certain are wooden roadways, providing safe passage across marshland, which can be dated to the second millennium B.C. by radiocarbon assay (Figure 6.14). Many of these exist in northwestern Germany, the Low Countries, Ireland, and southern England, and they provide almost all the evidence for woodworking and woodland control in the Bronze Age (Coles and Orme 1980; Hansen and Nielson 1977; Hayen 1957).

The other major source of transport for Bronze Age northwestern Europe was the boat, and fortunately there are a number of discoveries that have greatly increased our knowledge of sea and coastal traffic (Johnstone 1980). The ubiquitous logboat or dugout as pond, lake, stream, and river vehicle need not concern us because more ambitious craft are now known. The planked boats from the muds of North Ferriby, England, have been the subject of numerous treatises and reconstructions (Figure 6.15), and a flat-bottomed barge or punt

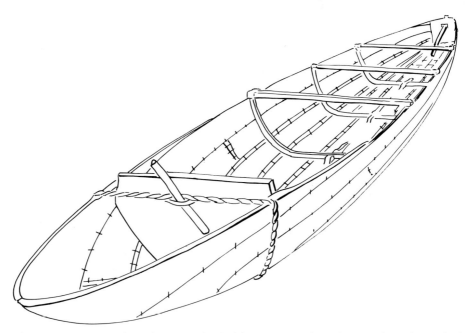

Figure 6.15 Provisional reconstruction of one of the Bronze Age boats from North Ferriby, England. (From Wright 1976.)

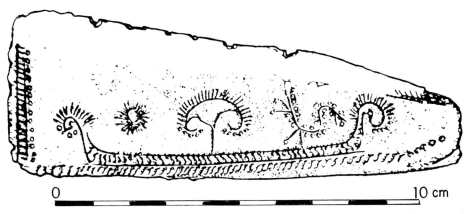

Figure 6.16 Engraving of a Bronze Age boat on a razor from Hadersleben. Such artifacts provide useful chronological indicators for the rock carvings of southern Scandinavia. (From *Bremer Archäologische Blätter*, Vol. 3, 1962, Fig. 26.)

from Brigg, near Ferriby, also demonstrates the very considerable craftsmanship available to boatbuilders of the Bronze Age (McGrail 1981). More intriguing are the discoveries of apparent cargoes of Bronze Age metal products from foundered and lost boats off the coast of England, at Dover and at Salcombe, Devon (Muckelroy 1981). These products, abundant on the seabed at Dover, may represent continental metals en route to Britain; hardly any comparable objects, axes and blades of particular types, have ever been found on land in Britain. No traces of the craft carrying these have been found, but the concept of such voyages poses highly interesting problems for Bronze Age merchandise. The recognition of a Bronze Age landing stage or wharf in the Thames River, at Runnymede, is just what we should expect to find (Needham and Langley 1980).

For northern Europe in particular, an intimate knowledge and understanding of boats would have been essential in the Bronze Age, as today (Figure 6.16). The area is, after all, a maritime-based region, and in the Bronze Age it is clear that land uplift through isostatic recovery was not as extensive as that of today, hence many more inlets, fjords, and straits existed for Bronze Age communities to utilize and negotiate (Figure 6.6) (Kaelas 1973). In southern Scandinavia, further but even more problematic evidence for water transport exists in profusion, pecked and carved in the living rocks from western Norway to eastern Sweden and from Denmark northwards to Rogaland, Østfold, and Uppland.

ROCK CARVINGS

The rock art of southern Scandinavia has been known and studied for many decades. From a period when simple descriptions seemed sufficient, there developed a widely subscribed school of thought that extracted particular elements from the art and provided interpretations based upon these alone. However, there has been a reaction against such subjectivity, and a return to documentation and landscape studies. Several of these deserve comment as representing real advances not only in the study of Bronze Age art, but also in the effort to incorporate such studies in consideration of Bronze Age societies (Nordbladh 1978).

The rock art consists of areas and panels of smooth, often stream-worn, rock near if not overlooking Bronze Age coastlands, entries to bays and fjords, and watershed boundaries; with pecked, rubbed, and ground lines and dots forming an extremely rich and varied representation of Bronze Age activities. Among the tens of thousands of artifacts depicted by these engravings are many thousands of boat-like designs (Figure 6.17). These vary in style and presentation as well as in size, from over 4 m long to merely a few centimeters, and there has been much speculation about the actual form or forms of craft that they represent. Because many other elements in the art appear to depict actual objects, such as animals, men with spears or bows, oxen with ard and plowman (Figure 6.18), it is at least a possibility that the boat designs represent actual craft. Many of these carry sets of short lines, or strokes, above the gunwale, and occasionally some of these are continued into human figures; the remainder stay as puzzles and no interpretation has been advanced to account for these yet.

The nature of the boats themselves, however, has been the subject of much conjecture, experimental reconstructions, and continuing arguments. The interpretation of some of the rock carvings as skin-covered boats is widely known and accepted, but there are other viewpoints, and plank-built boats still remain a possibility. The only way by which the matter might be resolved is through the discovery of an actual Bronze Age boat in Scandinavia, an event likely to occur given the intense interest in other and later craft from burial mounds and the Roskilde fjord. The other point worth emphasizing is that for all of northwestern Europe, maritime traffic is not a possibility but a certainty, and it cannot be long before we gain insights into the capacities of Bronze Age craft.

The remainder of the rock art of northern Europe also is under active investigation. Even in Britain, where the carvings tend to be severely restricted in content, some documentation is underway (Morris 1981), but this in no sense can match the quantity and variety of the southern Scandinavian art sites. In northern Scandinavia, a hunter–gatherer art province has for long been known, with representations of wild animals, humans, and geometric designs either carved or painted on rock surfaces. The recent discovery of such sites in southern Sweden, and the recognition of southern designs in the north, show that former ideas about mutual exclusiveness are incorrect. Nonetheless, the distribution of southern motifs coincides reasonably well with the defining features of the Bronze Age, agricultural settlements, burial monuments of characteristic content, and metallurgical products, and therefore the south Scandinavian art offers more direct help in understanding events of the Bronze Age in the area.

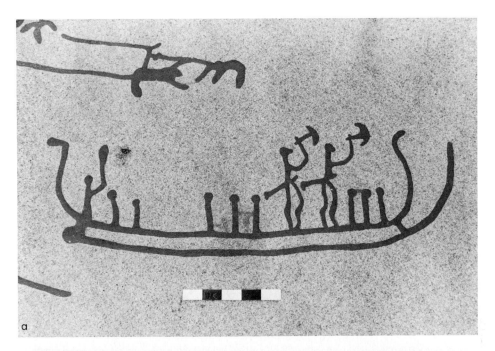

Figure 6.17 (a) Rock carving (painted red) of a Bronze Age boat from Vitlycke, Sweden. (b) Rock carving (painted white) of animals, humans, and boats from Aspeberget, Sweden. (Photographs by J. M. Coles.)

Figure 6.18 (a) Rock carving (unpainted) of oxen drawing an ard, with plowman, from Haga, Sweden. (b) Rock carving (chalked white) of wheeled vehicle and large boat near Vrångstad, Sweden. Note the water run on the rock surface, a characteristic feature. (Photographs by J. M. Coles.)

Current studies of Norwegian and Swedish rock carvings have at last begun to make progress in the documentation of sites, and several important catalogs have recently appeared (Fredsjö 1981; Kjellen 1976). Through these, and through the growing interest of many archaeologists, it can be suspected if not actually documented that the number of decorated sites in the Scandinavian Bronze Age is to be measured in tens of thousands. A very considerable proportion of these sites consist of representations of the objects noted above, although many more are of simple cupmarks only. It is most unlikely that we shall ever fully comprehend the significance of these sites to Bronze Age communities, but locational analyses not as yet published should at the very least open new suggestions and possibilities in terms of territorial indicators or social identifications, while not neglecting the very real expression of Bronze Age elements and events in the societies of the later second millennium and early first millennium. What has to be avoided in this work is the tendency to extract individual objects, such as "sun discs" or "battle-axe men," and to treat them as expressions of particular forms of worship or cult practice. Such tendencies have not always been resisted in the past, and one is tempted to describe these as opinions unencumbered by plausibility, except that to do so also seems subjective. Far better to treat the art sites as sites within a Bronze Age landscape, because to do so opens up possibilities for interpretation that are not otherwise available.

Several other lines of approach have recently become possible. The richly decorated slabs forming a great burial chamber in the largest cairn of all Scandinavia, at Kivik in Scania, have long been known (Figure 6.19), but recent excavations of a much smaller, damaged and outwardly unimpressive mound at Sagaholm, Småland, revealed an internal curb of sandstone slabs carefully carved to fit side by side and stand at a uniform height; one-third of the remaining 45 slabs were decorated by carvings of horses, as well as a few boats and humans (Wihlborg 1977–1978). The discovery of internal curbs of carefully fitted slabs is not unusual in burial mounds of the Early Bronze Age, as is Sagaholm.

0   1 m

Figure 6.19 Decorated slabs from the burial chamber in the Kivik cairn, one of the largest in Sweden. This is one of the few sites where elaborate rock carvings have been found as an integral part of a burial monument. (From Burenhult 1973.)

But it must be a possibility that, among the numberless monuments excavated in the past, some may have had decorated slabs unrecognized by both amateur and professional archaeologists. Equally important is the documentation at Sagaholm of art designs and associations of exact contemporaneity, a fundamental fact not capable of certainty from the carvings on living rock which will continue to provide material for interpretation with little hope of absolute proof. Nonetheless, the sheer quantity of this evidence suggests that it had an important role in Bronze Age society; its connection with burial monuments need not have been more direct than with settlements or territories, and the art remains a neglected field of study by a majority of archaeologists.

BURIAL MONUMENTS

More popular to many is the single most evident and visible monument of the Bronze Age in northwestern Europe, the burial mound (Glob 1974; Ashbee

Figure 6.20 (a) Aerial view of a group of barrows at Winterbourne Stoke, England. Among the cemetery are several large bell barrows (upper left), and small disc barrows (right) as well as the more common bowl barrows. (Photograph by John White, West Air Photography.) (b) Aerial view of ploughed out barrows near Winterbourne Stoke, England. (Photograph by J. K. S. St Joseph, Cambridge University Collection, Crown copyright reserved.)

1960). Although we are dealing with an episode of prehistory extending for more than one thousand years, the probable number of round barrows and cairns of earth and stone must have been of the order of several hundred thousand. A small proportion still remain in the landscape as upstanding monuments (Figure 6.20a); many more exist as fragments, plowed out; even more may be traced from aerial surveys as soil or crop discolorations (Figure 6.20b); and a majority are totally destroyed. The records of such monuments must serve the requirements of archaeology in its attempts to interpret the place of these mounds in Bronze Age society. Several approaches have been adopted in recent years.

Most of the round barrows and cairns of northwestern Europe belong essentially to the earlier part of the Bronze Age. The single-grave tradition, of individual inhumation or cremation beneath a small mound, had its origin in third millennium B.C. practices, but it became dominant and was apparently available to a larger part of the population in the second millennium B.C. Often the earthen mound, such as occurs in most areas of northwestern Europe, was built in a complex manner, with central turf stack or cairn of stones, a ring or arc of slabs, and external curb stones. The body might be in a shallow trench, or wooden coffin, or stone cist, and other mortuary structures concerned with the

b

actual funeral activity or the deceased's requirements were also provided (Figure 6.21). The internal arrangements of stone-built cairns, the common burial monument in upland Britain and parts of Scandinavia, are less well known due to inadequate excavation techniques. The earthen mounds themselves often contain evidence of formidable social undertakings. For example, one of the larger barrows of Denmark, at Lusehøj, was built of 3200 m^3 of turf, cut from 7 ha of fertile agricultural land.

The grave furnishings themselves were of course the original incentive for the excavations of long ago, an incentive not wholly abandoned today it must be admitted. Among the equipment placed with the dead were objects of valuable material and high technology, including gold, silver, faience, bronze, and amber. The ornaments and weapons as well as pottery and other equipment were placed in varying quantities in the graves. Archaeologists have occasionally had the opportunity to examine materials and artifacts not otherwise known from any other source. The textiles from the tree-trunk coffins of Jutland are an interesting example (original study: Broholm and Hald 1935). Although most of these were discovered long ago, the conservation procedures available in Denmark even then were often advanced enough to save the textiles for future research (Figure 6.22).

The dead, both male and female, were buried with funeral garments, some of which had certainly also been in use during the lifetime of the individuals. Males wore a kilt-like garment, a cloak, a cap, and foot-wrappings. Females wore either a short corded skirt or a long dress and a jacket, with hair net or hair band (Figure 6.23), socks and leather shoes. Apart from very detailed examination of the weaving techniques of these garments, few other studies have been made, but experimental work and investigation of the worn condition and repairs on the originals have prompted some new suggestions (Eskildsen and Lomborg 1976, 1977). Among these is the untested view that the two different female costumes might represent unmarried and married status, and that certain male garments might have been made from the long dresses worn by the unmarried female, before whatever form of "wedding" took place. It is unlikely that we will be able to pursue these interesting thoughts without further discoveries of individuals preserved within tree-trunk coffins.

Such studies as these, including the continuing investigations of carefully chosen barrows known or suspected to contain particular structures, represent a normal and legitimate archaeological activity that attempts to answer certain questions. Among these, the investigation of cenotaph barrows lacking burials, of internal mortuary structures, and of graves furnished with very elaborate

Figure 6.21 (a) Section through the central chamber of the tomb, with stone cairn enclosing the burial and sealed by earthen mound. The tomb contained a wealth of grave-goods of the earlier Bronze Age. (b) Plan of a massive burial mound of the Bronze Age at Kernonen, Brittany, with excavation trenches leading through the barrow to the central tomb. Much of the barrow remains undisturbed although its original edge has been obscured by wind and other weathering. (From L'Anthropologie, Vol. 74, 1970, p. 8.)

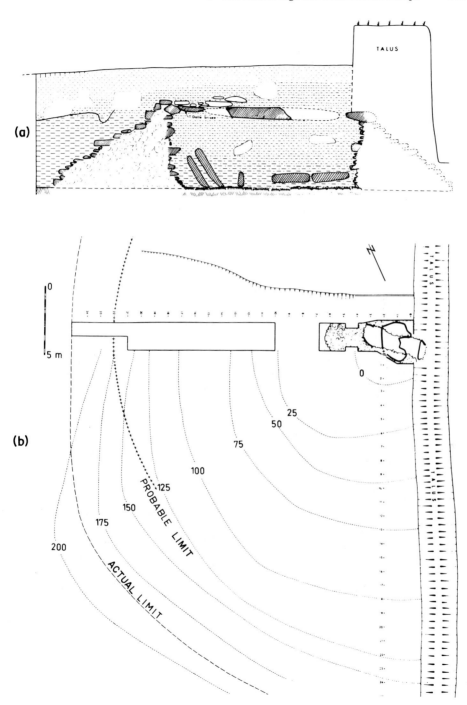

(a)

(b)

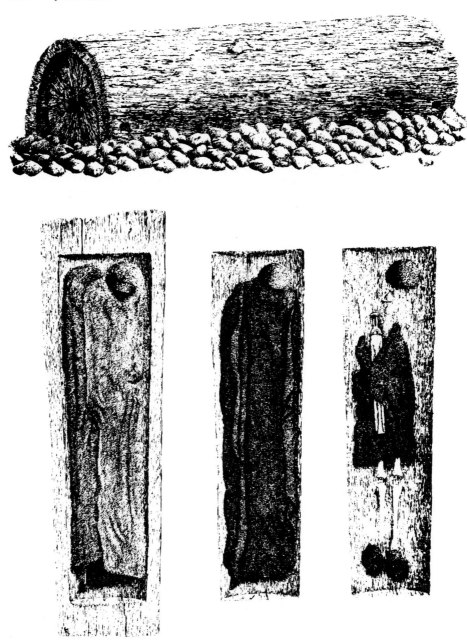

Figure 6.22   The tree-trunk coffin from Muldbjerg, Denmark, with its successive revelations, from hide covering down to the woven clothing around the disintegrated body of a male. (Reprinted by permission of Faber and Faber Ltd. from *The Mound People,* by P. V. Glob.)

Figure 6.23 The head of the young woman buried in a tree-trunk coffin at Skrydstrup, Denmark. Her ash-blonde hair, piled high on the head, rested on a thick pad of hair, and was held in place by a horsehair net. Gold earrings were coiled around the ears and held firm by strands of hair drawn through the loops. The woman was about 18 years in age; she wore a short-sleeved tunic with embroidered border, and a long skirt with belt. The burial had taken place in the summer, as shown by the presence of flowers and grasses in the coffin. (Reprinted by permission of Faber and Faber Ltd. from *The Mound People*, by P. V. Glob.)

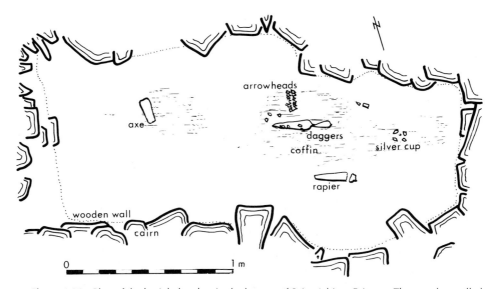

Figure 6.24 Plan of the burial chamber in the barrow of Saint-Adrien, Brittany. The wooden walled enclosure had decayed away, as had the wooden coffin and human remains. The body had been furnished with a wealth of goods, including 45 flint arrowheads. The contrast with the preserved remains of Figure 6.23 is remarkable. (Based on Giot *et al.* 1979.)

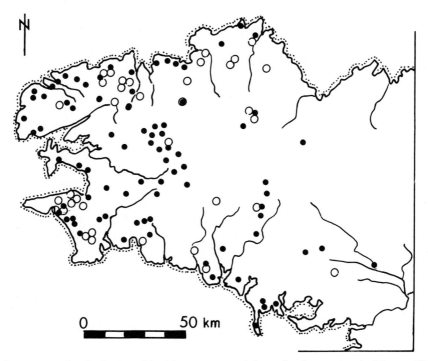

Figure 6.25 The distribution of burial monuments of the earlier Bronze Age in Brittany. Flint arrowheads and bronze weapons (○); graves with funerary pottery (●). (Based on Giot *et al.* 1979.)

306

material goods (Figure 6.24), has provided very striking sets of information from the Bronze Age of Brittany (Briard 1975). The problems of the earlier Bronze Age in Brittany are very considerable, and they include a record of execrable antiquarian digging, atrocious conditions of preservation, and an overly strong tradition of artifactual archaeology. Yet here, as in southern Britain as well, where only conditions of preservation are improved, the records have now been assembled which allow further thoughts to be developed about the implications of the evidence (Figure 6.25). Contemporary work is more concerned with the elucidation of cross-Channel connections between southern England and Brittany than with the social ordering of the segments of society placed in the tombs. It is surely a disappointment to those pioneering prehistorians who attempted to introduce concepts of social structure into this archaeological evidence that we can still be faced today by hypothetical propositions of warrior aristocracies providing patronage for privileged craftsmen, propositions still relentlessly undeterred by the facts and by the principles of methodological inquiry. Few modern excavations of these monuments, particularly of the mounds of Wessex, have yielded more than evidence already available through ancient antiquarian research, and neither typological inquiry nor radiocarbon dating has provided us with understandable information (Ashbee 1978).

SOCIAL ORDERING AND THE CULTURAL LANDSCAPE

A more fruitful trend in the study of funerary monuments of northwestern Europe concerns cemetery archaeology, the investigation of the whole population as it is represented by a complete cemetery, whether this be of barrows, cairns, flat graves, or combinations (Figure 6.26). By such examinations it has become clear to all but the most stubborn archaeologists that the careful typological separation and ordering of pottery shapes, burial practices, and other grave-goods, may represent convenient labels for descriptive purposes but they never were mutually exclusive in the early Bronze Age. The recent excavations at Cloughskelt, Ireland (Figure 6.27), yielded several varieties of pottery vessels, with cremations in pits, flat graves, or stone cists, the whole representing hardly more than one or two lifetimes (Flanagan 1976). Barrow cemeteries too have been shown to represent several combinations of ritual and grave-goods within a short period of time (Figure 6.28) (Glasbergen 1954). Where total excavation has been possible and conditions of preservation are adequate, modern studies have offered opportunities for assessment of population structure and social ordering; where these have been allied to environmental and economic data, exciting models and interpretations have been produced.

A pioneer study of the Early Bronze Age monuments of Denmark was based on the proposition that the regional settlement pattern was reflected by the distribution of graves (Randsborg 1974). From estimations of the agricultural potential of various zones of Denmark it was found that the distribution of

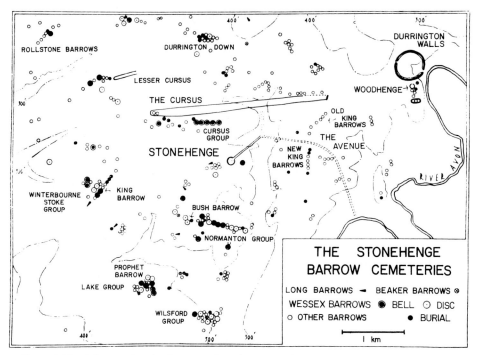

Figure 6.26 A Bronze Age landscape at Stonehenge, England. Neolithic monuments (Durrington Walls, Stonehenge and its avenue, and the Cursus) served as focal points for the establishment of small Bronze Age cemeteries, some of which appear to have had particularly important founders' barrows built early in the Bronze Age (Bush barrow, Prophet barrow, etc.). (From Ashbee 1960.)

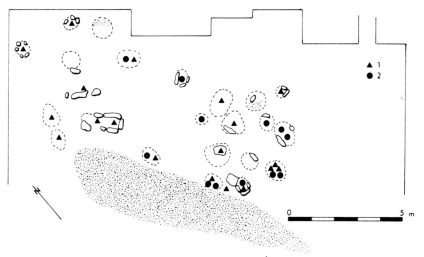

Figure 6.27 Plan of the Bronze Age cemetery at Cloughskelt, Ireland, with cremations placed in shallow scoops or pits, some lined with stones. The pottery vessels included food vessels (▲) and urns (●). Stipple indicates a granite outcrop. (Based on Flanagan 1976.)

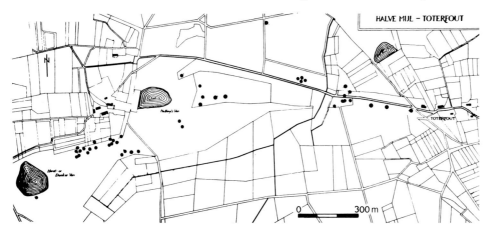

Figure 6.28   Field plan of the Bronze Age cemetery at Toterfout-Halve Mijl showing its linear character along a sand ridge. The excavation of much of this cemetery demonstrated the potential information to
be gained from "cemetery archaeology." (From Glasbergen 1954.)

graves was quite uniform in the earlier part of the Early Bronze Age, but not
uniform for a later part when northwestern Jutland contained a far higher density of graves than any other zone. That not all the population was buried in
recognizable graves is admitted; adult males outnumber females by a factor of
two, and children are hardly represented at all. However, if the increased density of graves really does reflect increased population, then some factors must be
responsible for allowing such increase to take place here and not elsewhere; this
could be improved or expanded farming practices, or a greater exploitation of
marine resources, either of which would permit population increase. Already
we have bypassed two problems, the destruction over much of Denmark of
many burial monuments without records, and the possibility that not all segments of society were equally treated to burial or not to burial in a mound in
every zone of Denmark.

A further interesting fact also emerges from this study. When the grave-goods
are considered, it can be seen that in other parts of Denmark, poorly furnished
graves outnumber rich graves except in the northwest of Jutland late in the Early
Bronze Age. Here, rich male graves actually outnumber poor male graves. What
is to be made of this evidence? One conclusion is that society was male-dominated, another is that it was not egalitarian; chiefdoms in the anthropological
sense are suggested. For northwestern Jutland, the close groupings and density
of rich graves may represent a more authoritarian society demanding and
strengthening production beyond normal previous levels.

This study has been followed, and complemented, by several other approaches to the problems of wealth and status identification in Bronze Age
Denmark (Kristiansen 1978a). These too involve zonation of the region in order
to draw contrasts and comparisons between east and west, north and south;

unfortunately, the zonation is not uniform with previous studies, and quantitative comparisons are not therefore possible. One study concerns the consumption of wealth, and introduces several of the subjects already noted in this chapter – the need for documentation of the primary evidence, the need for typological and technological analyses, and the need for detailed environmental and economic data to supplement and control the concepts. Archaeological societies tend to operate in an ecological vacuum, particularly when they are Bronze Age societies devised on the basis of surviving material culture.

Because all of the metal wealth of the Bronze Age in Denmark had to be imported, the consumption of this wealth through its deposition in graves and in hoards must have involved a deliberate and important set of decisions and actions. Objects were not consumed in this way at once, and careful study can detect the wear traces on metal products such as sword hilts, and deduce from these the circulation times of artifacts by area and chronological phase (Figure 6.29). This demonstrates that in northwestern Jutland there were many heavily worn bronzes in the later Early Bronze Age, perhaps passed by inheritance to

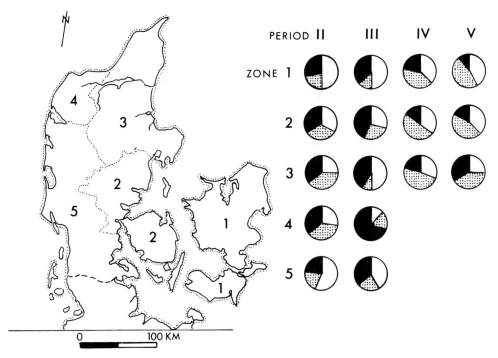

Figure 6.29 Zonation of Denmark in the Bronze Age with pie-diagram representations of the zonal variation in the circulation-time of swords (Periods II and III) and ornaments (Periods IV and V). The individual samples range from 12 to 78 artifacts. The diagrams are divided into three segments: white, artifacts without wear; dotted, artifacts with moderate wear; and black, artifacts with heavy wear. Note the high percentage of swords with heavy wear (long circulation time) in Zone 4, Period III. (Based on Kristiansen 1978a.)

new generations and perhaps serving as symbols of rank and authority. The relations between northern Europe and its suppliers of metal in central Europe may also have deteriorated at this time, and this was particularly marked in western Denmark; in the east, new alignments ensured a continued supply of metal. Such events will be reflected in the circulation time of objects, particularly those which may have denoted rank or wealth on the part of the owner.

The preference of Bronze Age communities for the lighter and more manageable soils, at the expense of the greater fertility of the heavier soils, must have meant that only periods of stress, with population increase, increased demands, or land exhaustion, would involve the dramatic adoption of and attack on the less easily cleared and worked soils. Northwestern Jutland, with rather low potential for agriculture, yet high in consumption according to estimates of its population demands, could hardly have maintained its position without some other factors such as marine resources, stockbreeding, and perhaps even textile manufacture; those textiles available for study from this area are of the highest quality and compare favorably with those from adjacent zones. However, western Jutland in general also experienced degradation of soils in the later Bronze Age, and perhaps depopulation, the result of mismanagement and overexploitation of grazing lands; could this have contributed to the gradual decline of the exchange networks too, which had brought valued materials from the south? It is possible. If so, it was reflected in the northwest of Jutland, where the prosperity evidenced by the male-dominated graves of the later Early Bronze Age came to a sudden end; its agricultural potential had been exploited fully and perhaps had created an ecological disaster. The conclusions of these studies point to all of western Denmark entering a period of crisis towards the end of the Bronze Age, with deteriorating soils and lower yields, with a population no less demanding but more isolated from exchange networks and hence consuming less and less bronze. At its expense, eastern Denmark and southern Sweden assumed a position of dominance not seen before in the north. It is of interest that independent work in southern Sweden provides a comment on this model of Bronze Age society and change.

Following a period of active research on general environmental and economic matters, with multiple pollen analyses and geomorphological observations, Swedish archaeologists have turned their attentions to problems of social organization and development through prehistory, and recently a particular effort has been made to create a model of land use and social ordering in the Bronze Age of Scania (Welinder 1977). The principle of the "filled cultural landscape" is under question here. Soil characteristics of the region demonstrate that the Scanian lands in the west and south, called central, were more suitable for cultivation than the massive marginal lands of the northeast (Figure 6.30). The distribution of Bronze Age material suggests that by the middle of the second millennium B.C., the entire central lands were filled and actively worked. In the later Bronze Age an expansion onto the marginal lands took place that presupposes a rise in the population of Scania in the centuries before and after 1000 B.C. How would

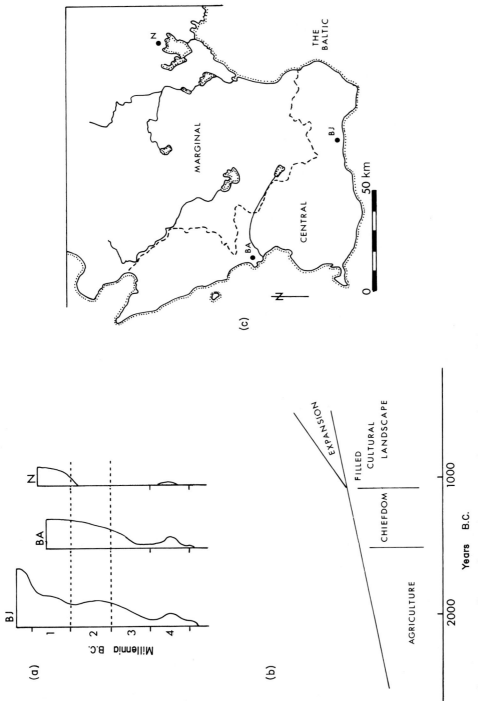

Figure 6.30 (a) Influence diagram from sites in the central area (Bjärsjöholmssjön [BJ] and Barsebäcks mosse [BA]) and marginal area (Näsums Gudahage [N]), with dashed lines marking the second millennium B.C. Note the lack of activity at Näsums Gudahage in the earlier Bronze Age. (b) A scheme to show the development of the cultural landscape, with metallurgy introduced about 1500 B.C., chiefdom structures formed thereafter, the central landscape filled about 1100 B.C. and expansion into marginal areas permitted and effected through social and political control. (c) Map of Scania, Sweden, with dashed line marking the boundary between the central and marginal areas exploited in the Bronze Age. (Based on Welinder 1977.)

this have occurred and under what social constraints? Here we encounter yet again the opposing viewpoints: "one cannot distinguish between the graves of the lower class and the aristocracy, and . . . the reason is, that no one of these classes has existed to any great extent" (Broholm 1943:262); "all over the picture is the same, a trade and navigation class rich but few in numbers with military and maritime power, able to control the commercial routes; and a numerous lower class. . . ." (Glob 1971:112).

The evidence from the burials of Scania suggests something more than the first view, if rather less exciting than the second. Because grave-goods with Early Bronze Age burials included exotic metals, their consumption must infer sacrifice of wealth, and only 20% of the known burials contained many such elegant products, with 80% containing fewer and more common objects. Of those not considered favorably enough to receive any such products we have little count but presume they outnumbered the other two classes. Hence we may be dealing with a population on three social levels of burial, one requiring an economically demanding ritual, another requiring a less-demanding ritual, and a third with no demand at all. The smallest archaeologically visible social unit in Scania is the group occupying a territory of 1 km², with a burial place and cult site, a population of 5–20 persons and 1–3 burials per generation. There are various ways by which such a unit might have operated in a population requiring land-sharing or cooperation from time to time (Figure 6.31), as well as permitting the passage of materials and products through the units. Although we know little about their economic activities, we may presume that food production and domestic requirements were met locally, that transport of materials between units was a shared service, and that more technical crafts such as weapon and ornament production were in the hands of specialists not necessarily resident within the unit in question. Such crafts, and the distribution of the products, could have been controlled by a segment of the whole population whose organizational talents were rewarded in the ways demonstrated by the burial monuments.

This introduces the concept of chiefdom and specialization in a more objective and logical manner than previously, but its weakness lies in a reliance upon metallurgy as the only tangible expression of this control (Figure 6.30). Ordinary settlements with small territories and limited numbers, based on cattle-breeding and long-fallow farming, might well have preferred to remain outside the redistribution pattern imposed on the area by the elite. The status of the elite is most unlikely to have been based entirely on one substance over which no direct control externally could be imposed. If we consider that the social units were locked together by a combination of both prestige material and the need for fundamental attachment to the land with its labor-intensive maintenance (Gilman 1981), then a case can be made for the expansion in the later Bronze Age from the central area into marginal areas. Little room for new territorial units would have existed centrally, the economic practices were already at maximum output, and the avoidance of social fracture through the collapse of the economic strategies, such as may have occurred in northwestern Jutland, could be

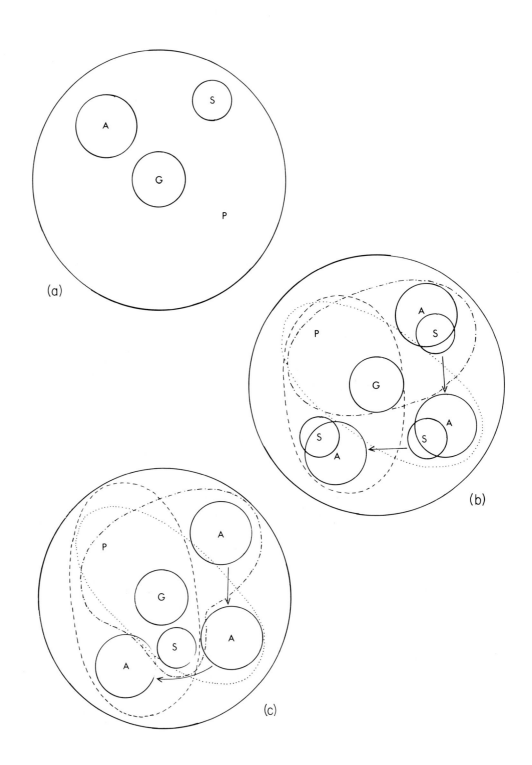

(a)

(b)

(c)

achieved by a strictly controlled and aided colonization movement from a part of the elitist population into the new lands, where traditional practices and behavior could be instituted.

Such an introduction may in fact be visible in part of the island of Fyn, Denmark, where abundant Bronze Age material has long tempted archaeologists; among the first was King Frederik VII who trenched into the enormous mound of Lusehøj, and recovered the richest Bronze Age burial in Denmark. Recent excavations in the barrow and at the Bronze Age settlement of Voldtofte nearby have pointed to the likelihood that these sites were linked, and formed the focal point of a very intensive and powerful occupation in southwestern Fyn in the later Bronze Age. The position of such a permanent occupation must be based upon its proximity to the Baltic shores to the south, its holding of the fertile lands of southern Fyn, and its ability to attract a disproportionate amount of tangible wealth in the form of bronze and particularly gold (Thrane 1980). Its source lies in the gradual evolution of powerful Bronze Age societies in the centuries before 1000 B.C., the development of trading and communication networks to the south, and the acquisition of new and fertile lands in Fyn and perhaps eastern Jutland. Its relationship with other areas has yet to be explained.

Although many archaeologists postulate the existence of ranked societies in the Bronze Age of Europe, few can agree on the definition of ranking. On the basis of the single-grave tradition of burial and the unequal distribution of wealth in the form of grave goods, it is clear that some form of individualizing societies existed. Whether or not these are to be seen as chiefdoms is perhaps too typological a decision to make, and there is no reason why Bronze Age ranked societies need conform to modern and recent anthropological definitions. One other element may also relate to this concept. The deliberate deposition of wealth as hoards or votive offerings can be interpreted as an act whereby material wealth was withdrawn from society in order to strengthen the prestige of those individuals able to control the supply of such desirable materials. This notion is difficult to document archaeologically, but one piece of evidence that links the strands of offerings, burials, and individuals is the rock carvings of southern Scandinavia. Such suggestive evidence, however, is lacking in other regions of northwestern Europe.

Figure 6.31   (a) A social and economic territory in southern Sweden during the Bronze Age, with central place for grave and other ritual activities (G), a settlement (S), cleared arable land (A), and wider areas controlled for pastoral and woodland activities (P). The whole territory of 1 km² is shown schematically: this area represents the smallest archaeologically visible unit in the landscape.

(b) A model of resources and development centered on the community grave and cult place, with settlement shifting along with arable land in a long-fallow process. Note the constant use of both central grave area and pastoral-woodland region. Outside connections are not shown.

(c) A model of resources and development in which the settlement is permanent, arable land is worked under a long-fallow process. Again, the central grave area and pastoral–woodland region are under constant use. (Based on Welinder 1977 with additions.)

The models and variations outlined above may help to explain the characteristic features of the Bronze Age in parts of northern Europe, but much more archaeological evidence is required to support the proposed conclusions and their implications. In particular, the consistent preference of farming communities for the most easily worked or fertile lands has ensured the destruction of many prehistoric traces in many areas. In contrast, marginal lands will tend to allow more complete preservation of sites, as we have seen in Britain as well as Scandinavia and the Low Countries. Problems such as this are implicit in archaeological investigations, and open yet again the age-old arguments about reliability and variability of the evidence. Most archaeologists of the Bronze Age tend to ignore such a fundamental problem.

It will be apparent to the reader that contemporary work on the Bronze Age of northwestern Europe is vigorously practised but lacks discipline, and is only now beginning to agree upon its aims. Theoretical, and theological, arguments about the nature of the study and the purpose of the study of prehistoric European societies are not rare (e.g., Hagen 1980), although this chapter has tried to steer clear of the semantic arguments; there are enough practitioners already. Nonetheless, the great retreat has begun, away from the acceptance of a view that the material evidence is an end in itself and will pose and answer its own questions. The new direction in which Bronze Age studies will proceed is not yet firmly established, but it is clearly towards those studies that will yield information about the formation and functioning of Bronze Age societies. Some of the recent advances in these studies must give encouragement for the future of the discipline.

REFERENCES

Aner, E., and K. Kersten
    1978   *Die Funde der älteren Bronzezeit des nordischen Kreises in Dänemark, Schleswig-Holstein und Neidersachsens. Band 4: Südschleswig-Ost.* Neumünster: Karl Wachholtz.
Ashbee, P.
    1960   *The Bronze Age round barrow in Britain.* London: Phoenix.
    1978   *The ancient British. A social-archaeological narrative.* Norwich: Geo-abstracts.
Bakker, J. A., R. W. Brandt, B. van Geel, M. J. Jansma, W. J. Kuijper, P. J. A. van Mensch, J. P. Pals, and G. F. Ijzereef
    1977   Hoogkarspel-Watertoren; towards a reconstruction of ecology and archaeology of an agrarian settlement of 1000 B.C. In *Ex Horreo,* edited by B. L. van Beek, A. W. Brandt, and W. Groenman-van Waateringe. Amsterdam: University of Amsterdam. Pp. 187–225.
Barker, G. (editor)
    1981   *Prehistoric communities in northern England: essays in economic and social reconstruction.* Sheffield: University of Sheffield, England.
Barrett, J., and R. Bradley (editors)
    1980   *The British Later Bronze Age.* Oxford: British Archaeological Reports.
Becker, C. J.
    1972   Hal og hus i yngre bronzealder. *Nationalmuseets Arbejdsmark 1972,* pp. 5–16.

Becker, C. J.
  1980   Bebyggelsesformer i Danmarks yngre bronsealder. In *Broncealderbebyggelse i Norden*, (Vol. 28), edited by H. Thrane. Odense: Historisk Institut. Pp. 127–141.

Bowen, C.
  1975   Pattern and interpretation: a view of the Wessex landscape. In *Recent work in rural archaeology*, edited by P. J. Fowler. Bradford-on-Avon: Moonraker. Pp. 44–56.

Bowen, C., and P. J. Fowler (editors)
  1978   *Early land allotment*. Oxford: British Archaeological Reports.

Bradley, R.
  1978   *The prehistoric settlement of Britain*. London: Routledge and Kegan.

Briard, J.
  1965   *Les Dépôts Bretons et l'age du bronze Atlantique*. Rennes: Laboratoire d'Anthropologie.
  1975   Nouvelles découvertes sur les tumulus Armoricains. *Archaeologia Atlantica*, **1**:17–32.

Broholm, H. C.
  1943   *Danmarks Bronzealder. I. Samlade fund fra den aeldre Bronzealder*. Copenhagen: Gyldendahl.

Broholm, H. C., and M. Hald
  1935   Danske Bronzealders Dragter. *Nordiske Fortidsminder*, Vol. 2, Hefte 5–6.

Brongers, J. A.
  1976   *Air photography and Celtic field research in the Netherlands*. Nederlandse Oudheden, Vol. 6. Amersfoort.

Brongers, J. A., and P. J. Woltering
  1973   Prehistory in the Netherlands: an economic-technological approach. *Berichten van de Rijksdienst voor het Oudheidkundig Bodemonderzoek*, Vol. 23, pp. 7–47.

Burgess, B.
  1980   *The age of Stonehenge*. London: Dent.

Burgess, C.
  1974   The bronze age. In *British prehistory: a new outline*, edited by C. Renfrew. London: Duckworth. Pp. 165–232, 291–329.

Burgess, C., and D. Coombs (editors)
  1979   *Bronze Age hoards: some finds old and new*. Oxford: British Archaeological Reports.

Burgess, C., and R. Miket (editors)
  1976   *Settlement and economy in the third and second millennia B.C.* Oxford: British Archaeological Reports.

Burenhult, G.
  1973   *The rock-carvings of Götaland*. Acta Archaeologica Lundensia, Vol. 8.

Butler, J. J.
  1969   *Nederland in de Bronstjid*. Bussum: Fibula-van Dishoeck.

Coles, J. M.
  1981   Metallurgy and Bronze Age society. In *Studien zur Bronzezeit. Festschrift für W. A. von Brunn*, edited by H. Lorenz. Mainz: von Zabern. Pp. 119–130.
  1982   Prehistoric roads and trackways in Britain: problems and possibilities. In *Routes and land transport*, edited by A. Fenton and G. Stell. Edinburgh: National Museum of Antiquities of Scotland.

Coles, J. M., and A. F. Harding
  1979   *The Bronze Age in Europe*. London: Methuen.

Coles, J. M., and R. A. Morgan
  1975   Timber and radiocarbon dates. *Antiquity* **49**:123–125.

Coles, J. M., and B. J. Orme
  1980   *Prehistory of the Somerset Levels*. Cambridge: Somerset Levels Project.

Ellison, A., and J. Harriss
  1972   Settlement and landuse in the prehistory and early history of southern England: a study based on locational models. In *Models in archaeology*, edited by D. L. Clarke. London: Methuen. Pp. 911–962.

Eskildsen, L., and E. Lomborg
    1976   Giftetanker. *Skalk* **1976**(5):18–26.
    1977   Skortejaegere. *Skalk* **1977**(4):3–6.
Flanagan, L. N. W.
    1976   The composition of Irish Bronze Age cemeteries. *Irish Archaeological Research Forum* **3**(part 2):7–20.
Fleming, A.
    1978   The prehistoric landscape of Dartmoor. Part 1: south Dartmoor. *Proceedings of the Prehistoric Society,* Vol. 44, pp. 97–123.
    1979   The Dartmoor reaves: boundary patterns and behaviour patterns in the second millennium bc. *Devon Archaeological Society: Prehistoric Dartmoor in its context,* Vol. 37, pp. 115–131.
Forsten, A.
    1977   A Bronze Age refuse fauna from Kökar, Aland. *Finskt Museum for 1974* (1977), pp. 56–60.
Fox, A.
    1954   Celtic fields and farms on Dartmoor. *Proceedings of the Prehistoric Society,* Vol. 20, pp. 87–102.
Fredsjö, A.
    1981   *Hällristningar. Kville härad i Bohuslän. Kville socken.* Studier i nordisk arkeologi. Göteborg: Fornminnesföreningen.
Gaucher, G.
    1981   *Sites et cultures de l'age du bronze dans le bassin de Paris.* Paris: Centre Nationale de la Recherche Scientifique.
Gerloff, S.
    1975   *The Early Bronze Age daggers in Great Britain and a reconsideration of the Wessex Culture.* Prähistorische Bronzefunde, Vol. VI, No. 2.
Gilman, A.
    1981   The development of social stratification in Bronze Age Europe. *Current Anthropology* **22**:1–23.
Giot, P-R., J. Briard, and L. Pape
    1979   *Protohistoire de la Bretagne.* Rennes: Ouest-France.
Glasbergen, W.
    1954   *Barrow excavations in the Eight Beatitudes.* Groningen: Wolters.
Glob, P. V.
    1971   *Danish prehistoric monuments.* London: Faber.
    1974   *The Mound People.* London: Faber.
Gräslund, B.
    1974   *Relativ datering. Om kronologisk metod i nordisk arkeologi.* Tor, Vol. 16.
    1976   Relative chronology. Dating methods in Scandinavian archeology. *Norwegian Archaeological Review* **9**:69–126.
Groenman-van Waateringe, W.
    1977   Palynologisch onderzoek van grafheurels te Weelde, Belgische Kempen. *Archaeologia Belgica* **193**:42–49.
Guilaine, J. (editor)
    1976   *La Préhistoire Française. Vol. II. Les Civilisations Néolithiques et Protohistoriques de la France.* Paris: Centre Nationale de la Recherche Scientifique.
Hachmann, R.
    1957   *Die frühe Bronzezeit im westlichen Ostseegebiet und ihre mittel- und südosteuropäischen Beziehungen.* Hamburg: Flemming.
Hagen, A.
    1980   Trends in Scandinavian archaeology at the transition to the 1980's. *Norwegian Archaeological Review* **13**:1–8.

Hansen, V., and H. Nielsen
1977   Prehistoric trackways and fords, elucidated by new investigations at Stevns, East Zealand. *Aarbøger for nordisk Oldkyndighed og Historie 1977*. Pp. 115–117.

Harding, A. F.
1980   Radiocarbon calibration and the chronology of the European Bronze Age. *Archeologické rozhledy* **32:**178–186.

Hartmann, A.
1970   *Prähistorische Goldfunde aus Europa*. Studien zu den Anfängen der Metallurgie (Vol. 3). Berlin: Mann.

Hayen, H.
1957   Zur Bautechnik und Typologie der vorgeschichtlichen, frühgeschichtlichen und mittelalterlichen hölzernen Moorwege und Moorstrassen. *Oldenberger Jahrbuch*, Vol. 56, pp. 83–170.

Herity, M., and G. Eogan
1977   *Ireland in prehistory*. London: Routledge and Kegan.

Jaanusson, H.
1971   Bronsaldersboplatsen vid Hallunda. *Fornvännen* **66:**173–185.
1981   *Hallunda. A Study of Pottery from a Late Bronze Age Settlement in Central Sweden*. Stockholm: Statens Historiska Museum.

Johnstone, P.
1980   *The sea-craft of prehistory*. London: Routledge and Kegan.

Junghans, S., E. Sangmeister, and M. Schröder
1968   *Kupfer und Bronze in der frühen Metallzeit Europas*. Studien zu den Anfängen der Metallurgie (Vol. 2). Berlin: Mann.

Kaelas, L. (editor)
1973   *Fyndrapporter 1973*. Göteborg: Göteborgs Arkeologiska Museum, pp. 237–258.

Kjellen, E.
1976   *Upplands Hällristningar*. Vitterhets Historie och Antikvitets Akademien. Lund: Kungl.

Kristiansen, K.
1974   En kildekritisk analyse af depotfund fra Danmarks yngre bronzealder (periode IV–V). *Aarbøger for nordisk Oldkyndighed og Historie 1974*, pp. 119–160.
1978a   The consumption of wealth in Bronze Age Denmark. A study in the dynamics of economic processes in tribal societies. In *New directions in Scandinavian archaeology*, edited by K. Kristiansen and C. Paludan-Müller. Studies in Scandinavian Prehistory and Early History (Vol. 1). Denmark: National Museum. Pp. 158–190.
1978b   Perioder og periodeovergange i neolitikum. *Hikuin* **4:**77–88.

de Laet, S. J.
1974   *Prehistorische Kulturen in het Zuiden der Lage Landen*. Wetteren: Universa.

Larsson, M.
1978   Review. S. Welinder, Ekonomiska processer i förhistorisk expansion. *Fornvännen* **73:**255.

McGrail, S. (editor)
1981   *The Brigg 'Raft' and her prehistoric environment*. Oxford: British Archaeological Reports.

Malmer, M. P.
1981   *A chorological study of north European rock art*. Stockholm: Kungl. Vitterhets Historie och Antikvitets Akademiens Handlingar Vol. 32.

Megaw, J. V. S., and D. D. A. Simpson
1979   *Introduction to British prehistory*. Leicester: University Press.

van Mensch, P. J. A., and G. F. Ijzereef
1975   Animal remains from a Bronze Age settlement near Andijk, province of North Holland. *Berichten van de Rijksdienst voor het Oudheidkundig Bodemonderzoek* **25:**55–68.

Mercer, R. (editor)
1981   *Farming practice in British prehistory*. Edinburgh: University Press.

Milisauskas, S.
    1978   *European prehistory.* New York: Academic Press.
Morris, R. W. B.
    1981   *The prehistoric rock art of southern Scotland.* Oxford: British Archaeological Reports, Vol. 86.
Muckelroy, K.
    1981   Middle Bronze Age trade between Britain and Europe: a maritime perspective. *Proceedings of the Prehistoric Society,* Vol. 47, pp. 275–298.
Müller-Karpe, H. (editor)
    1969–
    1980   *et seq. Prähistorische Bronzefunde.* Munich: Beck.
Musson, C. R.
    1970   House-plans and prehistory. *Current Archaeology,* No. 21:267–275.
Needham, S., and D. Langley
    1980   Runnymede Bridge, Egham: a Late Bronze Age riverside settlement. In *The British Later Bronze Age,* edited by J. Barrett and R. Bradley. Oxford: British Archaeological Report. Pp. 397–436.
Nordbladh, J.
    1978   Images and messages in society. Prolegomena to the study of Scandinavian petroglyphs and semiotics. In *New directions in Scandinavian archaeology,* edited by K. Kristiansen and C. Paludan-Müller. Studies in Scandinavian Prehistory and Early History · (Vol. 1). Denmark: National Museum. Pp. 63–78.
Oldeberg, A.
    1974   *Die ältere Metallzeit in Schweden.* Vitterhets Historie och Antikvitets Akademien. Lund: Kungl.
Ottenjann, H.
    1969   *Die nordischen Vollgriffschwerter der älteren und mittleren Bronzezeit.* Berlin: de Gruyter.
Piesker, H.
    1958   *Untersuchungen zur älteren Lüneburgischen Bronzezeit.* Hanover: Landesmuseums.
Pryor, F.
    1980   *Excavation at Fengate, Peterborough, England: the third report.* Archaeology Monograph (Vol. 6). Toronto: Royal Ontario Museum.
Randsborg, K.
    1974   Social stratification in Early Bronze Age Denmark: a study in the regulation of cultural systems. *Praehistorische Zeitschrift* **49**:38–61.
Rijksdienst voor het Oudheidkundig Bodemonderzoeg
    1965–
    1966   De periodisering van de Nederlandse prehistorie. *Berichten van de Rijksdienst voor het Oudheidkundig Bodemonderzoek* **15–16**:7–11.
Riley, D. N.
    1980   *Early landscape from the air.* Sheffield: University of Sheffield, England.
Rowlands, M. J.
    1976   *The organisation of Middle Bronze Age metalworking.* Oxford: British Archaeological Reports.
Ryan, M. (editor)
    1980   *The origins of metallurgy in Atlantic Europe.* Proceedings of the Fifth Atlantic Colloquium. Dublin: Stationery Office.
Smith, K., G. Coppen, J. Wainwright, and S. Beckett
    1981   The Shaugh Moor project: third report—settlement and environmental investigations. *Proceedings of the Prehistoric Society,* Vol. 47, pp. 205–274.
Stjernquist, B.
    1967   *Models of commercial diffusion in prehistoric times.* Lund: Scripta Minora.

Strömberg, M.
  1975   Untersuchungen zur Bronzezeit in Südostschonen. Probleme um die Besiedlung. *Meddelanden fran Lunds universitets historiska museum 1973–1974*, pp. 101–168.
Taylor, J. J.
  1980   *Prehistoric goldwork in the British Isles.* Cambridge: Cambridge University Press.
Thrane, H.
  1973   Bronzezeit in Nordeuropa. In *Reallexikon der Germanischen Altertumskunde*, edited by J. Hoops (Band 3, Lieferung 5). Berlin: De Gruyter. Pp. 519–540.
  1975   *Europaeiske forbindelser.* Copenhagen: National Museum.
  1980   Nogle tanker om yngre broncealders bebyggelse pa Sydvestfyn. In *Broncealderbebyggelse i Norden*, edited by H. Thrane. Odense: Historisk Institut. Pp. 165–173.
Thrane, H. (editor)
  1980   *Broncealderbebyggelse i Norden*, (Vol. 28). Odense: Historisk Institut.
Waterbolk, H. T.
  1964   The Bronze Age settlement of Elp. *Helinium* 4:97–131.
  1975   Evidence of cattle stalling in excavated pre- and protohistoric houses. In *Archaeozoological Studies*, edited by A. T. Clason. Amsterdam: North Holland. Pp. 383–394.
Welinder, S.
  1975   *Prehistoric agriculture in eastern Middle Sweden.* Acta Archaeologica Lundensia. Series in 8 Minore, Vol. 4.
  1977   *Ekonomiska processer i förhistorisk expansion.* Acta Archaeologica Lundensia. Series in 8 Minore, Vol. 7.
Wihlborg, A.
  1977–
  1978   Sagaholm. A Bronze Age barrow with rock-carvings. *Meddelanden fran Lunds universitets historiska museum 1977–1978.* Pp. 111–128.
Wright, E. V.
  1976   *The North Ferriby Boats.* London: National Maritime Museum.

7

Upper Pleistocene and Holocene Cultures of the Russian Plain and Caucasus: Ecology, Economy, and Settlement Pattern

PAUL M. DOLUKHANOV

INTRODUCTION

The development of prehistoric society was dependent on both ecological and social factors. Prehistoric society was highly adapted to the environment (Dolukhanov 1979) through the choice of optimal economic strategies by means of which energy entered the social system enabling it to function normally. The economy strongly affected both productive tools and population dynamics, and the mechanism of adaptation also influenced the settlement pattern, which provided for the optimal use of the surrounding landscape. The second important element in prehistoric society, culture *sensu lato,* is seen here mainly as an accumulator of traditions, or as a memory element. In certain cases this element may influence the choice of economic strategies and the tool kit.

The spatial manifestations of prehistoric cultural systems are distinguished by both discontinuity and inconsistency. On the basis of constantly recurring types or groups of artifacts, archaeologists (in most cases intuitively) try to define territorial and chronological entities, which are often labeled as *archaeological cultures.* Multivariate analysis of Upper Palaeolithic and Mesolithic stone assemblages (Dolukhanov *et al.* 1980) has substantiated the reality of these archaeological cultures, which, in all probability, reflect stable patterns of human behavior within finite limits. However, the same analysis also revealed that these entities are very complex in nature. The evolution of archaeological cultures was

ADVANCES IN WORLD ARCHAEOLOGY
Volume 1

largely determined by sociocultural and ecological–economic factors, but the relative significance of these factors altered in the course of the Pleistocene and Holocene.

In this chapter, an attempt is made to trace, on a regional basis, the relationships between the environment, economy, and settlement patterns of prehistoric populations during the Upper Pleistocene and the Early and Middle Holocene. Two contrasting areas are considered: the Caucasus and the Russian (or East European) Plain.

PLEISTOCENE

Caucasus

Environment

The Caucasus, an integral part of the Alpine orogenic belt, is a young mountain land, of which the structural elements are two complex anticlinal upfolds (Greater Caucasus and Minor Caucasus) separated by intermontane depressions. The contrasting nature of these major elements largely determines the peculiarity of the Caucasian environment. Other important environmental factors are altitudinal zonality and a general increase of aridity in the easterly direction.

Environmental change during the Pleistocene was caused by climatic changes, fluctuations in the levels of the Black and the Caspian seas and, indirectly, by recent movements of the earth's crust. There were two major glaciations in the Caucasus during the Upper Pleistocene, and these were separated by a mild interval (Tsereteli and Maisuradze 1976). The maximal depression of the snow line is estimated to have been 800–1000 m for the Greater Caucasus and 400–600 m for the Minor Caucasus.

Apart from large-scale changes, there were also minor climatic fluctuations. Palynological investigations by Levkovskaia (1980) of deposits in the Kudaro Caves (on the southern slopes of the central part of the Greater Caucasus; see the following) have enabled her to establish that, during the Mousterian occupation of the caves (Early and Middle Würm), the environment changed from coniferous forest to alpine meadows and then to subalpine birch forest. The last of these three phases has a radiocarbon date of 44,150 $^{+2400}_{-1800}$ B.P. (GrN-6079). Work in a bog situated in the Black Sea coastal area near the town of Sukhumi has shown that beech–fir forests were established at about 41,200 ± 710 B.P. Cold-resistant pine and alder forests then replaced the beech–fir forests about 38,000 years ago, and a new mild interval followed later (Arslanov et al. 1976; Arslanov et al. 1980). In eastern Georgia the maximum cooling has been dated to around 20,580 ± 680 B.P., at which time open pine forests covered the intermontane depressions and foothills (Gogichaishvili 1973). Reforestation of the area began about 14,000 years ago, and at approximately the same time arboreal vegetation also began to spread in the Zagros Mountains in northwestern Iran (van Zeist and Bottema 1977).

During the Upper Pleistocene there were major fluctuations in the level of the Black Sea. The Karangat transgression (27–35 m above sea level) in all probability coincided with the Riss-Würm interglacial (Ostrovskii *et al.* 1977:67), while the Surozh terrace, which is situated at 15–20 m above sea level, has uranium–thorium dates of 33,100 ± 280 B.P. years and 41,250 ± 340 B.P. (Kaplin *et al.* 1977:38). During the maximal stages of the Würm glaciation, the Black Sea dropped 100–120 m below its present level. This regression considerably enlarged the Black Sea coastal zone, and was thus an important environmental factor, which greatly stimulated human settlement in this area.

The Caspian Sea showed two peaks of transgression during the Upper Pleistocene. These were the Lower Khvalynian, which dated to about 65,000–35,000 B.P., and the Upper Khvalynian, which fell within the period 20,000–10,000 B.P.

Sites

The earliest site presently known from the Caucasus seems to be the Azykh Cave, on the piedmont of the Karabakh Ridge in the Minor Caucasus, Azerbaidjan Republic. The layers that contained the earliest claimed assemblage of pebble tools are reported to have reversed magnetic polarity. If this should be further substantiated, it would suggest that the assemblage was deposited during the Matuyama magnetic epoch, more than 700,000 years ago (Velichko *et al.* 1980). Yashtykh, in the Black Sea coastal area near the town of Sukhumi, is a group of open-air sites at which the artifacts were found in deposits covering the Ancient Euxine terrace (Korobkov 1967). This terrace corresponds to the Mindel–Riss interglacial, thus providing a *terminus post quem* for the assemblage. The valley of the Djodjori River, which crosses the southern slope of the Greater Caucasus, also contains a number of Acheulean cave sites, including Kudaro I and III and Tsona.

A considerable number of Mousterian sites appeared in the Caucasus during Early and Middle Würm. There are many such sites in the Djodjori Valley, as well as in other valleys in the central part of the Greater Caucasus (Figure 7.1). The latest Mousterian layer (3a) in the Kudaro I cave in the Djodjori valley has been radiocarbon dated to 44,150 +2400 and −1800 B.P. (Liubin 1977, 1980). There is a second cluster of Mousterian sites on the coastal area of the Black Sea and in the mountains that border the Colchis lowlands on the north. The Mousterian layer of Akhshtyr' Cave, near the town of Solchi, has a radiocarbon date of 35,000 ± 2000 B.P. (Vekilova and Grishchenko 1972). The third cluster of Mousterian sites is in the low and middle mountains of the Minor Caucasus. The Mousterian layers of Yerevan Cave, which belongs to this cluster, have been radiocarbon dated to 49,000–47,000 B.P. (Yeritsian, n.d.).

The Upper Paleolithic in the Caucasus approximately corresponds to the Late

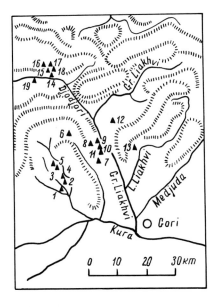

Figure 7.1 Topographical scheme of Mousterian sites in the Kura basin (Georgian Republic). (▲) Mousterian sites: (1) Koda; (2) Isak-Kau; (3) Alibar; (4) Naba Kebi; (5) Nedlat; (6) Djidjaita; (7) Kurseti 1; (8) Kurseti 2; (9) Kurseti 3; (10) Tamarasheni; (11) Karapusta-Kad; (12) Morgo; (13) Kokhati; (14) Kudaro 1; (15) Kudaro 3; (16) Kudaro 4; (17) Uchela; (18) Farsag; (19) Gorno. (After Liubin 1960.)

Würm Glaciation. Upper Paleolithic sites are much less common than are those of the Middle Paleolithic. They are known only from the coastal area of the Black Sea and from the middle mountains of western Georgia. The only reliable radiocarbon date for the Upper Paleolithic is from Akhshtyr' Cave, near Sochi, which gave a reading of 19,550 ± 550 B.P. (Vekilova and Grishchenko 1972).

Economy

Middle Paleolithic economies in the Caucasus were based primarily on the hunting of mountain–forest and mountain–steppe animals; cave bear was the most commonly hunted animal. The faunal assemblages of the Kudaro I (Vereshchagin and Baryshnikov 1980a) and Kudaro III (Vereshchagin and Baryshnikov 1980b) also included red deer and Caucasian wild goat. The hunting of birds (waterfowl, partridge, snow cock, blackcock, quail, and pheasant) and fishing (particularly for sturgeon) were also of considerable economic importance at these sites (Burchak-Abramovich 1980; Tsepkin 1980). Cave bear remains are also predominant in the faunal assemblages of the cave sites in the coastal area of the Black Sea, whereas red deer, wild goat, and bison are represented by single specimens (Vereshchagin 1959:104–110). In contrast, the Mousterian layers of cave sites in the Minor Caucasus have yielded remains of wild horse, wild ass, maral, elk, rhinoceros, and Caucasian tur (Aliev 1969; Yeritsian n.d.).

The structure of hunting in the Caucasian Upper Paleolithic was rather different. Caucasian wild goat is dominant in the faunal assemblages of the Upper Paleolithic cave sites in western Georgia, and wolf, fox, brown bear, wild cat, marten, wild pig, elk, and bison also occur. Species such as wild horse, wild sheep, and porcupine disappear in assemblages dating to the Final Pleistocene (Vereshchagin 1959:111–125).

Settlement Patterns

Most Paleolithic settlements in the Caucasus are cave sites in river valleys, or in low or middle mountains. Nearly all of them lay originally in the forest belts, but occupation sometimes penetrated into the subalpine meadows. Such locations enabled the occupants of the sites to utilize the resources of the river valleys, mountain slopes, and tablelands.

Based on the low volume of the archaeological deposits, the lack of permanent dwellings, and the character of faunal remains, Liubin (1977, 1980), as well as Vereshchagin and Baryshnikov (1980a,b) conclude that the majority of the Mousterian cave sites in the Djordjori Valley are the remains of short-term camping sites. Numerous interruptions in the archaeological deposits suggest that Mousterian man penetrated the area only during mild climatic episodes and in seasons suitable for hunting and fishing. This assumption seems valid for most of the areas of the Caucasus for which data are available. On this basis, one might speculate that the Mousterian population of the Caucasus consisted of small hunting groups who, during the short periods suitable for hunting or fishing activities, penetrated deep into the mountain valleys, which were particularly rich in biomass.

The question of origin of the Mousterian population of the Caucasus remains open. There exists a possibility that this population penetrated from the Near East, where there is an uninterrupted development of Early and Middle Paleolithic industries from at least Mindel. A similarity in the Levalloisian technique in both areas seems to point to that direction. Both the lithic inventory and the fauna of the open-air site of Il'skaya, situated in the basin of the Kuban River in the northern Caucasus, are quite distinct from those of the Transcaucasian sites. The fauna from Il'skaya is dominated by aurochs, and mammoth, wild horse, saiga, and red deer are also present (Vereshchagin 1959:95–99).

Russian Plain

Environment

The Russian (or East European) Plain corresponds geotectonically to the platform of the same name. It is limited by the Arctic Ocean in the north; by the Sudeten and Carpathian mountains in the west; by the Black Sea and the Crimean Mountains in the south; by the Caucasus Mountains in the southwest; and by the Ural Mountains in the east. The main relief features of the Russian Plain were formed during the lengthy period of its platform-type development. Minor forms of relief in the northwestern, central, and northeastern parts were created for the most part by glacial processes during the Last Glaciation. Areas beyond the extent of the glaciers were affected by periglacial processes.

The environments occurring on the Russian Plain are to a large extent determined by its central position in relation to the North Atlantic, Arctic, and Siberian centers of atmospheric activity, and the distributions of vegetation, animals,
and soils are also subject to latitudinal zoning. Both the limits and the structure
of natural zones changed during the course of the Pleistocene and Holocene.
Periods of cooling during the Pleistocene were, in several cases, accompanied by
the formation of extensive glaciers and by the development of a comparatively
uniform periglacial zone in the extraglacial areas. Interglacial conditions were
partly restored during mild phases (Velichko 1973).

According to the latest stratigraphical scheme by Zarrina *et al.* (1980), the
Würm (Weichselian or Valdai) glaciation may be divided into three stages: Early
(70,000–50,000 B.P.); Middle (50,000–25,000 B.P.) and Late (25,000–10,000
B.P.). According to Chebotareva and Makarycheva (1974), glacial phenomena
occurred only during the Late Würm. The Early Würm consisted of three cold
phases separated by two mild oscillations: Amersfoort-First Chereminian
(67,000–57,000 B.P.) and Brörup-Second Chereminian (60,000–57,000 B.P.). A
cool climate prevailed throughout the Middle Würm, and both mild and cold
oscillations occurred. The mild periods were accompanied by the spread of
forests (mostly coniferous). On the basis of the new geochronological data (Zarrina *et al.* 1980), one may propose the following paleoclimatic sequence for the
Middle Würm: 50,000–40,000 B.P., Grazhdanski Prospekt mild interval;
40,000–38,000 B.P., Bugrovo cold phase; 38,000–34,000 B.P., Kashino-Hengelo
mild interval; 34,000–32,000 B.P., Shensk cold phase; 32,000–29,000 B.P.,
Denekamp-Arcy mild interval; 29,000–25,000 B.P., Dunayevo-Kesselt mild interval. The Dunayevo-Kesselt interval, which coincided with the formation of the
Bryansk buried soil in the periglacial area, was probably the warmest (Velichko
1975:20). Spruce forests spread during this interval, and broad-leaved plant
species are established in the pollen spectra of the period in the Kostenki area
(Levkovskaia 1977:76–78; see the following).

During the Late Würm, the glaciation extended to its maximal size, after
which the glacial recession started. Several cold phases may be distinguished
within the Late Würm: the glaciation maximum (25,000–17,000 B.P.), Luga phase
(17,000–13,700 B.P.), Neva phase (13,200–12,400 B.P.), and Salpauselkä phase
(11,000–10,200 B.P.). During cold phases of the glaciation "periglacial plant associations" occurred in the ice-free areas. They consisted of arctic and steppic
species and have no analogies in present-day vegetation. The most important
warm oscillations were Lascaux (about 17,000 B.P.), Bölling (12,400–12,000 B.P.),
and Alleröd (11,800–11,000 B.P.). Predominantly coniferous forests existed during these intervals.

An important feature of the Late Glacial environment was the existence of
numerous ice-dammed lakes (Kvasov 1975). These lakes were created when the
ice sheet blocked the valleys of rivers flowing in northerly and northwesterly
directions, and prevented them from following their courses. The levels of the
ice-dammed rivers rose, filling all the low-lying depressions, and continued to

rise until they reached the height of the watershed. At that point, the ice-dammed lakes gained access to the rivers that flow in a southerly direction towards the Black and Caspian seas. These southward-flowing rivers became channels that drained the ice-dammed basins, and in many cases themselves turned into chains of lakes. Nearly all of the known Late Paleolithic sites were situated either on the shores of these channels or on the shores of the ice-dammed lakes.

Sites

Very little is known about the Mousterian settlement of the Russian Plain during the Early Würm; the population density was probably extremely low. Mousterian sites of that age do, however, exist in the coastal areas of the Azov Sea and on the lower River Volga, the best known being the site of Volgograd. Several Mousterian sites are known in the valley of the River Desna, in the vicinity of Bryansk. The Mousterian layer of the site of Khotylevo was deposited above the alluvium of the 22-m terrace of the Desna (Zaverniaiev 1978). Cores and intermediate products characteristic of a lithic workshop make up the bulk of the inventory from this site. The archaeological layer of another Mousterian site, Betovo, was deposited above bedrock on the right bank of the same river. Charcoal from deposits directly overlying the Mousterian layer gave a radiocarbon date of 36,100 ± 500 B.P. (GrN-9721). Arctic lemming dominates in the faunal remains, and there are also mammoth, woolly rhinoceros, bobac, hamster, vole, steppe pika, Arctic fox, and European hare. Pollen analysis indicates a landscape of forest–tundra type in the vicinity of the site. The lithic inventory contains high percentages of notched tools, denticulates, and scrapers (Tarasov 1977).

Sites belonging to the initial stage of the Upper Paleolithic date from the final episodes of the Middle Würm up to the onset of the glacial maximum, around 36,000–25,000 B.P. The earliest chronological position seems to be held by the Streletskian, which is represented at a number of sites in the Kostenki area (Kostenki 12, Layers 3 and Ia; Streletskaia; Kostenki 1, Layer 5), and possibly by Sungir' in the vicinity of Vladimir (Anikovich 1977b). The earliest occurrence of the Streletskian is Kostenki 12, Layer 3, which is deposited at the bottom of lower humus complex of the second terrace of the River Don. Layer Ia is deposited at the base of the upper humus complex in the same sequence and has a radiocarbon date of 32,700 ± 700 B.P. (GrN-7758). This could suggest that the transition from Mousterian to Upper Paleolithic on the Russian Plain may have taken place between 38,000 and 32,000 B.P. Anikovich (1977a:7–8) analyzed the stone inventory of the third layer of Kostenki 12, and stressed its archaic character (high percentages of Mousterian points and side-scrapers; the presence of Mousterian flaking and retouching techniques). I see the Streletskian as a transitional culture from Mousterian to Upper Paleolithic, although at present it cannot be linked with any known Mousterian assemblage.

The development of cultures belonging to the initial stage of the Upper Paleolithic occurred mainly during the Dunayevo-Kesselt mild interval, which is represented by the buried soil of Bryansk and the upper humus complex in the Kostenki area. According to Levkovskaia (1977:76–78), mixed coniferous and broad-leaved forests existed there at that time. The site of Sungir', near Vladimir, has radiocarbon dates of 22,500 ± 200 B.P. and 24,400 ± 400 B.P., and existed in a predominantly treeless environment, with patches of spruce and (rarely) of birch (Bader 1977:31–32). Khotylevo 2, which also belongs to the initial Upper Paleolithic, existed in a periglacial steppe environment with rare patches of birch and fir (Velichko *et al.* 1977; Kurenkova 1979). There are reasons to assume that the Gorodtsovian equally belongs to the initial stage. The sites which belong to this culture—Gorodtsovskaia, Markina Gora, Volkovskaia, and Uglianka (Grigor'ev, 1970:48)—occur only in the Kostenki area and are deposited within the upper humus. Bone from the second layer of Markina Gora has a radiocarbon date of 28,200 ± 700 B.P. (LU 59), while a bone sample from Gorodtsovskaia has been dated to 21,720 ± 570 B.P. (LE-1431) (Rogachev and Sinitsyn 1979a:75–77; 1979b:92–93).

The second stage of Upper Paleolithic includes those sites which existed during the glacial maximum and the early stages of glacial recession, from about 25,000 to 13,000 B.P. This stage is associated with the maximal density of Paleolithic sites on the Russian Plain, and several clearly defined archaeological cultures, such as the Kostenkian, Pushkarian, and Yeliseyevichian, as well as many other less distinct entities, existed during this stage. Sites attributed to the Kostenkian include several in the Don Valley, such as Kostenki I, Layer I, Gagarino, and others, such as Berdyzh, in the Valley of the Seim, a tributary of the Dnieper. Kostenki I, Layer I has a radiocarbon date of 22,300 ± 230 B.P. (GIN 1870) (Rogachev *et al.* 1979), and the dates available for Avdeievo are 22,700–22,200 B.P. (Gvozdover and Sulerzhitskii 1979:144), 16,565 ± 270 B.P. (QX-886) (O. Soffer, personal communication, 1981), and 13,900 ± 200 B.P. (IGAN 71) (Kurenkova 1979). The radiocarbon age of Gagarino is 21,800 ± 300 B.P. (GIN 1872) (Tarasov 1979). The numerous Paleolithic sites in the basin of the River Dnieper, attributed to the Pushkarian, Yeliseyevichian, Mezinian, and some minor cultural groupings, also belong to the second stage of the Upper Paleolithic. Recent work has provided a radiocarbon date of 18,690 ± 700 B.P. (LU-361) for the site of Pogon; of 17,340 ± 170 B.P. (LU-360) for Yeliseievichi; of 15,300 ± 700 B.P. (GIN-2003) for Timonovka 1; of 15,110 ± 530 B.P. (LU-358) for Timonovka 2; and, for Yudinovo, three dates of 15,660 ± 180 B.P. (LU-127), 13,830 ± 850 B.P. (LU-103), and 13,650 ± 200 B.P. (LU-153) (Kurenkova 1979).

Paleogeographical investigations (Velichko *et al* 1977; Levkovskaia 1977) show that most of the sites belonging to the second stage of the Upper Paleolithic existed during a period of cold and continental climate. The vegetation was of a periglacial tundra–steppe type, with patches of wood and brush of cold-resistant species restricted to the river valleys. Permafrost processes were widespread.

The warm Bölling oscillation (12,400–12,000 B.P.) marked the beginning of the final (Late Glacial) stage in the development of the Upper Paleolithic. During this stage the number of sites in the basins of the Don and the Middle Dnieper rivers seems to have decreased abruptly, while sites in the basins of the Upper Dnieper, Neman, and Western Dvina rivers grew in number. There is, however, very little evidence to determine the absolute age of these sites. On morphological grounds, Rimantiene (1971) suggests that the Late Paleolithic sites in Lithuania date back to Alleröd and to Younger Dryas, and morphological and palynological evidence indicates a comparable age for the Late Paleolithic sites in the Usvyaty area, Pskov oblast (Dolukhanov 1979:132).

Economy

At present, very little can be said about the Mousterian economy of the Russian Plain, except that it was based on hunting and food-gathering. The Upper Paleolithic economy was based on the highly efficient hunting of periglacial-forest and periglacial-steppe animals. During the initial stage of the Upper Paleolithic, the hunted animals were mainly wild horse, rhinoceros, red deer, and bison. During the second stage, mammoth, woolly rhinoceros, brown bear, cave lion, hare, and wolf were hunted most frequently (Vereshchagin and Kuz'mina 1979:15). The Upper Paleolithic populations were extremely well adapted to the periglacial environment, and some indication of the effectiveness of their hunting strategies may be gathered from the number of individual mammoths recovered during excavation of the sites: more than 55 from Kostenki I (Garutt and Urbanis 1979:19), 116 from Mezin, 25 from Gontsy, 70 from Kirillovskaia, 18 from Dobranichevka, and 95 from Mezherich (Vereshchagin 1971:214–215). Analysis of the faunal remains further indicates that sites of this stage were occupied year round; the mammoth were hunted mostly in autumn and winter; the reindeer in spring and in early summer; the fur-bearing animals in winter, and the waterfowl in summer (Korniets et al. 1981).

It seems reasonable to assume that at least an equally large amount of food was procured through the collecting of edible plants. The Upper Paleolithic sites of the Russian Plain contain numerous implements that might have been used for food-gathering. These include axe- and hoe-like tools made of reindeer antlers, mammoth ribs, or mammoth long bones (at Mezhirich, Dobdanichevka, Timonovka, and elsewhere); sandstone and quartzite slabs resembling grinding stones were found at Kostenki 4, Layer II, and at Chulatovo; and sites such as Kostenki 4, Layer 9, and Molodova 5 contain rounded granite and quartzite objects very similar to pestles. Rogachev (1973) sees these implements as indications of widespread food-gathering activities.

Coincident with the transition to the final stage of the Upper Paleolithic, there may have been a notable change in economy. The faunal evidence from contemporaneous sites in similar ecological settings in the northern German lowlands suggests that the economy of the Late Glacial sites may have been based on reindeer hunting. The morphological position of the sites themselves (in lake depressions and on low river terraces) and the high percentages of projectile points also seem to suggest that the hunting of waterfowl was important, while an increase in the extent of the forests, particularly during mild intervals, supports the suggestion that food collecting was more important during this stage. Archaeological deposits of Late Glacial sites are usually thin, and no traces of permanent or semipermanent dwellings have been found. All of this seems to indicate that nomadic hunting was the principal economic strategy during the Late Glacial.

Settlement Patterns

It was observed in the foregoing that, with the possible exceptions of the southern and southeastern areas, the population density of the Russian Plain during the Early Würm was very low. The first large-scale infiltrations of Mousterian populations occurred during the first half of the Middle Würm, around 50,000–40,000 B.P. These probably came from southeastern and central Europe, migrations from the Caucasus being less probable (see the preceding).

During the Middle Würm, socioeconomic, biological, and ecological processes, occurring simultaneously across vast territories of Europe and the Near East, resulted in the establishment of the Upper Paleolithic cultures. The processes that led to the appearance and the spread of these cultures are not yet fully understood, but there are reasons to speculate that the spread of the Upper Paleolithic was much facilitated by the formation of the periglacial zone in Europe. This zone, which combined both arctic and steppic elements, was extremely rich in biomass, with herds of large graminivores, such as mammoth and woolly rhinoceros.

Three stages may be distinguished in the development of the periglacial landscapes: the formative stage (35,000–25,000 B.P.), the stage of maturity (25,000–13,000 B.P.), and the stage of degradation (13,000–10,000 B.P.). Periglacial-forest landscapes spread largely during the formative stage. The thinness of the archaeological deposits and the lack of dwelling-like constructions (although very few sites have been excavated on a large scale) suggest that the early Upper Paleolithic population consisted of relatively small hunting groups that moved across the valleys of the Middle Don, the Upper Volga, and the Upper Dnieper basins. This population may have developed primarily from local Mousterian groups, but it is possible that there were also some limited immigrations, mainly from southeastern Europe, since there are similarities in the stone inventories.

The mature stage of the periglacial landscapes roughly coincided with the glacial maximum, and was characterized by a dominance of periglacial-steppic landscapes, by large-scale permafrost processes, by the transgressions of the ice-dammed basins and rivers, and by the existence of large herds of graminivores. During this stage, the prehistoric communities were highly adapted to the periglacial environment, the adaptation taking the form of an elaboration of highly efficient subsistence strategies, including the hunting of large herd animals and the gathering and processing of edible plants. The success of this adaptation is also reflected in a relatively stable settlement pattern. Settlements with permanent or semipermanent dwellings built of mammoth bones were usually situated on the edges of plateaux adjoining river valleys, on high terraces, or on promontories formed by deep ravines cutting the valley slopes (Figures 7.2 and 7.3). Such locations made it possible for the Paleolithic people to utilize the resources of the river, valley, and watershed plateau. Modes of life and of economic activities in particular seem to have been similar, and resulted in similarities between the major stone tool assemblages (Dolukhanov *et al.* 1980:70–71).

It is unlikely that there were any large-scale migrations during this stage. On the contrary, the whole area of Upper Paleolithic settlement formed a single economic zone, within which several archaeological cultures (such as the Kostenkian, Pushkarian, Yeliseyevichian, and Mezinian) may be distinguished. These cultures may be interpreted either in economic terms, as different seasonal or locational activities, or in ethnic terms, as stable cultural traditions within closed groups, or both. The most densely populated areas during this stage were the basins of the Upper and Middle Dnieper and the Middle Don. At a later phase settlements arose in the Lower Dnieper and in the coastal area of the Black Sea.

The stage of degradation coincided with the glacial recession, the spread of the forests and the lowering of the levels of the ice-dammed lakes and rivers. During this stage the large herd graminivores, such as mammoth and woolly rhinoceros, became extinct, while the population of reindeer increased dramat-

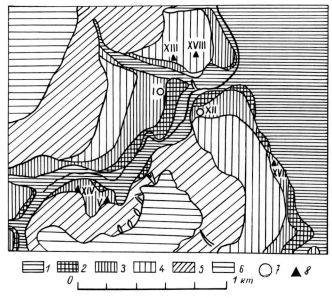

Figure 7.2 Geomorphological scheme of Don River Valley in the Kostenki area. (1) Floodplain; (2) first terrace; (3) second terrace; (4) third terrace; (5) slopes; (6) watershed; (7) Streletskian sites; (8) other Upper Paleolithic sites. (After Velichko and Rogachev 1969.)

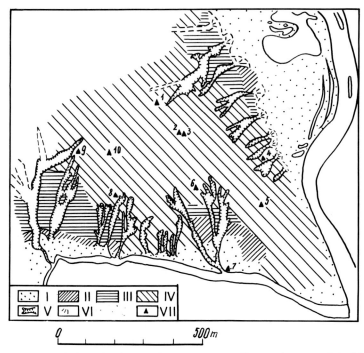

Figure 7.3 Geomorphological scheme of Desna River Valley in the area of Pushkari sites. (I) Floodplain; (II) first terrace; (III) second terrace; (IV) watershed plateau; (V) ravines; (VI) alluvial fans; (VII) Upper Paleolithic sites. (1) Pushkari 1; (2) Pogon; (3) Bugurok; (4) Davydok Berezniak; (5) Maidan; (6) Kravtsov Rov; (7) Ust'-Kravtsov; (8) Sosnitskii Rov; (9) Anikiev Rov 1; (10) Anikiev Rov 2. (After Velichko 1969.)

ically as the ice retreated. The human populations of the basins of the Middle Don and the Middle and Lower Dnieper rapidly diminished, while those of the Upper Dnieper (the Rivers Pripiat', Sozh, and Iput'), the Neman, and the Western Dvina expanded. Sites in these latter areas were usually situated on dunes developed either on low terraces or on floodplains (Rimantiene 1971; Isaienko 1973). Sites in the basins of the Upper Volga and the Oka rivers, belonging to the first stage of the Upper Volga culture as defined by Kol'tsov (1965, 1966), were probably also occupied during this stage, and numerous sites appeared on the shores of residual ice-dammed lakes (Dolukhanov and Mikliaiev 1966).

During the Late Glacial, a single economic zone included all the plains of northern and northeastern Europe. All known Late Paleolithic sites within this zone are interpreted as the remains of temporary hunting camps. There were large-scale migrations during this time in both south–north and east–west directions, but there did also exist stable archaeological cultures, which may be interpreted as relatively closed, traditional groups (Dolukhanov et al. 1980:71–84).

HOLOCENE

Caucasus

Environment

In the Caucasus, the transition from the Pleistocene to the Holocene is marked by changes in all elements of the ecosystem. According to Vereshchagin (1959:125), during the Final Pleistocene and Early Holocene such species as cave bear, cave lion, and cave hyena became extinct; xerophilous species, such as hamster, porcupine, and wild argali, retreated southward; and mountain forest species, such as bison, chamois, and roe deer, diminished in size. The evolution of the Caucasian ecosystems during the Early and Middle Holocene (10,000–5,000 B.P.) was determined mainly by the gradually increasing temperature and humidity. At the same time, differences between the various zones became more pronounced and this clearly affected the development of prehistoric cultures. Paleobotanical records indicate that the vegetation of western Georgia acquired its modern aspect during the Early Holocene, with alder forests on the floodplains of the numerous rivers; mixed, broad-leaved forests on the upper terraces; and coniferous forests in the upper mountain belts (Ramishvili and Shatilova 1973). In central Transcaucasia, on the other hand, broad-leaved forests covered the intermontane depressions and low mountain belts. The moist forests, which had appeared there by the end of the Early Holocene, disappeared during the Middle Holocene, and mixed oak forests with *Quercus longipes* dominated the landscape. The forested area diminished during the Late Holocene (Gogichaishvili 1973). Open pine forests spread around Lake Sevan during the Early and Middle Holocene. In the area of Van, in eastern Anatolia, the treeless desert-like vegetation that had prevailed there from 10,000 to 6,400 B.P. was replaced by oak–pistachio forests during the period 6,400–3,400 B.P. (van Zeist and Woldring 1978). A semidesert vegetation existed in the Middle Araxes depression throughout the Holocene, and desert and semidesert vegetation prevailed along the shores of the Caspian Sea during the Early Holocene. A general increase in aridity during the Middle Holocene resulted in the appearance of shrubs and even forests in some areas (Abramova 1980). Finally, the Caucasus is part of the Near Eastern center of plant domestication as defined by Vavilov (1965). More than 130 varieties of wheat (including forms intermediate between cultivated and wild) have been identified in Georgia (Dekaprelovich 1941), and more than 200 varieties are known in Armenia and Azerbaidjan (Lisitsina and Prishchepenko 1977:13).

Fluctuation in the levels of the Black and Caspian seas was also an important environmental factor. According to Fedorov (1978), the level of the Black Sea reached a peak of 10 m below sea level, during the Neo-Euxine transgression of around 11,000 B.P., after which the sea level dropped to about 20 m below sea level. A worldwide eustatic rise of sea levels, the Flandrian, locally known as the

New Black Sea transgression, reached its peak (1.5–2 m above sea level) twice, between 8000 and 7000 and between 5000 and 4500 years ago (Ostrovskii *et al.* 1977; Fedorov 1978). In the Caspian Sea, the pronounced Mangyshlak regression occurred about 11,000–8,000 B.P., and the Neo-Caspian transgression, which manifested itself in a series of minor fluctuations in sea level, began about 8000–7000 B.P. According to recent research (Maiev *et al.* 1977:69–74; Fedorov 1978), two peaks of this transgression occurred at 6000–5400 and 3400–3000 B.P.

Sites

Mesolithic sites are known only in western Georgia and on the Trialeti plateau, and are dated, mainly on typological grounds, to the Early Holocene (Gabunia 1976; Gabunia and Tsereteli 1977). In western Georgia, sites based upon food-gathering economies existed, during the Early and Middle Holocene, in the Black Sea coastal area (Kistrik and Nizhne-Shilovskaia), in the Colchis lowland (Odishi, Asenauli, and Gurianta), and in the piedmont of western Georgia (Samlde-kide and Belaia) (Munchaiev 1975:55–58).

During the eighth and seventh millennia B.P., Aeneolithic agricultural and stock-breeding sites appeared in the intermontane depressions of central Transcaucasia, in the Middle Araxes depression and on the adjacent foothills. Later, during the fifth millennium B.P., sites of the Bronze Age Kuro-Araxes culture developed in the same areas (Kushnareva and Chubinishvili 1970; Munchaiev 1975). By the end of the fifth millennium B.P., the number of agricultural sites in the lowland had dropped, while that in the foothills had increased (Piotrovskii 1955).

Economy and Settlement Pattern

The economy of Mesolithic sites in western Georgia was based on the hunting of predominantly forest animals, such as brown bear, wild pig, red deer, and badger, while on the Trialeti plateau, prey included wild horse, wild ass, maral, bison, and mouflon, caucasian tur, gazelle, and wild pig. Mesolithic sites in both areas are usually situated on low river terraces in densely forested areas. The lithic inventories retain numerous Upper Paleolithic elements, and in all probability, the Mesolithic population developed out of local Upper Paleolithic groups. The relatively stable forest ecosystems of western Georgia and of the coastal area of the Black Sea contributed to the stability of the food-gathering economy in these regions during the Early and Middle Holocene. Wild species (wild goat, bison, roe deer, red deer, wild pig, brown bear, and wolf) are exclusively represented in Neolithic cave sites there, but the presence of axe tools (probably intended for tilling), mortars, pestles, and grinding stones testifies to the great importance of collecting and processing edible plants (Solov'ëv 1967:18–23).

The spread of food-producing economies into the intermontane depressions and foothills of central Transcaucasia and the Araxes Valley coincided with the formation of the *agroclimatic potential* in these areas. By this term I mean temperatures and humidity suitable for domesticated plants and the availability of arable land and water resources. The economy of the Aeneolithic settlements was based on dry farming. At least seven species of wheat have been identified (*Triticum dicoccum, T. compactum, T. monococcum, T. spelta, T. aestivum, T. turgicum,* and *T. durum*). Barley was represented by a wild form (*Hordeum spontaneum*) as well as by naked two-row and six-row forms. Millet, oats, and legumes were also present, and a large number of wild edible plants has been identified (Lisitsina and Prishchepenko 1977). Almost 99% of the faunal remains are of domesticated animals (cattle, sheep or goat, and pig). All of this points to a stable food-producing economy supported by some food collecting.

Aeneolithic settlements were relatively small in size, from 1 to 4 ha, and included mud-brick, oval houses up to 3 m in diameter (Munchaiev 1975:80–148). Differences in geomorphic situation, such as between the lowland sites and those in the foothills, may reflect either economic specialization or seasonal movements of ethnically homogeneous populations (Figure 7.4). Development of Aeneolithic settlements in Caucasus seems to have been mainly due to the infiltration of population from agricultural areas in northern Mesopotamia.

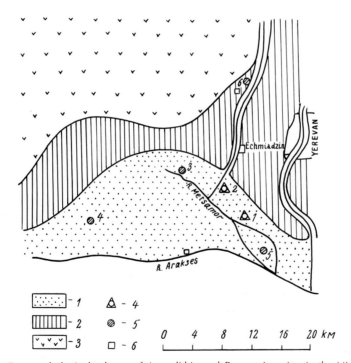

Figure 7.4 Geomorphological scheme of Aeneolithic and Bronze Age sites in the Middle Araxes valley: (1) low terraces; (2) upper terraces; (3) young volcanic relief; (4) Aeneolithic sites (1 Khatunarkh; 2 Karakishlag) (5); Bronze Age sites (3 Metsamor; 4 Arevik; 5 Djrahovit; 6 Voskevaz); (6) modern settlements. (After Dolukhanov 1980.)

Settlements of the Kuro-Araxes culture, which arose in the Caucasus during sixth and fifth millennia B.P., developed mainly from the local Aeneolithic groups. Changes in the subsistence pattern, the development of irrigated farming and developments in metallurgy led to a marked population growth without an influx from outside. The size of several settlements reached 4–10 ha, and complicated networks of stone or mud-brick structures, either oval or rectangular, have been uncovered on numerous sites. Several sites were fortified (Kushnareva and Chubinishvili 1970). Bronze Age settlements in the Caucasus were closely linked to contemporaneous centers in the Near and Middle East, with which there was exchange of raw material and products, as well as of ideas. This is attested, among other elements, by the similarities of several types of pottery, metal tools, and architecture (Kushnareva and Chubinishvili 1970:184).

By the end of the fifth millennium B.P. there was a marked decline of agricultural settlements in the lowlands, while, at the same time, the number of sites in the foothills increased. These latter sites had a predominantly pastoral, stockbreeding economy (Piotrovskii 1955). This apparent shift in population and associated change in economic strategy may have resulted from an increasingly arid climate, overpopulation of the lowlands, or a decline in the productivity of the soils (Dolukhanov 1980).

Russian Plain

Environment

The shift in the structure of ecosystems that occurred on the Russian Plain at the end of the Pleistocene and beginning of the Holocene manifested itself first in the disintegration of the relatively homogeneous periglacial zone and in the development of modern natural zones. The forest zone had begun to develop during the Late Glacial, and its development was completed during the Early Holocene. At the same time, the modern forms of tundra, forest–tundra, forest–steppe, and steppe developed. According to Vereshchagin (1971:221–224), no less than 10 animal species (including mammoth, woolly rhinoceros, and cave bear) became extinct at the end of the Pleistocene. Other species, such as reindeer, became extinct in the south, but expanded rapidly in the north. Steppe and semidesert species of ungulates migrated to the deserts of Central Asia, and the populations of elk, ducks, capercaillie, fish, and sea mammals expanded in the forest zone and adjacent coast.

The Holocene may be subdivided into three stages: the Early Holocene, including the Preboreal and Boreal (10,000–8,000 B.P.); the Middle Holocene, or Atlantic (8,000–5,000 B.P.); and the Late Holocene, including the Subboreal and Subatlantic (5,000 B.P. up to the present). During the Early Holocene the forest zone was similar in size to the present one, and pine and birch forests were predominant in northwestern and central parts of the plain, the same areas as were affected by the Last Glaciation. About 10,000–9,500 B.P., subarctic conditions were temporarily restored in many areas of the Russian Plain (Khotinski

1977). Steppe vegetation of xerotic type existed in the south, in the Black Sea coastal area, and in the Kerch peninsula (Dolukhanov and Pashkevich 1977:139).

During the Middle Holocene the forest zone expanded toward both north and south, and the forests were enriched in thermophilous species. Mixed broadleaved forests spread onto the clay moraine soils in northwestern and central areas, while the present-day forest–steppe zone was covered by light oak forests. True steppes were restricted to the Black Sea coastal area (Dolukhanov and Pashkevich 1977:14).

The forest zone shrank to its present size during the Late Holocene. According to Khotinski (1977:163–164), the Late Holocene included a cool phase (4600–4200 B.P.), a warm phase (4200–3400 B.P.), and a cool and humid phase (3400–2500 B.P.). During the first phase, forests were impoverished in thermophilous elements (the decline of elm was particularly marked), and, in central and northern areas, spruce forests rapidly expanded during the third phase. Human impact on vegetation steadily increased throughout the Middle and Late Holocene, as agriculture and stock-breeding gradually spread.

Sites

Mesolithic cultures occupied the Russian Plain during the Early Holocene and a considerable part of the Middle Holocene. Sites discovered in Estonia and in Latvia are considered to belong to the Kunda culture, of which the earliest site, Pulli, has been radiocarbon dated to 9700–9200 B.P., while the radiocarbon age of one of the latest sites, Osa, is 7200–7100 B.P. (Dolukhanov and Timofeiev 1972:59). The Neman Mesolithic culture is found in Lithuania and adjacent Belorussia, and the Upper Volga Mesolithic culture existed in the basins of Upper Volga and the Oka rivers. In the southern part of the Russian Plain Mesolithic cultures, such as the Grebeniki culture in Odessa oblast and in the south of the Moldavian Republic, are strongly microlithic. In the basins of the middle and upper Dnieper, on the other hand, Mesolithic assemblages may include both microlithic and macrolithic artifacts.

The Neolithic of the Russian Plain developed during the greater part of the Middle Holocene and the initial phases of the Late Holocene (around 7000–3800 B.P.). Three main phases may tentatively be distinguished within it: the Early Neolithic (around 7000–6000 B.P.); the Middle Neolithic (around 6000–4500 or 6000–4000 B.P.); and the Late Neolithic (around 4500–3800 or 4000–3800 B.P.). However, the Neolithic developed at different times and at different rates in the various parts of the Russian Plain. Thus, in the Ukraine and Moldavia, the Bugo-Dnestrian culture, the Sura-Dneperian culture and the Strumel-Gastiatin sites, which are dated to approximately 7000–6000 B.P., are attributed to the Early Neolithic. To the same phase belong the Narva culture in Estonia and Latvia, the Neman culture in Lithuania and Belorussia, the Dubiçiai-type sites in Lithuania, the Upper Volga culture, and Sperrings (also known as the I:I style) in Carelia. All of the groups are roughly dated to 6300–5000 or 6300–4500 B.P. (Gurina 1970; Dolukhanov 1979; Khotinski 1978).

In the Middle Neolithic are included the Gumelniţa culture (6000–5300 B.P.);

the Tripolye culture (6000–4500 B.P.) in the Ukraine and Moldavia; and the Dnepro-Donetsian (6000–4500 B.P.) and Sredni Stog cultures (5800–4600 B.P.) in the Ukraine (Telegin 1977; Dolukhanov 1979). Numerous sites with pit-and-comb decorated pottery in the central, eastern, and western parts of the Russian Plain and dated to approximately 5200–4000 B.P. also belong to this phase. Sites of the so-called Volosovo culture in the central and northeastern regions are dated to 5000–4500 B.P., and numerous radiocarbon dates place the Usviaty culture of the south Pskov oblast within the same period. The age of Piestina, Sarnate, and Šventoji-type sites in Latvia and Lithuania is approximately 4500–4000 B.P. (Dolukhanov et al. 1978).

Within the Late Neolithic or Early Bronze Age fall sites of the Pit Grave culture in southern Ukraine and the Black Sea coastal area (4500–3800 B.P.), and sites with corded-ware pottery in the northwestern (including the North-Belorussian culture) and central parts (the Fatianovo culture) of the Russian Plain (Telegin 1977; Dolukhanov et al. 1978; Charniauski 1979).

Economy and Settlement Pattern

During the Early Holocene and the greater part of the Middle Holocene, the economy of the population of the Russian Plain was based exclusively on the hunting of forest or steppe animals, on fishing, and on food collecting. Mesolithic sites in the extraglacial areas were usually situated on river floodplains, or on the shores of small lakes and of lagoons in the Black Sea coastal area. Roe deer, wild pig, wild horse, and aurochs were the most common prey of Mesolithic hunters. Within the areas affected by the Last Glaciation, Mesolithic sites were situated on floodplains or on low river terraces (numerous sites are known in the basins of the Neman, Upper Volga, and Oka rivers), and on shores of residual ice-dammed lakes and offshore lagoons (in the Baltic Sea coastal area). Nomadic hunting was the main economic strategy, with elk, brown bear, wild pig, and deer being most commonly hunted. In the coastal area, sea mammals were hunted, and fishing, fowling, and the collecting of edible plants and mollusks were of great economic importance. The Mesolithic population of the Russian Plain for the most part developed out of local Late Paleolithic groups through adaptation to the environment of the Early Holocene. There was no significant influx of population from outside.

The Early Neolithic of the Russian Plain roughly coincided with the middle part of the Atlantic—the postglacial climatic optimum. During this phase there was an increase in the population density, but the subsistence pattern and settlement pattern remained basically the same as during the Mesolithic. Sites were concentrated on river floodplains (Figure 7.5) and on the shores of lakes and offshore lagoons. Similarities in lithic inventories indicate that the Early Neolithic cultures developed at least partly from local Mesolithic groups. At the same time, however, affinities in the decoration on ceramic vessels point to an influx of population from the agricultural areas of southeastern Europe (Dolukhanov 1979). Also, the cereals and bones of domesticated animals discovered

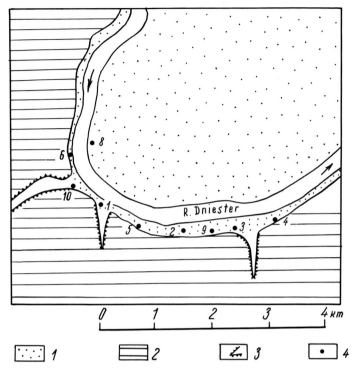

Figure 7.5   Geomorphological scheme of Soroki sites (Moldavian Republic). (1) Floodplain; (2) watershed plateau; (3) ravines; (4) sites (Soroki 1-10). (After Markevich 1974.)

at some Bugo-Dnestrian sites (Yanushevich 1976; Markevich 1974) suggest the existence of trade links with the agricultural and stock-breeding communities of the Balkan Neolithic.

The Middle Neolithic corresponds to the final Atlantic, or the beginning of the Sub-Boreal. During this stage at least two farming cultures, Gumelniţa and Tripolye, evolved in the southwestern Ukraine and in Moldavia. The Gumelniţa economy was of a stable food-producing nature, and cattle breeding was its most important branch (Tsalkin 1970). Three varieties of wheat (einkorn, emmer, and spelt), two varieties of barley (hulled and naked), oats, broom corn, and millet have all been identified (Yanushevich 1976). The Gumelniţa sites were situated on high promontories of the loessial plains flanking low stretches of rivers, in the Black Sea coastal area, or sea lagoons.

The initial phase of Tripolye culture, when some of the settlements were situated either on floodplains or on low terraces, had a mixed economy, and hunting, fishing, and food collecting remained important. Only in its middle phase, when some of the settlements were of considerable size (Bibikov 1965), did the Tripolye economy acquire a stable food-producing character. Cattle were the most important domestic animals, followed by pigs and ovicaprids (Tsalkin

1970). Einkorn, emmer, spelt, club wheat, hulled and naked barley, oats, millet, and pulses have been identified among the domesticated plants (Yanushevich 1976). The emergence of both the Gumelniţa and the Tripolye cultures is seen as a result of migrations from the Balkans. Apart from purely archaeological evidence, this is further supported by the similarity of species of domesticated plants in both areas (Yanushevich 1976:200).

Even during the Middle Neolithic, food-gathering economies continued to be practiced over the greater part of the Russian Plain, and successful adaptations to the environment of the Middle Holocene resulted in a marked population growth. In the Sredni Stog culture of the steppe zone, stock-breeding was very important, and domesticated horse dominates the faunal remains (Telegin 1973), but food gathering was the basis of settlements of the Dniepero-Donetsian culture, situated on the floodplains in the basins of the Middle and Upper Dnieper and of the Severski Donets (Telegin 1968). Nevertheless, impressions of domesticated cereal grains on pottery, such as that of *Hordeum sativum* at the Vita Litovskaia site (Telegin 1968), point to the existence of exchange links with agricultural communities, possibly including Tripolye. The Dniepero-Donetsian culture evolved at least partly as a result of the development of local Early Neolithic cultures. On the other hand, both the pottery decorations and the physical anthropological evidence suggest that some role in its development was played by the infiltration of population from the area of Funnel Beaker Culture in Central Europe (Dolukhanov and Tretiakov 1979).

Both the outer and inner zones of the area of the Last Glaciation were intensively populated during the Middle Neolithic. Large lake dwellings were constructed in residual ice-dammed basins, where investigations have shown (Dolukhanov 1979:151–164; Vereshchagin *et al.* 1979:363–368) that the dwelling sites were constructed on piles in offshore areas of the lakes. The catchment areas of these sites included the lake, the offshore area, the mixed broad-leaved forests on clay morainic soil, and the pine forests on sandy, glacial-lacustrine deposits (Figure 7.6). The economy of the lake-dwellings was based on hunting (elk, aurochs, brown bear, wild pig, roe deer, and waterfowl), food collecting (berries, mushrooms, acorns, hazelnut, and water nut), and fishing (perch, pike, and pike perch). Each lake basin harbored only a single dwelling site, and, according to demographic calculations, the population of a dwelling site numbered about 100 persons. Similarly, numerous Middle Neolithic settlements were situated in offshore lagoons in the coastal area of the Baltic Sea.

The Middle Neolithic sites in all of these areas are regarded as belonging to a variety of archaeological cultures. A large area with sites having pit-and-comb decorated pottery, among which several related cultures are distinguishable, was occupied as a result of the spread of population originating in the central part of the Russian Plain (Gurina 1973; Tretiakov 1972), while cultures such as Usvyaty, Piestina, Sarnate, and Šventoji arose as a result of both local development and infiltration of population from outside.

The Late Neolithic, or Early Bronze Age, roughly corresponds to the Sub-

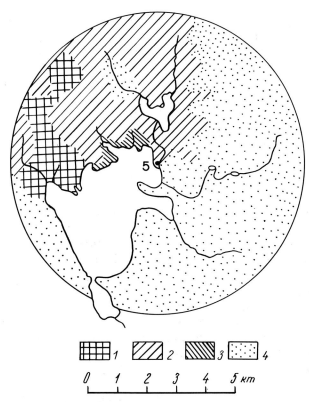

Figure 7.6 Geomorphological scheme of Naumovo site (Pskov oblast): (1) end moraine highland; (2) morainic plain; (3) glacial lacustrine plain; (4) lake terraces; (5) Neolithic dwelling site. (After Vereshchagin *et al.* 1979.)

Boreal warm phase (Khotinski 1977;163–164). During this phase, forests in both the north and the south were restricted to their present size. Increasing aridity and the decreasing agroclimatic potential disrupted the normal functioning of agricultural systems in the southern areas of the Russian Plain, which led to the gradual fading out of the Tripolye culture. In the Usatovo stage (4500–4400 B.P.), both the number and size of settlements decreased, and the economy acquired a pastoral character. Economic change was one of the important factors bringing about development of the Pit Grave Culture in the steppe zone (Merpert 1974). The earliest sites of the Pit Grave Culture are dated to about 5000 years ago, and most of the radiocarbon dates lie in the time span of 4500–3900 B.P. (Telegin 1977; 5–19; Sobotovich *et al.* 1980).

The Late Neolithic in the northwestern and central parts of the Russian Plain is marked by the appearance in the pottery assemblages of corded ware. Geochronological investigations of several sites in the southern Pskov oblast and in northern Belorussia have revealed that the transition from the Usvyaty culture to the North-Belorussian (corded ware) culture occurred about 4000 years ago (Mikliaiev 1975; Dolukhanov *et al.* 1978). Multivariate analysis of pottery decoration has established that this transition was marked by a profound transformation of the ceramic cultural subsystem, which was probably caused by the influx of a new population which was absorbed by the old one (Dolukhanov and Foniakov 1981). Some of the sites with corded ware have domestic animals (pigs and cattle) in their faunal assemblages, but the economy of the sites remains essentially that of food gathering.

CONCLUSIONS

On the basis of the evidence outlined in this chapter, it is possible to distinguish the following stages in the development of prehistoric cultures and of the environment in the Caucasus and on the Russian Plain (Figures 7.7–7.9).

1. 70,000–35,000 B.P. (Early and Middle Würm). This is marked by a succession of cold and of relatively mild climatic phases. Rather brief glaciations may have occurred in the higher latitudes of the Russian Plain and in the Caucasian mountains between 55,000 and 50,000 years ago. Periglacial-forest and periglacial-steppe formations dominated the vegetation of the Russian Plain. During this stage, the Mousterian cultures developed in Europe and in the Near and Middle East. A relatively high population density is recorded for the Caucasus, but population was extremely sparse on the Russian Plain (Figure 7.10).

2. 35,000–10,000 B.P. An extremely cold and dry climate prevailed in both areas, and the glaciations of both the Russian Plain and the Caucasus reached their maximal extent. Periglacial-steppe formations dominated the vegetation of the Russian Plain, while open pine forests and steppes existed in the intermontane depressions of the Caucasus. Complicated social and economic processes resulted in the development of the Upper Paleolithic cultures in Europe and in

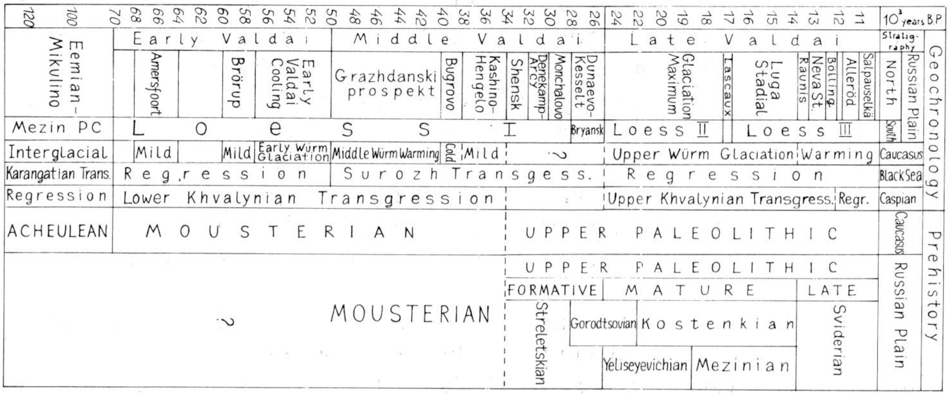

Figure 7.7 Geochronology of the Upper Pleistocene.

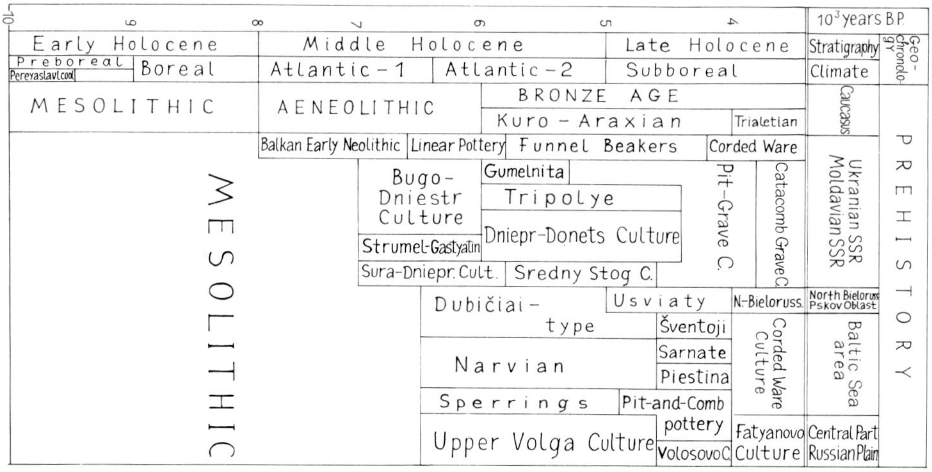
10³ years B.P.
10 9 8 7 6 5 4
Early Holocene
Middle Holocene
Late Holocene
Stratigraphy
Geo-chronology
Preboreal
Pereyaslavl cool
Boreal
Atlantic – 1
Atlantic – 2
Subboreal
Climate
MESOLITHIC
AENEOLITHIC
BRONZE AGE
Kuro – Araxian
Trialetian
Caucasus
Balkan Early Neolithic
Linear Pottery
Funnel Beakers
Corded Ware
Bugo-Dniestr Culture
Gumelnita
Tripolye
Dniepr-Donets Culture
Strumel-Gastyatin
Sura-Dniepr. Cult.
Sredny Stog C.
Pit-Grave C.
Catacomb Grave C.
Ukranian SSR Moldavian SSR
MESOLITHIC
PREHISTORY
Dubičiai-type
Usviaty
N.-Bieloruss.
North Bieloruss. Pskov Oblast
Šventoji
Sarnate
Piestina
Narvian
Corded Ware Culture
Baltic Sea area
Sperrings
Pit-and-Comb pottery
Upper Volga Culture
Volosovo C.
Fatyanovo Culture
Central Part Russian Plain

Figure 7.8 Geochronology of the Holocene.

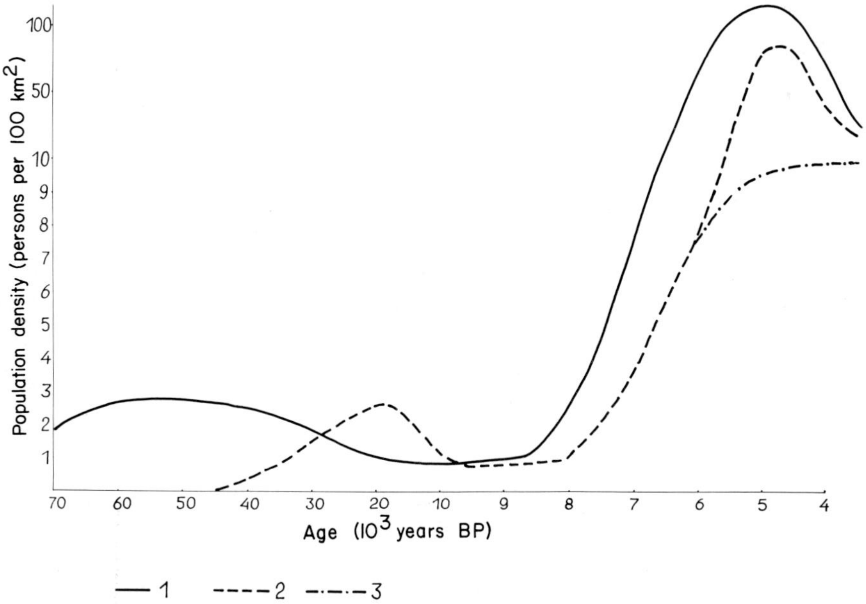
Population density (persons per 100 km²)
100
50
10
9
8
7
6
5
4
3
2
1
70 60 50 40 30 20 10 9 8 7 6 5 4
Age (10³ years BP)
—1 ----2 -·-·-3

Figure 7.9 Dynamics of prehistoric populations. (1) Caucasus; (2) South Russian Plain; (3) North Russian Plain. Note: the values given for population density are hypothetical (*cf.* Dolukhanov 1979:23–25.)

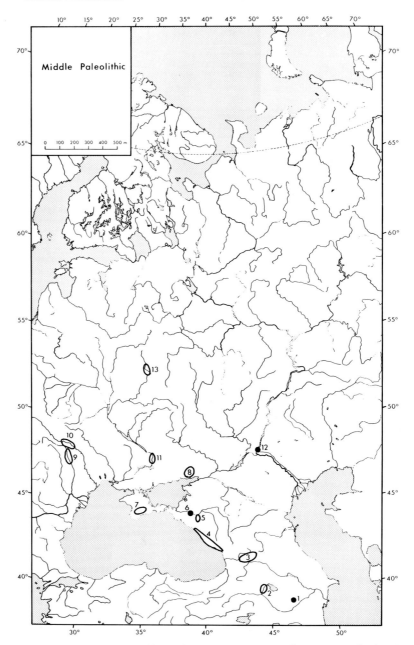

Figure 7.10 Mousterian. (1) Azykh, Aglar; (2) Yerevan, Lusakert; (3) South Ossetian sites, Tsutskhvati; (4) Black Sea coastal sites; (5) Gubskii Naves, Navalishenskaia; (6) Il'skaia; (7) Crimean sites; (8) Azov Sea sites; (9) Prut Valley sites; (10) Dniester sites; (11) Dnieper sites; (12) Volgograd site; (13) Desna sites.

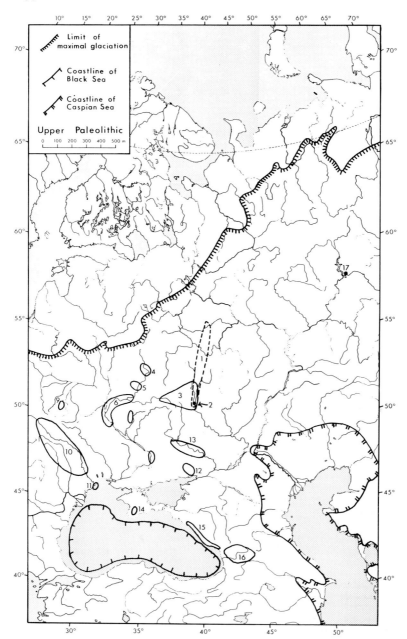

Figure 7.11 Upper Paleolithic. (1) Streletskian; (2) Gorodtsovian; (3) Kostenkian; (4) Yeliseievichian; (5) Pushkarevian; (6) Mezinian; (7) Gonsty, Zhuravka; (8) Zaporozh'e sites; (9) Lipian; (10) Molodovian; (11) Bol'shaia Akkarzha; (12) Azov Sea sites; (13) Severski Donets sites; (14) Crimean sites; (15) Black Sea coastal sites; (16) West Georgian sites; (17) Talitski site.

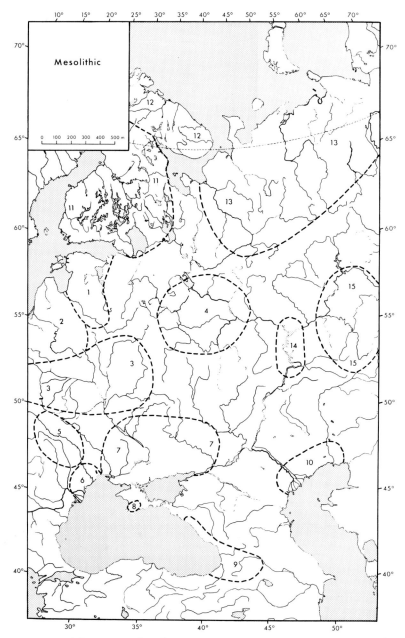

Figure 7.12 Mesolithic. (1) Kunda culture; (2) Neman culture; (3) Upper Dnieper Mesolithic; (4) Upper Volga culture; (5) Dniester sites; (6) Grebenikian culture; (7) Central Ukrainian Mesolithic; (8) Crimean sites; (9) West Georgian sites; (10) North Caspian sites; (11) Carelian Mesolithic; (12) Mesolithic of Kola Peninsula; (13) Mesolithic of the North of European part of USSR; (14) Volga-Kama culture; (15) Cisuralian culture.

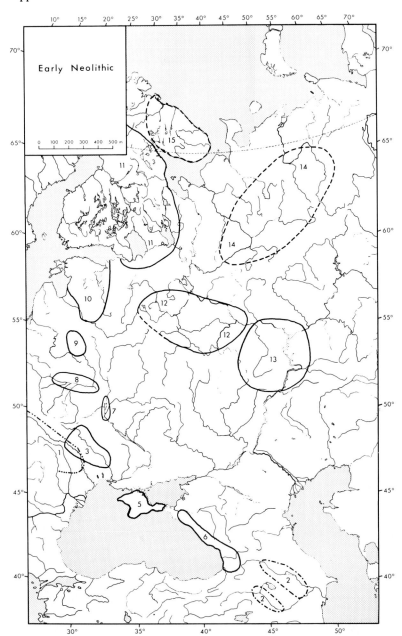

Figure 7.13   Early Neolithic. (1) Linear Pottery culture; (2) Transcaucasian Aeneolithic; (3) Bugo-Dnestrian; (4) Sura-Dneprian Culture; (5) Crimean Early Neolithic; (6) Black Sea coast Neolithic; (7) Stumel'-Gastiatin; (8) Polesse'e Early Neolithic; (9) Dubiçiai type sites; (10) Narva culture; (11) Sperrings; (12) Upper Volga culture; (13) Volgo-Kama culture; (14) Early Neolithic of the North of European part of USSR; (15) Early Neolithic of Kola Peninsula.

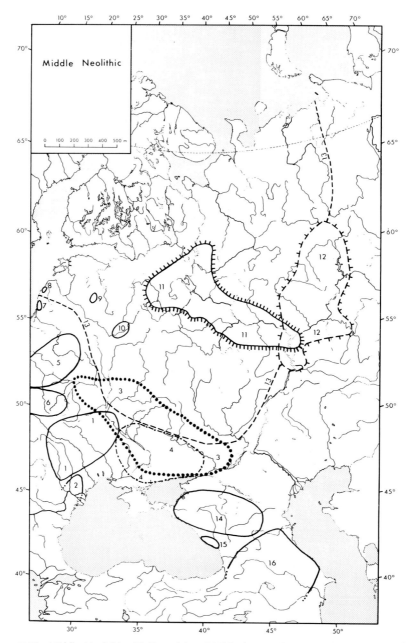

Figure 7.14 Middle Neolithic. (1) Gumelniţa; (2) Tripolye; (3) Dnepro-Donetsian; (4) Sredni Stog culture; (5) Neman culture; (6) Funnel Beaker culture; (7) Sviantoji culture; (8) Sarnate culture; (9) Piestina culture; (10) Usvyaty culture; (11) Volosovo culture; (12) Volgo-Kama culture; (13) maximum extention of pit-and-comb decorated pottery; (14) Maikop culture; (15) Ochamchiri culture; (16) Kuro-Araxes culture.

the Near and Middle East at the beginning of the stage. The population of Caucasus diminished, while that of the Russian Plain reached its maximal number for the Pleistocene. Three stages can be distinguished in the development of the Upper Paleolithic of the Russian Plain: the formative stage (35,000–25,000 B.P.); maturity (25,000–13,000 B.P.); and degradation (13,000–10,000 B.P.). The stage of maturity featured the optimal adaptation of social systems to the periglacial environment, while during the stage of degradation, the periglacial ecosystems disintegrated, population density diminished, and there occurred a general displacement of the population to the north (Figure 7.11).

3. 10,000–8,000 B.P. (Early Holocene). During this stage the modern structure of natural zones developed. Mesolithic cultures were formed as a result of adaptations of the local Late Paleolithic groups to the Early Holocene environment, but population density in both areas was low (Figure 7.12).

4. 8000–4000 B.P. (Middle and early Late Holocene; Post Glacial climatic optimum and subsequent cooling). During this stage, thermophilous forests spread both in the north and in the south, although they later retreated to their present size. Stable food-producing structures evolved in the intermontane depressions of central and southern Transcaucasia, as well as in the southwest of the Russian Plain. During the Middle Holocene these structures gradually spread to the north. At the same time, food-gathering economies, based on an effective adaptation to the forest ecosystems of Middle Holocene, continued in most of the Russian Plain. Large-scale migrations occurred in northerly, easterly, and westerly directions. Primarily because of increasing aridity, the area of agriculture diminished during the period 4500–4000 years ago, and in some areas of the steppe zone predominantly pastoral types of economy were established (Figures 7.13 and 7.14).

ACKNOWLEDGMENTS

The author wishes to express his gratitude to Prof. Fred Wendorf (Department of Anthropology, Southern Methodist University, Dallas, U.S.A.) and to Prof. Romuald Schild (Institute for the History of Material Culture, Polish Academy of Sciences, Warsaw) at whose instigation this chapter was written. The chapter was read and discussed at the Institute of Geography and at the Leningrad Branch of the Institute of Archaeology, U.S.S.R. Academy of Sciences. I am particularly grateful to my colleagues, N. A. Khotinski, G. P. Grigor'ev, L. M. Tarasov, G. M. Levkovskaia, and V. I. Timofeiev, whose comments are highly appreciated. My gratitude is also due to Mrs. Thelma L. Lowe (Department of South Asian Studies, University of California, Berkeley, U.S.A.), who read the paper and made valuable suggestions. I am indebted to Prof. W. G. Mook, Laboratorium voor Algemene Natuurkunde, Rijksuniversiteit Groningen, Netherlands, for the measurement of several important radiocarbon samples.

REFERENCES

Abramova, T. A.
    1980   Izmenenie uvlazhnënnosti Kaspiiskogo regiona v golocene po palynologicheskim dan-

nym (Change of humidity in Caspian region according to palynological data). In *Kolebaniia uvlazhnennosti Aralo-Kaspiiskogo regiona v golocene*, edited by B. V. Andrianov, L. V. Zorin and R. V. Nikolaieva. Moscow: Nauka. Pp. 71–73.

Aliev, S. D.
1969   Fauna Azykhskoi paleoliticheskoi stoianki (Fauna of the Azykh Palaeolithic site). Ph.D. dissertation, Baku State University.

Anikovich, M. V.
1977a   *Pamiatniki streletskoi kul'tury v Kostënkakh* (Sites of the Streletskian in Kostenki). Avtoreferat kandidatskoi dissertatsii, Moscow. Institute of Archaeology.
1977b   Stroienie verkhnei gumusirovannoi tolshchi v s.Kostënki i otnositel'nyi vozrast zalegaiushchikh v nei stoianok (Structure of the upper Humus series in Kostenki and relative age of the enclosed Palaeolithic sites). In *Paleoekologiia drevnego cheloveka*, edited by I. K. Ivanova and N. D. Praslow. Moscow: Nauka. Pp. 66–73.

Arslanov, Kh.A., N. A. Gei, V. V. Liadov and T. V. Tertychnaia
1980   Novye dannye o geokhronologii i paleogeografii srednego viurma Abkhazii (New data on the geochronology and palaeogeography of Middle Würm in Abkhazia). In *Geokhronologiia chetverichnogo perioda*, edited by I. K. Ivanova and N. V. Kind. Moscow: Nauka. Pp. 131–138.

Arslanov, Kh.A., N. A. Gei and B. L. Solov'ëv
1976   K paleogeografii i geokhronologii pozdnego pleistocena Abkhazii (Contributions to the palaeogeography and geochronology of the Late Pleistocene in Abkhazia). *Izvestiia AN SSSR, seriia geologicheskaia*, No. 6. Pp. 125–129.

Bader, O. N.
1977   Paleoekologiia i liudi stoianki Sungir' (Paleoecology and population of the site of Sungir'). In *Paleoekologiia drevnego cheloveka*, edited by I. K. Ivanova and N. D. Praslov. Moscow: Nauka. Pp. 31–39.

Bibikov, S. N.
1965   Khoziaistvenno–bytovoi kompleks razvitogo Tripolya, opyt izucheniia pervobytnoi ekonomiki (Economic–dwelling assemblage of a developed Tripolye site: paleoeconomic analysis). *Sovetskaia Arkheologiia*, No. 1, pp. 48–62.

Burchak-Abramovich, N. I.
1980   Ostatki ptic iz peshchery Kudaro I (Remains of birds from Kudaro I Cave). In *Kudarskie paleoliticheskie stoianki v Iugo-Osetii*, edited by I. K. Ivanova and A. G. Cherniakhovskii. Moscow: Nauka. Pp. 98–110.

Charniauski, M. M.
1979   Nealit Belaruskaga Paniamonnia (Neolithic of Nieman area in Bielorussia). Minsk: Navuka i Tekhnika.

Chebotareva, N. S., and I. A. Makarycheva
1974   Poslednee olodenenie Evropy i ego khronologiia (Last Glaciation in Europe and its geochronology). Moscow: Nauka.

Dekaprelovich, L. L.
1941   Rol' Gruzii v proiskhozhdenii pshenits (Role of Georgia in the origin of wheats). *Soobshcheniia AN Gruzinskoi SSR*, **2**:915–922.

Dolukhanov, P. M.
1979   *Ecology and economy in neolithic eastern Europe*. London: Duckworth.

Dolukhanov, P. M.
1980   Paleogeography and prehistoric settlement in Caucasus and in Central Asia during Pleistocene and Holocene. *Annali dell'Istituto Orientale di Napoli* **40**(N.S. XXX):49–87.

Dolukhanov, P. M., and D. I. Foniakov
1981   Mnogomernyi statisticheskii analiz keramicheskikh kompleksov na iuga Pskovskoi oblasti v sviazi s rasseleniem baltov (Multivariate analysis of the pottery assemblages in the south Pskov oblast' and the problem of the spread of the Balts). In *Problemy et-*

nogeneza i etnicheskoi istorii Baltov, edited by R. K. Volkaite-Kulikauskene. Vilnius. Pp. 20–21.

Dolukhanov, P. M., J. K. Kozlowski, and S. K. Kozlowski
  1980   *Multivariate analysis of Upper Paleolithic and Mesolithic stone assemblages. Typology and ecology.* Warsaw, Cracow: Uniwersytet Jagiellonski; Panstwowe Wydawnictwo Naukowe.

Dolukhanov, P. M., A. A. Liiva and A. M. Mikliaiev
  1978   Problemy absoliutnoi khronologii kul'tur V–II tysiacheletiia do n.e. v bassine Baltiiskogo moria (Problems of absolute chronology of cultures of 5th–2nd millenium B.C. in the basin of Baltic Sea). *Kratkie Soobshcheniia Instituta Arkheologii AN SSSR* **153**:25–30.

Dolukhanov, P. M., and G. A. Pashkevich
  1977   Paleogeograficheskíe rubezhi verkhnego pleistocenagolocena i razvitie khoziaistvennykh tipov na iugo-vostoke Evropy (Paleogeographic boundaries of the Upper Pleistocene-Holocene and evolution of prehistoric economic pattern in south-east Europe). In *Paleoekologiia drevnego cheloveka,* edited by I. K. Ivanova and N. D. Praslov. Moscow: Nauka. Pp. 134–145.

Dolukhanov, P. M., and V. I. Timofeiev
  1972   Absoliutnaia khronologiia neolita Evrazii po dannym radiouglerodnogo metoda (Absolute chronology of Neolithic in Eurasia according to radiocarbon method). In *Problemy absoliutnogo datirovaniia v arkheologii,* edited by B. A. Kolchin. Moscow: Nauka. Pp. 28–75.

Dolukhanov, P. M., and V. P. Tretiakov
  1979   Dnepro-Donetskii neolit i kul'tura voronkovidnykh kubkov. (Dniepro-Donetsian Neolithic and Funnel Beakers Culture). *Archaeologia Carpathica* **19**:37–50.

Fedorov P. V.
  1978   *Pleistocen Ponto-Kaspiia* (Ponto-Caspian Pleistocene). Moscow: Nauka.

Dolukhanov, P. M., and A. M. Mikliaiev
  1966   Paleogeografiia i absoliutnaia khronologiia pamiatnikov neolita i bronzy v basseine Zapadnoi Dviny (Paleogeography and absolute chronology of Neolithic and Bronze Age sites in the basin of the Zapadnaia Dvina). In *Golocen,* edited by M. I. Neishtadt. Moscow: Nauka. Pp. 120–128.

Gabunia, M. K.
  1976   *Trialetskaia mezoliticheskaia kul'tura* (Trialetian Mesolithic Culture). Tbilisi: Metsniereba.

Gabunia, M. K., and L. D. Tsereteli
  1977   Mezolit Gruzii (Mesolithic of Georgia). *Kratkie Soobshcheniia Instituta Arkheologii AN SSSR* **149**:39–40.

Garutt, V. E., and E. V. Urbanis
  1979   Mamont iz pozdnepaleoliticheskikh stoianok sela Kostënki (Mammoth from Upper Paleolithic sites in Kostenki). In *Verkhni pleistocen i razvitie paleoliticheskoi kul'tury v centre Russkoi ravniny,* edited by G. I. Goretskii. Voronezh State University. Pp. 19–20.

Gogichaishvili, L. K.
  1973   K istorii nizmennykh lesov zapadnoi Gruzii v golocene (The history of forests of west Georgian lowlands in holocene). In *Palinologiia golocena i marinopalinologiia,* edited by M. I. Neishtadt. Moscow: Nauka. Pp. 46–48.

Grigor'ev, G. P.
  1970   Verhknii paleolit (Upper Paleolithic). In *Kammenyi vek na territorii SSSR,* edited by A. A. Formozov. Moscow: Nauka. Pp. 43–63.

Gurina, N. N.
  1970   *Iz istorii drevnikh plemën zapadnykh oblastei SSSR* (From history of primitive tribes of western regions of USSR). *Materialy i Issledovaniia po Arkheologii SSSR* **114**.

Gurina, N. N.
  1973   Nekotorye obshchie voprosy izucheniia neolita lesnoi i lesostepnoi zon evropeiskoi

chasti SSSR (Some general problems related to the study of Neolithic in forest and forest-steppic zones of European part of USSR). *Materialy i Issledovaniia po Arkheologii SSSR* **172**:7–21.

Gvozdover, M. D., and L. D. Sulerzhitskii
1979   O radiouglerodnom vozdaste Avdeevskoi paleoliticheskoi stoianki (On the radiocarbon age of the Avdeievo paleolithic site). *Biulleten' komissii po izucheniiu chetvertichnogo perioda*, No. 49, pp. 144–146.

Isaienko, V. F.
1973   Topografiia i stratigrafiia pervobytnykh pamiatnikov Poless'ia (Topography and stratigraphy of prehistoric sites in Poless'ie). In *Problemy paleogeografii antropogena Belorussii.* Minsk: Vysheishaia shkola. Pp. 210–216.

Kaplin, P. A., O. K. Leontiev, G. I. Rychagov, O. B. Parunin, A. A. Svitoch and A. I. Shliukov
1977   Khronologiia i paleogeografiia Ponto-Kaspiia po dannym absoliutnogo datirovanniia (Chronology and paleogeography of Ponto-Caspian area on the evidence of absolute dating). In *Paleogeografiia i otlozheniia iuzhnykh morei SSSR*, edited by P. A. Kaplin and F. A. Shcherbakov. Moscow: Nauka. Pp. 33–42.

Khotinski, N. A.
1977   *Golocen Severnoi Evrazii* (Holocene of northern Eurasia). Moscow: Nauka.
1978   Paleogeograficheskie osnovy datirovki i periodizatsii neolita lesnoi zony evropeiskoi chasti SSSR (Paleogeographical foundations of dating and division of Neolithic in the forest zone of the european part of USSR). *Kratkie Soobshcheniia Instituta Arkheologii AN SSSR* **153**:7–14.

Kol'tsov, L. V.
1965   Nekotorye itogi izucheniia mezolita Volgo-Okskogo mezhdurech'ia (Some results of the investigations of Mesolithic in the Volga-Oka interfluve area). *Sovetskaia arkheologiia*, No. 4:17–26.
1966   Novye raskopki stoianki Ielin Bor (New excavations of Ielin Bor site). *Materialy i Issledovaniia po Arkheologii SSSR* **126**:178–184.

Korniets, N. L., M. I. Gladkikh, and A. A. Velichko
1981   Mezhirich. In *Arkheologia i paleogeografia pozdnego paleolita Russkoi Ravniny* (Archaeology and palaeogeography of the Upper Palaeolithic of the Russian Plain), edited by A. A. Velichko. Moscow: Nauka. Pp. 77–88.

Korobkov, I. I.
1967   Itogi piatiletnikh isslodovanii Iashtukhskogo paleoliticheskogo mestonakhozhdeniia (Results of five years of investigations of Yashtykh paleolithic site). *Sovetskaia areheologiia*, **4**:194–206.

Kushnareva, K. Kh, and T. N. Chubinishvili
1970   *Drevnie kul'tury Kavkaza* (Prehistoric cultures of Caucasus). Leningrad: Nauka.

Kurenkova, E. I.
1979   *Radiouglerodnaia khronologiia i paleogeografiia pozdnepaleoliticheskikh stoianok Verkhnego Podneprov'ia* (Radiocarbon chronology and paleogeography of Upper Paleolithic sites in Upper Dnieper basin). Ph.D dissertation, Institute of Geography, Moscow.

Kvasov, D. D.
1975   *Pozdnechetvertichnaia istoriia krupnykh ozër i vnatrennikh morei Vostochnoi Evropy* (Late Quaternary history of large lakes and inner seas in Eastern Europe). Leningrad: Nauka.

Levkovskaia, G. M.
1977   Palinilogicheskaia kharakteristika razrezov Kostënkovsko-Borshevskogo raiona (Palynological characteristics of sequences in Kostenki-Borshevo area). In *Paleoekologiia drevnego cheloveka*, edited by I. K. Ivanova and N. D. Praslov. Moscow: Nauka. Pp. 74–83.

Levkovskaia, G. M.
1980   Palinologicheskaia kharakteristika otlozhenii v peshcherakh Kudaro I i Kudaro III (Palynological characteristics of deposits in the caves Kudaro I and Kudaro III). In *Kudarskie*

peshernye paleoliticheskie stoianki, edited by I. K. Ivanova and A. G. Cherniakhovskii. Moscow: Nauka. Pp. 126–151.

Lisitsina, G. N., and L. V. Prishchepenko
1977   *Paleoetnobotanicheskie nakhodki Kavkazs i Blizhnego Vosoka* (Paleoethnobotanic finds of Caucasus and Near East). Moscow: Nauka.

Liubin, V. P.
1960   Nizhnepaleolithicheskie pamiatniki Iugo-Osetii (Low Paleolithic sites in South Ossetia). *Materialy i Issledovaniia po Arkheologii SSSR.* **79**:9–78.
1977   *Must'erskie kul'tury Kavkaza* (Mousterian cultures of Caucasus). Moscow: Nauka.
1980   Nekotrye itogi izuchenia litostratigraficheskikh i biostratigraficheskikh pokazatelei Kudarskikh peshcher (Some results of lithostratigraphic and biostratigraphic investigations of Kudaro caves). In *Kudarskie peshchernye paleoliticheskie stoianki*, edited by I. K. Ivanova and A. G. Cherniakovskii. Moscow: Nauka. Pp. 153–166.

Markevich, V. I.
1974   *Bugo-Dnestrovskaia kul'tura na territorii Moldavii* (Bugo-Dniestrian Culture on the territory of Moldavia). Kishinev: Shtiintsa.

Maiev, E. G., S. A. Maieva, and A. N. Kosarev
1977   Paleogeograficheskii analiz izmenchivosti urovnei Kaspiiskogo i Aral'skogo morei (Paleogeographical analysis of fluctuations in levels of Caspian and Aral seas). In *Paleogeografiya i otlozheniia pleistocena iuzhnykh morei SSSR*, edited by P. A. Kaplin and F. A. Shcherbakov. Moscow: Nauka. Pp. 69–74.

Merpert, N. Ia.
1974   *Drevneishie skotovody Volzhsko-Ural'skogo mezhdurech'ia* (Most ancient stock-breeders in the Volga-Ural interfluve area). Moscow: Nauka.

Mikliaiev, A. M.
1975   Svainye poseleniia III–II tysiacheletiia do n.e. v basseine verkhnego techeniia Zapadnoi Dviny (Dwelling sites on piles in the upper stretches of the Zapadnaia Dvina during 3rd–2nd millenium B.C.). *Biulleten' komissii po izucheniiu chetvertichnogo perioda* **43**:158–162.

Munchaiev, R. M.
1975   *Kavkaz na zare bronzovogo veka* (Caucasus at dawn of Bronze Age). Moscow: Nauka.

Ostrovskii, A. B., Ia. A. Izmailov, A. P. Shcheglov, Kh. A. Arslanov *et al.*
1977   Novye dannye o stratigrafii i geokhronologii pleistocenovykh terras Chernomorskogo poberezhia Kavkaza i Kerchensko-Tamanskoi oblasti (New data related to stratigraphy and geochronology of Pleistocene marine terraces of Black Sea and Kerch–Taman' coastal areas). In *Paleogeografiia i otlozheniia pleistocena iuzhnykh morei SSSR*, edited by P. A. Kaplin and F. A. Shcherbakov. Moscow: Nauka. Pp. 61–74.

Piotrovskii, B. B.
1955   Razvitie skotovodstva v drevneishem Zakavkaz'ie (Development of stock-breeding in the most ancient Transcaucasia). *Sovetskaia arkheologiia* **23**:5–15.

Ramishvili, I. Sh., and I. I. Shatilova
1973   O vormozhnostiakh ispol'zovaniia palinologicheskikh dannykh dlia stratigrafichiskogo raschleneniia pliocena i pleistocena Zapadnoi Gruzii (On possibility of utilisation of palynological evidence for stratigraphic division of Pliocene and Pleistocene in Western Georgia). In *Palinologiia pliocena i pleistocena*, edited by V. P. Grichuk. Moscow: Nauka. Pp. 133–136.

Rimantiene, R. K.
1971   *Paleolit i mezolit Litvy* (Paleolithic and Mesolithic of Lithuania). Vilnius: Mintis.

Rogachev, A. N.
1973   Ob uslozhnënnom sobiratel'stve kak forme khoziaistva ne Russkoi Ravnine (On complex food-gathering as a branch of the economy in the Upper Palaeolithic of the Russian Plain). In *Antropologischeskaia rekonstruktsia i problemy paleoetnografii*, edited by G. V. Lebedinskaia and M. G. Rabonovich. Moscow: Nauka. Pp. 127–142.

Rogachev, A. N., M. V. Anikovich and V. I. Beliaieva
    1979   Kostenki I. In *Verkhnii pleistocen i razvitie paleoliticheskoi kul'tury v tsentre Russkoi ravniny*, edited by G. I. Goretskii. Voronezh State University Press, Pp. 68–74.
Rogachev, A. N., and A. A. Sinitsyn
    1979a   Kostenki I4 (Markina Gora). In *Verkhnii pleistocen i razvitie paleoliticheskoi kul'tury v tsentre Russkoi ravniny*, edited by G. I. Goretskii. Voronezh State University Press. Pp. 75–78.
    1979b   Kostenki I5 (Gorodtsovskaia stoianka). In *Verkhnii pleistocen i razvitie paleoliticheskoi kul'tury v tsentre Russkoi ravniny*, edited by G. I. Goretskii. Voronezh State University Press. Pp. 92–94.
Sobotovich, E. V., D. Ia. Telegin, N. N. Kovaliukh and I. V. Sadol'skii
    1980   Radiouglerodnoie datirovanie pamiatnikov arkheologii Ukrainy (Radiocarbon dating of archaeological sites in the Ukraine). In *Geokhronologiia chetvertichnogo perioda*, edited by I. K. Ivanova and N. V. Kind. Moscow: Nauka. Pp. 97–101.
Solov'ëv, L. N.
    1967   Neoliticheskie poseleniia Chernomorskogo poberezh'ia Kavkaza (Neolithic sites in the Black Sea coastal area of Caucasus). In *Materialy po arkheologii Abkhazii*, edited by M. M. Trapsh. Tbilisi: Metsnierba. Pp. 3–38.
Tarasov, L. M.
    1977   Must'erskaia stoianka Betovo. (Mousterian site of Betovo). In *Paleoekologiia drevnego cheloveka*, edited by I. K. Ivanova and N. D. Prasvov. Moscow: Nauka. Pp. 18–30.
    1979   *Gagarinskaia stoianka i eë mesto v paleolite Evropy* (Gagarino site and its place in the Paleolithic of Europe). Moscow: Nauka.
Telegin, D. Ia
    1968   *Dnipro-Donets'ka kul'tura* (Dnepro-Donetsian Culture). Kiev: Naukova Dumka.
    1973   *Seredne-Stogivs'ka kul'tura epokhi midi* (Sredni Stog Culture of Copper Age). Kiev: Naukova Dumka.
    1977   Ob absoliutnom vozraste iamnoi kul'tury i nekotorye voprosy khronologii eneolita iuga Ukrainy (On absolute age of Pit-Grave Culture and some problems of Aeneolithic chronology in the south Ukraine). *Sovetskaia arkheologiia*, No. 2:5–19.
Tretiakov, V. P.
    1972   *Kul'tura iamochno-grebenchatoi keramiki v lesnoi polose evropeiskoi chasti SSSR* (Culture of pit-and-comb decorated pottery in the forest zone of the european part of USSR). Moscow: Nauka.
Tsalkin, V. I.
    1970   *Dreneishie domashnie zhivotnye Vostochnoi Evropy* (The most ancient domesticated animals of Eastern Europe). Moscow: Nauka.
Tsepkin, E. A.
    1980   Ostatki ryb iz pesccuery Kudaro I (Remains of fishes from Kudaro I Cave). In *Kudarski paleolithicheskie stoyanki*, edited by I. K. Ivanova and A. K. Cherniakovskii. Moscow: Nauka. Pp. 90–97.
Tsereteli, D. V., and G. M. Maisuradze
    1976   Osnovnye cherty paleogeografii Gruzii v verkhnem pleistocene (Main features of the Upper Pleistocene paleogeography in Georgia). In *Mezhdunarodnaia geografiia—'76* (Vol. 1), edited by I. P. Gerasimov. Pp. 354–357.
van Zeist, W., and S. Bottema
    1977   Palynological investigations in Western Iran. *Palaeohistoria* **19**:19–85.
van Zeist, W., and H. Woldring
    1978   A postglacial pollen diagram from Lake Van in East Anatolia. *Review of Palaeobotany and Palynology* **26**:249–276.
Vavilov, N. I.
    1965   *Tsentry proiskhozhdeniia kul'turnykh rastenii* (Centres of origin of cultivated plants). Izbrannye Trudy (Selected Works), vol. 5. Moscow: Nauka.

Vekilova, E. A., and M. N. Grishchenko
    1972   Rezul'taty issledovaniia Akhshtyrskoi peshchery v 1961–1965 godakh (Results of inves-
            tigations in the Akhshtyr Cave in 1961–1965). *Materialy i Issledovaniia po Arkheologii
            SSSR* **185**:41–54.

Velichko, A. A.
    1969   Paleogeografiia stoianok pozdnego paleolita basseina srednei Desny (Paleogeography
            of Upper Paleolithic sites in the basin of Middle Desna). In *Priroda i razvitie pervobytnogo
            obshchesva na territorii evropeiskoi chasti SSSR,* edited by I. P. Gerasimov. Moscow: Nau-
            ka. Pp. 97–103.
    1973   *Prirodny process v pleistocene* (Natural process in the Pleistocene). Moscow: Nauka.
    1975   Problemy korreliatsii pleistocenovykh sobytii v lednikovoi, perigliatsial'no-lëssovoi i
            primorskoi oblasthiakh Vostochno-Evropeiskoi ravniny (Problems of correlations of
            Pleistocene events in glacial, periglacial-loessic and maritime areas in the East Euro-
            pean Plain). In *Problemy regional'noi i obshchei paleogeografii lëssovykh i perigliatsial'nykh
            oblastei,* edited by A. A. Velichko. Moscow: Nauka. Pp. 7–25.

Velichko, A. A., G. V. Antonova, E. M. Zelikson, A. K. Markova, M. K. Monoszon, T. D.
Morozova, M. A. Pevzner, M. B. Suleimanova, and T. A. Khalcheva
    1980   Paleogeografiia stoianki Azykh, drevneishego poseleniia pervobytnogo cheloveka na
            territorii SSSR (Paleogeography of the Azykh site, the oldest settlement of prehistoric
            man on the territory of USSR). *Izvesiia AN SSR, seriia geograficheskaia,* No. 3, pp. 20–35.

Velichko, A. A., Iu. N. Gribchenko, and A. K. Markova
    1977   O vozraste i usloviiakh obitaniia stoianki Khotylëvo II na Desne (Age and environment
            of the Khotylevo 2 site on the Desna river). In *Paleoekologiia drevnego sheloveka,* edited by
            I. K. Ivanova and N. D. Praslov. Moscow: Nauka. Pp. 40–49.

Velichko, A. A., and A. N. Rogachev
    1969   Pozdnepaleoliticheskie poseleniia na srednem Donu (Upper Paleolithic sites on the
            Middle Don). In *Priroda i razvitie pervobytnogo obshchestva,* edited by I. P. Gerasimov.
            Moscow: Nauka. Pp. 75–88.

Vereshchagin, N. K.
    1959   *Mlekopitaiushchie Kavkaza* (Mammals of Caucasus). Moscow–Leningrad: Izdatel'stvo
            Akademii Nauk SSSR.

Vereshchagin, N. K.
    1971   Okhoty pervobytnogo cheloveka i vymiranie pleistocenovykh mlekopitaiushchikh v
            SSSR (Hunts of Primitive Man and extinctions of Pleistocene Mammals in the USSR). In
            Materialy po faunam antropogena SSSR (Vol. 49), edited by N. K. Vereshchagin. Trudy
            Zoologicheskogo Instituta AN SSSR. Leningrad: Nauka. Pp. 200–232.

Vereshchagin, N. K., and G. F. Baryshnikov
    1980a   Ostatki mlekopitaiushchikh v vostochnoi galleree peshchery Kudaro I (Remains of
            mammals in the eastern gallery of the Kudaro I Cave). In *Kudarskie paleoliticheskie
            stoianki v Iugo-Osetii,* edited by I. K. Ivanova and A. G. Cherniakhovskii. Moscow:
            Nauka. Pp. 51–62.
    1980b   Ostatki mlekopitaiushchikh iz ʼpeshchery Kudaro III. (Mammal remains from the
            Kudaro III Cave). In *Kudarskie paleoliticheskie stoianki v Iugo-Osetii,* edited by I. K.
            Ivanova and A. G. Cherniakhovskii. Moscow: Nauka. Pp. 63–78.

Vereshchagin, N. K., P. M. Dolukhanov, and A. M. Mikliaiev
    1979   Khoziaistvo i ekologiia svainogo poseleniia Naumovo v Pskovskoi oblasti (Economy
            and ecology of the Naumovo pile-dwelling site in the Pskov oblast'). *Izvestiia
            Vsesoiuznogo geograficheskogo obshchestva* **C1**(4):363–368.

Vereshchagin, N. K., and I. Ie. Kuz'mina
    1979   Ekologiia mlekopitaiushchikh Verkhnego Dona v epokhu pozdnego paleolita (Ecology
            of the Upper Don mammals during Upper Paleolithic). In *Verkhnii pleistocen i razvitie
            paleoliticheskoi kul'tury v centre Russkoi ravniny.* Voronezh State University Press. Pp.
            15–16.

Yanushevich, Z. V.

  1976   *Kul'turnye rasteniia Iugo-Zapada SSSR po paleobotanicheskim dannym* (Cultivated plants of south-western part of USSR according to paleobotanic evidence). Kishinev: Shtiintsa.

Yeritsian, B. G.

  n.d.   *Ierevanskaia peshchernaia stoianka* (Yerevan Cave Site). Yerevan: Izdatel'stvo AN Armianskoi SSR (in press).

Zarrina, Ie. P., I. I. Krasnov, and Ie. A. Spiridonova

  1980   Klimatostratigraficheskaia korrelaciia i khronologiia pozdnego pleistocena Severo-Zapada i Centra Russkoi ravniny (Climatostratigraphic correlations and chronology of Late Pleistocene of North-Western and Central parts of the Russian Plain). In *Chetvertichnaia geologiia i geomorfologiia,* edited by I. I. Krasnov. Moscow: Nauka. Pp. 46–50.

Zaverniaiev, F. M.

  1978   *Khotylëvskoie paleoliticheskoie mestonakhozhdenie* (Khotylevo Paleolithic Site). Leningrad: Nauka.

Index